Memoirs of Zehir-Ed-Din Muhammed Babur, Emperor of Hindustan

MEMOIRS
OF
ZEHĪR-ED-DĪN MUHAMMED BĀBUR

PORTRAIT OF THE EMPEROR BĀBUR.
SLIGHTLY ENLARGED FROM A MINIATURE IN THE BRITISH MUSEUM
(MS. ADD. 5717, FOL. 52.)

MEMOIRS OF
ZEHĪR-ED-DĪN MUHAMMED BĀBUR

EMPEROR OF HINDUSTAN

WRITTEN BY HIMSELF, IN THE CHAGHATĀI TŪRKĪ

AND TRANSLATED BY

JOHN LEYDEN, Esq., M.D.

AND

WILLIAM ERSKINE, Esq.

ANNOTATED AND REVISED BY

SIR LUCAS KING, C.S.I., LL.D., F.S.A.

PROFESSOR OF ARABIC AND PERSIAN, AND LECTURER IN INDIAN HISTORY
IN THE UNIVERSITY OF DUBLIN; LATE OF THE
INDIAN CIVIL SERVICE

IN TWO VOLUMES

VOLUME I

HUMPHREY MILFORD
OXFORD UNIVERSITY PRESS
LONDON   EDINBURGH   GLASGOW   COPENHAGEN
NEW YORK   TORONTO   MELBOURNE   CAPE TOWN
BOMBAY   CALCUTTA   MADRAS   SHANGHAI   PEKING
1921

PRINTED IN ENGLAND
AT THE OXFORD UNIVERSITY PRESS
BY FREDERICK HALL

CONTENTS

VOLUME I

	PAGE
EDITOR'S PREFACE	vii
ADVERTISEMENT TO THE FIRST EDITION	xvii
DEDICATION TO THE HONOURABLE MOUNTSTUART ELPHINSTONE	xviii
PREFACE	xxi

INTRODUCTION

    Part I. Containing Remarks on the Tartar Tribes, and on the Geography of Uzbek Turkestān . xlii

    Part II. Containing a Short Account of the Successors of Taimūr Beg, from the death of that Prince to the Accession of Bābur . . . xcviii

THE MEMOIRS OF BĀBUR, A. H. 908–911 . 1–324

VOLUME II

THE MEMOIRS OF BĀBUR, A. H. 912–937 . 1–432

APPENDICES

    A. An Account of Bābur's deliverance from imminent danger at Kirmān 433

    B. Hindāl's adoption. 435

    C. A plain account of the battle of Kānwāha . 436

    D. An account of Humāyūn's illness and of Bābur's self-devotion 440

    E. Biographies of Erskine and Leyden . . 443

INDEX 449

PORTRAIT OF BĀBUR . . . *frontispiece*

MAP . . . . . *at end of Vol. II*

EDITOR'S PREFACE

It is matter of surprise that a book so replete with interest as Erskine and Leyden's translation of Bābur's Memoirs has never been reprinted since its publication in 1826. For many years it has been so scarce and costly that it is practically unprocurable. An abridged edition was issued by Caldecott in 1824, and another by Colonel Talbot in 1909, but it is high time that a complete reprint should be made accessible to the public. The style of the translation, though somewhat old fashioned, is vigorous and direct, and is not disfigured by too close an adherence to the idioms of the original. According to Elphinstone, ' The translation seems to imbibe the very spirit of the original, and the style is singularly happy, strikingly characteristic, though perfectly natural.'[1] The literary and historical value of the Memoirs cannot be estimated too highly, and as a picture of the life of an Eastern sovereign in court and camp, the book stands unrivalled among Oriental autobiographies. In the words of the same historian : ' It is almost the only specimen of real history in Asia. . . . In Bāber the figures, dresses, habits, and tastes, of each individual introduced are described with such minuteness and reality that we seem to live among them, and to know their persons as well as we do their characters. His descriptions of the countries visited, their scenery, climate, productions, and works of art are more full and accurate than will, perhaps, be found in equal space in any modern traveller.' According to another high authority,[2] Bābar's ' place in biography and literature is determined by his daring adventures and persevering efforts in his early days, and by the delightful Memoirs in which he related them. Soldier of fortune as he was, Bābar was none the less a man of fine literary taste and fastidious critical perception. In Persian, the language of culture . . . he was an accomplished poet, and in his native Tūrki he was master of a pure and unaffected style, alike in prose

[1] *History of India*, p. 429 (9th edition, London, 1905).
[2] Lane-Poole's *Bābar*, pp. 10–12 (Oxford, 1899);

and verse.... Wit and learning, the art of turning a quatrain on the spot, quoting the Persian classics, writing a good hand, or singing a good song were highly appreciated in Bābar's world, as much perhaps as valour, and infinitely more than virtue. Bābar himself will break off in the middle of a tragic story to quote a verse, and he found leisure in the thick of his difficulties and dangers to compose an ode on his misfortunes. His battles as well as his orgies were humanized by a breath of poetry.

'Hence his Memoirs are no rough soldier's diary, full of marches and counter-marches ;... they contain the personal impressions and acute reflections of a cultivated man of the world, well read in Eastern literature, a close and curious observer, quick in perception, a discerning judge of persons, and a devoted lover of nature. . . . The utter frankness of self-revelation, the unconscious portraiture of all his virtues and follies ; his obvious truthfulness and fine sense of honour give the Memoirs an authority which is equal to their charm.'

Pavet de Courteille, a translator of the Memoirs, says of him :[1] ' D'une persévérance à toute épreuve, doué d'une résolution inflexible, brave de sa personne, alliant la ruse à l'audace, libéral et même magnifique dans ses dons, sachant punir, et pardonner au besoin, habile homme de guerre, général prévoyant, très capable de commander une armée et d'inspirer de la confiance à ses soldats, ... administrateur prudent et consommé, qui ne méprisait aucun détail, ce prince n'a pas été seulement un conquérant, mais encore un fondateur.' As to the value of the Memoirs the same author remarks : ' Il abonde en détails des plus instructifs sur les personnages politiques de la fin du xve siècle de notre ère et de la première partie du xvie, sur les célébrités littéraires et artistiques de cette époque, l'âge d'or de la littérature turque orientale ; surtout les hommes enfin, soit princes, soit chefs de clan, soit simples particuliers, dont le nom a mérité de ne pas tomber en l'oubli ; il renferme les notions les plus précises et les plus dignes de foi sur la partie de l'Asie centrale que son éloignement de nous et sa situation isolée au milieu de montagnes inaccessi-

[1] *Mémoires de Baber* (Paris, 1872), Preface, pp. i, ii.

bles et glacées . . . rendent presque inabordable pour le voyageur isolé ; il ne néglige même pas les détails purement techniques relatifs à la faune et la flore de ces provinces reculées, sans oublier, bien entendu, les considérations ethnographiques.'

The Memoirs are in the form of an irregularly kept diary. The first part (A. H. 899 to 914) contains a continuous narrative of his early life and troubles, and was probably elaborated at a later date in India. The succeeding portions consist of fragments of a Journal written from time to time and often from day to day, rough drafts in fact, for an autobiography. The style of the later portion is generally inferior to that of the earlier, and bears evidence of a lack of revision, although certain passages, as for instance the detailed description of India, may have been written up, as Lane-Poole points out, ' during the comparative leisure of Bābar's last year '. As Pavet de Courteille observes in the Preface to his translation, the fact that the first portion of the Memoirs was written, or revised, in India (1520–30) is proved by Bābur's frequent allusion to events that occurred during his residence in Hindustan, and his use of expressions that were only current in the cis-Indus region, and were so little known trans-Indus that he has to explain them, e. g. words to denote measures of distance, time, &c. Bābur was in the habit of recording rough notes of anything that struck his fancy, which were afterwards worked up in his Journal, as can be inferred from his remark on p. 245, vol. ii, of the Memoirs that ' hereafter if I observe anything worthy of being described I shall take notice of it, and if I hear anything worth repeating I will insert it.'

Five gaps occur in the Memoirs, viz. :

(*a*) From the end of 908 to the end of A. H. 909 (A. D. 1503–4).

(*b*) From the beginning of 914 to the beginning of A. H. 925 (A. D. 1508–19).

(*c*) From the beginning of 926 to the beginning of A. H. 932 (A. D. 1520–5).

(*d*) A. H. 934 (April 2nd to Sept. 18th, A. D. 1528).

(*e*) A. H. 936–7 (A. D. 1529–30).

At the end of the chapters, where two of these gaps occur

(*a* and *b*), the narrative breaks off suddenly in the middle of a sentence. In one of these the hiatus is supplied by Pavet de Courteille's French translation of the Tūrki text, but the authenticity of this passage, which will be found in Appendix A, is open to doubt. These blanks in Bābur's narrative, which afford evidence of the irregular manner in which the Journal was kept, have been partly filled by Erskine's historical supplements. Pavet de Courteille points out that these lacunae are as Bābur left them, a conclusion which is confirmed by the fact that they occur in all existing texts both Tūrki and Persian, so that they cannot be attributed to the ravages of time, the negligence of copyists, or any other accident independent of the author's will. Bābur has left no record of the last fifteen months of his life, about which little is known. Erskine in his concluding supplement has supplied almost all the available information on the subject, but this is necessarily meagre.

The principal Tūrki manuscripts of the Bābur-nāmeh are the following:

(*a*) The Russian Foreign Office MS. transcribed in 1757 by Dr. Kehr from an unknown source. This manuscript was used by Ilminski for the preparation of his Kāzān text printed in 1857, on which Pavet de Courteille's French translation is based, and, although old and therefore important, it is not, in the opinion of Mr. A. G. Ellis (late Assistant Librarian, India Office, whose knowledge of Oriental bibliography is unrivalled), of very great value, being at times ungrammatical, and even unintelligible.

(*b*) The Elphinstone MS., which was purchased by Mr. Elphinstone in Peshawar in 1809, and after many vicissitudes found a home in the Advocates' Library, Edinburgh. This manuscript, according to Mr. Ellis, was transcribed between 1543 and 1593. It is of high value, though unfortunately incomplete. Erskine collated his work from it.

(*c*) The Hyderābād Codex, which belongs to the library of the Sālār Jang family at Hyderābād, is the finest and most complete manuscript of the Bābur-nāmeh, and, though not so old as the last named, has proved of the utmost value in the preparation of a reliable text. Mr. Ellis is of the opinion that it was transcribed about

1700. To Mrs. Beveridge's indefatigable energy and resource is due the discovery of the last two manuscripts, one of which (Hyderābād Codex) she has edited with much scholarly care for the trustees of the Gibb Memorial. It is a matter of great regret to me that I am debarred from using her erudite translation of the Memoirs, based mainly on the Elphinstone and Hyderābād MSS., now in course of publication.

There are three Persian translations of the Bābur-nāmeh, all of which are based on the same text represented by both the Hyderābād and Elphinstone Manuscript, viz.:

(a) 'Abd ur Rahīm's translation (1590), which practically covers the whole text. This version, although it cannot possess the same value as the Tūrki source, faithfully respects the original text, and ' such variations as exist do not affect the essential accuracy of the document '.[1]

Of this translation a good many copies are preserved in the Public Libraries of this country, the Bib. Nat. of Paris has two (264 and 265), and there is one in my private library. The India Office MS. (Ethè No. 2989) is perhaps the most reliable. The British Museum possesses another fine copy (Or. 3714), illustrated with exquisite miniatures by Akbar's artists, but it does not present a very correct text.

(b) The version of Payandah Khan and Muhammed Quli (1586), based on the same text, but incomplete. All the MSS. accessible in this country are imperfect, the best being B. M. Add. 6588 II, and India Office 913.

(c) The translation of Shaikh Zain ud dīn Khwāfī (1590), which only covers eleven months (1525–6), and was probably never completed: There are two copies of this version in the B. M. (Or. 1999 and Add. 26202), both of which are fairly good.

The only European versions of the Memoirs are Pavet de Courteille's in French, and that of Erskine and Leyden in English. On the merits of the latter I have already enlarged. Pavet de Courteille's translation (Paris, 1871) is fairly good, but he has generally sacrificed style to accuracy, and in some passages, owing perhaps to the faulty nature of

[1] Lane-Poole's *Bābar*, p. 14.

Ilminski's text, his interpretation is defective, and even unintelligible.

Erskine tells us in his Preface that his work of translation was based on a collation of three manuscripts, viz. (*a*) 'Abd ur Rahīm's Persian translation, (*b*) Metcalfe's copy of another Persian version, and (*c*) a Tūrki text (the Elphinstone Codex). There can be little doubt that the two Persian translations referred to by him are those numbered Add. 26200 (a good sixteenth-century copy of 'Abd ur Rahīm's translation) and Add. 26201 (an inaccurate copy of the same version dated early nineteenth-century), which were among the manuscripts acquired by the British Museum after Erskine's death. He also possessed a copy of another Tūrki text (B.M. Add. 26324), which, although fragmentary, is a very good manuscript, dated 1629, and part of a copy of the Persian version by Shaikh Zain ud dīn Khwāfī (B. M. Add. 26202).

Pavet de Courteille was of opinion that Erskine had only a perfunctory knowledge of Tūrki, and that he relied chiefly on 'Abd ur Rahīm's Persian translation, which presents many difficulties of interpretation owing to its involved style, and the use of many Tūrki words and even whole verses, which are introduced without a translation, due to negligence, ignorance, or undue confidence in his reader's knowledge.

Leyden's MSS. passed into the possession of the India Office, but unfortunately, owing to the deficiency of records, it is impossible to identify them all. His MS. of the Tūrki text (No. 2538) is of little value, as it is a modern transcript dating from the beginning of the nineteenth century. As the Elphinstone Codex was in his possession, it is unlikely that he made use of this manuscript. It is doubtful if any of the India Office MSS. of the Persian version belonged to Leyden. If he can be assumed to have used any of them, it must have been 'Abd ur Rahīm's translation. My special thanks are due to Mr. A. G. Ellis for his invaluable assistance in the preparation of the foregoing account of the texts and translations of the Bābur-nāmeh, and other bibliographical notes.

We must remember that though Leyden was associated

with Erskine as joint translator of the Memoirs, the chief credit of the work belongs to the latter. Leyden translated less than half the Memoirs, and even this portion had to be substantially revised by his colleague. Erskine, on the other hand, contributed a valuable Preface and Introduction, supplied practically all the notes, and filled up the blanks in Bābur's Journal with scholarly memoranda.

I have carefully collated with Erskine and Leyden's translation Pavet de Courteille's French version, which is based on a comparatively accurate Tūrki text, and any important differences of interpretation are indicated in the foot-notes. These have been ruled off from the notes on the text, and are distinguished by small italic letters.

I have thought it advisable to correct the old-fashioned spelling of names and places and bring it up to date, though the modern system of transliteration has not been strictly adhered to where the pronunciation was not affected. In spite of the great care that has been taken over the matter it is possible that a few inconsistencies may remain. The greater part of Erskine's notes have been retained, but a few have been omitted as obsolete, some compressed, and others brought up to date. New notes have been added where necessary, and these are distinguished by square brackets. I have spared no pains to identify the animals and plants mentioned in the Memoirs, but the task is rendered difficult by the vagueness of Bābur's descriptions, the corruption of the texts, and the mistakes of the transcribers.

My friend Lt.-Col. D. C. Phillott has kindly placed his unique knowledge of Eastern bird-lore at my disposal, and I have also found much useful information in Jerdon's *Birds of India* (Calcutta, 1877), Sterndale's *Mammalia of India* (Calcutta, 1884), Blandford's *Fauna (Mammalia) of British India* (London, 1888–9), *The Fauna of British India* (Birds) by Oates and Blandford (London, 1889–98), Bonavia's *Cultivated Oranges and Lemons of India and Ceylon* (London, 1890), and Watts' *Dictionary of the Economic Products of India*, but some names of animals and plants still remain unidentified or doubtful.

The original map attached to the Memoirs, being incomplete and obsolete, has not been reproduced, and Waddington's note thereon has also been omitted. A new map has been prepared under my directions by Messrs. J. Bartholomew & Sons to illustrate Bābur's campaigns in Turkestan, Afghanistan, and India, and I take this opportunity to acknowledge the careful manner in which this work has been performed. A number of place-names occurring in the Memoirs defy identification owing to the corruption of the texts, the changes of nomenclature, or the fact that they are too insignificant to be shown in any map. I have, however, been able to identify the more important places on Bābur's routes with the assistance of the following maps : Major J. Rennell's map in his *Memoir of a Map of Hindustan* (2nd ed., London, 1792), Waddington's map prefixed to the first edition of Erskine and Leyden's translation of the Memoirs (London, 1826), Elphinstone's map in his *Account of Caubul and its Dependencies* (London, 1839), Sir H. Yule's map in Woods' *Journey to the source of the Oxus* (London, 1872), Elias' map of Central Asia in the *Tarīkh i Rashīdī* (London, 1895), Lane-Poole's map in his *Bābar* (Oxford, 1899), and the Atlas of the *Imperial Gazetteer of India*, by Hunter and Meyer (Oxford, 1907–9).

Among the many works consulted in the preparation of my notes on history, ethnography and religion, the following may be specially mentioned : *History of Baber.* by W. Erskine (London, 1854), referred to as E. B. ; *The Encyclopaedia Britannica* (last edition) ; *History of India*, by Elliott and Dowson (London, 1867); *Notes on Afghanistan*, by Major Raverty (London, 1888) ; *Oriental Biographical Dictionary*, by T. W. Beale, revised by H. G. Keene (London, 1894); *A Dictionary of Islām*, by T. P. Hughes (London, 1895) ; *Tarīkh i Rashīdī*, translated by Elias and Ross (London, 1895), referred to as T. R. ; the Provincial Gazetteers of the Panjāb and United Provinces.

The portrait of Bābur, which forms the frontispiece of the first volume, has been printed from a heliogravure plate, the property of the trustees of the Gibb Memorial, to whom my cordial thanks are due for kindly permitting me to use it. The portrait is a slightly enlarged copy of a miniature in the B. M. (Add. 5717, fol. 52). This portrait, the work of which is very fine, appears in Lane-Poole's *Bābar*, but the reproduction was so much enlarged that the likeness has become faint and indefinite. From its style the miniature would appear to have been executed in Turkestān, and it preserves the Tūrki characteristics of feature. It is undated, but, if not contemporary, ' it doubtless represents a tradition, and probably copies an earlier miniature ' (Lane-Poole's *Bābar*, p. 7).

Pavet de Courteille's version contains four long passages of doubtful authenticity, which are omitted in Erskine and Leyden's translation, and these I have thought it best to include in this edition as Appendices A, B, C, and D. The first describes Bābur's miraculous deliverance from imminent danger at Kirmān; the second supplies an account of Hindāl's adoption by Humāyūn's mother; the third furnishes a plain account of the battle of Kānwāha; and the fourth gives the story of Humāyūn's illness and Bābur's self-devotion. Appendix E contains short biographies of the joint authors of the translation, the material for which has been obtained from the *Dictionary of National Biography* (1st ed., London, 1885). A copious analytical index is provided.

I am under deep obligation to the late Mr. Vincent A. Smith, without whose encouragement and advice I should not have attempted the task of editing this work. My cordial acknowledgements are also due to Dr. Stanley Lane-Poole, Sir George Grierson, Mr. L. A. Storey, Assistant Librarian, India Office, and Mr. G. F. Finney of the Record Department, India Office Library, for much valuable help.

LUCAS WHITE KING.

ROEBUCK HALL,
    CO. DUBLIN.

ADVERTISEMENT TO THE FIRST EDITION

THE following Volume was sent from India as it now appears, and reached England in the course of the year 1817, but was not then published, in consequence of circumstances which it is unnecessary to mention. It is thought proper to take notice of the fact, chiefly in order to account for the silence of the notes as to any works of a later date.

EDINBURGH, *July* 22, 1826.

TO THE

HONOURABLE MOUNTSTUART ELPHINSTONE,

BRITISH RESIDENT AT THE COURT OF POONA, ETC. ETC. ETC.

My dear Sir,

WHILE employed in completing the following Translation, and in arranging the various prefatory and supplementary observations which accompany it, I have often indulged the wish of inscribing them with your name, as being the only appropriate return I could make for the perpetual assistance received as well from your advice and judgement, as from your valuable manuscript collections, which contain more information regarding the Geography, Manners, and Political Situation of the Countries that were the scene of the two first periods of Bābur's History, than are to be found in all the printed and written authorities which exist in any other quarter.

That the work is still very imperfect, no one can be more sensible than myself. I might explain some of the difficulties which occasioned this imperfection, were such apologies ever attended to. Some of them, perhaps, should have deterred me from the undertaking, and others a more resolute scholar might have overcome. Had the work indeed been finished by the same hand by which it was begun, no such apologies would have been required. For the task, whether of translating or illustrating any work on Oriental history, Dr. John Leyden was eminently qualified, as well as for greater things. The number and variety of the literary undertakings of that extraordinary man, many of which he had conducted far towards a conclusion, would have excited surprise, had they been executed by a recluse scholar, who had no public duties to perform, and whose time was devoted to literature alone. As he was cut off in the full vigour of his mind indeed, but suddenly, and without warning, he was prevented from putting the last hand to any of his greater works; yet from the knowledge which you possess of his researches, you will perhaps agree with me in thinking, that the full extent of his powers cannot be justly estimated from anything that he has published. The facility with which he mastered an uncommon number of languages, ancient and modern, European and Oriental, the extent and ingenuity of his antiquarian inquiries into the Literary History of his own country, and even the beauty of his poetical genius, are surpassed by the sagacious and philosophical spirit which he evinced, in the latter period of his life, in his different Memoirs regarding the languages of the East, and particularly those of Hindustan, Bengal, the Dekhan, and Northern India. The acute discrimination, the various and patient research which he brought to the task, combine to render them, unfinished as they unfortunately are, and imperfect as, from the nature of the subject, they necessarily must be, one of the most valuable literary gifts that India has yet bestowed on the West. These, or the substance of them, will, it is hoped, be given to the world under the care of some one who may do justice both to them and their author. The turn of mind that directs to the successful prosecution of studies so remote from the beaten tracts of literature, is so rare, that even the unfinished essays of an accomplished observer, with all their defects, are of singular value, and inconceivably lessen the happier labour of succeeding inquirers.

If the share which I have had in completing and correcting for the press the following papers, which, however, are of a very different kind, shall enable the Public to benefit by one of the lesser labours of Dr. Leyden, of which it would otherwise have been deprived—or if it adds, in any degree, to the idea justly entertained of his learning, industry, and judgement, I shall be satisfied. I could have wished, on his account, that the execution had been more perfect. It would have been pleasing to me to have offered a tribute worthy of a friend endued with so many rare and valuable talents, warmed by every manly and generous feeling, and rendered doubly dear to me, as the only companion of my youthful studies and cares, whom I have met, or can ever hope to meet, in this land of exile.

Though I well know, that no man is so likely as yourself to be alive to the defects of the following pages, no European having seen so much of the countries described in them, or inquired so successfully into their history, yet I present them to you with more confidence than I might otherwise have done, as I seem only to pay you a debt which I owe in common with my excellent friend. And perhaps you will not judge me too hardly, should it seem that I am not uninfluenced by the vanity of letting it be known, that I too may pride myself in having shared some portion of your regard. Believe me to be,

Yours very faithfully,

WM. ERSKINE.

Bombay, April 12, 1816.

PREFACE

The Memoirs of the Emperor Bābur, of which the following pages contain a translation, are well known, by reputation, to such as are conversant with the history of India. They were written by that prince in the Jaghatāi or Chaghatāi Tūrki, which was his native language, and which, even down to the present time, is supposed to be spoken with more purity in his paternal kingdom of Ferghāna than in any other country. It is the dialect of the Tūrki tongue which prevails in the extensive tract of country that formed the dominions of Jaghatāi or Chaghatāi Khan, the son of Chingiz Khan, the celebrated conqueror, which extended from the Ulugh-Tāgh mountains on the north to the Hindūkūsh mountains on the south, and from the Caspian sea on the west to the deserts of Gobi, beyond Terfān, Kāshghar, and Yārkand, on the east. It was, however, chiefly the language of the deserts and plains, as the cities, especially along the Jaxartes, and to the south of that river, continued to be, in general, inhabited by persons speaking the Persian tongue, while the inhabitants of most of the hills to the south retained their original languages.

The Chaghatāi Tūrki was a dialect of the language of that extensive division of the Tartaric nations, which, in order to distinguish them from the Mongals, or Moghuls, have recently, though perhaps erroneously, been more peculiarly denominated Tartars or Tatārs. The language really spoken by that great race is the Tūrki; and the language of Kāshghar, of the Crimea, of Samarkand and Bokhāra, of Constantinople, and the greater part of Turkey, of the principal wandering tribes of Persia, and, indeed, of one half of the population of that country, of the Turkomāns of Asia Minor, as well as of those east of the Euxine, of the Uzbeks, the Kirghiz, the Kazzāks, the Bāshkirs, and numerous other tribes of Tartary, is radically the same as that of the Chaghatāi Tūrks. The most mixed, and, if we may use the expression, the most corrupted of all the dialects of the

Tūrki, is that of the Constantinopolitan Turks,[1] which, however, for some centuries, has been the most cultivated and polished. The others all still very closely approximate, and the different tribes speaking them can easily understand and converse with each other.

The Tūrki language had been much cultivated before the age of Bābur, and at that period had every title to be ranked among the most perfect and refined in the East. The sovereigns of the different Turkomān and Tūrki dynasties to the south of the Caucasian range, the Caspian sea, and the river Sirr, (the ancient Jaxartes,) though many of them had been distinguished encouragers of Arabic literature in the kingdoms which they had conquered, and though several of the earliest and most eminent of the Persian writers flourished in their courts, had still continued to speak their native tongue in their families and with the men of their tribe. When Sir William Jones decided [2] that the Memoirs ascribed to Taimūr could not be 'written by Taimūr himself, at least as Caesar wrote his Commentaries, for one very plain reason, that no Tartarian king of his age could write at all,' he probably judged very correctly as to Taimūr, who seems to have been unlettered, though, as to the other princes of Tartarian descent, his contemporaries, he perhaps did not sufficiently consider that two centuries had elapsed since the conquest of Chingiz Khan, and two more since the reign of Mahmūd of Ghazni, during all which time the territories to the east of the Caspian, as well as a great part of Persia, had been subject to Tūrki dynasties, and the country traversed by tribes of Tūrki race and speech; and that this period was far from being one of the darkest in the literary history of Persia. The want of a suitable alphabet, which he gives as a reason for doubting whether the language was a written one before the days of Chingiz Khan,[3] was soon remedied. The Arabic character is now

---

[1] In order to discriminate the Constantinopolitan or Osmanli Turks from the Chaghatāi and other original Tūrks, I shall in the following pages denominate the former *Turks*, and their language *Turkish*; the latter *Tūrks* and their language *Tūrki*, pronounced *Toorks* and *Toorki*.

[2] Discourse on the Tartars. *Works*, vol. i, p. 69, 4to ed.

[3] Ibid., p. 68.

PREFACE

used, as it was at least as early as the thirteenth century,[1] the age of Haitho. The fact only proves that the Tūrki language was, as Sir William Jones justly concluded, very little cultivated before the Tūrki tribes entered those provinces which had formed part of the immense empire of the Arabian Khalifs, in which the Arabian literature still prevailed, and the Arabian character was still used.

I may be permitted to add, that there seems to have been some mistake or confusion in the account given to Sir William Jones of the *Tūzuk*, or Institutes of Taimūr. 'It is true,' says he, ' that a very ingenious but indigent native, whom Davy supported, has given me a written memorial on the subject, in which he mentions Taimūr as the author of two works in Turkish ; but the credit of his information is overset by a strange apocryphal story of a King of Yemen, who invaded, he says, the Amīr's dominions, and in whose library the manuscript was afterwards found, and translated by order of Alisher, first minister of Taimūr's grandson.'[2] He tells us in the same discourse,[3] that he had ' long searched in vain for the original works ascribed to Taimūr and Bābur.' It is much to be regretted that his search was unsuccessful, as, from his varied knowledge of Eastern languages, he would have given us more ample and correct views than we yet possess of the Tūrki class of languages, with the Constantinopolitan dialect of which he was well acquainted. The preface to the only copy of the complete Memoirs of Taimūr which I have met with in Persian, and which is at present in my possession, gives an account of the work, and of the translation from the original Tūrki into the Persian tongue ; but does not describe the original as having been

---

[1] Haitho observes that the *Jogour* 'literas habent proprias' (*Hist. Orientalis*, c. 2, ed. 1671). The inhabitants of Turkestān, he says, 'vocantur *Turchae*, literas non habent proprias, sed utuntur Arabicis in civitatibus, sive castris'. Ib., c. 3. See also *Hist. Orient.*, c. 3, ap. Bergeron, p. 7. [The Uighurs are credited with having been the first to reduce the Tūrki language to writing by borrowing the Syriac written characters from the Nestorian Missions, which, during the Middle Ages (thirteenth century), were spread over Central Asia (T.R., p. 95). Tūrki now denotes the language spoken by the tribes of E. Turkestān and Kāshgar.]

[2] Jones's *Works*, vol. i, p. 69.   [3] Ibid., p. 60.

found in the library of a King of Yemen, but of Jaaffer, the Turkish Pasha of Yemen. Now, Sir Henry Middleton, in the year 1610, met with a *Jaffer Basha*, a Turk, in the government of Senna,[1] or Yemen. It is curious, too, that we are told by the author of the *Tārīkh i dilkushā*, that a copy of the Memoirs, kept in Taimūr's family with great care and reverence, fell into the hands of the Sultan of Constantinople, who suffered copies of it to be made. Some confused recollection of these facts seems to have been working in the mind of Sir William Jones's informant, and to have produced the misstatements of his memorial. The mistake of a copyist writing *Pādshah* (king) for *Pasha*, might have produced part of the error.

The Tūzuk, or Memoirs themselves, contain the history of Tamerlane, in the form of annals, and conclude with the Institutes, which have been translated by Major Davy and Dr. Joseph White.[2] The Persian translation, in the manuscript to which I have alluded, differs considerably in style from the one published by the learned professor, which is an additional proof that there was a Tūrki original of some kind, from which both translations were made ; a fact confirmed by the number of Tūrki words which are scattered over both translations ; in which respect the Persian translation of Bābur's Memoirs strongly resembles them. Whether these Memoirs of Taimūr are the annals written by Tamerlane, or under his inspection in the manner described by Sherīf-ed-din Ali Yezdi in his preface,[3] I have not

---

[1] Astley's *Collection of Voyages*, vol. i, p. 326. [A person of this name was Pasha of Yemen in 1610, *Elliott's History of India*, p. 389, vol. iii.]

[2] [The *Tūzukāt i Taimūrī* were translated into English by Major Davy, and published under the editorship of Professor White at Oxford in 1783.]

[3] That author tells us that Taimūr had always with him Tartar and Persian secretaries, whose business it was to describe all his remarkable words and actions, and whatever related to religion or the state ; and as many officers and great lords of the Court had got accounts made of particular events of which they were eye-witnesses, or of which they had had the principal direction, he had all these collected, ' et eut la patience de les arranger lui-mème, apres quoi il les fit verifier en sa presence de la manicre suivante. Un lecteur lisoit un de ces memoires : et lorsqu'il en etoit sur quelque

examined the manuscript with sufficient care to venture to affirm or deny. They contain, in the earlier part of Taimūr's life, several little anecdotes, which have much the air of autobiography; while throughout there are many passages in a more rhetorical style than we should expect from that rough and vigorous conqueror; but that they are a work translated from the Tūrki, the same that has long passed in the East as being the production of Tamerlane, which Dr. White, in his preface, regrets could no longer be found, and for which Sir William Jones sought in vain, there seems no reason to doubt. I confess that the hypothesis of the Nawāb Muzaffer Jung appears to me the most probable, that they were written, not by the Emperor, but by Hindu Shah, Taimūr's favourite, under the direction of Taimūr [1] himself. If the European public are not already satiated with works on Oriental history, they might easily be translated.

The period between the death of Tamerlane and that of Bābur formed the golden age of Tūrki literature. From every page of the following Memoirs it will be seen that the spirit and enthusiasm with which Persian poetry and learning were then cultivated had extended itself to the Tūrki. I do not find that any works on law, theology, or metaphysics, were written in that tongue. But the number of poems of various measures, and on various subjects, the number of treatises on prosody and the art of poetry, on rhetoric, on music, and on other popular subjects, is very considerable. The palm of excellence in Tūrki verse has long been unani-

fait important, ou quelque action remarquable, il s'arrêtoit, les temoins oculaires faisoient leur rapport, et verifioient les circonstances du fait, les rapportant telles qu'ils les avoient vues; alors l'Empereur examinoit lui-même la verité du fait, et ayant bien confronté ce que les temoins rapportoient avec le contenu des memoires, il dictoit aux secretaires la maniere dont ils devoient l'inserer dans le corps de l'ouvrage, et se le faisoit relire ensuite, pour voir s'il étoit tel qu'on ne pût y rien trouver, ni à ajouter, ni à diminuer.'—*Hist. de Timur-Bec*, traduite par M. Petis de la Croix, preface de l'Auteur.

[1] Sir William Jones's works, vol. i, p. 69. Major Davy was quite wrong in confounding the Tūrki and Moghul tongues. A Chaghatāi Tūrk will not suffer his language to be called Moghul. No one marks the distinction more clearly than Bābur himself in the first part of his Memoirs.

mously assigned to Ali Sher Beg Nawāi, the most eminent nobleman in the court of Sultan Hussain Mirza Baikera, of Khorasān, and the most illustrious and enlightened patron of literature and the fine arts that perhaps ever flourished in the East. Many of the principal literary works of that age are dedicated to him. He is often praised by Bābur in the following Memoirs, and his [1] own productions in the Tūrki language were long much read and admired in Māweralnaher and Khorasān, and are not yet forgotten. Many Tūrki princes were themselves poets; and although the incursions of barbarians, and the confusion and unsettled state of their country for the last three centuries, have broken the continuity of the literary exertions of the Tūrki nations, they still cling with uncommon affection to their native tongue, which they prefer extremely to the Persian for its powers of natural and picturesque expression; and they peruse the productions of the fifteenth and sixteenth centuries with a delight that reminds us of the affection of the Welsh, or of the Highlanders of Scotland, for their native strains. Unfortunately, however, as the Mullas, or schoolmasters, in the cities of the countries north of the Oxus, regard the Arabic as the language of science, and the Persian as the language of taste, and measure their own proficiency, as scholars and men of letters, chiefly by the extent of their acquaintance with the language and literature of Arabia and Persia, the earlier works written in the Tūrki language run some risk of being lost, unless speedily collected. From these causes, and from the air of literary superiority which a knowledge of Persian confers, few works are now written in Tūrki, even in Tūrki countries. In the great cities of Samarkand and Bokhāra, though chiefly inhabited by men of Tūrki extraction, Persian is the language of business.

[1] [Ali Sher Beg Nawāi was born in A. D. 1440, and became Prime Minister to Sultan Hosain Mirza, Ruler of Khorasān, in 1469. After some time he resigned this office, and devoted the remainder of his life to the composition of works in Tūrki and Persian. He was the patron of the celebrated poet Jāmi.—He wrote in Tūrki a collection of odes under the pen-name of Nawāi—(of which I possess a beautifully written copy with a number of exquisite miniatures) as well as a Quintet in the style of Nizāmi's *Khamsah* In Persian he composed a *Diwan* under the *nom de plume* Fanāi. He died in A. D. 1500.]

Though the present royal family of Persia are Tūrks, and though Tūrki is the ordinary language spoken in their families, and even at their [1] court, as well as by one-half of the population of Persia, particularly by the tribes around the capital, who compose the strength of the army, Persian is the usual and almost only channel of written communication ; nor am I aware that any work of note has, of late years, been written in the Tūrki tongue.

The Chaghatāi Tūrki, as contained in the Memoirs of Bābur, is evidently not the same language which was brought from the wilds of Tartary by the Turkomāns in the ninth century, or by the Tūrki tribes who accompanied Chingiz Khan in the thirteenth. It has received a very strong infusion of Arabic and Persian words, not merely in the terms of science and art, but in its ordinary tissue and familiar phrases. These words are all connected by the regular grammar of the Tūrki ; but so extensive is the adoption of foreign terms, that perhaps two words in nine in the Chaghatāi dialect may be originally derived from a Persian or Arabic root. The language itself is, however, remarkable for clearness, simplicity, and force ; the style far less adorned than that of the modern Persian, and as free from metaphor and hyperbole as that of a good English or French historian ; and on the whole the Tūrki bears much more resemblance to the good sense of Europe than to the rhetorical parade of Asia. The style of all Tūrki productions that I have ever happened to meet with, is remarkable for its downright and picturesque naïveté of expression.

It is not difficult to discover how these Persian words flowed into the Tūrki language. The cities of Samarkand, Bokhāra, Akhsi, Andejān, and Tāshkend, as well as the other towns to the north of the Oxus and Jaxartes, were chiefly inhabited by Persians, the Tūrks long retaining their aversion to the life of a town, and refusing to submit to the drudgery of agriculture for the sake of supporting them-

[1] The same was the case even under the Safavi dynasty, as we learn from Kaempfer. See *Amoenitat. Exotic.* It may appear singular, that while all the neighbouring courts used Persian as the language of polite intercourse and diplomacy, Tūrki was the court language in Persia itself ; but it arose from its being the mother-tongue of the sovereign, who belonged to a Tūrki tribe.

selves on *the top of a weed,* as they call wheat in derision. The cities and market towns in Māweralnaher were therefore chiefly peopled, and the grounds were cultivated solely by the old inhabitants, the Sarts or Tājiks, who had used, and continued to retain the Persian tongue. The courts of the Kings and Princes were usually held in the great cities, which necessarily became the resort of the chieftains and head men of the tribes that still kept the open country. The Tūrks, some time after leaving their deserts, had exchanged their former superstition for the religion of Muhammed. All religious, moral, and literary instruction proceeded from their priests and Mullas, men trained to Arabic literature, and whose native language was Persian. It became necessary for every Tūrk to know something of Persian, to enable him either to conduct his purchases or sales in the public markets, or to comprehend the religion to which he belonged; and the course of five hundred years, from the days of the Samanian dynasty to the birth of Bābur, gave ample space for that corruption or improvement of the language, which a daily and regular intercourse with a more refined people in the common business of life must necessarily produce.

Bābur does not inform us, nor do we learn from any other quarter, at what period of his life he began to compose his Memoirs.[1] Some considerations might lead us to suppose that he wrote them after his last invasion of India. That they must have been corrected after that period is certain, since in the first part of them he frequently refers to that event, and mentions some of his Begs as holding appointments in Hindustān. Perhaps, too, the idea of writing his Memoirs was more likely to have occurred to him after his success in India, than at any previous time, as he had then overcome all his difficulties, was raised to eminence and distinction, and had become not only an object of wonder and attention to others, but perhaps stood higher in his own

[1] [The Memoirs were probably written at various dates; the earlier portion having been revised and enlarged after Bābur's invasion of India, while the latter part remains in its original form of a rough diary which he had not time to revise (S. L.-Poole's *Bābur,* pp. 13–14).]

estimation. His Memoirs may be divided into three parts, the first extending from his accession to the throne of Ferghāna, to the time when he was finally driven by Sheibāni Khan from his paternal kingdom, a period of about twelve years; the second reaching from his expulsion from Ferghāna to his last invasion of Hindustān, a period of about twenty-two years; and the third containing his transactions in Hindustān, a period of little more than five. The whole of the first part, and the three first years of the second, are evidently written chiefly from recollection; and the style and manner in which they are composed, appear to me far to excel that of the rest of the work; not only from the clearer connexion given to the various parts of the story, and the space given to incidents in proportion to their importance, but from the superior unity and rapidity of the narrative. This is, perhaps, in other respects also, the most agreeable portion of the Memoirs. During a great part of the period to which they relate, he was unfortunate, and often a wanderer; but always lively, active, and bold; and the reader follows him in his various adventures with that delight which inevitably springs from the minute and animated recital of the hazardous exploits of a youthful warrior. The narrative, when renewed in the year 925 of the Hijira, after an interval of twelve years, partakes too much of the tedium of a journal, in which important and unimportant events find an equal space, and seems to be in a great measure the copy of one kept at the time. The same remark applies perhaps even more strongly to the greater part of the concluding portion of the work. In the earlier portions of the Memoirs we have a continuous narrative of details, such as a lively memory might furnish at the distance of many years. In the latter parts, trifling incidents are often recorded, which, if not committed to writing at the time, would soon have met the oblivion they merited. We are informed of minute particulars which can interest even the writer only by recalling particular events or peculiar trains of association—how often he ate a maajūn, or electuary—how often he got drunk, and what nameless men were his boon companions. These incidents, however curious as illustrative of manners

A.D. 1519.

or character, are repeated even to satiety. Yet these parts also contain the valuable accounts of Kābul and of Hindustān; he gives an occasional view of his aims and motives, of the management of some of his expeditions, and particularly of his conduct during the alarming mutiny of his troops; while the concluding portion of his Memoirs, where the form of a journal is resumed, appears to be hardly more than materials for his private use, intended to assist him in recalling to his memory incidents as might have enabled him to furnish a connected view of the transactions of that period. Still, however, all the three parts of his Memoirs, though the two last are evidently unfinished, present a very curious and valuable picture of the life and manners of a Tartar Prince, and convey an excellent idea of Bābur's policy, and of his wars in Māweralnaher, Afghānistān, and India, as well as of his manners, genius, and habits of thinking; and perhaps no work ever composed introduces us so completely to the court and council, the public and private life of an Eastern Sultan.

A question may arise whether we have the Memoirs of Bābur at the present day as perfect as he wrote them; and in spite of the various *hiatus* which they exhibit, one of which extends to a period of twelve years, I am inclined to believe that they never were much more perfect than we now possess them. This opinion I entertain first from the fact that all the copies and translations which I have seen or heard of, are deficient in the same important passages; and next, from the remarkable fact, that the narratives of the different authors who treat of Bābur's reign, are more or less particular, exactly where the Memoirs, as we now possess them, are more or less minute. In many instances there are chasms in his history which no succeeding writer has supplied. This would not have been the case had he written and published the whole events of his reign in a continuous narrative. It is remarkable too, that, in commencing his fifth invasion of India, he makes a sort of recapitulation, which would have been unnecessary, had the events alluded to been explained immediately before, as they must have been, had he written an unbroken history of his reign.

Bābur himself seems to have been satisfied with his labours, for, towards the close of his life, we find him sending a copy of his work from Hindustān to a friend in Kābul. The Memoirs continued to be held in the greatest veneration at the Courts of Delhi and Agra after his death. From some marginal notes which appear on both copies of the translation, as well as on the Tūrki original, it appears that the Emperor Humāiūn, even after he had ascended the throne, and not long before his death, had transcribed the Memoirs with his own hand. In the reign of Akber, they were translated from the original Tūrki into Persian by the celebrated Mirza Abdal-Rahīm, the son of the Bairām Khan, who acted so conspicuous a part in the reigns of the Emperors Humāiūn and Akber.[1]

[1] As his translation is so often referred to in the following pages, and may be regarded as in some degree a second original, a few anecdotes of the life of the author may not be here misplaced :— When Humāiūn, after his long misfortunes, was restored to the throne of Delhi, in order to attach to his interests the chief men of the various principalities of Hindustān, he encouraged intermarriages between their families and those of his chief Tartar officers. He himself married one daughter of Ismael Khan, the nephew of Hassan Khan of Mewāt, so often spoken of in the third part of these Memoirs, and gave another daughter to Bairām Khan, his minister and favourite. Of this last marriage, Mirza Abdal-Rahīm was born at Lahore on the 17th of December, 1556, in the first year of Akber's [1] reign. His father, who was thus connected with the imperial family, and who was unfortunately too powerful for a subject, after having been goaded into rebellion, was killed in Gujerāt when on his way to perform the pilgrimage of Mekka. Abdal-Rahīm, his son, then only four years of age, was conveyed in safety to Ahmedābād by his faithful attendants, who sustained repeated attacks of the assailants up to the very gates of that city. He was carried from thence to Lahore and Agra. When he came of age, Akber bestowed on him the title of Mirza Khan, and married him to Mahbānu, the sister of Khan Azīm Goge, an officer of high distinction. At the age of twenty-one, he got the government of Guzerāt, and in his twenty-fifth year was promoted to the office of Mīr Arz (or Master of Requests). When twenty-eight years of age, he was made Atālik, or Governor, of Sultan Selīm, the Emperor's eldest son, who afterwards

[1] 14 Safer, A. H. 964. See the *Maāsir al umarā*, vol. i, folio, art. Abdal-Rahīm, MS. This work, which is well known in India, is a curious and very correct Biographical Dictionary of all the eminent statesmen and warriors who have flourished in that country since the time of Bābur. It is in two large folio volumes.

The translation which he executed of the Memoirs of Bābur is extremely close and accurate, and has been much praised for its elegance. But, though simple and concise, a close adherence to the idioms and forms of expression of

mounted the throne under the name of Jehāngīr; and in the same year was sent into Gujerāt against Muzaffer Shah, the King of that country, who, after being compelled to take refuge among the Katti with the Jām at Jūnager,[1] had collected an army of forty thousand men, defeated the imperial generals, and seized Ahmedābād. The Mirza's army consisted of only ten thousand, and he had received instructions not to hazard the safety of the province by engaging in battle. But he did not decline an engagement, and the armies having come close upon each other, Daulat Khan Lodı, a very gallant officer, told him, that now was the moment either to make himself Khān i Khānān,[2] or to fall in battle. Abdal-Rahīm attacked the enemy at Sarkaj,[3] four or five miles from Ahmedābād. The conflict was bloody, and maintained with various success. At one period the battle seemed to be lost, and Abdal-Rahīm found himself obliged with three hundred men to face a firm body of six or seven thousand. Some of his friends seized the reins of his horse to carry him from the field; but he refused to retreat, and stood his ground with such bravery and conduct, that he changed the fortune of the day. Muzaffer in the end was defeated, and fled to Cambay,[4] whence, after plundering the merchants of the place, he sought refuge among the mountains of Nadot.[5] Muzaffer soon after again ventured into the field, but, being once more defeated, fled to the Rājpīpli[6] hills, on the south of the Nerbudda. Where disobedience is eminently successful, the disobedience is generally forgotten, and the success only remembered. Abdal-Rahīm, according to the prediction of Daulat Khan, was promoted to the rank of an Amīr of five thousand horse, with the high title of Khān i Khānān. It is said, that on the day of battle, after he had distributed all his jewels and property among his troops, a soldier having come to him and complained that he had had no share in the division, the Mirza, to satisfy him, took out and gave to him his enamelled inkstand, richly adorned with jewels, being the only article which he had retained. In the thirty-fourth year of his own age, and of the reign of Akber, he translated the Memoirs of Bābur, which he presented to the

---

[1] In the western part of the Peninsula of Gujerat.

[2] Khan of Khans (Commander in Chief), the title of one of the chief officers of the empire of Delhi.

[3] [Sarkaj is three kos distant from Ahmedābād.]

[4] Kambāit. [This town is situated at the head of the gulf of Cambay on the north of the estuary of the Myhee river.]

[5] [Nadot is probably Nandod, between the Nerbadda and Rājpīpla.]

[6] [Rājpīpla is south of the Nerbadda.]

PREFACE   xxxiii

the Tūrki original, joined to a want of distinctness in the use
of the relatives, often renders the meaning extremely obscure,
and makes it difficult to discover the connexion of the
different members of the sentence. The style is frequently
not Persian, and a native of Persia would find it difficult
to assign any sense to some of the expressions. Many of the
Tūrki words are not translated, sometimes because they had
no corresponding term in Persian, and sometimes perhaps
from negligence, or, it may be, because they were then
familiar to the Tūrki nobility of the court of Agra. But the
whole is uncommonly valuable, and probably there are few
persons now living even in Mālweralnaher, who could give

Emperor, by whom he was highly complimented. We are told by
Abulfazel, that they were translated at the desire of Akber when
he was on a progress to Kashmīr and Kābul. The same year he was
raised to the distinguished rank of Vakīl-e-Sultanet, or Lord Lieutenant of the Empire, a title very rarely conferred. It would be tedious
to follow him to the governments of Jaunpūr, Multān, and Sinde, which
he successively held. He completely defeated the Hākim (or chief)
of Sinde, obliged him to cede Sehwān and some other districts, and
married his son Mirza Irej to the Hākim's daughter. A revolt having
ensued, Abdal-Rahīm obliged the Hākim and all his family to repair
to Agra. The long wars that followed in the Dekhan, particularly
that against Ahmednagger, gave him great opportunities to signalize
his military talents. During the whole reign of Akber he was employed in the most important commands, and the relation in which
he stood to the imperial family was drawn closer by the marriage of
his daughter Jāna Begum to Daniāl the Emperor's son. His influence
continued under the Emperor Jehāngīr his former pupil, and he was
selected for the chief direction of affairs wherever great talents were
required, in the wide range of country from the Dekhan [1] to Kandahār, to which last place he was sent with Sultan Khurram, afterwards
the Emperor Shah Jehān, to repel the invasion of Shah Abbās the
Persian King. The history of his life would be a history of the public
affairs of the empire of Delhi during half a century. He died at Delhi
in the year 1626 or 1627, at the age of seventy-two, with the highest
reputation for talents, valour, generosity, and learning.[2]

---

[1] It was during one of his battles in the Dekhan when his troops
were broken, that some of his officers came to ask what was to be their
rallying place in case of defeat, and where they were to look for him.
His answer was, *under the slain*! He gained a bloody victory.
(*Maāsir al umarā*, as above.)

[2] These details are chiefly taken from the *Maāsir al umarā*, and
from Ferishta.

an accurate translation of the original Tūrki of Bābur's Memoirs without the aid of Mirza Abdal-Rahīm's Persian translation. To account for this fact, it must be recollected that the study of the language of past ages is peculiar to that antiquarian refinement which exists only in highly improved times, and may be regarded as one of the last luxuries of literary curiosity. The learned Langlés, in the article 'Babour' of the *Biographie Universelle Ancienne et Moderne*, affirms that the Commentaries were translated into Persian by Abdal-Rahīm after being enlarged by Jehāngīr. I know not on what authority he hazarded this assertion, which is certainly erroneous. The Prince Selīm, who was afterwards Emperor under the name of Jehāngīr, was indeed twenty years of age when the translation was published ; and, at a former period, Abdal-Rahīm, who was his *Atālik* or Governor, may have prescribed to him a perusal of the Memoirs in the original as an exercise in the language of his forefathers ; but the coincidence of all the copies, the marginal notes of Humāiūn, and the nature of the work itself, may satisfy us that the other assertion is unfounded, and we certainly possess the Memoirs of Bābur, whatever their value may be, in the state in which they were originally written by their imperial author.

The English translation now presented to the public was begun by the late Dr. John Leyden, a man whose inquisitive mind left no department of literature unexplored. He found, I am uncertain whether in the Library of the College of Fort William, or in the collection of the Honourable Mountstuart Elphinstone, a copy of the original Tūrki. Being delighted with the novelty and merit of the work, he began translating it with all his characteristic ardour. He soon, however, found difficulties which his instructor, a Persian Tūrk of Ganj, could not solve. I had fortunately some time before procured at Bombay a copy of Mirza Abdal-Rahīm's translation, which is found in several of the public libraries of Europe, but of which Dr. Leyden had been unable to meet with any copy in Bengal. At his desire, I had begun sending him the sheets of a transcript which I caused to be made, when he was called to accompany the late Earl of Minto in the expedition against Java. This interrupted his labours, and his premature death followed soon after in August 1811.

Feeling a warm interest in the preservation of his manuscripts, and desirous that nothing which could add to his reputation should be lost, I wrote to our common friend, Dr. James Hare, junior, of Calcutta, in whose possession his papers then were, offering my assistance in completing the translation of Bābur, which I knew was imperfect. Perhaps I engaged too rashly in the undertaking. At that time I happened to have in my service the Persian who had assisted Dr. Leyden in his translation, and who had become pretty well versed in the language of the Memoirs. But before my letter reached Calcutta, Dr. Leyden's papers and manuscripts had been sent home to Mr. Richard Heber, his principal literary executor, and I relinquished all idea of seeing the work completed, at least in India. Some years before, I had translated a small portion of the Memoirs from the Persian, and was now strongly urged by General Sir John Malcolm and the Honourable Mountstuart Elphinstone, who were struck with their merit as a literary curiosity, to complete an English translation of the whole from the Persian alone. As both of these gentlemen had been on missions into the countries described by Bābur, and were peculiarly versed in the manners and history of the Tūrki dynasties, more competent judges could not be found, and their advice had its natural weight with me. I accordingly undertook the task, which I had brought to a close, when, in the end of the year 1813, I was surprised by receiving from London a copy of Dr. Leyden's translation, which, in consequence of my letter to Dr. Hare, had been procured and forwarded by the kindness of that gentleman, who was then in England.

This acquisition reduced me to rather an awkward dilemma. The two translations differed in many important particulars; but as Dr. Leyden had the advantage of translating from the original, I resolved to adopt his translation as far as it went, changing only such expressions in it as seemed to be inconsistent with the context, or with other parts of the Memoirs; or such as seemed evidently to originate in the oversights that are unavoidable in an unfinished work. This labour I had completed with some difficulty, when Mr. Elphinstone sent me the copy of the Memoirs of Bābur in the original Tūrki, which he had procured when he went to Peshāwer on his Embassy to Kābul. This copy, which he had supposed to have been sent home with Dr. Leyden's manuscripts from Calcutta, he was now fortunate enough to recover.

The discovery of this valuable manuscript reduced me, though heartily sick of the task, to the necessity of commencing my work once more. Being now possessed of the original, it was necessary to compare the whole translation with it. It appeared to me that, in many instances, Dr. Leyden's translation was less accurate than the Persian, a fact not to be wondered at, as he had only recently begun the study of the Chaghatāi Tūrki, and no part of the translation had received his last corrections, or perhaps been twice gone over. I therefore examined the whole with minute attention, comparing it with the Tūrki and Persian texts, and made such alterations as I was persuaded my friend would not have disapproved of, had he assisted in the labour. The rest of the Memoirs I then completed by the aid of the Tūrki original, of my own copy of the Persian translation, and of another copy, which Mr. Elphinstone, with that readiness with which he invariably lends his aid to whatever has the semblance of forwarding useful knowledge, procured for me from Delhi, through Mr. Metcalfe, the British Resident at that Court. From this last copy, though much less accurate than the other, I was enabled to correct many errors, and to supply several chasms in the Persian translation which I previously possessed. The Tūrki original, which is very correct, is unfortunately incomplete. The continued narrative closes before the great battle in which Sultan Ibrahīm of Delhi was slain, and there is only one short fragment of a later period. Mr. Metcalfe's copy of the Persian translation, though the most incorrect, is the most perfect of the three. It contains the whole Memoirs, with such errors and omissions alone as arose from the negligence of the copyist. My own copy has lost three leaves in different parts of the work, and is deficient in the journal of several months at the end. This last period is filled up on the authority of Mr. Metcalfe's manuscript alone.

I ought to observe, that my own knowledge of the Chaghatāi Tūrki would not have enabled me to complete the translation from the original, and that I relied principally on the Persian. The Persian Tūrk, on whose assistance I had at first relied, had unfortunately left Bombay before I received Mr. Elphinstone's Tūrki copy. With the assistance of some natives of Uzbek Tartary, who happened to be in Bombay, but chiefly aided by the patience and skill of my worthy friend Mulla Firūz, so well known to all who have made the antiquities of ancient Persia their study, I went over the Tūrki text, and compared it with the translation. I hope that few errors have escaped. But this long account of the origin and progress of the translation, which at first sight may seem needless, was rendered necessary in order to account for any want of uniformity that may probably be discovered in its various parts, and for any errors that may have crept in, in the course of the different transmutations it has undergone. The Memoirs of Bābur would undoubtedly have appeared to more advantage if clothed in the simple picturesque style, and illustrated by the varied erudition of Dr. Leyden, whose success in the study of languages has rarely been equalled, and whose industry was indefatigable. My aim in the following work has been limited to exhibiting that part of the translation which he executed, as much as possible in the state in which he would have wished it to appear, had he been spared to revise it; and to completing what he left unfinished. Dr. Leyden's translation is without notes, except occasionally verbal explanations; nor am I aware that he made any historical or geographical collections for completing or illustrating the Memoirs. The translation is close and literal to a degree which many will think faulty, and which few works written in an Eastern language would admit of; but such closeness is not without its use, as the style of a people generally exhibits in some degree the dress of their mind, and often leads to more just conclusions regarding their habits of thinking, than can easily be attained in any other way.

Of the Historical Introduction, and of the Supplements which fill up the various blanks in the Memoirs, little need be said. They were compiled from such books and manuscripts as were within my reach. For the copies of Khāfi Khan,[1] and of the *Maāsir al umarā*,[2] the former of which was of great use to me throughout, I was indebted to the kindness of Henry Russell, Esq., the British Resident at the Court of the Nizām, to whom I owe many similar obligations; the copy of the *Ālim-ārāi-Ābbāsi*,[3] which I have followed in the account of Bābur's latest transactions in Māwcralnaher, was furnished me by my friend Claudius James Rich, Esq., the British Resident at Bagdad. The curious anonymous history,[4] which contains the singular anecdote regarding the succession of Humāiūn, I owe to Captain William Miles of the Bombay Establishment. Nor must I forget to acknowledge the use of a corrected copy of Dow's translation of Ferishta's *Life of Bābur*, part of a revisal of the whole of Dow's translation of the *History of Hindostān*, by Captain John Briggs of the Madras Establishment, assistant to the Resident at Poona. The important and gross mistakes

---

[1] [Khāfī Khān (the concealed) was the pen-name of the celebrated historian, Muhammed Hāshim, the author of the work here referred to, the *Muntakhab ul lubāb*. This was a history of India from Bābur to Rafi'ud darajāt, and was published in 1732.]

[2] [The *Ma'āsir ul 'umarā*, or 'Peerage of the Mughal Empire', which has been printed for the *Bibliotheca Indica*, was commenced in 1742 by Shāh Nawāz Khān, Samsām ud daulah, and finished by his son, Mīr 'Abd ul Hai, in 1780 (Rieus' *Catalogue of Persian MSS.*, vol. i, p. 340). Shāh Nawāz Khān was born in 1700, and died by the hand of an assassin in 1758. He was Dīvān of Berār under Āsaf Jāh, *subahdār* of the Deccan, and subsequently became the Prime Minister of his successor Salābat Jang.]

[3] [The *Tārīkh i 'Ālam ārāi Abbāsī*, a history of the Persian Kings of the Safawī dynasty from Shāh Ismaīl to Shāh Abbās I, was compiled by Iskander Beg Munshi, who completed it in 1628 (Rieus' *Catalogue*, vol. i, p. 185).]

[4] [This must be the *Tabaqāt i Akbari*, a general history of India, compiled by Khwājā Nizām ud dīn Ahmed, and dedicated to Akbar in 1593. He became Bakhshī of Gujerāt under that Emperor, and died in 1594. The author's father was Muhammed Muqīm Herawī, who was Dīvān of Bābur's household and subsequently rose to be minister to 'Askari in Gujerāt'. Erskine's MSS. in the B.M include two copies of this work.]

in names, in geography, and in the sense of the author, with which Dow's translation abounds, makes it to be wished that Captain Briggs would communicate to the public the result of his studies, either by presenting a more accurate translation of that excellent author, or by giving an original work on these periods of the history of India, which he has studied with so much industry and success.[1]

For the materials from which the Geographical Sketch of the countries north of the Hindū-kūsh range are compiled, I am indebted almost solely to the Honourable Mountstuart Elphinstone. The description of these countries contained in geographical works and in books of travels, is very defective, and often erroneous. When Mr. Elphinstone went on his Embassy to Kābul, he exerted himself to procure, from merchants and travellers, such accounts as were to be had, of all the range of country as far as the borders of Russia. These he committed to writing, and even after his return to Hindustān and the Dekhan, he continued to add to his geographical treasures by conversing with such intelligent natives of these northern countries as happened to visit India, and securing the information which they afforded. Many of them he induced to write accounts of their own districts, or itineraries of their travels, in the Persian tongue. The unreserved use of the whole of these collections, with his own remarks and corrections, Mr. Elphinstone threw open to me, with that perfect frankness which belongs only to superior minds. Nor have I to acknowledge to him my obligations only in this part of the work. I received similar assistance from his accurate researches into the geography of Afghānistān and the Panjāb, and many of Bābur's marches, particularly that of Chotiāli and Āb-īstādeh, with the whole course of his progress to Khorāsān and return from that country, would have

[1] [The first edition of Briggs' *Ferishtah* was published in 1829 (London, 4 vols.). A reprint was issued in Calcutta in 1908–10. Ferishtah, who is so frequently referred to in these notes, was the *nom de plume* of Muhammed Kāsim, the author of the *Tārīkh i Ferishtah*, a history of India, which was written in 1614, and dedicated to Ibrahīm 'Ādil Shah II of Bījapūr. According to Mohl, he was born in Asterābād in A.D. 1550 and died in 1623. (Beale's *Dict. Or. Biog.*)]

been unintelligible to me without the assistance which his descriptions and maps afforded; and I may add that I have rarely had occasion to consult him regarding the manners of the age, or difficulties of the language, without feeling the benefit of the same extensive and accurate knowledge.

Besides my obligations for the use of his own papers, my thanks are further due to him for the communication of some valuable manuscripts of the late Lieutenant Macartney and of Captain Irvine of the Bengal Establishment, regarding the provinces to the north and west of Hindustān, from which I have freely drawn; and for procuring from Mr. Moorcroft the use of a very curious journal in the Persian language, kept by Syed Izzet-ullah, who had been sent by that gentleman on a route hitherto little frequented by travellers. The Syed went from the Sind to Kashmīr, thence across the hills to Leh or Ladāk, from thence to Yārkend and Kāshghar, whence he returned by Ush, Khojend, Uratippa, Samarkand, Bokhāra, and the Afghān country. This route traverses a very great proportion of the little-frequented districts so often spoken of by Bābur, and lies through the heart of that Prince's paternal kingdom. The instructions of Mr. Moorcroft appear to have been so judicious, that the Journal of Syed Izzet-ullah, besides giving an accurate itinerary of the country through which he passed, contains many amusing facts regarding the manners and state of society of the inhabitants, and was found of the greatest service in the construction of the map.

The countries which were the scene of Bābur's early transactions are so little known, and so imperfectly laid down in all our maps, that I was desirous that a chart of at least Ferghāna and Māweralnaher should be constructed with the assistance of the new materials afforded from different quarters, and my friend Mr. Charles Waddington of the Bombay Engineers kindly undertook the labour. The mode which he adopted for laying it down, will be best explained by his own Memoir. Having only one fixed point by which to correct his positions, the difficulties he had to encounter were very great. How well he has overcome them the map itself is the best evidence.[1] The additions and improvements made in the geography of all the country beyond the Oxus, but especially in the country of Ferghāna and the districts near Samarkand, will be visible by comparing his delineation with any previous one of these countries. Mr. Waddington laid me under the greatest obligations by the ready politeness with which, for a considerable period of time, he devoted to the completion of the map most of the few hours allowed him for relaxation from his professional duties ; and it is not a little to his honour, that while still only in the first step of his professional career, he has exhibited not only a love of knowledge, but a judgement and science in the use of his materials, that would have done no discredit to the most experienced officer of the scientific corps to which he belongs. Of the following work this portion will very generally be considered as the most valuable.

Before concluding, it may be necessary to say something of the orthography adopted in writing Asiatic words. I have in general preserved that used by Dr. Leyden. The vowels have the sound that is given to them in Italian ; *i* has the sound of the English *ee* ; *u*, of the English *oo* ; of the consonants the *ghain* is expressed by *gh* ; the two *kāfs* are not discriminated ; *g* has always its hard sound ; *shīn* is expressed by *sh* ; *che* by *ch*, which has the sound of *ce* in Italian, and *j* expresses the Italian *gi*.[2]

[1] [The map here referred to being out of date and incomplete another has been substituted.]
[2] [See Editor's Preface, p. xiii.]

INTRODUCTION

PART FIRST

CONTAINING

REMARKS ON THE TARTAR TRIBES

AND ON

THE GEOGRAPHY OF UZBEK TŪRKESTĀN

THE Emperor Bābur was of Tartar race, and the language in which his commentaries are written was that spoken by the tribes who inhabited the desert to the north and east of the Caspian. On the very edge of this desert he was born, but the changes of his fortune in the course of his eventful life carried him sometimes as a fugitive, and sometimes as a conqueror, into various provinces of Asia. Some correct general idea of the character of the race to which he belonged, and of the geography of the several countries which he visited, is absolutely necessary, to enable the reader to follow him with pleasure in his chequered career. But the geography of the provinces which form the scene of his early story, and in particular that of the countries beyond the great river Oxus or Amu, one of which was his native country and hereditary kingdom, is peculiarly obscure; insomuch, that by one of our latest and best-informed geographers, it has been justly characterized as being 'chiefly conjectural', and as 'remaining, to the disgrace of science, in a wretched state of imperfection'.[1] Some of these imperfections Mr. Elphinstone's valuable collections, and the Memoirs of Bābur themselves, may assist in removing. But the principal object of the following remarks is to give such an idea of the natural divisions of the country as may render the position and extent of the

[1] Pinkerton's *Geography*, vol. ii, p. 37. Third ed., 4to.

various provinces mentioned by Bābur, distinctly understood, as some of them are not to be found in the geographical systems of the present day.

The whole of Asia may be considered as divided into two parts by the great chain of mountains which runs from China and the Burman Empire on the east, to the Black Sea and the Mediterranean on the west. From the eastward, where it is of great breadth, it keeps a north-westerly course, rising in height as it advances, and forming the hill countries of Assām, Bootān, Nepāl, Sirinagar, Tibet, and Ladāk. It encloses the valley of Kashmīr, near which it seems to have gained its greatest height, and thence proceeds westward, passing to the north of Peshāwer and Kābul, after which it appears to break into a variety of smaller ranges of hills that proceed in a westerly and south-westerly direction, generally terminating in the province of Khorasān. Near Herāt, in that province, the mountains sink away, but the range appears to rise again near Meshhed, and is by some considered as resuming its course, running to the south of the Caspian and bounding Mazenderān, whence it proceeds on through Armenia, and thence into Asia Minor, finding its termination in the mountains of ancient Lycia. This immense range, which some consider as terminating at Herāt, while it divides Bengal, Hindustān, the Panjāb, Afghanistān, Persia, and part of the Turkish territory, from the country of the Moghul and Tūrki tribes, which, with few exceptions, occupy the whole extent of country from the borders of China to the sea of Azof, may also be considered as separating, in its whole course, nations of comparative civilization from uncivilized tribes. To the south of this range, if we perhaps except some part of the Afghān territory, which, indeed, may rather be held as part of the range itself than as south of it, there is no nation which, at some period or other of its history, has not been the seat of a powerful empire, and of all those arts and refinements of life which attend a numerous and wealthy population, when protected by a government that permits the fancies and energies of the human mind to follow their natural bias. The degrees of civilization and of happiness possessed in these various regions may have been extremely different;

but many of the comforts of wealth and abundance, and no small share of the higher treasures of cultivated judgement and imagination, must have been enjoyed by nations that could produce the various systems of Indian philosophy and science, a drama so polished as the *Sakuntala*, a poet like Ferdousi, or a moralist like Sadi. While to the south of this range we everywhere see flourishing cities, cultivated fields, and all the forms of a regular government and policy, to the north of it, if we except China and the countries to the south of the Sirr or Jaxartes, and along its banks, we find tribes who, down to the present day, wander over their extensive regions as their forefathers did, little if at all more refined than they appear to have been at the very dawn of history. Their flocks are still their wealth, their camp their city, and the same government exists of separate chiefs, who are not much exalted in luxury or information above the commonest of their subjects around them.

The belt of mountains that forms the boundary between the pastoral and civilized nations is inhabited, in all its extent, by hill-tribes who differ considerably from both of the others. The countries to the east of Kashmīr, at least those lying on the southern face of the range, are chiefly of Hindu origin, as appears from their languages; while the countries to the west of Kashmīr, including that of the Dards, Tibet-Balti or Little Tibet, Chītral and Kāferistān,[1] which speak an unknown tongue, with the Hazāras and Aimāks,[2] contain a series of nations who appear

[1] [The following note, for which I am indebted to the kindness of Sir George Grierson, summarizes the modern view on the subject. The languages of the East of Kashmīr, and indeed all Kashmīr territory including Baltistān and Ladākh, are all various forms of Tibetan. To the North of Kashmīr (Dardistān) the speech is Shina. Immediately to the West of Kashmīr the language is a form of Western Panjābi (Indo-Aryan). In Chitral the Khowār language, and beyond the Kunar River, the Kāfir dialects are spoken. Kashmīri, Shina, Khowār and the Kāfer languages all belong to the Pisācha Group, i.e they are partly Eranian and partly Indo-Aryan. Kashmīri, which is spoken in Kashmīr itself, though its basis is Pisācha, has become much mixed with Indian forms.]

[2] [The external characteristics of the Hazāras and Chār Aimāks are Mongolian, and they are probably a relic of the Mongol invasion. Their language is West Mongolian though it bears strong marks of Persian influence.]

never to have attained the arts, the ease, or the civilization of the southern states ; but who at the same time, unlike those to the north, have in general settled on some particular spot, built villages and towns, and cultivated the soil. No work of literature or genius has ever proceeded from this range. The inhabitants, justly jealous of their independence, have rarely encouraged any intercourse with the civilized slaves to the south, and do not appear, till very recently, to have had much commerce with their northern neighbours. The labour of providing for subsistence, the remoteness of their scattered habitations, and the limited means of intercourse with each other, appear, in all ages, to have stifled among them the first seeds of improvement.[1] Yet even among these mountains, the powerful influence of a rich soil and happy climate, in promoting civilization, is strongly visible. The vale of Kashmīr is placed near their centre ; and such has been the effect of the plenty and ease resulting from these circumstances, that that fortunate country has not only been always famous for the richness of its productions, and the skill of its manufacturers, but was, at one period, the seat of a considerable empire ; and its historians furnish us with a long catalogue of its authors on every art and in every department of literature, some of whom are still held in deserved estimation.

Bābur was descended from one of the tribes that inhabited to the north of this range. That immense tract of country which is known by the general name of Tartary, extends over nearly all the north of Asia, and over a considerable part of the south-east of Europe. It corresponds very nearly with the ancient Scythia. The tribes that inhabit it differ from each other in manners, features, and language. Of these, the most powerful and numerous seem to belong to three races : first, the *Mandshūrs*, called also *Manjūrs* and *Manchūs*, to the east, who extend from the Eastern Ocean along the north of China. Secondly, the *Mongols or Moghuls*, who chiefly occupy the central regions between the other two : and thirdly, the people, by Europeans, and particularly the Russians and later

[1] The same may be said of the indigenous population of Afghānistān, particularly of the hill country.

travellers, exclusively called *Tartars or Tatārs*, and sometimes *Western Tartars*, names not acknowledged by themselves, but who may with more propriety receive their original name of *Tūrks*, by which their principal branches still designate themselves.[1]

[1] [Manchu (= pure) was the name adopted by a ruler who rose to power in the beginning of the thirteenth century. Before that the Manchus were a shifting population, broken up into a number of tribes, which took the name of the particular clan whose chief exercised lordship over them. Their first appearance as a nation was in the tenth century, when under the name of Khitans they established the 'iron' dynasty in the Northern portion of the Chinese Empire. These were driven out two centuries later by another horde from Manchuria, who took the name of Kin or the 'golden' dynasty.

The history of the Mongols is extremely obscure. The name is said to be derived from *mong* (= brave). From the earliest notice we have of the Mongols in the history of the T'ang dynasty of China (A. D. 617-90) it appears that their original camping ground was along the course of the Kerulen, Upper Nouni, and Argūn rivers. A petty chief, Budantsar, by craft and violence, gained the headship of his particular clan, and the power of his descendants gradually increased until Yasukai, who was eighth in descent from Budantsar, extended his authority over a wide area, and his son, the great Chinghiz Khan, ruled an Empire which stretched from the China Sea to the Dneiper. Linguistically the Turks are easily defined as they all speak an Ural-Altaic language, but it is difficult to differentiate them ethnographically from the Finno-Ugrians, Mongolians, and Manchus, who have many Turkish characteristics. From a linguistic point of view Turks include the Yakūts of Siberia, the Tatārs of Kazān and Astrakhān, the Bashkīrs, the Nogais of the Crimea and Caucasus, the Kirghiz, the Kara Kapāks of the South-eastern shores of the Sea of Aral, the Uzbegs of Central Asia, the Sarts, the Moghuls, the Uighurs of Kashgar, Yārkand, and Khotan, the Turkomāns, and the Persian Turks of Azarbaijān. According to tradition the Turks and Mongols sprang from two brothers, but the early history of the Turks is very obscure. The Chinese Annals refer to certain warlike nomads, known as the Hiung-nu (or ten tribes), who even before the Christian era were considered a danger to the Empire. Their power was broken up by the Wei dynasty. In A. D. 433 a Hiung-nu tribe, called Asena, moved away from the Wei dominions and joined with another people called Jwen-jwen or Avārs. These they served near Shantun (in Kansuh), where there was a hill called from its shape *Turkai* (helmet), a somewhat fanciful derivation of the tribal name. They were first called Turks by the Chinese in A. D. 525, when the descendants of the Asena revolted and crushed the Jwen-jwen. They afterwards defeated the White Huns,

The country of the Mānchūs, containing all that lies east of the Siolki Mountains, and north of the range of Kinchan,[1] may be neglected on the present occasion; the influence of its inhabitants having been confined chiefly to China, of which they are now the rulers.

The Moghul and Tūrki tribes have exercised a far more important influence on the nations around them. The Moghuls extend over all the country between the Siolki Mountains and China on the east; the mountainous country from China towards Leh or Ladāk on the south; a line from Leh through the desert of Cobi to the east of Terfān, and thence by the Ulugh Tāgh,[2] the Ghiū river, and the Kūchik Tāgh hills[3] on the west; and by a very indefinite line north of the Altaian chain on the north. The Tūrki nations have the western boundary of the Moghuls as their eastern frontier; on the south they have the Muz-Tāgh,[4] the Belūt-Tāgh,[5] the Hindū-kūsh, and the limits of the cultivated country of Khorasān down to the Caspian, a line drawn across that sea to the Caucasian range, the northern shore of the Euxine as far as the sea of Azof, including the Krim, and thence their western boundary extends along the eastern limits of Europe to the Ural and Altai mountains. Some Tūrki tribes, however, have settled even south of the Danube, and others far in Russian Siberia; and in like manner detached tribes of Kalmuks still inhabit along the

who were possibly another tribe of the Hiung-nu, in A. D. 560. In 582 they split up into two sections, the Northern Turks round Lake Baikal and the Yenessei, and the Western in the neighbourhood of Tāshkend. This account of the origin of the Turks, if true, would seem to show that they were a branch of the Hiung-nu. It was not till A. D. 1250 that the Turks settled in Asia Minor under Ertoghrul, the father of Osmān, the founder of the Ottoman Empire (A. D. 1288–1326).—*Encyc. Brit.* The Tartars were properly certain tribes living in the N.E. corner of Mongolia, and partially, at least, of Tungusic race, whose descendants are found among the Solons of Northern Manchuria. They were divided into six tribes whose principal camp was at Buyur.—Howorth's *History of the Mongols*, vol. i, p. 25–6.]

[1] [The modern Khingang, a range, which running North and South, separates Manchuria from Mongolia.]
[2] Great mountains. [3] Little mountains.
[4] Ice hills. [5] Dark or cloudy mountains.

Volga, and down to Astrakhān, and probably may be found insulated even in more remote situations.

In a country so extensive, there is, as may be imagined, almost every variety of climate and of soil; but by much the greater part of the land, particularly that to the eastward, is barren, mixed in many instances with sandy deserts, while the climate is inhospitable, so that the difficulty of procuring subsistence on one spot, or at a moderate distance from their habitations, has compelled the inhabitants in all ages to adopt a wandering life. The many noble rivers which intersect the country, of course supply numerous fertile tracts along their banks; but in the greater part of this region, the districts capable of profitable cultivation are too few, too remote from each other, and too much surrounded by desolate sands, to admit of the formation of a permanent kingdom or state devoted to agriculture sufficiently extensive to protect the cultivator, and to check the predatory tribes of the desert by which it would be surrounded on all sides. The cities that have been built, and the districts that have been cultivated, in the flourishing times of any particular tribe, have always therefore rapidly declined.

The country lying between the Amu and Sirr rivers (the Oxus and Jaxartes of antiquity), and usually called Great Bucharia, or Māweralnaher, though now overrun and governed by Tūrki tribes, was not perhaps originally a part of Tartary, and must be excepted from this description. It is a region abounding with fine tracts of land, defended by inaccessible mountains and barren deserts, and watered by numerous streams. The natural condition of this country is that of a civilized and commercial state, abounding with large towns; a situation which it has always rapidly attained, when its governors possessed sufficient power to secure it from foreign enemies.

The Moghul and Tūrki tribes, though now confined to the limits that have been described, have, however, successively changed the aspect of the civilized world. The Huns (whom their historian the learned Des Guignes regards as being of Tūrki race, though some circumstances in the hideous description given of them by the Roman

INTRODUCTION

historians would lead us to conclude that, with a mixture of Tūrks, they consisted chiefly of the Moghul tribes),[1] passing from their deserts beyond the Caspian, poured into the richest provinces of the empire of the Romans, and under the ferocious Attila, the scourge of the human race, broke the already declining force of that mighty people. Still later, in the tenth century, the rich and

[1] The Empire of Hiung-nu, or Huns, had its origin north of the Great Wall of China, and conquered as far as Korea and the Caspian. It is said to have begun twelve hundred years before Christ (Des Guignes, *Hist. des Huns*, vol. i, p. 213), and the tribes composing it do not appear to have been conquered or driven westward by the Chinese, till the 93rd year of the Christian era. Those who retired to Aksū, Kāshghar, and the Jaik, or who had maintained their possessions there, entered Europe at a later period in the reign of Valens. As this empire had its origin in the centre of Tartary, extending both ways, it is probable that it originated among the Moghul tribes, and that the chiefs even of the minor divisions were of the ruling race of Moghuls. This presumption is confirmed by the descriptions preserved of Attila, which bear such strong marks of Moghul extraction, that Gibbon justly characterizes them as exhibiting the genuine deformity of a modern Kalmuk. It is almost unnecessary to remark that the Kalmuks are one of the most numerous tribes of Moghul extraction. But though the chief, and many of the tribes that accompanied him, were Moghuls, he probably, like his countryman Chingiz Khan in later times, had in his army numerous bodies of men of different nations, comprising the inhabitants of the various parts of his Empire, and particularly many of Tūrki origin, as tribes of that race appear, from the earliest accounts in history, to have extended from the Volga to the desert of Gobi. The observation made on the composition of the Empire of Attila will equally apply to most of the other great empires mentioned in the history of the Huns. They were not composed purely of one race, but of races of various descent, Tūrki, Moghul, Finnic, and Manchū.
[The identity of the Huns cannot be fixed with any certainty. The name has been given to at least four peoples, viz. (1) the Huns under Attila, (2) the Magyars, (3) the Ephthalites or White Huns, and (4) the Hunas. The last two appear to be racially identical, and, though it cannot be proved, it is probable that all four belonged to the same stock. After the defeat of the Hiung-nu (who are by some authorities identified with the Huns) by the Chinese in the first century A. D., one body of Huns, after a long sojourn in Transoxiana, passed on through Afghānistān to India (A.D. 450–500), while another horde pushed westward to the Caspian Sea, whence they invaded Europe in the end of the fourth century A. D. The Magyars speak a Finno-Ugric language, but we have no warrant for assuming that the language of the Huns was the same.]

cultivated provinces of Samarkand and Khwārizm, at that period the seats of Oriental science and learning, were subdued by the Tūrki hordes. In the following century the Ghaznevide dynasty, whose dominion spread over great part of India and Persia, the dynasties of the Seljuks in Persia, the vassalage of the Khalifs of Baghdad to their Turkomān guards, and the final destruction of the Khalīfat itself, the successive conquest of Armenia, Asia Minor, and in the end of the whole Empire styled the Turkish, from its founders, attest the valour and enterprise of the Tūrki tribes. The Moghuls were unknown beyond the wilds of Tartary, from the age of Attila till the thirteenth century, when their leader, the celebrated Chingiz Khan, after having subdued all the neighbouring Tartar tribes, particularly those of Tūrki extraction, who, under the dynasty that existed down to his time, had possessed the ascendancy over the Moghuls, burst into the provinces of Turān, Māweralnaher, Khwārizm, and Khorasān, subdued part of India, reduced Azarbaijān, and a considerable portion of Persia, the Tūrki tribes of Kipchāk, and a great part of China, leaving those vast countries, which were much more extensive than the Roman Empire at the period of its widest dominion, to be governed by his posterity. His successors pursuing the tract of conquest, traversed Russia, marched over Poland, and poured their troops into Hungary, Bohemia, and Silesia; accident alone, perhaps, prevented the cities of Germany from undergoing the fate of Samarkand and Bokhāra, cities at that time the seats of greater refinement and politeness than any in Europe; and it has been truly observed that the disordered digestion of a barbarian on the borders of China, by withdrawing the Moghul armies from the west, may have saved us from the misfortune of witnessing at this day a Tartar dynasty in the richest countries of the west of Europe. The superiority acquired by Chingiz Khan, a Moghul, over the Tūrki tribes, has never been entirely lost. His empire, after his death, having been divided among his sons, who seem to have been accompanied to their governments by numerous families, and even by tribes, or parts of tribes, of Moghuls, who followed their princes, the chief authority in all the conquered countries continued for a series of years to be in the hands of that race; and even the chiefs of Tūrki tribes, if not Moghuls themselves, appear to have been ambitious of connecting themselves by intermarriages with Moghul families; so that, at the present day, the greater part of them trace up their descent to Chingiz Khan. The descendants of these Moghuls and Moghul families, however, being placed among a people who spoke a different language, gradually adopted that of their subjects, as is usual in all conquered countries where the conquerors are few and the conquered many; so that the Tūrks and their chieftains, being now freed from any dependence on the Moghuls, are once more completely separated from them both by government and language, and regard them as strangers and foreigners.

Whether the Moghul and Tūrki languages differ from each other essentially, or only as very different dialects of the same tongue, is a question which I have never seen clearly decided. Of the Moghul I possess no vocabulary by which a comparison could be instituted with the Tūrki.[1] An examination of the lists in the Comparative Vocabulary made by order of the Empress of Russia, or of those in the Mithridates of the learned Adelung, would go far towards deciding the question, which is one of considerable curiosity. If the Tūrks, as is probable, inhabited the neighbourhood of the Caspian as early as the days of Herodotus, by whom the *Turkai* are mentioned,[2] and if they always inhabited

[1] [The Mongol tongue belongs to the Ural-Altaic branch of languages, which also includes Finno-Ugric, Turkish, Manchu, and Samoyede. The Turkish group differs from the Mongol-Manchu group by the greater development of its system of inflections, the freer use of pronominal affixes, and its more thoroughly agglutinative character, a difference due, perhaps, to Chinese influence. There is no resemblance in their vocabularies. The Mongol language is divided into three branches, (a) East Mongolian (Mongolian proper), (b) West Mongolian (including the Kalmak and Hazāra dialects), (c) Buriatic, and all these groups are closely inter-related, and all are characterized by the curious system known as the 'harmony of vowels'. The characters, which, like the Manchu, are written from above downwards, are lineal descendants of the original Uighurian forms derived from the Syriac.]

[2] The Khozāri, a Tūrki tribe, inhabited to the north of the Caspian in the middle of the fifth century, and, according to Moses of Chorene, had their Khākān (or great Khan) and their Khātūns or Princesses.

the country from Tibet to the Black Sea, their language may reasonably be supposed to have had some influence on that of their neighbours. But if, in addition to this, we consider the frequency of their irruptions into the south of Asia for the last fourteen hundred years, under their own name, and probably for a much longer period under that of Scythians; that one-half of the population consists of Tūrki tribes, or of Tūrks settled in towns, but still speaking their native tongue; that the most numerous race next to the Slavonians, in the extensive empire of Russia, are the Tūrks;[1] that several Turkomān tribes also traverse the wastes of Turkey, and that the Ottoman Empire itself, as well as the Turkish language, owes its origin to the northern Tūrks, we shall probably feel some surprise that a language so extensively spoken, and which seems to promise so rich a field to the industry of the philologist, should have been so much overlooked,[2] and even its existence scarcely known, except in the Osmanli dialect of Turkey, the dialect, to the antiquary and philologist, of all others the least valuable, as most widely deviating from its primitive form. The Chaghatāi Tūrki furnishes a variety of finished works, both in prose and verse; but that dialect having been carried to its perfection in the provinces between the Amu and Sirr,[3] where the Persian was formerly spoken, is full of words borrowed with very little change from that language and from the Arabic. In the Tūrki of Bābur, perhaps the purest specimen now extant of the language of his times, probably two-ninths of the whole extent may be traced to an Arabic or Persian root. Specimens of the language of the different wandering Tūrki tribes, compared with the language of Bābur and with that of the Moghul tribes, would enable us to form tolerably decided notions of the affiliations of the Tūrki and Moghul races.

'Rex autem aquilonarius appellatur *Chacanus*, qui est Chazirorum dominus, et regina vocatur *Chathunia*, quae est Chacani conjux ex Barsiliorum gente orta.' (Moses Choren., *Geog. ad calcem Hist. Armen.*, p. 356, London, 1736, 4to.) This, I imagine, is the earliest contemporary mention of these tribes.

[1] See Tooke's *View of the Russian Empire*, vol. i, p. 449.

[2] [Modern research has done much to remove this reproach, and here is a copious literature extant on the subject.]

[3] The Oxus and Jaxartes.

INTRODUCTION

Another question, which has been a good deal agitated, and which to me appears to have been erroneously decided, is that which regards the application of the name of *Tartar*, or more properly *Tatār*, by which we denominate these nations. It is applied by Europeans as a general term comprehending a variety of different tribes in the northern division of Asia, and is quite unknown to the inhabitants themselves, as well as to the Indians ; which last, very improperly, call all of these tribes, as well as all Persians, and indeed any Mussulman with a whitish face, Moghuls. The term Tartar seems to have been first used by our historians and travellers about the thirteenth century. Joannes de Plano Carpini, who travelled A.D. 1246, informs us that the country of the Moghuls, in his time, not long after the death of Chingiz Khan, was inhabited by four nations (or populi), the Yeka Mongols,[1] the Sū-Mongols, or Water Mongols,[2] *who call themselves Tartars from a certain river called Tartar which runs through their territory,*[2] the Merkat and Metrit ; and adds that all these nations speak the same language. Chingiz belonged to the Yeka Mongols, and subdued the other three divisions. All of these nations lived in the middle division of Tartary. Carpini, after describing his passage eastward through the country along the Sirr or Jaxartes, and the lands of the Tūrks whom he calls Black Kythai,[3] adds, ' On leaving the country of the Naymans ' (which was the last of the Tūrks), ' we then entered the country of the Mongols, whom we call Tartars.'[4] This name of Tartar, however, by which we are accustomed to designate Chingiz Khan and his successors as well as their empire, these princes themselves rejected with disdain. Rubriquis, who visited the court of Sartakh, Chingiz Khan's grandson, about the year 1254, was cautioned, therefore, to call him Moal (that is Moghul), and not Tartar ; ' for they wish to exalt their

---

[1] Chief or superior Moghuls.

[2] Hakluyt, vol. i, p. 30. See also Petis de la Croix's *Life of Gengis Can*, p. 63, who calls the river *Tata*, whence *Tatārs*. [Howorth (*History of the Mongols*, vol. i) denies the existence of this river.]

[3] That is Kara Khitāi.

[4] ' Deinde terram Mongolorum intravimus, quos Tartaros appellamus.' (Hakl., vol. i, p. 55.)

name of *Moal* above every name, and do not like to be called Tartars; for the Tartars were a different tribe;'[1] meaning, I presume, the Sū-Mongols, conquered by Chingiz; and hence the victorious family did not choose to receive the name of their subject vassals. Rubriquis informs us that Chingiz Khan, after the union of the kindred tribes of Moghuls and Tartars under his government, generally made the Tartars take the advance, and that, from this circumstance, they being the tribe who first entered the territory of their enemies, and whose name was first known, the appellation of Tartar was by foreigners applied to the whole race, to the exclusion of the superior name of Moghul. It was by the united strength of these two tribes of Moghuls that Chingiz Khan destroyed the powerful kingdom of Kara Khita, and subdued the Tūrki tribes.

As, in the time of the early successors of Chingiz Khan, the name of Tartar was erroneously transferred from one, and applied to the whole Moghul tribes; so, in latter times, and at the present day, it is, with still greater impropriety, applied by European writers to designate exclusively the tribes of Tūrki extraction, who are in reality a very different race. The French, as well as the German and Russian writers, regard the name of Tartar as properly applicable only to the western Tartars. D'Herbelot, Petis de la Croix, Pallas, Gmelin, as well as the Editor of Astley's *Collection of Voyages*, all agree in the propriety of this limitation. Tooke, who follows the best-informed Russian travellers, after dividing the country called Great Tartary among the Mongols, Tartars, and Mandshūrs, adds that the appellative Tartars 'is so much misapplied, that, with some inquirers into history, a doubt has even arisen whether there ever was a peculiar people of that name. Under this denomination have been implied all tribes beyond Persia and India, as far as the Eastern Ocean, however differing from each other in regard to their origin, language, manners, religion, and customs. Now', he continues, ' that we are better acquainted with these nations, we know that the Tartars in reality compose a distinct nation, which originally

---

[1] Hakluyt, vol. i, p. 93.

INTRODUCTION

belonged to the great Turkish stock.'[1] This opinion seems to be that at present universally received. The general name of Tartar, however, is not recognized by any of the tribes on whom it is thus bestowed. These tribes, who have the best right to fix their own appellation, know themselves only by the particular name of their tribe, or by the general name of Tūrk: their language they call the Tūrki, and if the name of Tartar is to be admitted as at all applicable peculiarly to any one of the three races,[2] it belongs to the Moghuls, one of whose tribes the ancient Tatārs were, with much greater propriety than to either of the others.

It is curious that, in like manner as in modern Europe, the name of Tatār, taken from a Moghul tribe, was bestowed on all the inhabitants of these vast regions; so, among the Arab conquerors of Asia, and the Arab and Persian geographers, they were all of them, Moghuls as well as Tūrks, known as Tūrks, by a name taken from a different race; while the country as far as China received the name of Tūrkestān. This singularity arose from a very obvious cause, the relative position of the Arabs and Tūrks. The country of Tūrkestān enclosed the Arab conquests in Māweralnaher on three sides. Being in immediate contact with Tūrki tribes, and unacquainted with the varieties of race or language among the more distant wanderers of the desert, whose manners, from similarity of situation, probably were, or at least to a stranger appeared to be, nearly the same, they applied the name of Tūrki to all the more distant nations in these quarters, though differing from each other in many important respects. It has already been remarked that the Indians use the term Moghul with still greater latitude.

But the difference between the Tūrks and Moghuls, if we may believe the best-informed travellers, is more marked than any that language can furnish. The Mongols, says

[1] Tooke's *View of the Russian Empire*, vol. i, p. 346.
[2] It may be remarked as singular that, though no large tribe, or union of tribes, bears at the present day the name of Tatar, it is sometimes to be found in the subdivisions of the tribes or septs. Thus the Kachar are divided into six Aimāks, the Shulask, the *Tatār*, Kuban, Tubin, *Mungal*, and Jastyn. See *Dic. Russ.*, vol. v, p. 183. Other similar instances occur.

Gmelin, have nothing in common with the Tartars (meaning the Türks) but their pastoral life, and a very remote resemblance in language. The Mongols differ, on the contrary, from all the races purely Tartar (Türki), and even from all the western nations, in their customs, in their political constitution, and, above all, in their features, as much as in Africa the Negro differs from the Moor. The description of their features, indeed, marks a race extremely different from the Türki. 'Les traits caracteristiques de tous les visages Kalmucs et Mongoles sont des yeux dont. le grand angle, placé obliquement en descendant vers le nez, est peu ouvert et charnu : des sourcils noirs peu garnis. et formant un arc fort rabaissé ; une conformation toute particuliere du nez, qui est generalement camus et ecrasé vers le front : les os de la joue saillans ; la tête et le visage fort ronds. Ils ont ordinairement la prunelle fort brune, les levres grosses et charnues, le menton court, et les dents tres blanches, qu'ils conservent belles et saines jusques dans la vieillesse. Enfin leurs oreilles sont generalement toutes enormement grandes et detachées de la tête.'[1] Gmelin observes, that indeed 'they have not the shadow of a tradition which could justify a suspicion that they ever composed one nation with the Tartars. The name of Tartar, or rather Tatār, is even a term of reproach among them ; they derive it in their language from *tatanoi*, to draw together, to collect : which, to them, means little better than a robber.'[2] It is singular that a name thus rejected among the nations to whom it is applied should have had so much currency. The resemblance between Tartar and the infernal Tartarus, joined with the dread and horror in which the Tartar invaders were held, while they scattered dismay over Europe, probably, as has been well conjectured, preserved the name in the west.

While all accounts of the Moghuls concur in giving them something hideous in their appearance, the Türks, on the other hand, appear to have been rather distinguished as a comely race of men. The Persians, themselves very handsome, considered them as such. Hāfiz and the other Persian poets celebrate their beauty. They seem to have very much

[1] *Hist. des Decouvertes Russes*, vol. iii, p. 209. [2] Ibid., p. 210.

of the European features, but with more contracted eyes;
a peculiarity which they probably owe to intermarriages
with the Moghuls, or perhaps to something in their local
situation in the deserts whence they issued. But, whatever
may have been the difference between these two nations,
certain it is that a marked distinction did exist between
them from very early times.

The manners of these roving and pastoral tribes, as
described by the ancient Greek and Roman writers, agree
precisely with those of their descendants at the present day;
but they have been painted with so much liveliness and
truth by Gibbon, in a work which is in every one's hands,
that nothing need be added to what he has sketched.
The first historical period, a knowledge of which is of consequence to the understanding of the following Memoirs,
is that marked by the conquests of Chingiz Khan. In
the earlier days of that Prince, the Kara Khitan was the
most powerful Tartarian dynasty. Within the extensive
range which their empire embraced, from the Chinese wall
to the Ala Tāgh mountains, though the population was
chiefly Tūrki, were included several tribes of different races,
Tūrks, Uighurs, and Moghuls. Their power was broken
in the year 1207 by the Naimans, another Tūrki race;
and soon after, the Moghul tribes, impatient of a foreign
yoke, rose under Chingiz Khan, shook off the authority of
the Kara Khitans, and, under his conduct, rapidly subdued
them in their turn. The name of Kara Khita indicates their
connexion with Khita [1] or northern China, on which their
chiefs acknowledged a dependence. It was, however, a
dependence that originated in a previous conquest of that
very country made by their predecessors the Khitans, or
Leao, to whom the Chinese had paid tribute; and the
dependence, in the first instance, was on the emperor
rather than the empire. The title of Ung-Khan given to
the chief prince of the Kara Khitans, and assumed by him,
shows that they were not ashamed of their dependence on
China; the title *Ung* being one purely Chinese, and bestowed

---

[1] There is reason to think that, though the term Khita is now
applied to northern China and its Tartar dependencies, it was at first
given to a Tartar tribe who overran that country.

on mandarins of the highest class. The Tūrki population at that time probably extended farther east than it does at the present day, and tradition informs us that the Kirghiz and some other tribes, now far to the west, then occupied ground close to the Chinese wall. They migrated westward, flying from the vengeance of their enemies when the Moghuls proved victorious. On the other hand we have heard of Kalmuks on the borders of Poland, and several Moghul tribes may now be found as far west as the Volga, and pushed in between Tūrki tribes, who still differ from them in aspect, language, and religion. These last appear to have been chiefly the tribes that were induced to settle in the west, after the conquests of Chingiz Khan. They accompanied that conqueror, and remained with his sons for their protection, or to overawe the conquered. One of the most remarkable of these was the grand tribe of Moghuls, who, in the age of Bābur, were settled, one branch on the territory of Tāshkend and the plains in its vicinity, in a country by Bābur called Moghulistān, and the other probably in the present Sungaria,[1] the Jetteh of the Institutes of Taimūr, or on the river Illi. They seem to have been part of the royal horde of Chaghatāi Khan, the son of Chingiz, who fixed his capital at Bishbāligh on the Illi; and many particulars of their manners, which continued extremely rude, are detailed in a very picturesque manner by Bābur in his Memoirs.

In the division of the empire of Chingiz Khan among his sons, one of them had the provinces to the east of the Tūrki frontier; Chaghatāi had the country westward as far as the Sea of Aral, and perhaps nearly to the river Jaik; while a third had all the other regions to the west, along the Caspian, and far into modern Russia. The country occupied by Chaghatāi Khan was long afterwards held by his descendants, and the inhabitants acquired the name of Jaghatāi or Chaghatāi Tūrks, and the country itself that of Jaghatāi. The connexion subsisting between the different tribes, in consequence of their having a point of union by being under the same government, seems to have favoured

[1] [Sungaria is a district in Mongolia lying north of Kuldja and east of the Ala-tau range which divides it from W. Siberia.]

an approximation in language; and their dialect, which became highly cultivated, has continued down to the present day, and is still spoken, especially in towns and by the stationary Tūrks, over nearly the whole extent of the ancient Chaghatāi territories. The power of the Khans of Chaghatāi was nearly [1] lost before the age of Taimūr, who founded a new dynasty, the capital of which he fixed at Samarkand. He, in common with Chingiz Khan,[2] traced up his descent to Toumeneh Khan, a Moghul prince, so that both were of the royal race of the Moghuls; but the family and dependent tribe of Taimūr had been settled for nearly two centuries at Késh, to the south of Samarkand, and, being in the midst of a country inhabited by Tūrks, spoke the language, and had adopted the manners and feelings, of those among whom they dwelt. The families descended from Taimūr, therefore, though strictly Moghul, always regarded themselves as Tūrki.

Bābur had a close connexion with both races of Tartars. He traced up his descent on the father's side in a direct line to the great Taimūr Beg, whence he always speaks of himself as being a Tūrk; while by the mother's side he was sprung from Chingiz Khan, being the grandson of Yunis Khan, a celebrated prince of the Moghuls. All Bābur's affections, however, were with the Tūrks, and he often speaks of the Moghuls with a mingled sentiment of hatred and contempt.

In spite of the various changes that have occurred in the course of six hundred years, the limits of the Tūrki language are still not very different from what they were in the days of the imperial Chingiz. These limits have already been roughly traced. The object of this Introduction does not require that we should enter farther into any details concerning these countries, the cradle of the Tartarian ancestors of Bābur. Our attention is more immediately

[1] Gibbon, vol. xii, p. 4, speaks of the Khans of Chaghatāi as extinct before the rise of Taimūr's fortunes. But they still existed though stripped of their power; and, accordingly, in the progress of the historian's narrative, p. 28, we find that the nominal Khan of Chaghatāi was the person who took Bajazet prisoner.

[2] See D'Herbelot, *Bibliothèque Orientale*, art. 'Genghis' and 'Timour'; and the Shujret-ul-Itrāk.

called to that division of it generally called Great Bucharia, but which may with more propriety be denominated Uzbek Tūrkestān, which not only contains his hereditary kingdom, but is the scene of his early exploits. It will, in the first place, however, be necessary to give some idea of the high country of Pamīr and Little Tibet, whence the rivers flow that give their immediate form to all the surrounding countries.

It has been already remarked that the Himalaya Mountains, those of Tibet, Kashmīr, Hindū-kūsh, and Paropamisus, form a broad and lofty barrier, separating the countries of northern from those of southern Asia. The mountains, as they advance west, acquire a very great height; and measurements made at various places, towards Nepāl and Hindū-kūsh, by assigning to these ranges a height of upwards of 20,000 feet, would make them rank with the highest in the world.[1] Nearly parallel to this great chain, on the north, runs a considerable range, which has been called the Muz-tāgh, or Ice-Mountains. It extends on the east, at least from the northward of the Tibet range, near Leh or Ladāk, and has a north-westerly direction, skirting Eastern or Chinese Tūrkestān on the south, till it meets the Belūr,[2] or Belūt-tāgh Mountains, in the latitude of about 40° 45′, and longitude 71°; whence it seems to proceed on westward, as far as Khojend and Uratippa,

[1] Very recent measurements give to the highest of the Himalaya Mountains an altitude of 28,000 feet, which would make them decidedly the loftiest in our globe. [The height of Mount Everest is now stated to be 29,002 feet.]

[2] This name, in our older works on geography, is written Belūr. It is now generally called Belūt, or the Dark or Cloudy Mountain. Yet Marco Polo, after travelling twelve days over the elevated plain of Pamīr, travels for forty more over the country called Beloro. (Ramusio, vol. ii, p. 11.) Add to this, that Nasīrudīn of Tūs, in his geographical tables, places Belūr four degrees east of Badakhshān. (*Hudsoni Geograph. Min. Graec.*, vol. iii, p. 110.) There seems, therefore, to be some uncertainty as to the tract of country to which the name was at first applied. The name, at least, of Belor, is also given to this country by Rabbi Abraham Pizol. (Kircher's *China Illustrata*, p. 48. See also Bergeron, in cap. 27 of *Marc. Paul.*, p. 31.) [The Belūt-tāgh appears to be a range that runs northward from the Hindū-kūsh on the eastern boundary of Badakhshān. The country of Bolor is marked on the map in the *T.R.* as extending NE. from Chitrāl to the Taghdum-bāsh Pamīr.]

under the name of the Asfera[1] mountains, and then divides into three or four principal branches, as will afterwards be mentioned. Connecting these two great ranges of Kashmīr or Hindū-kūsh, and of Muz-tāgh, a third range proceeds northward from that part of the Hindū-kūsh which lies near Kaferistān, in longitude 72°, and meets the Muz-tāgh, as already mentioned. This range is called by geographers the Belūr, or Belūt-tāgh. It seems to revive again to the north of the Muz-tāgh, running, under the name of the Ala,[2] or Alāk-tāgh, and according to others of the Ming Bulāk, or Arjun Hills, first to the north as far as north latitude 42°, and next to the westward towards Tāshkend, when it terminates in the desert of Aral, about the 65th or 66th degree of east longitude.

The extensive country which lies between the three grand ranges of mountains, the Kashmirian, Muz-tāgh, and Belūt-tāgh, does not properly belong to Tūrkestān, though some parts of it at the present day are traversed by Tūrki tribes. It seems rather, with the country immediately east of the Ala, or Alāk-tāgh, to have belonged to one of the mountain races which inhabit the grand range of Hindū-kūsh, in an independent state to this day. Bābur mentions a curious fact, which seems to throw some light on the ancient history and geography of that country. He tells us that the hill-country along the upper course of the Sind (or Indus) was formerly inhabited by a race of men called Kas ; and he conjectures that, from a corruption of the name, the country of Kashmīr was so called, as being *the country of the Kas*.[3] The conjecture is certainly happy, and the fact on which it is founded important ; for its leads us farther, and permits us to believe that the Kasia Regio and the Kasii Montes of Ptolemy, beyond Mount Imaus,

---

[1] [This range runs a little south of the modern Isfara (40° 18′ N., 70° 45′ E.), which lies south-west of Khokand, and is marked on the ordnance survey map as the Kharlitan Mountains. I am indebted for this note and the last to the kindness of Dr. O. Codrington.]

[2] That is, the Chequered Mountain. It is said to be ' bare of forest and as if studded all over with rocks '. (Tooke's *View of the Russian Empire*, vol. i, p. 121.)

[3] Mīr is still united with the names of several districts, as *Jeselmīr Ajmīr* [and is said to mean hill].

were inhabited by this same race of Kas, whose dominion, at some period, probably extended from Kāshghar to Kashmīr, in both of which countries they have left their name. The country at this day called Kāshkār, and included within the triangular range just described, probably derived its appellation from the same origin, being only a corruption of Kāshghar, within the territory of which it was long included, the name having survived the dominion.

The mountains by which this country is buttressed on every side are very lofty, and bear snow on their summits the greater part of the year. It has been conjectured that, if we except some parts of the Greater Tibet, it is the highest table-land in Asia. In confirmation of which, it has been observed that, from this high land, which, for want of a general denomination, may be called Upper Kāshghar, the rivers take their course in opposite directions, and to different seas: the Sind or Indus, and the Kāshkār or Cheghānserāi river, flow through the mountains to the south, and after uniting near Attok, proceed to the Indian Ocean; while the Amu, which originates from the snows and springs of Pushtekhar, in the same high table-land, pours down the western mountains of Belūt-tāgh and, after keeping for some time along the Hindū-kūsh range, pursues its course towards the Sea of Aral. No river is known to cross the Muz-tāgh; but the rivers which originate on its northern face proceed down to the desert and the lake of Lop-nor. Of these which flow north, some originate not very far from the Indus, which flows from the eastward by Ladāk, between the two ranges, in the earlier part of its course.

This elevated country of Upper Kāshghar, though plain when compared with the huge and broken hills which rise and inclose it on all sides, is, however, crossed in various directions by numerous hills and valleys. As the slope of the country is from the north and east, the Muz-tāgh, though certainly of less height than the other ranges, probably rises from a more elevated base. Of this high and thinly-peopled country, the south-west part is called Chitrāl, the north-west portion Pamīr, or the Plain, whence the whole country is often denominated. The country of the

INTRODUCTION lxiii

Dards lies in the south-east, and the rest of it is occupied by Little Tibet, which on the east stretches away into Great Tibet.

The country of Uzbek Tūrkestān may be considered as a large basin, hollowed out by the waters descending from the Paropamisan and Hindū-kūsh hills on the south, and those of Belūt-tāgh and Alā-tāgh on the east and north, but formed into two divisions by the Asfera mountains; on the south of which lies the vale of the Amu or Oxus, and on the north the vale of the Sirr or Jaxartes. Both of these great rivers, after receiving all the tributary streams that pour into them from the valleys and smaller branches of hills which they meet with in their course, force their way with difficulty through extensive sandy plains to the Sea of Aral. Uzbek Tūrkestān on the south, after the termination of the Paropamisan hills, may be considered as divided from Persian Khorāsān by a line beginning north of Herāt, in latitude 35°, and running north-west along the south verge of the Desert, so as to terminate on the Caspian, about latitude 39°. The Caspian forms its western boundary; and a line, from the Caspian to the Sea of Aral, and thence again to the Alā-tāgh, or Ming Bulāk mountains, which run north of the Sirr, or Jaxartes, as far as Tāshkend, completes its northern frontier.

That part of Uzbek Tūrkestān which lies south of the Asfera mountains may be divided into the countries south of the Amu, or Oxus, and those to the north of that river.

The divisions to the south of the Amu, including also those that extend to both its banks, or which are contained between its branches, are four: 1. Badakhshān; 2. Balkh; 3. Khwārizm; and, 4. The Deserts of the Turkomāns.

The divisions to the north of the Amu are five: 1. Khutlān; 2. Karatigīn; 3. Hissār, or Cheghāniān; 4. Késh, or Shaher e sebz, including Karshi and Khozār; and, 5. The Vale of Soghd, in which are the celebrated cities of Samarkand and Bokhara.

The countries lying along the Vale of the Sirr, or Jaxartes, may be considered as being six in number: 1. Ferghāna, now called Kokān and Nemengān; 2. Tāshkend; 3. Uratippa, or Ushrushna; 4. Ghaz, or the Aral desert; to which may perhaps be added, 5. Ilāk, extending between Uratippa and Tāshkend; and, lastly, the district of Tūrkestān Proper.

I. DIVISIONS SOUTH OF THE AMU

It may be convenient, in reviewing the different divisions of Uzbek Tūrkestān, to follow the course of the two great rivers, as they proceed from the hills to the Sea of Aral.

It will not be necessary to say much of the southern divisions, as they are, in general, sufficiently well known.

1. BADAKHSHĀN

Badakhshān is the first district to the south of the Amu. In the age of Bābur it was considered as being bounded on the south by Kaferistān, on the east by Upper Kāshghar, on the north by Khutlān, and on the west by Kunduz and Anderāb. It is chiefly mountainous, and appears to be formed by the course of two considerable rivers that unite to form the Amu. That river of the two which has the longest course and the greatest body of water is the Panj, called also the Hammū,[1] which appears to be the Harat of the Arabian geographers. It has lately been ascertained to rise in the high grounds east of the Belūt-tāgh range, issuing from under the snow of the lofty mountains of Pushtekhar, and working its way by the lower grounds of Shighnān and Derwāz. The second river, which is called the Kokcha, or Badakhshān river, is inferior in magnitude and length of course to the first, rising to the south of it, in that high mountainous ridge of Belūt-tāgh, which separates Badakhshān from Chitrāl, and the course of the Kāshkār or Cheghānserāi river; and on the north, divided from the course of the Panj by a chain of lofty hills, which intervene and form the ridge of the opposite valleys. Badakhshān Proper lies along the Kokcha river, though the dominion of the King of Badakhshān generally embraced all the country south of the Panj. The country north of the Panj belonged to Khutlān. The mountainous tracts

[1] Hence probably the name of Amu.

INTRODUCTION lxv

near its source still called Wakhān, and by Marco Polo, Vochan, are probably part of the Wakhsh of the Oriental geographers. Besides the two great valleys which run along the river, through all the extent of the country, there are numerous others which wind among the hills, particularly on the south, towards Kaferistān, and which transmit several streams of considerable size to the larger rivers. The Panj and Kokcha unite just below the Badakhshān territory.

The soil in the valleys is fertile, and the country has always been famous for producing precious stones, especially rubies and turquoises. It was visited in the thirteenth century by Marco Polo, whose account of this and the neighbouring provinces is far more correct than has been generally supposed. It belonged to Bābur in the latter period of his life, but was not the scene of any of his more eminent exploits. He mentions that its native king claimed descent from Sikander, or Alexander the Great; a claim which is continued down to the present day. The family may, perhaps, be descended from the Grecian dynasty of Bactriana, which subsisted so long unconnected with the empire of Alexander's successors.

2. BALKH

The country between Badakhshān and the desert of Khwārizm, on the east and west, and the Hindu-kūsh hills and the Amu, on the south and north, which, following Mr. Elphinstone, I include under the general name of Balkh,[1] comprehends a variety of districts that, at the present day, are under several different governments. They are chiefly valleys formed by rivers that descend from

[1] This is the ancient Bactria, a term probably taken from its old Persian name of Bakhter-zemīn, or Eastern country, which is given it as late as the Institutes of Taimūr. Khorasān is sometimes made to include this, as well as the whole country below the hills, as high up as Badakhshān on the one side, and round their ridges to Kandahār on the other. The name of Khorasān may be derived either from its being the country east of Persia, or that west of Bakhter-zemīn; as, by an odd singularity, *Khawer*, in the ancient Persian, is used to signify either east or west. The first certainly seems to be the more probable.

the Hindū-kūsh hills, and which, after forming glens and dales, frequently of considerable extent and fertility, discharge themselves into the Amu. The principal districts mentioned by Bābur are Anderāb, Tālikān, Kundūz, and Khulm, to the east ; Balkh, in the centre, in a plain below the Dareh Gez, or Valley of Gez, and Shiberghān, Andek-hūd, and Meimana, to the west. The eastern districts are generally level and fertile towards the mouth of their different rivers ; but the valleys become narrower, and contract into glens as they are followed towards the sources of their parent streams on the Hindū-kūsh. The country round Balkh is level and rather sandy. The Dehās, or Balkhāb, as it approaches that city, after leaving the Dareh Gez, diminishes in size till it nearly disappears in the barren plain ; and the western districts are ill watered, and indicate, by their sandy soil, the approach to the desert.

3. Khwārizm [1]

Bābur never visited this country, which lies near the mouth of the Amu or Oxus ; and, being surrounded on all sides by desert, may be considered as an island formed in the waste by the Amu ; by innumerable branches and cuts from which, the whole country is enriched. Its geography is very defective and erroneous, though considerable materials exist for correcting it. The Amu, soon after it passes the cultivated country of Urgenj, meets the sandy desert, in which it is nearly swallowed up, so that the river is of no great volume when it reaches the sea of Aral.

4. Desert of the Turkomāns

This desert, which extends from Khwārizm and the borders of Balkh to the Caspian, and from the limits of the Persian Khorasān to the sea of Aral, and the country of the Kirghiz,

---

[1] The Chorasmin of the Persarum Syntaxis (see *Geograph. Gr. Minor*, vol. iii, p. 5) is, I presume, the two Khwārizms ; and indeed it includes places both in Khwārizm and Balkh. [Khwārizm is the modern Khiva.]

s inhabited by wandering Turkomāns,[1] some of whom own submission to the chiefs of Khwārizm, or Urgenj, and others to the Persians; while a considerable portion of them yield scarcely even a nominal submission to either.

II. DIVISIONS NORTH OF THE AMU

It has already been remarked, that these divisions are bounded on the east by the Belūt-tāgh mountains, which extend northward from the Hindū-kūsh to the Asfera mountains, are very lofty and precipitous, and bear snow on their summits the greater part of the year, some of them without intermission. They are probably very broken and abrupt, as no pass is known to cross them, except from Badakhshān. And it is remarkable that, in consequence of the height and abruptness of the mountains which enclose the country that has been denominated Uzbek Tūrkestān on the east, there appear in all ages to have been only two passes across them for caravans and armies, both of which are gained by following the course of the two great rivers, the Amu and the Sirr, to which the country appears to owe many of its most obvious features. One of these grand passes leads through Badakhshān, and is the route taken by the caravan of Kābul, and frequently by that of Samarkand and Bokhāra, on its road to Khutan and Kāshghar. This was the road followed by Marco Polo, in the thirteenth century, and more recently by De Goes, the last European who is known to have crossed these mountains. The second pass, which ascends by the sources of the Sirr, lies in the hills that separate Ferghāna from Kāshghar, to the eastward of Ush. This is the road by which the ambassadors of Shahrokh returned from China. Some inroads of Taimūr's generals, by this pass, are recorded; and the caravan of Kāshghar seems to have taken this road in going between that city and Samar-

[1] [Erskine favoured the antiquated derivation of the name from Turk-Komān (=Komān Turks), but *mān* is probably the Persian suffix signifying 'like'; hence Turkomāns=Turk-like. The Turkomāns—a branch of the Western Turks—is the term now applied to the nomadic tribes who inhabit the country between the Oxus and the Caspian.]

kand in the time of Bābur's father, as it does at the present day. The route pursued by the caravan of Tāshkend, on its way to Kāshghar and China, is not quite clear; but, in some instances, it seems to have gone up the right bank of the Sirr; and after passing the Julgeh Ahengerān, or Blacksmiths' Dale, to have crossed the range of hills that encloses Ferghāna on the west, near Akhsi; to have proceeded on thence to Uzkend, and from that place by the same pass as the caravan of Samarkand. There is, however, reason to imagine that the caravan of Tāshkend frequently kept a more northerly course, skirting the Ala-tāgh hills that enclose Ferghāna on the north and east; and that after rounding them, and passing near Almāligh, it proceeded straight to Kāshghar. These are the only routes by which Eastern Turkestān appears to have been reached from the west; and an attention to this fact will explain several difficulties in the earlier historians and travellers. If the supposed route to the north of the Ala-tāgh hills was really one of those followed by the caravan of Tāshkend, it will perhaps explain a difficulty stated by Major Rennell, in his *Memoir of a Map of Hindostān*. After mentioning that Kāshghar was twenty-five days' journey from Samarkand, he observes that one account differs so much from the rest that he will draw no conclusion from it. It is one that makes twenty-seven journeys from Tāshkend to Kāshghar, ' although Tāshkend is supposed to be five journeys nearer to it than Samarkand is.' If the Tāshkend route led round the hills to the north of Ferghāna, whence the traveller had to return southward towards Kāshghar, the itinerary in question will not be so inconsistent with the others as it might at first seem to be.

1. KHUTLĀN

The two districts of Khutlān and Karatigīn, which stretch along the Belūt-tāgh mountains, are more inaccessible and less known than most of the others. The name of Khutl, or Khutlān, does not appear to be known at the present day; but it was applied in the time of Bābur, and as far back as the age of Ibn Haukal, to the country lying between the upper branch of the Amu, called Harat, or Panj, which divided it from Badakhshān on the south; the Wakhshāb or Surkhrūd, which separated it from Cheghāniān or Hissār on the west; the hill country of Karatigīn on the north; and the Belūt-tāgh on the east. Khutlān is broken in all quarters by hills. Its few valleys are said to be narrow, and overhung with lofty mountains. The glens of Shighnān and Derwāz, which lie near the source of the Panj, are fertile. The country of Wakhsh, which is always joined with Khutlān by the earlier geographers, probably extended between Khutlān and Karatigīn, or may have included Karatigīn itself. Its name is still to be found not only in the uncertain district of Wakhīka, but in the country of Wakhān, the Vochan of Marco Polo, which lies above Badakhshān, near the source of the Panj, close upon Pushtekhar. The name Wakhshāb, anciently given to the river which divided Cheghāniān from Khutlān, is said, by Ibn Haukal, to be derived from that of the country of Wakhsh, where it originates. It ran by Weishgird, the ancient capital of the country, and joined the Amu above Kobādiān. On this river was the Pul-e-sangīn, or Stone-bridge, so often mentioned in the history of Taimūr Beg. While some circumstances seem to point to the river which joins the Amu above Kobādiān, opposite to Kunduz, others certainly accord much better with the Surkh-āb, or the river of Karatigīn, which has a course of upwards of 160 miles before it falls into the Amu. The Wakhi language still remains in many districts in the hills of Badakhshān and Khutlān; and it is not improbable that the Wakhi or Wakhshi race were the most ancient inhabitants of this hilly region. Many of the rivers that flow into the Amu in the earlier part of its course descend from the hill-country of Khutlān. It is said to have been the seat of a splendid dynasty, before the Musulman conquest; and Abulfida[1] mentions the magnificent palaces of its kings. In Bābur's time it was generally subject to Hissār.

[1] [Abulfidā became Prince of Hamāt in Syria in 1342; and died in A.D. 1345. He was the author of a geographical work, *Taqwīm ul buldān*, edited by Hudson, Oxford, in 1712. He also compiled an abridgement of universal history down to his own time, entitled *Tārīkh i mukhtasir*, Beale's *Biog. Dict.*]

2. Karatigīn

This country, which is seldom mentioned in history, lies along the southern range of the Asfera mountains, and appears to extend, on the east, as far as those of Belūt-tāgh; on the south, it has part of Khutlān and Wakhīka, and the country of Hissār; on the west, it extends to the hill-districts of Uratippa and Yār-Ailāk. It is altogether mountainous. The height of the Asfera and Belūt-tāgh mountains, the former covered with perpetual snow, prevents it from having much communication with the countries to the north and east.

3. Hissār

Before proceeding to make any remarks on this district, it is necessary to point out, in a few words, the course taken by the branches of the Asfera mountains, when they diverge, somewhat to the east of the longitude of Khojend, as has been already mentioned. All along the south of Ferghāna, their summits are everywhere covered with perpetual snow. As they approach Uratippa, they appear suddenly to lose their height, and to divide into three or perhaps four branches. One of these, running south by Derbend or Kohlūgha (the Iron Gate), under the name of Kara-tāgh, or the Black mountains,[1] divides the country of Hissār from that of Késh. The northern part of this range, as described by Bābur, is lofty and precipitous in the extreme; but it evidently declines in height as it approaches the desert along the Amu, where it probably altogether disappears. The second branch, running south-west from Karatigīn, extends to the south of Samarkand and Bokhāra, though much inferior in height to the former, and seems, like it, to die away in the desert towards the Amu. This may be called the Késh branch, and the country between it and the Kara-tāgh forms the territories of Késh and Karshi. The hill between Samarkand and Késh is, by Sherīfeddīn,

[1] [This is a range of mountains in the district of Karatigīn lying to the south of the Karlitau mountains and situated about 100 miles south-east of Samarkand.]

called the hill of Késh. Ibn Haukal tells us [1] that the mountain of Zarkah, as he calls the same range, runs from Bokhāra, between Samarkand and Késh, joins the border of Ferghāna, and goes on towards the border of Chīn. The Arabian geographer, therefore, evidently considered the range south of Samarkand as connected with the Asfera, and probably with the Muz-tāgh ranges. The third range, called the Ak-tāgh, or Ak-kāya, the white mountains, and by the Arabian geographers [2] Butum, or Al-Butum,[2] extending to the westward, runs to the north of Samarkand and Bokhāra, and declines down to the desert. Where it leaves the Asfera mountains it forms, with the Kara-tāgh and Késh hills, the country of Yār-ailāk, and, lower down, one boundary of the celebrated valley of Soghd. This branch is lofty, and bears snow in its hollows all the year. The fourth branch is that which appears to run, but very ruggedly and uncertainly, to the north-west, through the country of Uratippa. It slopes down towards the sea of Aral, and a portion either of this, or of the last branch, crosses the Amu below the cultivated country of Khwārizm, before that river works its way into the sea of Aral. This may be called the Uratippa branch, as that country lies chiefly among its offsets, and towards the Ak-tāgh hills. The Uratippa hills approach very closely to the Sirr, or Jaxartes.

The country of Hissār, which was often traversed by Bābur, and which, for some years in the middle period of his life, formed his head-quarters, is by the Arabian geographers denominated Saghāniān, while the Persians called it Cheghāniān and Jeghāniān, from the city of that name which lies on the Cheghān-rūd, more frequently, how-

[1] [Ibn Haukal was the author of the *Ashkāl ul bilād*, which he wrote in A. D. 977.]
[2] [This place is referred to in Yākūt's *Geographical Dictionary* (ed. Wüstenfeld) as a fort in Ferghāna. Le Strange, in his *Land of the Eastern Caliphate*, p. 436, says that the two rivers of Kubādiyān and Saghāniān join the Oxus on its right or northern bank and have their sources in the Buttam mountains, which form the watershed between the rivers of Soghd and those of Saghāniān and Wakhshāb. The slopes of this range, though steep, were covered with villages.]

ever, called the river of Cheghānīān. This country received, in later times, the name of Hissār (or the Castle), from the fort of Hissār-Shādmān, which was long the seat of government of all the neighbouring regions. At the present day, this country is known by the name of Deh-nau (or New-Town), from a town of that name, where the chief resides; and in general it may be remarked that all over the East, where the governments are fluctuating, there is a disposition to designate the government rather by the name of the city where the king or governor resides, than by a general name taken from the whole country which he governs. And, in like manner, as to rivers, and ranges of mountains, it is seldom, except in books, that they have any general name; the former are usually described by the name of the nearest large town, the latter by that of some remarkable summit, and consequently change their denomination many times in their course. Frequent instances of this kind will be found in the Memoirs of Bābur.

Hissār, on the south, was bounded by the river Amu or Oxus, on the east by the hill country of Wakhsh and Khutlān, from which it was divided by the Surkhrūd or Karatigīn river, formerly called the Wakhshāb, on the north by Karatigīn, and on the west by the Kara-tāgh mountains. It is hilly, but not mountainous, in its chief extent. The soil is in general sandy, and inclining to degenerate into desert; but, being on the whole well watered, is capable of high cultivation. The river Weish or Wakhshāb, which proceeds from the north-west, joins the Oxus considerably to the east of Kobādiān. The river of Cheghānīān, and that of Hissār or Kafernihān, are the other streams of chief note in this district. In the days of Bābur, the most important places in this division were Hissār, Cheghānīān, Kobādiān and Termez. The city of Termez or Termed has always been famous as covering the best passage over the Amu; but somewhat higher up is the passage of Ubāj, lying between Cheghānīān and Khulm, which is several times mentioned, both in Bābur's Memoirs and in the History of Taimūr. The country towards Weishgird, where the natives were protected by the sudden rise of the hills, was the scene of many bloody battles

INTRODUCTION   lxxiii

between the ancient inhabitants and the Arabs, during
their conquest of Māweralnaher. The inhabitants of the
hill countries were never fully subdued. Bābur gives a
very particular account of his passage up one of the long
valleys of this country, called the valley of Kāmrūd, which
he ascended in his flight from Hissār to Yār-ailāk, after his
defeat near Samarkand. The valley of Kāmrūd leads up
to the summit of the Kara-tāgh range.

4. KÉSH

This division has already been described as bounded on
the east by the Kara-tāgh mountains dividing it from
Hissār; on the south by the Amu or Oxus; and on the
north and west by the Késh hills, which divide it from
Yār-ailāk and the valley of Soghd.

The chief cities now, and they are the same that existed
in the time of Bābur, are Késh, also called Shahr-i-sabz
(or the Green City), and to the south Karshi, also called
Nakhsheb, and by the Arabs Nasef. Khozār also has always
been a place of consequence, and lies south-east of Karshi,
in a desert tract. The country round Késh is uncommonly
fertile, full of streams, and rather marshy, but degenerates
as it approaches the Amu, and becomes a perfect desert,
insomuch that the rivers of this district disappear before
reaching that great river. The famous Pass of Kohlūgha
(the Iron Gate), or Derbend, lies in the hills between Késh
and Hissār. Fazlullah[1] pretends that it was cut in the rock,
which only proves that it was narrow and difficult, and
perhaps improved by art. Near Késh, the native town of
the great Taimūr, is the plain of Akiār, where, close by the
river Koshka, were held the *Kurultais* or annual reviews
of his armies, and what have been called the diets of his
states. It was celebrated for its beautiful verdure and the
rich profusion of its flowers.

5. SAMARKAND AND BOKHĀRA

The country which composes the territory of these famous
cities, has always been deemed one of the most fertile and

[1] [Fazlullah Rashīd ud dīn (A.D. 1247-1318) was the author of
the *Jāma' ut tawārīkh*, a history of the Moghals, which he completed
in A.D. 1310; Beale's *Biog. Dict.*]

beautiful in the world. It lies between the Késh hills on the south, the Desert of Khwārizm on the west, and the Uratippa and Ak-tāgh mountains dividing it from Uratippa, on the north. On the east, it has the hill country of Karatigīn and the Kara-tāgh mountains. It is traversed, in nearly its whole extent, by the Kohik or Zarefshān [1] river, which, coming from the north-east angle of the hills that rise out of Karatigīn, flows down by Yār-ailāk to Samarkand and the vale of Soghd, passing to the north and west of Bokhāra, considerably below which the small part of it that is not swallowed up in the sand runs into the Amu. The country near the sources of the Kohik is hilly and barren, and in the time of Bābur was full of petty forts, especially along the skirts of the hills. This is the district so often mentioned under the name of Yār-ailāk or Bār-ailāk. It seems to comprise the countries at the present day called Karatippa and Urgūl. Uratippa extends over the opposite side of the hills, to the north-west, except only the district called the Ailāks of Uratippa, which is higher up on the same side of the hills, and not far distant from Yar-ailāk. The vale of Soghd, which commences lower down [2] than the Ailāks, is an extensive plain, a great part of which is admirably watered and cultivated, by means of cuts from the river. Bābur has given so correct and detailed an account of this whole country in his Memoirs that little need be added regarding it. This tract of plain is the Sogdiana of the ancients, so called from the river Soghd, the ancient name of the Kohik. Samarkand was a city of note at least as far back as the time of Alexander the Great, when it was known under the name of Marakanda, a name which may lead us to suspect that even then the country had been overrun by Tūrki [3] tribes. The country beyond the Amu, called by the Arabs Māweralnaher (i.e. beyond the river), was conquered by them as early as the years 87, 88, and 89 of the Hijira; and their geographers present us with the most dazzling picture of its prosperity

---

[1] i.e. gold-bedding.

[2] Abulfida tells us that it commences twenty farsangs (about eighty miles) higher up than Samarkand.

[3] *Kend* is the Tūrki for a *town*, as in Tāshkend, Uzkend.

INTRODUCTION lxxv

at an early period. Ibn Haukal, who is supposed to have
lived in the tenth century, speaks of the province as one
of the most flourishing and productive in the world. The
hospitality of the inhabitants he describes, from his personal
observation, as corresponding to the abundance that
prevailed. The fortunate situation of the country, and the
protection which it enjoyed under the Arabian Khalifs,
produced their ordinary effects, and the arts of civilization,
the civilities of social life, and the study of literature, all
made a distinguished progress. We are told that the
inhabitants were fond of applying their wealth to the
erection of caravanserais or inns, to the building of bridges
and similar works, and that there was no town or stage in
Mäweralnaher without a convenient inn or stage-house [1]
for the purpose of accommodating travellers with every
necessary. One of the governors of Mäweralnaher, which
included all the Arabian conquests north of the Amu,
boasted, probably with considerable exaggeration, that he
could send to war three hundred thousand horse, and the
same number of foot, whose absence would not be felt in
the country. The Vale of Soghd was reckoned one of the
three paradises of the world, the Rūd-Ābileh and the
Ghūteh of Damascus [2] being the other two; over both of
which, however, Ibn Haukal assigns it the decided preference, both as to beauty and salubrity. The glowing
description which he gives of it in the tenth century is
confirmed by Abulfida in the beginning of the fourteenth;
and early in the sixteenth, Bābur informs us, that there
was no more delightful country in the world. The beauty
and wealth of these cities had rendered the names of
Samarkand and Bokhāra proverbial among the poets of
Persia. Several streams from the hills, on both sides, join
the Kohik in its course. As you recede from the Soghd
river or approach the Amu, the soil becomes sandy and
desert.

The chief cities in the days of Bābur, as at the present
time, were Samarkand and Bokhāra. The former lies

[1] *Geography of Ibn Haukal*, p. 235.
[2] Abulfida ap. *Geog. Graec. Min.*, vol. iii, p. 32, in Chorasmiae
Descript., adds the Shi'bi Bauwan [the ravine of Bauwan] in Persia.

on the south of the Kohik on a rising ground, and has always been very extensive, the fortifications having varied, by different accounts, from eight to five miles in circumference; but a great part of this space was occupied by gardens. When D'Herbelot and Petis de la Croix [1] give the city a compass of twelve farsangs, or forty-eight miles, they have not observed that the whole garden-grounds around it must have been included in the range. A wall one hundred and twenty farsangs in length, said to have been built by Gushtasp, king of Persia, to check the incursions of the Tūrks, and to protect the province of Samarkand, is probably fabulous, no notice being taken of any remains of it in latter times. Yet a similar one certainly existed, lower down the river, for the defence of the highly-cultivated districts of Bokhāra.

A town of considerable note in the northern part of the country is Jizzikh or Jizik, better known in history by the name of Dizak. It lies towards the Ak-tāgh mountains, on the road to the Pass of Ak-Kūtel. To the south of Jizzikh, on the road to Samarkand, is Shirāz, which has long been in ruins.

Down the river, below Samarkand, was the town of Sir-e-pul (or Bridgend), so frequently mentioned by Bābur. It is probably the place noticed by Abulfida under the name of Khushūfaghan,[2] and by the Arabs called Rās-al-kantara, a translation of its Persian name.

The town and castle of Dabūsi or Dabūsīa, often mentioned in the history of Bokhāra, lie between that city and Samarkand.

The city of Bokhāra, which is now the capital of the country, as it frequently was in former times, has given its name in Europe to the countries of Great and Little Bucharia. These names, however, are unknown in Asia, the name of Bokhāra being confined to the city of that name and the

[1] See *Bibl. Orientale*, art. Samarkand; and *Hist. de Ghengiz-can*, p. 220.

[2] [This place is referred to in the *Geographie d'Abulfida*, ed. Reinaud and de Slane, p. 485, and also in Yākūts' *Geographical Dictionary* (ed. Wüstenfeld), as one of the villages of Soghd. Le Strange, in his *Lands of the Eastern Caliphate*, p. 466, states that it was an important village which lay eight leagues to the north-east of Samarkand.]

country subject to it. It lies far down in the Valley of Soghd, in the middle of a rich country intersected by numerous water-courses. It is said, at the present day, to contain a hundred thousand inhabitants, and it is, perhaps, the most eminent seat of Musulman learning now existing. Thompson, who visited it in 1740, gives an amusing account of the city and its trade.[1] It was visited by Jenkinson in the reign of Queen Elizabeth,[2] and in 1812 by Izzet ullah, whose account of its present state is highly interesting.

The fort of Ghajhdewān, which lies north-west of Bokhāra, close on the desert of Khwārizm, is remarkable for a great defeat sustained by Bābur and his Persian auxiliaries, when he was compelled to raise the siege.

The hills of Nūrattāu lie ten miles north from Bokhāra, and run from east to west for about twenty-four miles. This is probably the *Nūr* of the Arabian geographers, with the addition of *tau*, a hill.

Miānkāl, which is several times mentioned by Bābur, includes Katta-Kurghān, Yung-Kurghān, Panjshembeh, Khattichi, and some other places on both sides of the Kohik near Dabūsi.

But the minuteness of Bābur's own description of the country, its rivers and mountains, precludes the necessity of any further remarks.

III. COUNTRIES ALONG THE SIRR, OR JAXARTES

The countries along the Sirr have always been much less considerable than those on the Amu. The Sirr, or Jaxartes, rises among the lofty mountains which divide Ferghāna from Kāshghar. The chief source appears to lie east from Ush, nearly two degrees. On the west side of the Ala-tāgh range are the sources of the Sirr, and on the east side, at no great distance, is the source of the Kāshghar river. The Sirr, after dividing Ferghāna, takes a turn to the north-west, passes to the south of Tāshkend,

---

[1] Hanway's *Travels*, vol. i, p. 240.
[2] Hakluyt's *Voyages*, vol. i.

and, flowing down through the sandy desert, is nearly lost in the sands before it reaches the Sea of Aral.

1. FERGHĀNA

The particular account of this country with which the Memoirs of Bābur open renders it needless to enter into any description of it. It now forms the powerful kingdom of Khokand, whose capital, of the same name, is the ancient Khuakend, lying between Khojend and Akhsi. Though Ferghāna is in general fertile, yet several small deserts are to be found within its extent. It is divided into two parts by the Sirr. That on the left bank has for its boundary on the south the snowy mountains of Asfera, which on their northern face slope down into the hill countries of Wadil, Warukh,[1] Hushiār, Sukh, &c.; while their southern side forms the frontier of Karatigīn. On the west it has Uratippa, from which it is divided by the river Aksū, which flows into the Sirr. The portion of Ferghāna on the right bank of the Sirr has for its western boundary a range of hills running south from the Ala-tāgh, past Akhsi to Khojend, on the Sirr, and dividing Ferghāna from Tāshkend. The north appears to be protected by the lofty and barren mountains called Ala-tāgh, which are probably always covered with snow, and which also wind round to its eastern frontier, where they separate it from the territory of Kāshghar. The country north of the Sirr, which formerly contained Akhsi and Kāsān, is now called Nemengān. The Ala-tāgh mountains are generally represented as being joined, on their north-east angle, by a range of mountains running far eastward, and connecting them with those of Ulugh-tāgh. None of them, however, are probably high, where they join in with the hills that bound Ferghāna, as we find that the Kirghiz pass freely at all seasons, on the north and east of that country, from Tāshkend to the vicinity of Kāshghar; and the whole tract is, indeed, generally designated as belonging to the same pastoral range: thus, in the accounts of the Russian travellers, when speaking of the Great Horde of Kirghiz, we find Kāshghar, Tāshkend,

---

[1] [Wadil is due east and Warukh due south of Asfera.]

and Otrār put together, as constituting their range along the Ala, or Alak-tāgh mountains, without adverting to any intervening hills. One Uzbek traveller, from whom I had an account of his journey from Kāshghar to Astrakhān, mentioned that he passed some broad low hills near Almāligh; so that, if any connecting range runs from the Ala-tāgh to the Ulugh-tāgh, it is probably a very low one, and easily surmounted.

Bābur justly describes his native country as encircled with hills on every side except towards Khojend, where, however, the opening between the hills and the Sirr is very narrow.

Abulfida mentions that in the mountains of Ferghāna they have black stones which burn like charcoal, and, when kindled, afford a very intense heat. The fact of the existence of coal in the Ala-tāgh range, and to the east of it, is confirmed by recent travellers. It is found in great plenty, and forms the ordinary fuel of the natives.

2. Tāshkend

The country of Tāshkend lies along the north bank of the Sirr, having that river on the south, and the Ala-tāgh mountains, running parallel to it, on the greater part of its northern frontier; the hills near Akhsi bound it on the east, and the desert of the Kara Kilpāks on the west. The ancient Türkestān proper stretched considerably to the north and westward of this country. The range of Ala-tāgh mountains which extend along its northern boundary, run from east to west, at no great distance from the Sirr, and decline in height toward the western desert. The inferior range of hills that run from the Ala-tāgh, between Tāshkend and Akhsi, within eight miles of the latter place,[1] we find several times crossed by armies that marched from Tāshkend to Kāsān, Akhsi, and the northern provinces of Ferghāna. In this route lies the Julgeh Ahengerān, or Ironsmiths' Dale, and Kundezlik and Amāni, so often mentioned in the Memoirs of Bābur. It was probably by

[1] D'Herbelot says (art. Aksiket) that the plain reaches to the hills, which are only two leagues (perhaps farsangs) off. Abulfida says they are at the distance of one farsang.

this road that the caravan of Tāshkend proceeded to Uzkend, on the route to Kāshghar; though it appears sometimes to have gone to Kāshghar by keeping to the north of the Ala-tāgh hills. The road generally pursued from Tāshkend to Akhsi did not follow the course of the Sirr, but went eastward directly towards Akhsi, cutting off, to the south, the large tract of country surrounded on three sides by the river which runs south-west from Akhsi to Khojend, and north-west from Khojend to Tāshkend. The city of Shahrokhīa lay between Khojend and Tāshkend, on the Sirr, while Seirām lay north-west of Tāshkend, still lower down. Magnificent accounts of the wealth, cultivation, and populousness of Tāshkend, and the country along the rich banks of the Sirr, in the time of the Arabs, and of the Khwārizmian dynasty, are given by Ibn Haukal, Abulfida, and the historians of Chingiz Khan; and the many works of learning and science which issued from this country at that era sufficiently attest that these praises were not altogether gratuitous. The dynasty of Khwārizmian kings, destroyed by Chingiz Khan, were eminent encouragers of letters. In Bābur's time, Tāshkend and Shahrokhīa were its chief towns. A considerable traffic has of late years been carried on at Tāshkend, between the Russians and the inhabitants of Bokhāra, but the country is not in a flourishing state. The range of the Great Horde of the Kirghiz extends from Tāshkend all round the Ala-tāgh mountains, through the western part of the country of Kāshghar and Yārkend, and even into Upper Kāshghar and Pamīr, close to Derwāz and Badakhshān. They are Tūrks, and speak a dialect of the Tūrki language, though probably mingled with Moghul words.

3. Uratippa

The country of Uraṭippa, which is also called Ustrūsh, Ustrūshta, Setrūshta, Isterūshān, and Ushrūshna, is the hilly tract which lies west of Khojend, whence it is separated by the river Aksū. It has that river and the Asfera mountains, including part of Karatigīn, on the east; on the south-east, in the days of Bābur, it seems to have stretched over to the Kara-tāgh mountains, which divided it from Hissār, while Yār-ailāk completed its boundary in that quarter. On the south, the Ak-tāgh and Uratippa mountains divided it from Samarkand and Bokhāra; on the north, the Sirr, and probably the districts of Ilāk, separate it from Tāshkend; and on the west it has the desert of Ghaz (by Abulfida, called Ghazna), or the Kara Kilpāks, towards the sea of Aral. It is full of broken hill and dale, and anciently was studded with small and nearly independent castles, each of which had its separate district. The slope of country is towards the desert of Aral. It is now subject to Bokhāra. Uratippa and Ramīn, or Zamīn, are its chief towns. It has been celebrated from early ages for the quantity of sal ammoniac which it produces in some natural caverns in the hills. It has no considerable river, but several smaller streams, most of which probably disappear in the sandy desert. In all our maps, the Kizil (or Red River) is made to rise in the hill country of Uratippa, and to proceed downward to join the Amu, below the cultivated country of Khwārizm. Yet Ibn Haukal tells us that in all Setrushta (or Uratippa) there is not one river considerable enough to admit of the plying of boats; and the river, after leaving Uratippa, would have to run for several days' journey through a desert sand. It rather seems that no such separate river exists; but that the Kizil is only a branch that proceeds from, and returns to, the Amu. Hazārasp, which certainly stands on the Amu, is said to lie on the north side of the Kizil. This must be just where the Kizil runs off from the great river. Kāt, or Kāth, the old capital of Khwārizm, which was six farsangs, or twenty-four miles, from Hazārasp down the Amu, and certainly stood on that river, is, however, said to lie on the north side of the Kizil. The different branches of the Amu, in passing through Khwārizm, or Urgenj, have different names, like the various branches of the Ganges in Bengal. This, with some other causes, has spread a good deal of confusion over the geography of the former country. In the instance in question, a great river being found, and its connexion with the Amu not being known, it was natural to search for its sources in the hills to the east.

4. The Desert of the Kara Kilpāks

The desert country which is bounded by the sea of Aral on the west, the river Sirr on the north, Uratippa on the east, and Bokhāra and Khwārizm on the south, is now traversed by the wandering Tūrki tribe of Kara Kilpāks [1] (or Black Bonnets), who, according to the general opinion, are Turkomāns, though some accounts describe them as Uzbeks. This district, which was, by the Arabian geographers, called Ghaz, and sometimes, if we may trust the readings of the manuscripts, Ghaznah, probably extends a little to the north, beyond the place where the Sirr loses itself in the sand. These wanderers have a considerable range, but are few in number. The desert is six or seven days' journey from east to west, and upwards of ten from north to south.

5. Ilāk

Ilāk, probably, is not a separate district, but comprehends the rich pastoral country on both sides of the Sirr, on the southern side, reaching up the skirts, and among the valleys of the hills of Uratippa that branch towards the Sirr, and belong to Uratippa ; and on the north having some similar tracts subject to Tāshkend and Shāhrokhīa. It is by some ancient geographers made to comprehend the whole country between the northern hills of Tāshkend and the river, including Tāshkend and Benāket, or Shāhrokhīa. It is little known, and is probably dependent on Tāshkend to the north of the Sirr, and on Uratippa to the south.

6. Turkestān

The country peculiarly called Turkestān by Bābur, lies below Seirām, between it and the sea of Aral. It lies on the right bank of the Sirr, and stretches considerably to the north, along the banks of some small rivers that come from

[1] [Howorth says they were Mongols, and that they were formerly divided into two sections, the Upper and the Lower, of which the former were settled on the lower Sirr Darya from its mouth to Tāshkend, and the latter on the sea of Aral and the Kuvan Darya.]

the east and north. Some part of it was rich, and had been populous. A city of the same name stands on one of these inferior streams. In the time of the Arabs it is said to have been a rich and flourishing country, full of considerable towns, such as Jund, Yangikent, &c. In the time of Bābur it seems to have had few towns, but was the chief seat of the Uzbeks, who had recently settled there, and whose territories extended a considerable way to the north; though Sheibāni Khan never recovered the great kingdom of Tūra, whence his grandfather Abulkhair had been expelled, the succession of which was continued in another branch of the family. It was to this Turkestān that Sheibāni Khan retired when unsuccessful in his first attempt on Samarkand; and it was from the deserts around this tract, and from Tāshkend, which they had conquered, that his successors called the Tartars, who assisted them in expelling Bābur from Māweralnaher, after Sheibāni's death.

Such is a general outline of the divisions of the country of Uzbek Turkestān, which may deserve that name, from having had its principal districts chiefly occupied for upwards of three centuries past by Uzbek tribes. The face of the country, it is obvious, is extremely broken, and divided by lofty hills; and even the plains are diversified by great varieties of soil, some extensive districts along the Kohik river, nearly the whole of Ferghāna, the greater part of Khwārizm along the branches of the Amu, with large portions of Balkh, Badakhshān, Késh, and Hissār, being of uncommon fertility; while the greater part of the rest is a barren waste, and in some places a sandy desert. Indeed, the whole country north of the Amu has a decided tendency to degenerate into desert; and many of its most fruitful districts are nearly surrounded by barren sands; so that the population of all these districts still, as in the time of Bābur, consists of the fixed inhabitants of the cities and fertile lands, and of the unsettled and roving wanderers of the desert, the Īls and the Ulūses of Bābur, who dwell in tents of felt, and live on the produce of their flocks. The cultivated spots are rich in wheat, barley, millet, and cotton; and the fruits, particularly the peaches, apricots, plums, grapes, apples, quinces, pomegranates, figs, melons, cucumbers, &c., are among the finest in the world. The mulberry abounds, and a considerable quantity of silk is manufactured. The cultivation is managed, as far as is practicable, by means of irrigation. The breed of horses is excellent. The less fertile parts of the country are pastured by large flocks of sheep. They have also bullocks, asses, and mules, in sufficient numbers, and some camels. The climate, though in the low lands extremely cold in winter,[1] and hot in summer, brings to perfection most of the fruits and grains of temperate climates ; and perhaps there are few countries in the world to which Nature has been more bountiful.

This felicity of climate and fruitfulness of soil have, in most ages of the world, rendered the country along the Kohik the seat of very considerable kingdoms. The earliest inhabitants, at least, of the desert tracts, were probably the Scythians, who, in this quarter, appear to have been of the Tūrki race. When Alexander advanced to the Sirr, he marched by Marakanda, a name the termination of which, as has already been remarked, seems to speak a Tūrki origin. The Turanian monarchs, so long the rivals and terror of those of Irān, seem also to have been Tūrks. After the Arab conquest, in the first century of the Hijira, many Persians were probably induced, by the security of the government and fertility of the soil, to settle to the north of the Amu ; though it is likely that long before, when Balkh was the chief seat of the Persian government, the rich lands of Māweralnaher were cultivated and the larger towns inhabited chiefly by men of Persian extraction, and speaking the Persian tongue. Down to the age of Chingiz Khan, when the grand desolation of the country began, the Persian was the common language all over the towns and cultivated lands from the Amu to the Sirr, as well as in the great and flourishing cities that then existed along the northern banks of that river, such as Tāshkend, Benāket, Jund, and Yangikent ; the Tūrki being, however,

---

[1] Snow lies on the ground for several days at a time everywhere to the north of the Késh hills. The Sirr, or Jaxartes, is frozen over every winter, and passed in that state by the Russian caravans. The Amu is also frozen for a considerable extent above Khwārizm.

understood and familiarly used in the bazars and markets of all these northern districts. The Persian language also crossed the Ala-tāgh hills, and was the language of the towns of eastern Tūrkestān, such as Kāshgar and Yārkand, as it continues to be at this day as far east as Terfān. A proof of the remote period from which the language of Persia was spoken in Māweralnaher is to be found in the present state of the hill country of Karatigīn. The language of that mountainous and sequestered tract is Persian; and as it has not been exposed to any conquest of Persians for many hundred years, it would seem that the Persian has been the language in familiar use ever since the age of the Khwārizmian kings, if not from a much more remote era. It is probable, therefore, that, in the days of Bābur, the Persian was the general language of the cultivated country of the districts of Balkh, Badakhshān, the greater part of Khutlān, Karatigīn, Hissār, Késh, Bokhāra, Uratippa, Ferghāna, and Tāshkend, while the surrounding deserts were the haunts of various roving tribes of Tūrki race, as in all ages, from the earliest dawn of history, they appear to have been.

While the Tūrks and Persians, the pastoral and agricultural races, thus from the earliest times divided the country north of the Amu, and considerable tracts to the south, the hills of Belūt-tāgh, towards the source of that river, extending for a considerable extent to the north and north-west, as well as those of Hindū-kūsh, which stretch along its southern course, were occupied by men of a different language and extraction. The progress of the Arabian conquest through the mountains was extremely slow. Though all the low countries were in the possession of the Arabian Khalifs in the first century of the Hijira, yet in the fourth or fifth, when their power was beginning to wane, the Kāfers, or Infidels, still held the mountains of Ghor, and the lofty range of Hindū-kūsh.[1] Down to the time of

[1] [Sir T. Holdich (vide *India* (London, 1904), p. 98) remarks that the hills of Kāfiristān contain ' as strange an agglomeration of tribal survivals as can be found in the whole world ', including, perhaps, those of the Greek dominion which was the result of Alexandra's conquest of the Persian Empire. The Kāfirs are divided into three main groups, Siāhposh, Wargulis, and Pressungulis. They are to a

Marco Polo, in the thirteenth century, the language of Badakhshān was different from that of the lower country, though we cannot ascertain whether it was the same as that of the Kāfers or Siāhposhes, whose country he calls Bascia, or that of Wakhān, which he denominates Vochan. It is not improbable that one radical tongue may have extended along the Hindū-kūsh and Belūt-tāgh mountains, though the continuity of territory was afterwards broken off by the interposition of the province of Badakhshān, which, being rich and fertile, was overrun earlier than the others. Indeed, Kāferistān, or the country of the Siāhposhes, is still a country untouched, except during one expedition of Taimūr Beg, who crossed the snowy tracts of their mountains with incredible labour, but was unable to reduce them under subjection to his yoke. Some correct specimens of the language of the Dards near Kashmīr, of Kāferistān, of Wakhān, of Wakhīka, of the Pashāi,[1] or any other of the barbarous dialects of these hills, would be of singular curiosity, and of very great value in the history of the originization of nations. The present Afghān language,[2] if I may judge of it from the specimen which I have seen, is certainly in a great degree composed of Hindu and Persian, with the usual sprinkling of Arabic terms. It would be desirable to ascertain what proportion of the unknown terms can be referred to any of the languages still spoken by the inhabi-

large extent descended from the border tribes of Afghānistān, who, refusing to accept Islām in the tenth century, were driven into the hills of Kāfiristān, the unwarlike inhabitants of which they subjugated and enslaved.]

[1] [Wakhān is inhabited by Ghalchas (cf. Ghalchah = clown in Persian), the so-called Aryans of the Hīndū-kūsh. They speak an Eranian tongue (Ghalchah), and conform physically to the European Alpine race. Ghalchah is the language of the Pamīrs. Pashai is a Pisāchah language which is spoken by the inhabitants of the Laghmān valley in Afghānistān. Under the same head may be classed Shinā, the language of the Dards, who are inhabitants of Gilgit, Chilās, and the neighbourhood; Khowār, the speech of Chitrāl, and a number of Kāfir dialects, such as Bashgāli, Wai, and Kalasha.]

[2] [Pushtu, the language of British and independent Afghānistān, belongs, according to Sir G. Grierson, to the Medic branch of Eranian speech. It has an alphabet of its own based on the Persian characters, and a considerable literature. It is quite distinct from the language spoken by the tribes inhabiting the mountainous district to the north.]

tants of the hills to the north. The settlement of the Afghān tribes in the districts to the north of the road from Kābul to Peshāwer, is not of very ancient date. Their peculiar country has always been to the south of that line.

Besides the Tūrki tribes that have been mentioned, a body of Moghuls had taken up their residence for some years in the country of Hissār; and the whole of Tāshkend, with the desert tract around the Ala-tāgh mountains as far as Kāshgar, though chiefly inhabited by Tūrks, was subject to the principal tribes of the Western Moghuls, who were then ruled by two uncles of Bābur, the brothers of his mother, the elder of whom had fixed the seat of his government at Tāshkend. Where the Moghulistān,[1] so often mentioned by Bābur, may have lain, is not quite clear, though it probably extended round the site of Bishbāligh, the place chosen by Chaghatāi Khan for the seat of his empire, on the banks of the Illi river, before it falls into the Balkash, or Palkati Nor. The eastern division of the tribe, which had remained in its deserts, was governed by the younger brother. They were probably the same race of Moghuls who are mentioned by Taimūr, in his Institutes, as inhabiting Jattah.

The Kazāks, frequently mentioned by Bābur, are the Kirghiz,[2] who to this day call themselves *Sahrā-Kazāk*,

[1] [The boundaries of Moghulistān proper, or Jatta, are given as follows in the T.R. (pp. 52-3): On the west it was bounded by Shāsh (Tāshkend) and the watershed of the Upper and Lower Talās valleys; on the north-west the boundary ran from the Kara Tau mountains to the southern extremity of Lake Balkash, and was continued again from its other extremity to the Tarbagatai mountains; thence south-eastward to a point near Urumtsi at the northern foot of the Tian Shan range. The Tian Shan range formed the southern limit as far west as the head of the Narin river, and thence westward again the boundary ran along the watershed between the Narin and Lake Issigh Kul as far as the heads of the Talās valleys.]

[2] [The Kirghiz, according to the *Encyclopaedia Britannica*, consist of two main divisions: the Kara Kirghiz of the Uplands (800,000), and the Kirghiz Kazaks of the Steppes (two millions). They occupy an area of three million square miles, stretching from Kulja westward to the Lower Volga, and from the head-streams of the Ob southwards to the Pamīr and the Turkomān country. They are related in speech to the Tatārs and ethnically to the Mongolians, though both belonged originally to the same racial stock.]

or *robbers of the desert*, a name which its etymology proves to be of later origin than the Arabian settlement on the Sirr. It is not clear what country they traversed with their flocks in his age, but they probably occupied their present range, and were dependent on the Moghuls.

The Uzbeks [1] lived far to the north in the desert, along the Jaik river, and on as far as Siberia, as will afterwards be mentioned; but they had more recently occupied the country called Turkestān, which lies below Seirām, and stretches north from the Sirr or Jaxartes, along the Tarās, and the other small rivers that flow into the Sirr, between Tāshkend and the Aral.

The general state of society which prevailed in the age of Bābur, within the countries that have been described, will be much better understood from a perusal of the following Memoirs, than from any prefatory observations that could be offered. It is evident that, in consequence of the protection which had been afforded to the people of Māweralnaher by their regular governments, a considerable degree of comfort, and perhaps still more of elegance and civility, prevailed in the towns. The whole age of Bābur, however, was one of great confusion. Nothing contributed so much to produce the constant wars, and eventual devastation of the country, which the Memoirs exhibit, as the want of some fixed rule of succession to the throne. The ideas of regal descent, according to primogeniture, were very indistinct, as is the case in all oriental, and, in general, in all purely despotic kingdoms. When the succession to the crown, like everything else, is subject to the will of the prince, on his death it necessarily becomes the subject of contention; since the will of a dead king is of much less consequence than the intrigues of an able minister, or the sword of a successful commander. It is the privilege

---

[1] [The Uzbeks are of Turco-Tatār origin and speak pure (Chaghatāi) Tūrki, but they are now much mixed with Persians, Kirghiz, and Mongols. Under settled conditions they are mostly called Sarts, who include the Kalmaks. Uzbeg is a political and not an ethnological denomination, as the name is derived from Uzbeg Khan, Khan of the Golden Horde (A. D. 1312-40), and was used later to designate the ruling tribes of the Central Asian Khanates (cf. the term Osmanli) in opposition to Kirghiz, Sarts, &c. (*Encycl. Brit.*)]

of liberty and of law alone to bestow equal security on the rights of the monarch and of the people. The death of the ablest sovereign was only the signal for a general war. The different parties at court, or in the haram of the prince, espoused the cause of different competitors, and every neighbouring potentate believed himself to be perfectly justified in marching to seize his portion of the spoil. In the course of the Memoirs, we shall find that the grandees of the court, while they take their place by the side of the candidate of their choice, do not appear to believe that fidelity to him is any very necessary virtue. They abandon, with little concern, the prince under whose banner they had ranged themselves, and are received and trusted by the prince to whom they revolt, as if the crime of what we should call treason was not regarded, either by the prince or the nobility, as one of a deep dye. While a government remains in the unsettled state in which it is often found in Asiatic countries, where the allegiance of a nobleman or a city, in the course of a few years, is transferred several times from one sovereign to another, the civil and political advantages of fidelity are not very obvious; and it is not easy for any high principles of honour or duty to be generated. A man, in his choice of a party, having no law to follow, no duty to perform, is decided entirely by those ideas of temporary and personal convenience which he may happen to have adopted. There is no loyal or patriotic sentiment, no love of country condensed into the feeling of hereditary attachment to a particular line of princes, which in happier lands, even under misfortune and persecution, in danger and in death, supports and rewards the sufferer with the proud or tranquil consciousness of a duty well performed. The nobility, unable to predict the events of one twelvemonth, degenerate into a set of selfish, calculating, though perhaps brave partisans. Rank, and wealth, and present enjoyment become their idols. The prince feels the influence of the general want of stability, and is himself educated in the loose principles of an adventurer. In all about him he sees merely the instruments of his power. The subject, seeing the prince consult only his pleasure, learns on his part to consult only his private convenience. In such societies, the steadiness of principle that flows from the love of right and of our country can have no place. It may be questioned whether the prevalence of the Mahommedan religion, by swallowing up civil in religious distinctions, has not a tendency to increase this indifference to country, wherever it is established. A Musulman considers himself as in a certain degree at home, wherever the inhabitants are Musulmans. The ease with which one even of the highest rank abandons his native land, and wanders as a fugitive and almost a beggar in foreign parts, is only exceeded by the facility with which he takes root and educates a family wherever he can procure a subsistence, though in a land of strangers, provided he be among those of the true faith. Unity of religion is the single bond which reconciles him to the neighbours among whom he may be, and religion fills up so much of the mind, and intermingles itself so much with the ordinary tenor of the habitual and almost mechanical conduct of persons of every rank, that of itself it serves to introduce the appearance of considerable uniformity of manners and of feeling in most Asiatic countries.

In Bābur's age the power of the prince was restrained in a considerable degree, in the countries which have been described, by that of his nobles, each of whom had attached to him a numerous train of followers, while some of them were the heads of ancient and nearly independent tribes, warmly devoted to the interest of their chiefs. It was checked also by the influence of the priesthood, but especially of some eminent Khwājehs or religious guides, who to the character of sanctity often joined the possession of ample domains, and had large bands of disciples and followers ready blindly to fulfil their wishes. Each prince had some religious guide of this description. Bābur mentions more than one, for whom he professes unbounded admiration. The inhabitants were in general devoted to some of these religious teachers, whose dictates they received with submissive reverence. Many of them pretended to supernatural communications, and the words that fell from them were treasured up as omens to regulate future conduct. Many instances occur in the history both

INTRODUCTION

of India and Māweralnaher, in which, by the force of their religious character, these saints were of much political consequence, and many cities were lost and won by their influence with the inhabitants.

The religion of the country was mingled with numerous superstitions. One of these, which is wholly of a Tartar origin, is often alluded to by Bābur. It is that of the *yadeh*-stone. The history of this celebrated superstition, as given by D'Herbelot,[1] is that Japhet, on leaving his father Noah, to go to inhabit his portion of the world, received his father's blessing, and, at the same time, a stone, on which was engraved the mighty name of God. This stone, called by the Arabs *hajar-al-mater*, the rain-stone, the Tūrks call *yadeh-tāsh*, and the Persians *sang i yadeh*. It had the virtue of causing the rain to fall or to cease; but, in the course of time, this original stone was worn away or lost. It is pretended, however, that others, with a similar virtue, and bearing the same name, are still found among the Tūrks; and the more superstitious affirm, that they were originally produced and multiplied, by some mysterious sort of generation, from the original stone given by Noah to his son.

Izzet-ullah, the intelligent traveller to whom I have already alluded, in giving a description of Yārkand, mentions the *yadeh*-stone as one of the wonders of the land. He says that it is taken from the head of a horse or cow; and that, if certain ceremonies be previously used, it inevitably produces rain or snow. He who performs the ceremonies is called *yadehchī*. Izzet-ullah, though, like Bābur, he professes his belief in the virtues of the stone, yet acknowledges that he was never an eyewitness of its effects; he says, however, that he has so often heard the facts concerning its virtues stated over and over again, by men of unimpeachable credit, that he cannot help acquiescing in their evidence. When about to operate, the *yadehchī*, of whom there are many at this day in Yārkand, steeps the stone in the blood of some animal, and then throws it into water, at the same time repeating certain mysterious

[1] *Biblioth. Orient.*, art. 'Turk'. See also the Supplément de Visdelou et Galand, p. 140, folio edition.

words. First of all, a wind is felt blowing, and this is soon succeeded by a fall of snow and rain. The author, aware of the incredulity of his readers, attempts to show that, though these effects certainly follow in the cold country of Yārkand, we are not to look for them in the warm region of Hind; and, further, ingeniously justifies his opinions regarding the unknown and singular qualities of the rainstone by the equally singular and inexplicable properties of the magnet.

The branch of literature chiefly cultivated to the north of the Oxus, was poetry; and several of the persons mentioned in the progress of the following work had made no mean proficiency in the art. The age which had produced the great divines and philosophers, the Būrhāneddīns and the Avicennas,[1] was past away from Māweralnaher; but every department of science and literature was still successfully cultivated on the opposite side of the southern desert, at Herāt in Khorasān, at the splendid court of Sultan Hussain Mirza Baikera.[2] It is impossible to contemplate the scene which Khorasān then afforded, without lamenting that the instability, inseparable from despotism, should, in every age, have been communicated to the science and literature of the East. Persia, at several different eras of its history, has only wanted the continuous impulse afforded by freedom and security, to enable its literature to rank with the most refined and useful that has adorned or benefited any country. The most polished court in the west of Europe could not, at the close of the fifteenth century, vie in magnificence with that of Herāt; and if we compare the court of Khorasān even with that of Francis the First—the glory of France, at a still later period—an impartial observer will be compelled to acknowledge that in every important department of literature—in poetry, in history, in morals and metaphysics, as well

[1] [Burhān ud dīn (1135-97) was the celebrated author of the *Hidāya*, a work on Muhammedan Jurisprudence, which was translated by Charles Hamilton (London, 1791). Abū 'Alī Sīnā (983-1037) was a famous philosopher and physician. His chief works were *Shifa* on physics, and a great medical encyclopaedia entitled *Iānūn*.]

[2] [Sultan Hosain Mirza (1469-1506) was himself an author of merit, having composed the *Majālis ul 'ishq*, and a *Dīvān* in Tūrki.]

perhaps as in music and the fine arts—the palm of excellence must be assigned to the court of the oriental prince. But the manners of Bābur's court, in the early part of his reign, were not very refined; the period was one of confusion, rebellion, and force; and his nobles probably bore rather more visible traces of the rude spirit of the inhabitants of the desert from which their Tūrki ancestors had issued, and in which their own followers still dwelt, than of the polished habits of the courtiers who crowd the palaces of princes that have long reigned over a prosperous and submissive people.

Bābur frequently alludes to the *Tūreh or Yāsi*, that is, the Institutions of Chingiz Khan; and observes that, though they were certainly not of divine appointment, they had been held in respect by all his forefathers. This *Tūreh*, or *Yāsi*, was a set of laws which were ascribed to that great conqueror, and were supposed to have been promulgated by him on the day of his enthronization. They seem to have been a collection of the old usages of the Moghul tribes, comprehending some rules of state and ceremony and some injunctions for the punishment of particular crimes. The punishments were only two—death and the bastinado;[1] the number of blows extending from seven to seven hundred. There is something very Chinese in the whole of the Moghul system of punishment; even princes advanced in years, and in command of large armies, being punished by bastinado with a stick, by their father's orders. Whether they received their usage in this respect from the Chinese, or communicated it to them, is not very certain. As the whole body of their laws or customs was formed before the introduction of the Musulman religion, and was probably in many respects inconsistent with the Korān, as, for instance, in allowing the use of the blood of animals, and in the extent of toleration granted to other religions, it gradually fell into decay. One of these laws ordered adulterers to be punished with death; in consequence of which we are told that the inhabitants of Kaindu, who, from remote times, had been accustomed to resign their wives to the strangers who visited them, retiring from their own houses during their stay, represented to the

---

[1] D'Herbelot, *Biblioth. Orient.*, art. 'Turk'.

Tartar Prince the hardship to which this new enactment would subject them, by preventing the exercise of their accustomed hospitality, when they were relieved by a special exception from the oppressive operation of this law.[1] It is probable that the laws of Chingiz Khan were merely traditionary, and never reduced into writing. In Bābur's days they were still respected among the wandering tribes, but did not form the law of his kingdom. The present Moghul tribes punish most offences by fines of cattle.

We are so much accustomed to hear the manners and fashions of the East characterized as unchangeable, that it is almost needless to remark that the general manners described by Bābur as belonging to his dominions are as much the manners of the present day as they were of his time. That the fashions of the East are unchanged is, in general, certainly true; because the climate and the despotism, from the one or other of which a very large proportion of them arises, have continued the same. Yet one who observes the way in which a Musulman of rank spends his day will be led to suspect that the maxim has sometimes been adopted with too little limitation. Take the example of his pipe and his coffee. The *kaliūn*, or *hukka*, is seldom out of his hand; while the coffee-cup makes its appearance every hour, as if it contained a necessary of life. Perhaps there are no enjoyments the loss of which he would feel more severely; or which, were we to judge only by the frequency of the call for them, we should suppose to have entered from a more remote period into the system of Asiatic life. Yet we know that the one (which has indeed become a necessary of life to every class of Musulmans) could not have been enjoyed before the discovery of America; and there is every reason to believe that the other was not introduced into Arabia from Africa, where coffee is indigenous, previously to the sixteenth century;[2] and what marks the circumstance more strongly,

---

[1] For a further account of this code, see Notes to Langle's *Instituts politiques et militaires de Timour*, p. 396; *Hist. des Découvertes russes*, tom. iii, p. 337; and Tooke's *Russia*, vol. iv, p. 23; whence further particulars may be gleaned.

[2] La Roque, *Traité historique de l'Origine et du Progrès du Café*, &c., Paris, 1716, 12mo.

both of these habits have forced their way in spite of the remonstrances of the rigorists in religion. Perhaps it would have been fortunate for Bābur had they prevailed in his age, as they might have diverted him from the immoderate use first of wine, and afterwards of deleterious drugs, which ruined his constitution and hastened on his end.

The art of war in the countries to the north of the Oxus was certainly in a very rude state. No regular armies were maintained, and success chiefly depended upon rapidity of motion. A prince suddenly raised an army, and led it, by forced marches, into a neighbouring country, to surprise his enemy. Those who were attacked took refuge in their walled towns, where, from the defects in the art of attacking fortified places, they were for the most part secure. The two countries harassed each other by predatory inroads and petty warfare. Sometimes the stronger party kept the field, blockaded a fort, and reduced it by wasting the surrounding country; but peace was usually made with as much levity as war had been entered upon. Great bravery was often exhibited in their desperate forays; and the use of the sword and the bow was carefully studied. Some matchlocks were beginning to be introduced into their armies; but the sabre and the charge of horse still generally decided the day. They were not ignorant of the art of mining. Their most skilful miners were from Badakhshān, where they probably learned the art from working the ruby mines and beds of lapis lazuli. A few cannon had begun to be used in sieges, and latterly even in the line. Their military array, however, was still formed according to the rules given by Taimūr Beg. They had indeed, a right and left wing, and a centre, with a body in advance, and a reserve;[1] they had also parties of flankers on their wings; but they seem seldom to have engaged in a regular battle. Most of the armies mentioned by Bābur were far from being numerous; and the day seldom appears to have been decided by superior skill in military tactics.

These are the only remarks that seem necessary regarding the countries north of the Hindū-kūsh mountains; and little need be added concerning those to the south, which

[1] See White's *Translation of the Institutes of Timour.*

were subdued by Bābur. The labours of Major Rennell throw sufficient light on the geography of that monarch's transactions in India; and long before this volume can appear, a similar light must have been shed over his marches in Afghanistān, by the publication of the work of Mr. Elphinstone on that country. It may only be briefly remarked, that the Hindū-kūsh range, after passing to the north of Kābul, breaks into numerous hills running west and southwest, which constitute the ancient kingdom of Bāmiān and the modern countries of the Hazāras and Aimāks; that the Belūt-tāgh mountains, formerly mentioned as running north from Hindū-kūsh, seem also to shoot south by Sefīd Koh, forming the Suleimān range which traverses the whole of Afghanistān, as far as the country of Beluchistān, running in the greater part of its course nearly parallel to the Indus; and that this range, soon after it passes the latitude of Ghazni, seems to divide into three or more parallel ridges that run south; but that though the mountains run north and south, the slope of the land is from west to east; in consequence of which, some of the rivers that rise in the high lands of Ghazni and Kābul, appear to be obliged to force their way through a rupture in the transverse ranges, when they pursue their course eastward to the Indus. Such is the case with the river of Kābul, when it bursts its way first through the Logar range, and lower down, through the Suleimān hills, near Jelālābād; and, in an inferior degree, with the Kurram and Gumal rivers, which have wrought themselves a course through the more southern branches of the same range.

From this long range, which runs south, there issue three minor branches of some note, that run eastward. The most northerly is the Kheiber, or Kohāt range, which extends from Sefīd Koh to Nilāb on the Indus, running all the way nearly parallel to the Kābul river, and to the road from Kābul to Peshāwar. The next, which by Bābur is called the Bangash hills, and by Mr. Elphinstone is designated as the Salt Range, runs from Sefīd Koh southeast to Kālabagh, where it is crossed by the Indus, but pursues its course in its original direction to the Behāt or Jhelam river, the Hydaspes of antiquity, beyond Pind-

Dādan-Khan. The third, which runs from Bāzār to Paniāla, on the Indus, may be called the Dūki Range. Between the two first lies the valley of Kohāt, so particularly mentioned by Bābur; and between the two last, Bannu, part of Bangash, and several other districts. The other places in this direction will be noted when they occur.

From the west of the Sefīd Koh runs a range which passes to the south-west of Kābul, Ghazni, and Kandahār, whence it runs down to the desert of Sīstān.

Between this range and that of Paropamisus, the level country of Kābul rises up to Ghazni, which is the highest table-land in Afghānistān, the rivers descending on the one side north to Kābul, on the other west to Kandahār, and on the eastward to the Indus. The western slope of Ghazni is by Kandahār, to the Lake of Sīstān and the desert. This level country is of no great breadth.

But the part of Afghānistān which is most frequently alluded to by Bābur is the tract lying along the southern slope of the Hindū-kūsh mountains and the angle formed by the Paropamisan hills as they advance to the south. It consists of a number of mountainous mounds, pushed forwards from the higher hills, and forming steep and narrow, but beautiful and finely watered, valleys between, which transmit their streams to swell the Kābul river. Most of these, from Ghorbend and Panjsher, down to Panjkora and Sawād, are particularly commemorated by Bābur himself, in his lively description of the country. His account of the different roads from Hindustān is a curious portion of the geography of Afghānistān.

With the assistance of Major Rennell's and Mr. Elphinstone's maps, it will be easy to follow Bābur through all the journeys mentioned in the two last parts of the Memoirs; and the Memoir and map of Mr. Waddington will give a clearer idea than is elsewhere to be found of the country north of the Oxus, the scene of the first part of the Memoirs.[1]

[1] [The Memoir and map referred to have been omitted as they were found to be imperfect and out of date. The new map which has been substituted for that of Mr. Waddington includes Afghānistān and northern India.]

INTRODUCTION

PART SECOND

CONTAINING

A SHORT ACCOUNT OF THE SUCCESSORS OF TAIMŪR BEG FROM THE DEATH OF THAT PRINCE TO THE ACCESSION OF BĀBUR

BĀBUR begins his Memoirs abruptly, by informing us, that he mounted the throne of Ferghāna at the age of twelve. As he often alludes to events that occurred previous to that time, and speaks familiarly of the different princes who had governed in the neighbouring countries, supposing the reader to be well acquainted with their history, it becomes necessary, for the better understanding of his text, to give a short review of the succession of the most eminent of those who had ruled in his kingdom and in the adjoining countries for some years before his accession; and as the whole of these princes were descended from the famous Tamerlane, or Taimūr Beg, as all their kingdoms were only fragments of his immense empire, and their claims and political relations derived from him, the reign of that prince is the most convenient period from which to commence such a review.

Death of Taimūr Beg.

Taimūr Beg, after having spread his empire over the fairest provinces of Asia, died in the year 1405,[1] near the city of Otrār, beyond the river Sirr. His dominions, however, though extensive, were ill compacted and ill governed. He had conquered countries, but he had not the genius to found an empire. Though a conqueror, whatever his encomiasts may assert, he was no legislator. He had marched

[1] 17 Shābān, A. H. 807. Wednesday, February 18, A. D. 1405.

into Tartary, into Hindustān, into Mesopotamia, into Syria and Asia Minor, and had subdued a great portion of all these countries; but in the course of a very few years his native country of Māweralnaher, with Persia and Kābul, alone remained in his family, and Persia also very soon after escaped from their grasp, and was overrun by the Turkomāns.

In his lifetime, he had given the immediate government of different quarters of his extensive dominions to his sons and their descendants, who, at the period of his death, were very numerous; and the Tūrki and Moghul tribes, like other Asiatics, having no fixed rules of succession to the throne, various princes of his family set up for themselves in different provinces. The nobles who were about his person at the time of his death proclaimed his grandson Khalīl, an amiable prince of refined genius and warm affections, but better fitted to adorn the walks of private life than to compose the dissensions of a distracted kingdom, or to check the ambitious designs of a turbulent nobility. He reigned for some years, with little power, at Samarkand, his grandfather's capital; but was finally dethroned by his ambitious nobles. His uncle Shahrokh, the youngest son of Taimūr Beg, a prince of solid talents and great firmness of character, on hearing of this event, marched from Khorasān, which was the seat of his dominions, took possession of Samarkand, and reduced all the rest of Māweralnaher under his obedience. He governed his extensive dominions with a steady hand till his death, which happened in 1446. *He is succeeded in Samarkand by Khalīl. A.D. 1412. Shahrokh Mirza seizes Māweralnaher. A.D. 1415. His death. A.D. 1446.*

On his death, his sons, according to the fashion of their country and age, seized the different provinces which they had held as governors, each asserting his own independence, and aiming at the subjugation of the others. He was succeeded in Samarkand by his eldest son Ulugh Beg, a prince illustrious by his love of science, and who has secured an honest fame, and the gratitude of posterity, by the valuable astronomical tables constructed by his directions, in an observatory which he built at Samarkand for that purpose. Ulugh Beg, who had long held the government of Samarkand in his father's lifetime, soon after *Is succeeded in Samarkand by Ulugh Beg Mirza.*

his accession, led an army from that city against his nephew Alā-ed-daulat, the son of his brother Baiesanghar, who was the third son of Shahrokh. Alā-ed-daulat, who had occupied the kingdom of Khorasān, being defeated by his uncle Ulugh Beg, on the river of Murghāb, fled to his brother, the elder Bābur Mirza. That prince had taken possession of Jorjān, or Korkān, on the south-east of the Caspian, the government of which he had held in the lifetime of his grandfather, Shahrokh, and now asserted his independence. Bābur led the forces of his principality towards Herāt, to restore his brother Alā-ed-daulat; but being defeated, and hard pushed by Ulugh Beg, was forced to abandon even his capital, Asterābād, and to take refuge, in company with Alā-ed-daulat, in Irāk, which was then held by another of their brothers, Muhammed Mirza. Ulugh Beg having soon afterwards returned across the Amu to Bokhāra, Bābur Mirza again entered Khorasān, and took possession of Herāt; while Ulugh Beg's own son, Abdallatīf, revolted and seized upon Balkh.

In Khorasān by Alā-ed-daulat, who is dethroned by Ulugh Beg.

In Korkān by Bābur Mirza, who marches to restore his brother; but is defeated, and flies to Irāk. 1448.

Conquers Khorasān.

Revolt of Abūsaīd Mirza.

To complete Ulugh Beg's misfortunes, Abūsaīd Mirza, who was the son of Muhammed Mirza, the grandson of Taimūr Beg, by that conqueror's second son Mirānshah, but who is better known by his own conquests, and as the grandfather of the great Bābur, also appeared in arms against him. Abūsaīd had been educated under the eye of Ulugh Beg. When his father, Muhammed Mirza, was on his death-bed, Ulugh Beg had come to visit him. The dying man took Abūsaīd's hand, and, putting it into Ulugh Beg's, recommended his son to his protection. Ulugh Beg was not unworthy of this confidence, and treated the young prince with great kindness and affection. One of Ulugh Beg's friends having remarked to him that his young cousin seemed to be attached and active in his service, 'It is not my service in which he is now employed,' said the generous Sultan; 'he is busy acquiring the rudiments of the arts of government and of policy, which will one day be of use to him.'[1] Abūsaīd, during the disorders that followed the death of Shahrokh, had for some time held

---

[1] *Tārikh i Khāfi Khan.*

the province of Fārs; but, being stripped of that possession by Muhammed Mirza (the brother of Alā-ed-daulat and of Bābur Mirza), had again taken refuge at the court of Ulugh Beg, who had given him one of his daughters in marriage. Believing, probably, according to the maxims of his age and country, that the pursuit of a throne dissolved all the obligations of nature or of gratitude, he now availed himself of the prevailing confusions, and of the absence of Ulugh Beg, who had marched against Abdallatīf, his rebellious son, to seize on Samarkand. Ulugh Beg, on hearing of this new revolt, had turned back to defend his capital, but was followed from Balkh by Abdallatīf, who defeated and slew him, after a short reign of three years. Death of Ulugh Beg.
1449.

Abdallatīf, after the murder of his father, continued his march, defeated Abūsaīd Mirza, took him prisoner, and recovered Samarkand. But Abūsaīd, who was destined to act an important part in the history of Asia, was fortunate enough to effect his escape, and found shelter and concealment in Bokhāra. While in this retreat, he heard that Abdallatīf had been murdered by a mutiny in his army, and had been succeeded by his cousin Abdallah,[1] who was the son of Ibrahīm, the second son of Shahrokh, and consequently a nephew of Ulugh Beg. The ambitious hopes of Abūsaīd Mirza were revived by this event. He succeeded in forming a party, seized upon Bokhāra, and marched against Samarkand, but was defeated and forced to take shelter in Turkestān,[2] beyond the Sirr. Next year, however, having engaged the Uzbeks of the desert to assist him, he returned towards Samarkand, defeated Abdallah in a great battle, and occupied all Māweralnaher. His new allies appear to have indulged in great excesses, and were with difficulty prevailed upon to retire from the fertile plains and rich pillage of the valley of the Soghd.[3]

[1] [This Abdullah Mirza had succeeded his father, Ibrahīm, son of Shahrokh, in the government of Fārs about 1443. Four years later, in 1447, he was dispossessed by Abu Sa'īd Mirza, and fled to his uncle Ulugh Beg, who then reigned in Transoxiana. He was killed in a battle with Abu Sa'īd Mirza in 1451. (Beale's *Biog. Dict.*)]

[2] This is the Turkestān below Tāshkend, and north-west from that country.

[3] D'Herbelot, in voce Abousaīd. De Guignes, vol. v, p 84

Meanwhile Bābur Mirza had not remained long in possession of Herāt, having been driven from it by Yār-Ali, a Turkomān chief. Bābur, however, retired slowly, and with reluctance; and, returning soon after by forced marches, came upon him by surprise in that capital, took him prisoner, beheaded him in the public market-place, and succeeded in occupying all Khorasān. But repose was not an enjoyment of those unquiet times. Before he could establish himself in his new conquest, he was attacked and defeated by his two elder brothers, Alā-ed-daulat and Muhammed Mirza, the kings of Fārs and Irāk. He retired for some time to the strong fortress of Umad, whence he took the field and defeated the governor whom Muhammed Mirza had left in charge of Asterābād; but having been closely followed by that prince, and overtaken before he could gain the town, he found himself once more compelled to seek safety in flight, and was fortunate enough to escape back to his fastness. Muhammed Mirza did not long remain in Khorasān. Disgusted with some circumstances in the conduct of his brother, Alā-ed-daulat, he withdrew to his own territories; whereupon Bābur once more issued from his retreat, drove Alā-ed-daulat out of Khorasān, following him to Balkh, which he took, as well as all the low country up to Badakhshān, where the fugitive prince sought refuge. He then returned back to Herāt. Alā-ed-daulat soon after fell into his hands.

This success of Bābur Mirza recalled his brother Muhammed into Khorasān, in an evil hour. He met with a fatal discomfiture, was taken prisoner, and put to death by the command of Bābur;[1] who, at the same time, to free himself from all apprehensions from his surviving brother, ordered the fire-pencil to be applied to the eyes of Alā-ed-daulat. The operation, however, from accident, or the mercy of the operator, was imperfectly performed, and Alā-ed-daulat did not lose his sight. Bābur Mirza, for the purpose of improving his victory to the utmost extent, now marched against Muhammed Mirza's kingdom of Fārs. He had made some progress in the conquest of it, when he was recalled into Khorasān by the alarming intelligence

[1] [A. D. 1452.]

that Alā-ed-daulat had escaped from custody, and was at the head of a numerous and increasing army. On his return to Khorasān, he found the revolt suppressed, and Alā-ed-daulat expelled from his territories; but Jehān Shah, the powerful chief of the Turkomāns of the Black Sheep, now descended from Tabrīz, and after occupying Persian Irāk, pursued his conquests, and in a few years subdued Fārs and the remaining territories of Muhammed Mirza. To regain these provinces, Bābur Mirza led a formidable army into Persian Irāk and Azarbaijān; but had scarcely set his foot in the country when he learned that Abūsaīd Mirza had entered his dominions from the north. Enraged at this insult, he measured back his steps, followed Abūsaīd across the Amu, and laid siege to Samarkand; but after lying before it forty days, he concluded a peace, which left the Amu or Oxus the boundary between the two countries. Bābur then returned to Khorasān, and enjoyed several years of comparative peace. He was carried off in the year 1457, by a disease originating in his habitual excesses in wine.[1]

1457. Death of Bābur Mirza.

His death was the signal for Abūsaīd Mirza again to attempt the conquest of Khorasān. From this enterprise he was, however, recalled towards Balkh, by a revolt of the sons of Abdallatīf Mirza, one of whom he slew, while the other, Muhammed Jūki, took refuge in the deserts of Tartary, with Abulkhair, one of the Khans of the Uzbek principality of Tura, a part of the empire of Kipchäk that lies to the east of the Ural mountains, and who dwelt in summer towards the banks of the river Jaik, and in winter on the Sirr.[2] Abūsaīd soon after returned into Khorasān, a great part of which he overran, and repressed the commotions excited by the restless Alā-ed-daulat. But he was glad to retire before the formidable irruption of Jehān Shah, the Turkomān chief, who entered Herāt, which was cruelly plundered by his troops. When the first fury of the invasion was over, the Turkomāns began to divide their forces. Abūsaīd, watching the opportunity, fell

Abūsaīd invades Khorasān.

---

[1] D'Herbelot, in voce Abūsaīd; de Guignes, vol. v, p. 88.
[2] Abulghāzi Khan's *Gen. History of the Turks*, &c., vol. i, p. 289, London, 1730. 8vo.

furiously on Jehān Shāh's son, near Marghūb, defeated the detachment under his command, and compelled his father to sue for a peace, and retreat from Khorasān. A treaty was concluded, by which it was agreed that the town of Semnān, which lies between Khorasān and Persian Irāk, should be the boundary between the territories of these two princes.

1458.
And conquers the country.

In these times of confusion, Sultan Hussain Mirza, a prince of great talents, and who is often mentioned in the Memoirs of Bābur, had fixed himself in the possession of Asterābād and Mazenderān. He was descended from Taimūr Beg [1] by his son Omer-Sheikh Mirza. Not contented with the peaceable enjoyment of the rich provinces which he held, he had pushed on his plundering parties into Khorasān as far as Sabzewār. Abūsaīd, having disengaged himself of the Turkomāns, and defeated Alā-ed-daulat, who had once more invaded his territories on the side of Meshed, now marched to chastise Sultan Hussain Mirza. The contending armies met, Abūsaīd was victorious, and, pursuing his advantage, entered his enemy's capital, Asterābād, in which he left one of his sons, Sultan Mahmūd Mirza.

Sultan Hussain Mirza invades Khorasān.

1459.

Driven from Asterābād.

But Abūsaīd was not yet destined to enjoy repose. Muhammed Jūki, the son of Abdallatīf, and grandson of Ulugh Beg Mirza, who, after his defeat, had fled, as has been mentioned, to Abulkhair, the Khan of the Uzbeks, [2] had meanwhile returned, accompanied by his new allies, and was ravaging Abūsaīd's territories beyond the Amu. Abūsaīd once more hastened to Samarkand, and the predatory bands of his enemies, on his approach, retired beyond the Sirr. From the prosecution of this war, Abūsaīd was recalled by the unwelcome intelligence of the defeat of his son, Mahmūd Mirza, whom Sultan Hussain Mirza had driven from Asterābād. Not contented with this success, Sultan Hussain had advanced into the very heart of Khorasān, and had even laid siege to the capital, Herāt. The return of Abūsaīd speedily raised the siege. He

Muhammed Jūki invades Samarkand.

1460.
Retires before Abūsaīd Mirza.

Sultan Hussain Mirza recovers Asterābād.

---

[1] He was the son of Mansūr, the son of Baikara, the son of Omer-Sheikh, the son of Taimūr Beg. See D'Herbelot, art. 'Taimūr'.

[2] Abulkhair's wife was sister of Muhammed Jūki's father. *Gen. History of the Turks*, vol. i, p. 212.

drove the Sultan out of his territories, and, following him into his own, stripped him of all that he held in Jorjān and Māzenderān.

This success enabled Abūsaīd to turn his undivided force to complete the destruction of Muhammed Jūki. He besieged that prince in Shahrokhīa, a strong and populous city on the Sirr, and, after a siege of one year,[1] took the place and his rival. Being finally disengaged of this enemy, he now returned across the Amu, where Sultan Hussain Mirza had availed himself of his absence to enter Khorasān. That active prince was once more compelled to fly, and sought shelter in Khwārizm. Abūsaīd, being now delivered from all his enemies, gave his attention, for some time, to the extension of his territories on the side of Sīstān and India, by means of his generals, and to the settling of his extensive dominions. He soon after went to Merv, where he gave a splendid feast, which lasted five months, to celebrate the circumcision of the princes his sons. It was on this occasion that his son, Omer-Sheikh Mirza, Bābur's father, received the government of Ferghāna, as is mentioned in the Memoirs.

While Abūsaīd was yet at Merv, Hassan Ali, the son of Jehān Shah, the prince of the Turkomāns of the Black Sheep, arrived from Irāk, where, by one of those reverses so frequent in the East, his father had been defeated and slain by the celebrated Ūzūn Hassan, the Beg of the Turkomāns of the White Sheep. Hassan Ali now solicited the protection and assistance of Abūsaīd, who gladly undertook to restore him to his paternal dominions. The expedition which followed is famous in eastern history, and is often alluded to by Bābur, under the name of 'the disaster of Irāk'. Abūsaīd Mirza advanced into Azarbaijān with a powerful army, subduing the country in his course. He sent two detachments to take possession the one of the Persian Irāk, the other of Fārs. As he pushed on towards Ardebīl and Tabrīz, among the hills of Azarbaijān, Ūzūn Hassan, alarmed at his progress, sent repeated embassies to sue for peace ; but in vain, as Abūsaīd, to all his offers, annexed the condition that the Turkomān

Again dispossessed by Abūsaīd, who besieges Shahrokhīa, and takes Muhammed Jūki.

1463.

1465.

1466. Hassan Ali solicits the assistance of Abūsaīd,

1467. who marches into Azarbaijān.

[1] Abulghāzi Khan says of four months. Vol. i, p. 215.

should appear in his presence, and humble himself before the descendant of Taimūr Beg. To this Ūzūn Hassan refused to submit, and, reduced to despair, betook himself to the hills and fastnesses in which the country abounds, and employed himself indefatigably in harassing and cutting off the supplies of the enemy, whom he prudently avoided meeting in the field. What the sword could not achieve was completed by famine. The large but tumultuary army of Abūsaīd began to suffer from the pressure of want, and no sooner suffered than it began to fall away.

The disaster of Irāk. The various chieftains and tribes of which it was composed gradually withdrew each to his own country. The army fell to pieces. Abūsaīd was compelled to seek safety in flight, was pursued, taken prisoner, and soon after beheaded. Of his mighty army few returned to their homes. The greater part were taken prisoners, or slaughtered in the course of their long retreat.

1468. Abūsaīd beheaded.

His sons. The dominions of Abūsaīd, who was by far the most powerful prince of his time, extended, at the period of his death, from Azarbaijān to the borders of India, and from Mekrān to the deserts of Tartary. Of his sons, Sultan Ahmed Mirza, who was the eldest, retained possession of Samarkand and Bokhāra, the government of which he had held in the lifetime of his father. Another of them, Sultan Mahmūd Mirza, held the government of Asterābād, from whence, after the 'disaster of Irāk', he marched to take possession of Herāt ; but the inhabitants preferring the government of Sultan Hussain Mirza, called him in ; and Sultan Mahmūd Mirza, expelled from Khorasān, and forced to cross the Amu, took refuge in Samarkand, with his brother, Sultan Ahmed Mirza, having lost Asterābād in his attempt to gain Khorasān. In the course of a few months, he fled privately from his brother's protection, and by means of Kamber Ali Beg, a Moghul nobleman of great influence, who was at that time the governor of Hissār, gained possession of all the country, from the straits of Kolugha or Derbend, to the Belūt mountains, and from the hills of Asfera to the mountains of Hindū-kūsh, an extensive tract of country, that included Hissār, Chegāniān, Termiz, Kunduz, Badakhshān, and Khutlān. Another of Abūsaīd's

Sultan Ahmed Mirza, king of Samarkand and Bokhāra.

Sultan Mahmūd Mirza, king of Hissār, Kunduz, and Badakhshān.

INTRODUCTION cvii

sons, Ulugh Beg Mirza, retained possession of Kābul and Ghazni, which he had governed in his father's lifetime. Another, Omer-Sheikh Mirza, the father of the illustrious Bābur, and the fourth son of Abūsaīd, continued to reign in Ferghāna. Sultan Murād Mirza, another of Abūsaīd Mirza's sons, who had held the government of Garmsīr and Kandahār, had advanced, at the period of his father's death, to occupy Kermān. He was forced to retreat by the ensuing events, and found that he could not maintain himself even in Kandahār. He repaired to the court of Sultan Hussain Mirza, by whom he was sent to Samarkand, to his brother, Sultan Ahmed Mirza; but he soon after returned to Herāt, after which he is little mentioned. It is needless to detail the fortunes of the other sons, as they had no influence on the history of Bābur.

Ulugh Beg Mirza, king of Kābul and Ghazni. Omer-Sheikh Mirza, king of Ferghāna. Sultan Murād Mirza.

Sultan Hussain Mirza was no sooner relieved of his formidable enemy, by the death of Abūsaīd, than he once more entered Khorasān, invited, as has been already mentioned, by the wishes and affections of the inhabitants. He quickly drove from Asterābād, Yādgār Mirza, a son of Muhammed Mirza, the late sovereign of Irāk and Fārs, who had been selected by Ūzūn Hassan and the Turkomāns to fill the throne of Khorasān, and compelled him to take refuge in Tebrīz, at the court of his patron. Next year, however, Yādgār Mirza returned, supported by a formidable body of Turkomāns, penetrated into Khorasān, and took Herāt, which Sultan Hussain, unable to resist the first impulse of the enemy, was glad to abandon. The Sultan retired to Balkh, but it was only to watch the favourable moment for returning; and he had no sooner learned, by a secret correspondence which he maintained with some of the chief officers about Yādgār Mirza's person, that that young prince had given himself up to all the enjoyments of a luxurious capital, than, returning by forced marches, he came upon him by surprise, while overpowered with wine, in the Bāgh-e-zāghān,[1] near Herāt, took him prisoner, dispersed his troops, and put him to death.

Sultan Hussain Mirza occupies Khorasān. Drives Yādgār Mirza from Asterābād. 1469. Surprises and puts him to death near Herāt. 1470.

The remaining years of the reign of Sultan Hussain Mirza were little disturbed, except by the rebellion of his

Reigns in Khorasān.

---

[1] The Raven Garden.

sons, and, towards its close, by the invasion of Sheibāni Khan. But these events will be best explained by Bābur himself in his Memoirs, where copious details will be found regarding the family, dominions, and court of this monarch.[1]

<small>Reign of Omer-Sheikh Mirza in Ferghāna.</small>

Sultan Omer-Sheikh Mirza, the sovereign of Ferghāna, and the father of Bābur, has by some writers been supposed to have had his capital at Samarkand, and by others to have extended his dominions even into India. His dominions, however, never extended beyond the narrow limits of Ferghāna and Uratippa, unless for a short time, when he received Tāshkend and Seirām from his eldest brother, Sultan Ahmed, and gained Shahrokhīa by stratagem. These acquisitions he soon lost, having given them up to his brother-in-law, Sultan Mahmūd Khan, in return for assistance afforded him in his wars; and at his death, which happened in 1494, he only retained possession of Ferghāna, Uratippa having just been taken from him by his brother, Sultan Ahmed Mirza of Samarkand. He was a restless, profuse, good-humoured man, who left his dominions in considerable disorder to his eldest son, the illustrious Bābur, then only twelve years of age.

<small>State of Māweralnāher at the accession of Bābur.</small>

It is from this event that Bābur commences his Memoirs. At that period, his uncle, Sultan Ahmed Mirza, was still king of Samarkand and Bokhāra. Another of his uncles, Sultan Mahmūd Mirza, was the sovereign of Hissār, Termiz, Kunduz, Badakhshān, and Khutlān. A third uncle, Ulugh Beg Mirza, was king of Kābul and Ghazni; while Sultan Hussain Mirza Baikera, a descendant of the great Taimūr, and the most powerful prince of his age, was king of Khorasān. To the west and north of Ferghāna, Sultan Mahmūd Khan, a Moghul prince, Bābur's maternal uncle, and the eldest son of Yunis Khan, so often alluded to by Bābur, held the fertile provinces of Tāshkend and Shahrokhīa, along the Sirr or Jaxartes, as well as the chief power over the Moghuls of the desert as far as Moghulistān, where

---

[1] The seventh volume of the *Rawzat-us-safā*, the Garden of Purity, or rather Pleasure Garden, by Mīr Khāwend Shah, contains a very detailed account of all the incidents of Sultan Hussain Mirza's reign. [The history of Mīr Khāwand (1433-98) was translated by David Shea and published with illustrative notes for the Oriental Translation Fund in 1832.]

Sultan Ahmed Khan, his younger brother, appears to have governed a separate division of the same tribe. Three daughters of Yunis Khan, the sisters of these two princes, had been married to the three brothers, the kings of Samarkand, Hissār, and Ferghāna ; and the relations of affinity arising from these marriages are often alluded to by Bābur.

To prevent the necessity of hereafter interrupting the narrative, it may be proper, in addition to these remarks, to observe that Sheibāni Khan, a name which occurs in every page of the earlier part of the following history, was still in the deserts of Tartary. He was descended from Chingiz Khan, by his eldest son, Tūshi or Jūji Khan, the sovereign of Kipchāk. Bātu, the eldest son of Tūshi, having returned from his expedition into the north of Europe, bestowed on one of his younger brothers, Sheibāni Khan, a large party of Moghuls and Tūrks, who fed their flocks in the champaign between the Ural hills and the sea of Aral, and along the river Jaik, or Yaik, which flows into the Caspian ; and he became the founder of the Khanate of Tūra, which, in process of time, extended its conquests considerably into Siberia. One of his descendants, Uzbek Khan, was so much beloved by his tribes that they are said to have assumed his name, and hence the origin of the Uzbek nations. Abulkhair Khan, the grandfather of the second Sheibāni, was a contemporary of Abusaīd Mirza. When that monarch had expelled Muhammed Jūki Mirza from Samarkand, the young prince, as has already been mentioned, had fled for protection to Abulkhair Khan, who sent him back, accompanied by one of his sons, with a powerful army, which took Tāshkend and Shahrokhīa,[1] and occupied all the open country of Māweralnaher. The approach of Abusaīd compelled them to retire beyond the Sirr.

The ambition and power of Abulkhair Mirza were so formidable as to justify a combination of all the neighbouring Tartar princes against him, by which he was defeated and put to death with several of his sons ; the

Account of the family of Sheibāni Khan.

The elder Sheibāni.

Uzbek Khan.

Abulkhair Khan.

1460.

His death [1465].

---

[1] Tāshkend and Shahrokhīa, as well as all the cultivated country down the Sirr, were at that period subject to Samarkand.

others saved themselves by flight. But his grandson Sheibāk or Sheibāni Khan, the son of Borāk or Budāk, regained at least a part of his hereditary dominions, and not only retrieved the honour, but greatly extended the power of the family. The confused state of the country between the Amu and the Sirr, soon after attracted him into the territories of Samarkand; an expedition to which the Uzbeks were probably equally called by the invitation of the contending princes of the country, and by the remembrance of the plunder and spoil which they had carried off from these rich and ill-defended countries twenty-four years before. From some expressions used by Bābur, it seems pretty clear that, in spite of the extent of his conquests along the banks of the Oxus, Sheibāni Khan had never regained the power enjoyed by his grandfather in his native deserts, and was confined to the range of territory around the town and country of Turkestān, to the north-west of Tāshkend, which was a recent conquest made by that division of his tribe that adhered to his interests. His subjects were a mass of tribes of Tūrki, Moghul, and probably of Finnic race, moulded down into one people, but with a great preponderance of Tūrks. His army was latterly swelled by volunteers from all the Tūrki and Moghul tribes from Kāshghar to the Volga;[1] and he appears, even under the partial colouring of his enemy Bābur, as a prince of great vigour of mind, and of no contemptible military talents.

Such was the general division of the neighbouring countries when Zehīr-ed-dīn Muhammed, surnamed Bābur, or the Tiger, ascended the throne. Immediately before the death of his father Sultan Omer-Sheikh Mirza, his neighbours Sultan Ahmed Mirza of Samarkand and Sultan Mahmūd Khan of Tāshkend, displeased with some parts of his conduct, had entered into a coalition, in consequence of which they had invaded his country.

[1] The Khanship of Kipchāk expired in A. D. 1506, and broke into several smaller divisions. That of Tūra seems to have continued under a different branch of the family of Sheibāni Khan until the year 1598, when the kingdom of Tūra fell into the hands of the Russians.

INTRODUCTION

Few incidents of the life of Bābur previous to his mounting the throne are known. It may be remarked, however, that he was born[1] on the 6th Muharrem 888, and that when a boy of five years of age he had paid a visit to his paternal uncle, Sultan Ahmed Mirza, at Samarkand, on which occasion he was betrothed to his cousin, Āisha Sultān Begum, the daughter of that prince. This lady he afterwards married. *(Feb. 14, 1483.)*

Bābur ascended the throne about two years after the discovery of America by Columbus, and four years before Vasco de Gama reached India. The year in which he mounted the throne was that of the celebrated expedition of Charles VIII of France against Naples. His contemporaries in England were Henry VII and Henry VIII; in France, Charles VIII, Louis XII, and Francis I; in Germany, the Emperors Maximilian and Charles V; in Spain, Ferdinand and Isabella, and Charles. The discovery of America, and of the passage to India by the Cape of Good Hope, the increase of the power of France by the union of the great fiefs to the crown, and of Spain by the similar union of its different kingdoms under Charles, the destruction of the empire of Constantinople, and the influence of the art of printing, introduced about that time a new system into the west of Europe, which has continued with little change down to our times. The rise and progress of the Reformation formed the most interesting event in Europe during the reign of Bābur.

---

[1] The date of his birth is recorded in a Persian couplet, preserved by Abul-fazl, who makes some characteristic remarks on them, founded on his fondness for astrology: 'As that generous prince was born on the sixth of Muharrem; the date of his birth is also (*Shesh Muharrem*) the sixth of Muharrem.' The numeral letters in these two words happen to give 888.

THE
MEMOIRS OF BĀBUR

IN the month of Ramzān,[1] in the year eight hundred and ninety-nine, and in the twelfth year of my age, I became King of Ferghāna.

Account of Ferghāna.

The country of Ferghāna is situated in the fifth climate,[2] on the extreme boundary of the habitable world. On the east, it has Kāshgar; on the west, Samarkand; on the south, the hill-country on the confines of Badakhshān; on the north, although in former times there were cities such as Almāligh,[3] Almātu, and Yangi,[4] which is known in books of history by the name of Otrār; yet, at the present date, in consequence of the incursions of the Uzbeks, they are desolate, and no population remains.

Boundaries

Ferghāna is a country of small extent, but abounding in grain and fruits; and it is surrounded with hills on all sides except on the west, towards Samarkand and Khojend, where there are none; and on that side alone can it be entered by foreign enemies. The river Seihūn, which is generally known by the name of the river of Khojend, comes from the north-east, and after passing through this country, flows

---

[1] The month of Ramzān, A. H. 899, begins on June 6, A.D. 1494. This was the year of Charles VIII's expedition to Naples.

[2] [The habitable world, according to Arabic geographers, was divided into seven climates (Arabic *iqlīm*).]

[3] *Almāligh* or *Almālig*, in Tūrki, signifies 'a grove of apple trees'. Almātu, in the same language, signifies 'abounding in apples'. Almāligh is a city which lies [on the Ili river near the modern town of Kuldja] north-east from Kāsān, on the other side of the Alā-tāgh Mountains. Otrār lies between Tāshkend and the sea of Arāl; and in the days of Taimūr was a place of great note. He died there while preparing for his expedition against China.

[4] [There are several towns with the appellation of Yangi (= new). Among these is Tarāz, or Tarāzkent, which is situated on the Talās river near the modern Aulia Ata, at the foot of the extreme western limit of the Alexander Mountains (*T. R.*), and is substituted for Yangi in Pavet de Courteille's French version.]

towards the west. It then runs on the north of Khojend and south of Finākat,[1] which is now better known as Shahrokhīa; and thence, inclining to the north, flows down towards Tūrkestān; and meeting with no other river in its course, is wholly swallowed up in the sandy desert considerably below Tūrkestān, and disappears.

In this country there are seven districts, five on the south of the Seihūn, and two on the north.

Divisions. 1. Andejān. Of the districts on the south of the river, one is Andejān, which has a central position and is the capital of Ferghāna. It abounds in grain and fruits, its grapes and melons are excellent and plentiful. In the melon season it is not customary to sell them at the beds.[2] There are no better *nāshpātis*[3] produced than those of Andejān. In Māweralnaher, after the fortresses of Samarkand and Kĕsh, none is equal in size to Andejān. It has three gates. The citadel is situated on the south of the city. The water-courses of the mills by which the water enters the city, are nine; and it is remarkable that of all the water that enters the city, none flows out of it. Around the fortress, on the edge of the stone-faced moat,[a] is a broad highway covered with pebbles. All round the fort are the suburbs, which are only separated from the moat by this highway that runs along its banks.

The district abounds in birds and beasts of game. Its pheasants[4] are so fat, that the report goes that four persons may dine on the broth[5] of one of them, and not be able to finish it. The inhabitants of the country are all Tūrks, and there is none in town or market who does not understand the Tūrki tongue. The common speech of the people of this country is the same as the correct language of composition, so that the works of Mīr Ali Sher, surnamed Nawāi, though

[a] on the outer edge of the ditch,

---

[1] Finākat is also called Benākat and Fiākat. It is situated on the Seihūn or Sirr, between Tāshkend and Khojend.
[2] i. e. passengers eat them gratuitously.—*Leyden*.
[3] The *nāshpāti* is a species of melon. [It usually means 'pear'.]
[4] [*Qargāval* = *tazarv* (*Phaseanus Colchicus*).]
[5] The broth here mentioned is called *ıshkaneh*, and is a sort of stew, or rather jelly broth.

he was bred and flourished at Heri,[1] are written in this dialect. The inhabitants are remarkable for their beauty. Khwājeh Yūsef, so famous for his science in music, was a native of Andejān. The air is unwholesome, and in the autumn agues are prevalent.

Another district is Ush, which is situated to the south-east of Andejān, but more to the east, and distant from Andejān four farsangs[2] by the road. The air of Ush is excellent. It is abundantly supplied with running water, and is extremely pleasant in spring. The excellencies of Ush are celebrated even in the sacred traditions.[a][3] On the south-east of the fort is a mountain of a beautiful figure, named Barakoh, on the top of which Sultan Mahmūd Khan built a small summer house, beneath which, on the shoulder of the hill, in the year 902,[4] I built a larger palace and colonnade. Although the former is in the more elevated situation, yet that built by me is the more pleasant of the two ; the whole town and suburbs are seen stretched out below. The river of Andejān, after passing through the suburbs of Ush, flows on towards Andejān.[5] On both of its banks there are gardens, all of which overlook the river. Its violets are particularly elegant. It abounds in streams of running water. In the spring its tulips and roses blow in great profusion. On the skirt of this same hill of Barakoh,[6] between the hill [b] and the town, there is a mosque, called the Mosque of Jouza ;[7] and from the hill there comes a great and wide stream of

2. Ush.

[a] Many traditions are current in praise of its excellent climate.
[b] pleasure garden

[1] The ancient name of Herāt.
[2] The *farsang* may in general be taken at four English miles. It is the ancient *parasanga*. [P. de C. substitutes the Türki word *igadj* (*yighach*) for parasang *passim*. *Yighach* is a variable unit, and may mean any distance from 4 to 6 miles.]
[3] The *Hadīs*.
[4] A.D. 1496.
[5] The river of Andejān is one of those that form the great river Sirr.
[6] [Schuyler identifies Barakoh with the Takht i Suleimān, which, he says, is a bare high ridge of rugged stone standing out of the midst of the plain on the edge of the town (*Turkistan*, vol. ii, p. 43. London, 1877).]
[7] [Twin mosque.]

water. Beneath the outer court of the mosque there is a meadow of clover, sheltered and pleasant, where every traveller and passenger loves to rest. It is a standing joke among the common people at Ush to carry across the three streams all such as fall asleep there.[1] On this hill, about the latter end of the reign of Omer-Sheikh Mirza, there was discovered a species of stone finely waved red and white, of which they make the handles of knives, the clasps of belts, and other things of that sort, and it is a very beautiful stone. In all Ferghāna for healthiness and beauty of situation, there is no place that equals Ush.

3. Marghinān.

Another is Marghinān,[2] which lies on the west of Andejān, at the distance of seven farsangs, and is a fine district. It is noted for its pomegranates and apricots. There is one species of pomegranate named *dana-kalān* (or great seed), which, in its flavour, unites the sweet with a sweet acid, and may even be deemed to excel the pomegranate of Semnān.[3] They have a way of taking out the stones of the *zerd-ālu* (or apricot), and of putting in almonds in their place, after which the fruit is dried. When so prepared, it is termed *seikkhāni*,[a] and is very pleasant. The game and venison are here also excellent. The white deer[4] is found in its vicinity. All the inhabitants are Sarts;[5] the race are great boxers, noisy and turbulent, so that they are famous all

[a] Seihānī,

[1] [The French version has ' to turn the water of this stream on all such as sleep there ', which makes the meaning clear.]
[2] Mr. Metcalfe's MS. has Marghilān, which is its present name. It is a considerable town, and the capital of Ferghāna proper. Its trade consists chiefly in silk and shawl-wool.
[3] Semnān, a town between Khorasān and Irāk, near Damghān.
[4] The *āhu e werak* is said to be the *arkāli*, described in many books of natural history. See *Voyages de Pallas*, vol. iv, p. 325. [The *argali* is a wild sheep, and apparently the *Ovis Ammon*.]
[5] The Sārts or Tājiks of these countries are the inhabitants of the towns and villages, and the cultivators of the ground, who speak the Persian tongue; as opposed to the Tūrks. They appear to be the remains of the more ancient population, and probably received the name of Tājik from the Tūrks as being subjects of the Arab or *Tāzi* government; the Persians and Tūrks having first known the Arabs by the name of Tāzi or Tāji.

over Māweralnaher for their blustering and fondness for boxing, and most of the celebrated bullies of Samarkand and Bokhāra are from Marghinān. The author[1] of the *Hidáya* was from a village named Rashdān, a dependency of Marghinān.

Asfera is another district. It is situated at the foot of the mountains, and possesses numerous streams and beautiful gardens. It lies south-west of Marghinān, at the distance of nine farsangs.[2] Many species of fruit-trees abound there; but, in the gardens, the almond trees are most numerous. The inhabitants are all mountaineers and Sarts. Among the small hills to the south-east of Asfera[a] is a slab of stone called *sang aineh* (the stone-mirror); its length is about ten gez. It is in some places as high as a man, in others not higher than his middle; everything is seen in it as in a glass.

The district of Asfera is separated into four divisions, all situated at the foot of the hills; one of them is Asfera, another Warūkh, another Sukh, and the fourth Hūshiār. When Muhammed Sheibani Khan defeated Sultan Mahmūd Khan and Ilcheh Khan,[3] and took Tāshkend and Shahrokhīa, I spent nearly a year in Sūkh and Hūshiār among the hills, in great distress; and it was from thence that I set out on my expedition to Kābul.

Khojend, another of the districts, is situated on the west of Andejān, at the distance of twenty-five farsangs, and it is also at the same distance from Samarkand. This is a very ancient city. Sheikh Maslehet and Khwājeh Kemāl[4] were of Khojend. Its fruits are very good, particularly its pomegranates, which are so celebrated, that the apples of Samarkand and the pomegranates of Khojend have passed

4. Asfera.

5. Khojend

---

[a] Among the hills to the south a *shar'i kos* from Asfera,

[1] Sheikh Burhān-ed-dīn Ali [1135–97].
[2] It is not easy to convert the Tartar and Indian measures used by Bābur into English ones, with any degree of certainty. [Bābur's *gaz* may be taken as nearly equal to a yard, the *kos* as 1½ miles, and the *shar'i* or long *kos* as 2 miles.]
[3] [Alacha Khan, or Sultan Ahmed.]
[4] These were two men eminent for their sanctity. [Kamāluddin Khujendi, a celebrated lyric poet and author of a *divān*, was a contemporary of Hāfiz. He died in A. D. 1390 (Beale).]

into a proverb ; but excellent as the latter are, they are greatly excelled at present by the pomegranates of Marghinān. The fortress of Khojend is situated on an eminence, having on the north the river Seihūn, which flows past at the distance of about a bowshot. On the north of the fort and of the river Seihūn there is a hill, which is named Myoghil,[a][1] where they say that there are turquoise and other mines. In this hill there are many serpents. Khojend is a good sporting country ; the white deer, the mountain goat,[2] the stag,[3] the fowl of the desert,[4] and the hare are found in great plenty ; but the air is extremely noisome, and inflammations of the eyes are common ;[b] insomuch, that they say that even the very sparrows have inflammations in the eyes. This badness of the air they ascribe to the hill on the north.

Kandbā-dām.
Kandbādām is one of the districts belonging to Khojend. Though of no great extent, yet it is rather a fine little district, and its almonds, from which it derives its name,[5] are of excellent quality, and are exported to Hindustān, Hormuz, and other quarters. It is distant from Khojend five or six farsangs to the east. Between Kandbādām and Khojend there is a desert, named Ha-dervīsh, where a sharp wind prevails, and constantly blows from the desert in the direction of Marghinān, which lies to the east of the desert, or in the direction of Khojend, which lies to the west, and this wind is excessively keen. It is said that certain Dervīshes having encountered the wind in this desert, and being separated, were unable to find each other again, and perished, calling out, 'Ha, Dervīsh ! Ha, Dervīsh !'[6] and that hence the desert is denominated Ha-dervīsh unto this day.

[a] Mtoughil,
[b] in the autumn fevers are common ;

[1] [Moghaltav (Schuyler).]
[2] [This may be either the Ibex of Asia Minor (*Capra aegagrus*), which had a wide range, or the Markhor (*Capra megaceros*).]
[3] [This is evidently the *Cervus maral*, an animal allied to the Bara-singha of Kashmir (*Cervus cashmerianus*).]
[4] [The pheasant.]
[5] *Kand* or *kend* signifies a town in Tūrki, and *bādām* an almond.
[6] 'Help, Dervīsh ! help, Dervīsh !'

Of the districts to the north of Seihūn, one is Akhsi, which in histories is called Akhsīkat.[1] Hence Asīr-ed-din, the poet, is termed Asīr-ed-din Akhsīkati.[2] There is no town in Ferghāna after Andejān, which is more considerable than this. It lies to the west of Andejān, at the distance of nine farsangs. Omer-Sheikh Mirza made it his capital. The river Seihūn flows under the walls of its castle. The castle is situated on a high precipice, and the steep ravines around serve instead of a moat. When Omer-Sheikh Mirza made it his capital, he, in one or two instances, scarped the ravines outside of the fort. In all Ferghāna there is no fortified town so strong as this. The suburbs are rather more than a shiraa kos from the fort. The proverb, 'Where is the town, and where are the trees?'[3] applies in a particular manner to Akhsi. The melons here are excellent; there is one species which is termed Mīr Taimūri, no such melons are known to exist in the world. The melons of Bokhāra are also celebrated; but, at the time when I took Samarkand, I had melons brought from Akhsi and Bokhāra, and cut open at an entertainment, when those of Akhsi were judged beyond comparison the best. There is good hunting and hawking. From the river of Akhsi to the town there is a desert, in which the white deer are very numerous. Towards Andejān is a waste, abounding with the stag, the fowl of the desert, and the hare, all of which are extremely fat.

6. Akhsi.

Another district is Kāsān,[4] which lies to the north of Akhsi, and is of small extent. As the river of Andejān comes from Ush, so the river of Akhsi comes from Kāsān. The air of Kāsān is extremely good, and its gardens are beautiful. In consequence of its gardens being all sheltered [a] along the

7. Kāsān.

[a] The gardens which border both banks of the stream are called

---

[1] [This place is said to have stood near the site of the present Namangān (*T. R.*, p. 9).]

[2] [He was a contemporary of the poet Khakānī, and died in A.D. 1211.]

[3] i. e. 'where are your houses and gardens?'—*Leyden.*

[4] [This is a town now called Kuchar, situated on the main road leading towards Kara Shahr (*T. R.*, p. 9).]

banks of the stream, they call it the mantle of five lambskins.[1] There is a standing quarrel between the inhabitants of Kāsān and those of Ush concerning the beauty and climate of their respective districts.

All around the country of Ferghāna, among the mountains, there are excellent *yailāk*[2] (or summer stations). The *tabulghū*[3] wood is found here among the mountains, and in no other country. The *tabulghū*, which has a red bark, is a wood of which they make walking-staves, whip-handles, and bird-cages. They also cut it into the forked tops of arrows.[4] It is an excellent wood, and is carried to a great distance, as a rarity in much request. In many books it is related that the Yabruj-us-sannam[5] grows on these hills; but now it is quite unknown. There is, however, a species of grass which is produced on the mountains

---

[1] *Postīn-pīsh-burra.* The Persian has *postīn e mish burra*, or lambskin mantle. [The phrase clearly conveys the meaning of fine or beautiful.]

[2] The wandering tribes all over Persia and Turkestān are accustomed to shift their ground according to the season. In summer they move northward, or ascend the hills and higher grounds. The Persian Court is often transferred to these summer quarters, for the purpose of shunning the excessive heats. They are called *yailāks*, from the Tūrki word *yai*, summer. In winter they move southward, or descend to warm and sheltered valleys, to their winter stations, which are called *kishlāks*, a word derived from *kīsh*, which in the Tūrki signifies winter. The custom is as old as the age of Cyrus.—See Xenoph. *Inst. Cyr.*, lib. viii, p. 222.

[3] [The Red Willow.]

[4] *Gīz.* [Steingass describes this as 'an arrow without wing or point, the two ends thin and the middle thick'.]

[5] i.e. the mallow consecrated to idols.—*Leyden*. The *Yabruj-us-sannam* is the plant called the mandragora or mandrake.—See the *Alfāz adwīyeh*, or Materia Medica of Noureddeen Mohamed Abdallah Shirāzi, published with a translation, by Gladwin, Calcutta, 1793. The name *aikoti* is derived from the Tūrki word *ayek*, vivacity, and *oti*, grass. *Mehergiah* seems to be merely a Persian translation of the name, from *meher*, affection, and *gīah*, grass. It is, however, called *atikoti*, or dog-grass, a name which comes from the way in which it is said to be gathered. They have a fancy that any person who plucks up this grass dies; on which account they are said to dig round its roots, and when these are sufficiently loosened, tie it to the neck of a dog, who, by his endeavours to get away, pulls it out of the earth.—See D'Herbelot, art. Abrousanam.

of Bete-kend,[1] and which the people of the country term *aikoti*, that is said to have the virtue of the *mehergīah*, and is what passes under the name of *mehergīah*. In these hills, also, there are mines of turquoise and of iron.

The revenues of Ferghāna may suffice, without oppressing the country, to maintain three or four thousand troops.

As Omer-Sheikh Mirza was a prince of high ambition and magnificent pretensions, he was always bent on some scheme of conquest. He several times led an army against Samarkand, was repeatedly defeated, and as often returned back disappointed and desponding. He oftener than once called in to his assistance his father-in-law, Yunis Khan, who was descended from Chaghatāi Khan, the second son of Chinghiz Khan, and who was at that time the Khan of the tribe of Moghuls in the dominions of Chaghatāi Khan.[2] He was also my maternal grandfather. Every time that he was called in, Omer-Sheikh gave him some province; but as things did not succeed to the Mirza's wish, Yunis Khan was unable to keep his footing in the country, and was therefore repeatedly compelled, sometimes from the misconduct of Omer-Sheikh Mirza, sometimes from the hostility of other Moghul tribes, to return back to Moghulistān.[3] The last time, however, that he brought his force, Omer-Sheikh Mirza gave Yunis Khan the country of Tāshkend, which was then in the possession of the Mirza. Tāshkend is sometimes denominated Shāsh, and sometimes Chāch, from whence comes the phrase, *a bow of Chāch*.[4] From that time

Reign of Omer-Sheikh Mirza.

[A.D. 1485.]

---

[1] [The Elphinstone (Tūrki) copy has Yeti Kent, and this is also P. de C.'s reading. The site of this place, called in Persian Haftdih, or Seven Villages, is uncertain, but in the *T. R.* (p. 181) it is suggested that it was situated in the south-west extremity of Moghulistan on the northern slope of the range which forms the limit of the Sirr valley.]

[2] It would seem that when Jaghatāi or Chaghatāi Khan received possession of his share of the empire of Chinghiz Khan, he also got a tribe of Moghuls to attend him, and to confirm his authority over the Tūrki population. The same appears to have been the case in Kipchāk, which was given to another brother; and also in the formation of the kingdom of Tūra, under Sheibāni.

[3] [According to the *T. R.*, p. 96, the Mirza took offence at the Khan's wintering in Akhsi. The battle of Tika Sagurt Ku followed, in which Omar Sheikh was defeated.]

[4] [Kamāni Chach is a bow made of wood that is unaffected by damp or heat.]

[A.D. 1502-3.]

[A.D. 1494.]
A. H. 899.
Alliance against him.

June 9, 1494.

His death.

His early life.
A.D. 1456.

to the year 908, the countries of Tāshkend and Shahrokhīa remained subject to the Chaghatāi Khans. At this time the Khanship of the (Ulūs or) tribe of Moghuls was held by my maternal uncle, Sultan Mahmūd Khan, the eldest son of Yunis Khan. He and Sultan Ahmed Mirza, the King of Samarkand, who was my father Omer-Sheikh Mirza's elder brother, having taken offence at Omer-Sheikh Mirza's conduct, entered into a negotiation, the result of which was, that Sultan Ahmed Mirza having given Sultan Mahmūd Khan one of his daughters in marriage, they this year concluded an alliance, when the latter marched an army from the north of the river of Khojend, and the former another from the south of it, against that prince's dominions.

At this very crisis a singular incident occurred. It has already been mentioned that the fort of Akhsi is situated on a steep precipice, on the very edge of which some of its buildings are raised. On Monday, the 4th of the month of Ramzān, of the year that has been mentioned, Omer-Sheikh Mirza was precipitated from the top of the steep, with his pigeons, and pigeon-house,[1] and took his flight to the other world.

He was then in the thirty-ninth year of his age. He was born at Samarkand in the year 860. He was the fourth son of Sultan Abūsaīd Mirza, being younger than Sultan Ahmed Mirza, Sultan Muhammed Mirza, and Sultan Mahmūd Mirza. Sultan Abūsaīd Mirza was the son of Sultan Muhammed Mirza, the son of Mirza Mirānshah, who was the third son of Taimūr Beg, being younger than Omer-Sheikh Mirza and Jehāngīr Mirza, and elder than Shahrokh Mirza. Sultan Abūsaīd Mirza had at first given Kābul to the Mirza, and sent him off for that country, attended by Baba Kābuli as his *Beg-atkeh* (or Protector and Regent). He, however, recalled him to Samarkand, when he had reached the Dera-

[1] The Musulman princes of Asia are often ridiculously fond of training tame pigeons. These are taught to take circular flights, to tumble in the air, to attack each other when on the wing, and to stand on the defensive. Abul-fazl tells us (*Ayeen e Akberi*, vol. i, p. 251) that in Akber's pigeon-houses each pigeon, before he received his allowance of grain, performed fifteen circular flights and seventy tumbles. In the same place may be found a curious account of the mode of training them.

Gez,[1] in order that he might be present at the festival of the circumcision of the Mirzas.[2] After the festival, as Taimūr Beg had given Omer-Sheikh Mirza the elder the country of Ferghāna, Abūsaīd was induced, by the coincidence of names, to bestow on his son Omer-Sheikh the country of Andejān,[3] appointed Khuda-berdi Taimūrtāsh his guardian and regent, and sent him off to his government.

Omer-Sheikh Mirza was of low stature, had a short bushy beard, brownish hair, and was very corpulent. He used to wear his tunic extremely tight ; insomuch, that as he was wont to contract his belly while he tied the strings, when he let himself out again the strings often burst. He was not curious in either his food or dress. He tied his turban in the fashion called *destār-pēch* (or plaited turban[4]). At that time all turbans were worn in the *chār-pēch* (or four-plait) style. He wore his without folds, and allowed the end to hang down. During the heats, when out of the Divān,[5] he generally wore the Moghul cap. {His person.}

As for his opinions and habits, he was of the sect of Hanīfah,[6] and strict in his belief. He never neglected the five regular and stated prayers,[7] and during his whole life he rigidly performed the *kaza*[8] (or retributory prayers and fasts). He devoted much of his time to reading the Korān. He was extremely attached to Khwājeh Obeidullāh, whose {His opinions and habits.}

---

[1] The valley of Gez (tamarisk), which lies on the Dehās, or Balkhāb, south of Balkh.

[2] The festival given by Abusaīd Mirza at Merv, A. D. 1465, to celebrate the circumcision of his sons, lasted five months, and was famous for its uncommon splendour.

[3] Andejān, it will be recollected, was the capital of Ferghāna, and the name is often given to all that country.

[4] [i. e. in a single fold.]

[5] [Council chamber.]

[6] [One of the four schools of Quranic interpretation among the Sunnis, the founder of which was Imām Abu Hanīfah (born A. D. 702), the great oracle of jurisprudence. (Hughes's *Dict. of Islam*).]

[7] It is very well known that the Musulmans must, by their law, pray five times a day regularly ; at dawn, at noon, between noon and sunset, at sunset, and about an hour and a half after sunset.

[8] These are prayers and fasts *performed*, if the expression may be allowed, by pious Musulmans, to make up for any omissions at the stated times. If sick, if on a journey, or in war, they are not bound to fast at the time, but should do so afterwards.

disciple he was, and whose society he greatly affected. The reverend Khwājeh, on his part, used to call him his son. He read elegantly: his general reading was the *khamsahs*,[1] the *mesnevis*,[2] and books of history, and he was in particular fond of reading the *Shahnāmeh*.[3] Though he had a turn for poetry, he did not cultivate it. He was so strictly just, that when the caravan from Khita[4] had once reached the hill-country to the east of Andejān, and the snow fell so deep as to bury it, so that of the whole only two persons escaped; he no sooner received information of the occurrence, than he dispatched overseers to collect and take charge of all the property and effects of the people of the caravan; and, wherever the heirs were not at hand, though himself in great want, his resources being exhausted, he placed the property under sequestration, and preserved it untouched; till, in the course of one or two years, the heirs, coming from Khorasān and Samarkand, in consequence of the intimation which they received, he delivered back the goods safe and uninjured into their hands.[5] His generosity was large, and so was his whole soul; he was of an excellent temper, affable, eloquent and sweet in his conversation, yet brave withal, and manly. On two occasions he advanced in front of the troops, and exhibited distinguished prowess; once, at the gates of Akhsi, and once at the gates of Shahrokhīa. He was a middling shot with the bow; he had uncommon force in his fists, and never hit a man whom he did not knock down. From his excessive ambition for conquest, he often exchanged peace for war, and friendship for hostility. In the earlier part of his life he was greatly addicted to drinking

[1] Several Persian poets wrote *khamsahs*, or poems, on five different given subjects. [The most celebrated are Nizāmi and Amīr Khusru.]

[2] The most celebrated of these *mesnevis* is the mystical poem of Moulavi Jalāleddīn Muhammed.

[3] The *Shahnāmeh*, or Book of Kings, is the famous poem of the great Persian poet Ferdausi [d. A. D. 1025], and contains the romantic history of ancient Persia.

[4] North China, but often applied to the whole country from China to Terfān, and now even west to the Ala-tāgh Mountains.

[5] This anecdote is erroneously related of Bābur himself by Ferishta and others.—See Dow's *Hist. of Hindostan*, vol. ii, p. 218.

būzeh and *talar*.[1] Latterly, once or twice in the week, he indulged in a drinking party. He was a pleasant companion, and in the course of conversation used often to cite, with great felicity, appropriate verses from the poets. In his latter days he was much addicted to the use of maajun,[2] while under the influence of which, he was subject to a feverish irritability. He was a humane man. He played a great deal at backgammon, and sometimes at games[3] of chance with the dice.

He fought three great battles; the first with Yunis Khan, to the north of Andejān, on the banks of the Seihun, at a place called Tīka-Sakaratkū,[4] which derives its name from this circumstance, that the river, in flowing past the skirt of a hill, becomes so much contracted in breadth, that it is said that, on one occasion, a mountain-goat leaped from the one bank to the other. Here he was defeated, and fell into the hands of Yunis Khan, who treated him with great generosity, and sent him back to his own country. This is termed the battle of Tīka-Sakaratkū, because it was fought at that spot; and it is still used as an era in that country. Another battle he fought in Tūrkestān, on the banks of the river Aras,[5] with the Uzbeks, who, having plundered the territory of Samarkand, were on their return back. The Aras being frozen over, he passed it on the ice, gave them a severe defeat, and recovered the prisoners and effects which they had carried off, all of which he restored to their families and owners, retaining nothing to himself. The third battle was fought with Sultan Ahmed Mirza, between

His wars.

---

[1] *Būzeh* is a sort of intoxicating liquor somewhat resembling beer, made from millet. *Talar* I do not know, but understand it to be a preparation from the poppy. There is, however, nothing about *būzeh* or *talar* in the Persian, which only specifies *sherāb*, wine or strong drink. [These are probably interpolations, as P. de C. only says, ' he was much addicted to drinking '.]

[2] Any medical mixture is called a *maajūn*; but in common speech the term is chiefly applied to intoxicating comfits, and especially those prepared with *bang*.

[3] These to Musulmans are unlawful.

[4] 'The he-goat's leap.'

[5] [P. de C. notes that the Aras was one of the affluents on the right bank of the Seihūn (Sirr) to the north of Tāshkend.]

14 MEMOIRS OF BĀBUR A. H. 899

Shahrokhīa and Uratippa, at the place named Khawās, where he was defeated.

His dominions.
His father gave him the country of Ferghāna. He held for a short period Tāshkend and Seirām,[1] which his eldest brother Sultan Ahmed Mirza had given him. He was also, at one time, in possession of Shahrokhīa, which he gained by a stratagem. Finally, however, he lost both Tāshkend and Shahrokhīa, and only retained Ferghāna, Khojend, and Uratippa, the original name of which is Usrūshta,[2] and which is also called Austerūsh. Many do not reckon Khojend to be included in Ferghāna. When Sultan Ahmed Mirza went to Tāshkend against the Moghuls, whom he engaged, but was defeated on the banks of the river Chir,[3] Hāfiz Beg Duldāi, who was in Uratippa, delivered it up to Omer-Sheikh Mirza, from which period it continued in his possession.

His children. Bābur. Jehāngīr.
He had three sons and five daughters. Of the sons I, Zehīr-ed-dīn Muhammed Bābur, was the eldest. My mother was Kūtluk Nigār Khānum. The second son was Jehāngīr Mirza, who was two years younger than myself. His mother was sprung of one of the chiefs of the race of the Moghul Tumāns,[4] and was named Fātima Sultan. The third

Nāsir.
was Nāsir Mirza, whose mother was of the country of Andejān, and a concubine, by name Umeid. He was four years younger than I. Of all the daughters, the eldest was

Khanzādeh Begum.
Khanzādeh Begum, who was born of the same mother as myself, and was five years older than I. The second time that I took Samarkand,[5] although my army was defeated at Sir-e-pul, I threw myself into the town, and sustained a siege of five months; when, no succour or assistance coming from any of the neighbouring kings or Begs, in despair, I abandoned the place. During the confusion that ensued, Khanzādeh Begum fell into the hands of Muhammed Sheibāni Khan, and had by him a son named Khurram

[1] [Sairām lies on the Bādām tributary of the Arys, 10 miles east of Chimkent.]
[2] [P. de C. calls this Usrushna, and adds that it lies at a distance of 26 parasangs from Samarkand.]
[3] [The Chir is a tributary of the Sirr, and the battle referred to was fought in 1488 (*E. B.*, p. 63).]
[4] [The chief tribal subdivision, nominally of ten thousand men.]
[5] [In A.D. 1500.]

Shah, a fine young man, who had the country of Balkh assigned to him; but, a year or two after his father's death, he was received into the mercy of God.[1] When Shah Ismael defeated the Uzbeks at Merv,[2] Khanzādeh Begum was in that town; out of regard for me, he paid her every attention, and caused her to be conducted in the most honourable manner to join me at Kunduz.—We had been separated for ten years, when I and Muhammed Gokultāsh went out to meet her; the Begum and her attendants did not know us, not even after I had spoken; but in a short while they recognized me. The second daughter was Mcherbānu Begum, who was born of the same mother as Nāsir Mirza, and was two years older than I. The third daughter was Sheherbānu Begum, who was likewise born of the same mother with Nāsir Mirza, and was eight years younger than I. The fourth daughter was Yādgār Sultan Begum, whose mother, Agha Sultan, was a concubine. The youngest daughter was Rokhīa Sultan Begum, whose mother, Sultan Makhdūm Begum, went by the name of Karagūz Begum (the black-eyed princess). These two last were born after the Mirza's death. Yādgār Sultan Begum was brought up by my grandmother Isān Doulet Begum. When Muhammed Sheibāni Khan took Andejān and Akhsi, Yādgār Sultan Begum fell into the hands of Abdallatīf Sultan, the son of Hamzeh Sultan. When I defeated Hamzeh Sultan and the other Sultans in Khutlān, and took Hissār, Yādgār Sultan Begum came and joined me. During those same troubles, Rokhīa Sultan Begum had fallen into the hands of Jāni Beg Sultan, by whom she had one or two sons, who died young. I have just received information that she has gone to the mercy of God.

The principal wife of Omer-Sheikh Mirza was Kūtluk Nigār Khānum, who was the second daughter of Yunis Khan, and the elder sister of Sultan Mahmūd Khan and Sultan Ahmed Khan by the same mother. Yunis Khan was of the race of Chaghatāi Khan, the second son of

Meherbānu Begum. Sheherbānu Begum.

YādgārSultan Begum.

Rokhīa Sultan Begum.

A. D. 1503.

A. D. 1511.

His wives. Kūtluk Nigār Khānum.

Descent of Yunis Khan.

---

[1] A well-educated Musulman is very unwilling to say directly that a man died. He uses some circumlocutory expression, which gives the fact by inference.

[2] [In 1510 (*E. B.*, p. 303).]

Chingiz Khan, and his genealogy runs thus : Yunis Khan, the son of Weis Khan, the son of Sher Ali Oghlān, the son of Muhammed Khan, the son of Khizer Khwājeh Khan, the son of Tughluk Taimūr Khan, the son of Aishbugha Khan, the son of Dawa Khan, the son of Burāk Khan, the son of Isān-bugha, the son of Mutukān, the son of Chaghatāi Khan, the son of Chingiz Khan.[1]

History of the Khans of the Moghuls.

Since the opportunity thus presents itself, I shall now briefly state a few particulars regarding the history of the Khans. Yunis Khan and Isān-bugha Khan were the sons of Weis Khan. The mother of Yunis Khan was of Turkestān, and was either the daughter or grand-daughter of Sheikh Nūr-ed-dīn Beg, who was one of the Amīrs of Kipchāk, and had been brought forward by Taimūr Beg. On the death of Weis Khan, the Ulūs (or Horde) of the Moghuls divided into two parties, one of which adhered to Yunis Khan, while the majority sided with Isān-bugha Khan. This occasioned a separation of the tribe. Before this time the elder sister of Yunis Khan had been engaged by Ulugh Beg Mirza to be married to his son Abdal-azīz Mirza. This connexion induced Airzīn, who was a Beg of the Tumān of Nārin, and Mīrak Turkman, who was a Beg of the Tumān of Khirās, to carry Yunis Khan, attended by three or four thousand families [2] of the tribe of Moghuls, to Ulugh

Yunis Khan

leaves Moghulistān.

---

[1] [In P. de C. as well as in the genealogy recorded on p. 49 of the *T. R.*, Isun-bugha and Isun-tawa are substituted for Aish-bugha and Isān-bugha respectively. The following table explains Bābur's connexion with the line of Timur :

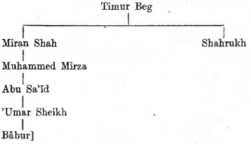

Bābur]

[2] Literally houses ; the Tartars reckon the numbers of the families in their tribes by households, tents, and sometimes by kettles.

Beg Mirza; in the expectation that, with the assistance which he could afford them, they might reduce the whole of the Moghul tribe under the authority of the Khan. The Mirza did not give them a favourable reception, but with great unkindness,[1] imprisoned some, and dispersed the rest in all directions over the face of the country; so that 'the Dispersion of Airzīn' has become an era among the Moghuls. The Khan he sent into Irāk. Yunis Khan accordingly remained in Tabrīz for upwards of a year, at the time when Jehān-Shah Barani Kara-koilūk[2] (of the black sheep) was sovereign of Tabrīz. Thence he proceeded to Shirāz, where Shahrokh Mirza's second son, Ibrahīm Sùltan Mirza, then reigned. Five or six months after his arrival, this prince died, and was succeeded by his son Abdallah Mirza. The Khan engaged in the service of Abdallah Mirza, and remained in Shirāz and that country for seventeen or eighteen years. When the disturbances between Ulugh Beg Mirza and his sons broke out, Isān-bugha Khan, seizing the opportunity, came and plundered the country of Ferghāna, as far as Kandbādām, took Andejān, and made all the inhabitants prisoners. Sultan Abūsaīd had no sooner mounted the throne than he collected an army, advanced beyond Yāngi,[3] and gave Isān-bugha Khan a severe defeat, at a town in Moghulistān, named Ashpera. In order still more effectually to secure himself from such inroads, he was induced by his connexion with Yunis Khan, to invite him back from Irāk and Khorasān, Yunis Khan's elder sister having been married to Abdal-azīz Mirza. On the Khan's arrival he made a great feast, received him in the most friendly manner, acknowledged him as Khan of the tribe of Moghuls, and sent him into their country to assert his rights. At that time it happened that all the Begs of the Tumān of Sagharichi

[1] This happened in the lifetime of Shahrokh Mirza, Ulugh Beg's father, who had given the government of Samarkand to his son.
[2] The Kara-koilūk or Kara-koinlū Tūrkomans, that is, the Tūrkomans of the black sheep, so called from their banner, are celebrated in the history of Persia and of Baghdad.
[3] [Erskine and P. de C. identify this with Otrār, but it is probably Tarāz on the Talās river near the modern Aulia Ata (*T. R.*, pp. 80–1). Ashpera is the modern Isfara, which is situated (40° 18′ N., 70° 45′ E.) south-west of Khokand.]

had come to Moghulistān, highly displeased with Isān-bugha Khan. Yunis Khan went among them. The greatest of the Begs of the Sagharichi was then Sher Hāji Beg, whose daughter Isān Doulet Begum, Yunis Khan married. Sher Hāji Beg having seated the Khan and Isān Doulet Begum on a white felt,[1] according to the Tūreh, or ancient Institutions of the Moghuls, they proclaimed him Khan.

Marries Isān Doulet Begum.

The Khan had three daughters by Isān Doulet Begum, of whom the eldest was Meher Nigār Khanum, whom Sultan Abūsaīd Mirza took for his eldest son Sultan Ahmed Mirza. By the Mirza she had neither son nor daughter. In the succeeding wars she fell into the hands of Sheibāni Khan; but after I went to Kābul, she accompanied Shah Begum from Samarkand to Khorasān, and thence to Kābul. When Sheibāni Khan invested Nāsir Mirza in Kandahār, I proceeded to Lamghān, and Khan Mirza, Shah Begum, and Meher Nigār Khanum, set out for Badakhshan. Mubārek-shah having invited Khan Mirza to the fortress of Zafer,[2] they were met on the road, attacked and plundered by one of Ababeker Kāshghari's marauding parties, and Shah Begum and Meher Nigār Khanum, with their whole family and attendants, were taken prisoners; and, in the prisons of that wicked miscreant, they departed from this perishable world.

Yunis Khan's children.

Meher Nigār Khanum.

The second daughter, Kūtluk Nigār Khanum, was my mother, and accompanied me in most of my wars and expeditions. Five or six months after the taking of Kābul she departed to God's mercy, in the year 911.

Kūtluk Nigār Khanum.

A.D. 1505.

The third daughter was Khūb Nigār Khanum, who was married to Muhammed Hussain Korkān Dughlet.[3] He had

Khūb Nigār Khanum.

[1] Petis de la Croix, in his history of Genghiscan, describing the general diet held by that prince at Tonkat, says, 'They erected a magnificent throne for Genghiscan, and forgot not to place on an eminence the black felt-carpet on which this prince was seated when he was proclaimed Grand Can. And this emblem of the poor estate of the Mogols at that time was always held in great veneration by them so long as their Empire lasted.'—P. 358, Eng. translation. See also *Hist. de Timur-Bec*, vol. i, p. 78. [P. de C. translates this 'they were lifted off the ground in token of sovereignty', alluding to the ancient custom.]

[2] [This place was situated on the river Kokchah.]

[3] Muhammed Hussain Korkān Dughlet held the government of U'ratippa under Sultan Mahmūd Khan.

by her one daughter and one son. The daughter married Ubeid Khan, and when I took Bokhāra and Samarkand, was residing there, and being unable to effect her escape, stayed behind: when her paternal uncle Syed Muhammed Mirza came to me in Samarkand as ambassador from Sultan Saīd Khan,[1] she accompanied him back, and was married to Sultan Saīd Khan. She had a son, Haider Mirza,[2] who, after his father was slain by the Uzbeks, entered my service and remained in it three or four years; he then took leave of me and went to Kāshghar to the Khan; but as [A D. 1511.] [A D. 1503.]

> Everything returns to its original principles,
> Whether pure gold, or silver, or tin;

it is said that he has now adopted a commendable course of life and become reformed. He excels in penmanship, in painting, in fletchery, in making arrow-heads, and thumblets for drawing the bow-string. He is remarkably neat at all kinds of handiwork. He has also a turn for poetry, and I have received an epistle from him, the style[3] of which is by no means bad.

Another of the Khan's wives was Shah Begum; though he had other wives besides these, yet he had children by these two only. Shah Begum was the daughter of Shah Sultan Muhammed, King of Badakhshān. The Kings of Badakhshān are said to trace back their descent to Sikander Filkūs.[4] This Sultan Muhammed had also another daughter, elder than Shah Begum, who was married to Sultan Abūsaīd Mirza, and bore to him Ababeker Mirza. Yunis Khan had two sons and two daughters by Shah Begum. Among these, Sultan Mahmūd Khan was younger than the three daughters

Shah Begum

Sultan Mahmūd Khan.

---

[1] Sultan Saīd Khan was Prince of Kāshghar.

[2] [This was the celebrated author of the *Tarīkh-i-rashīdi*, the *History of the Moghuls* (A.D. 1499-1551).]

[3] *Insha*, or art of letter-writing, in Persian, is quite a science, requiring a long study to be perfectly understood. It is generally the art of telling insignificant things in an involved and rhetorical style. The number of *bienséances* to be observed is quite overwhelming.

[4] Alexander the son of Philip, concerning whom the Persians have many traditions and idle stories. The King of Derwāz, a small territory north of Badakhshān, still claims descent from the Macedonian hero.

who have been mentioned, and elder than the other three children. In Samarkand and these quarters he is generally called Khānikeh Khán. Sultan Ahmed Khan was younger than Sultan Mahmūd Khan, and is well known by the name of Ilcheh Khan.[1] He received this denomination from the following circumstance: In the language of the Kilmāks[2] and Moghols, they call a slayer Ilaji; and, as he several times overcame the Kilmāks with great slaughter, he on that account was generally spoken of under the name of Ilaji, which, in pronunciation, was converted into Ilcheh. It will often be necessary to make mention of these Khans in this history, when their transactions and affairs shall be fully detailed. Sultan Nigār Khanum was the youngest of all the family, except one daughter. She was given in marriage to Sultan Mahmūd Mirza (the son of Sultan Abūsaīd Mirza), by whom she had one son, named Sultan Weis, who will be mentioned in the sequel. After the death of Sultan Mahmūd Mirza, this princess, having taken her son along with her, without giving any notice of her intention, proceeded to Tāshkend to her brothers. A few years afterwards, her brother married her to Uzbek Sultan,[3] one of the Sultans of the Kazāks,[4] who was descended of Juji Khan, the eldest son of Chinghiz Khan. When Sheibāni Khan defeated the Khans, and took Tāshkend and Shahrokhīa, she fled with ten or twelve of her Moghul attendants to Uzbek Sultan, by whom she had two daughters: one of them was given to one of the Sheibāni Sultans, and the other to Rashīd Sultan, a son of Sultan Saīd Khan.[5] After the death of Usbek Sultan, she married Kāsim Khan,[6] the chief of the horde of the Kazāks. It is said that no one of the Khans or Sultans of the Kazāks ever kept the horde in such complete

---

[1] [Alacha Khan from Alachi = he who kills.]
[2] The Kilmāks, or Kalemāks, are our Kalmuks, one of the chief divisions of the Moghuls.
[3] [P. de C. has Adik Sultan. He was the son of Jāni Beg, son of Burak (*T. R.*, p. 373).]
[4] The Kirghis tribes at this day call themselves *Sahrā-kazzāk*, or robbers of the desert, and occupy the deserts about Tāshkend. The name Cossack is a corruption of the same word.
[5] The Chief of Kāshghar.
[6] [Her husband's brother (*T. R.*, p. 373).]

order as Kāsim Khan. His army amounted to nearly three hundred thousand fighting men. After the death of Kāsim Khan, she went to Kāshghar to Sultan Saīd Khan Kāshghari. Doulet Sultan Khanum, who was the youngest daughter of all, at the sack of Tāshkend fell into the hands of Taimūr Sultan, the son of Sheibāni Khan. By him she had one daughter. She left Samarkand along with me, and lived three or four years in Badakhshān, after which she went to Kāshghar to Sultan Saīd Kāshghari.

Doulet Sultan Khanum.

Another of Omer-Sheikh Mirza's wives was Ulūs Aghāi, the daughter of Khwājch Hussain Beg; by her he had one daughter, who died young. A year, or a year and a half after her marriage, she was removed from the haram.

Omer-Sheikh's other wives. Ulūs Aghāi.

Another of his wives was Fātima Sultan Agha, who was the daughter of one of the Begs of the Moghul Tumāns. Omer-Sheikh Mirza married her first of all his wives.

Fātima Sultan Agha.

There was yet another named Karagūz Begum (or the black-eyed Princess), whom he married towards the end of his days. She was tenderly beloved by Omer-Sheikh Mirza, and, in order to flatter him, they affected to derive her origin from Manucheher Mirza, the elder brother of Sultan Abūsaīd Mirza.

Karagūz Begum.

He had many women and concubines. One of them was Omeid Aghācheh, who died before the Mirza. In the Mirza's latter days he had one called Yūn Sultan, of Moghul extraction. Another was Agha Sultan.

His concubines.

Of his Amīrs, one was Khuda-berdi Taimūrtāsh,[1] who was of the family of the elder brother of Akbugha Beg, the Hākim[2] of Heri. When Sultan Abūsaīd Mirza besieged Juki Mirza in Shahrokhīah, he gave the country of Ferghāna to Omer-Sheikh Mirza, and sent Khuda-berdi Taimūrtāsh with him as Master of his Household.[3] At that time Khuda-berdi Taimūrtāsh was only about twenty-five years of age, but young as he was, his method, his arrangements, and regulations were excellent. One or two years afterwards, when Ibrahīm Begchik ravaged the territory of Ush, Khuda-

His Amīrs. Khuda-berdi Taimūrtāsh. [A.D.1464.]

---

[1] Most Tūrki names, both of persons and places, have some signification. Thus *Khuda-berdi* means given-of-God, and *Taimūrtāsh*, iron-stone.
[2] Governor.
[3] That is, as Prime Minister.

berdi Taimūrtāsh having pursued and overtaken him, a severe battle ensued, in which Khuda-berdi was defeated and slain. When this event occurred, Sultan Ahmed Mirza was among the *yailāk* (or summer habitations) of Uratippa, called Ak Kechghai, eighteen farsangs to the east of Samarkand, and Sultan Abūsaīd Mirza was at Babakhāki, which is twelve farsangs to the east of Heri, when this intelligence was transmitted to him express by Abdal Wahāb Shaghāwel. The messenger accomplished this distance, which is one hundred and twenty-six farsangs, on horseback in four days.

Hāfiz Beg Duldāi.

Another of his Amīrs was Hāfiz Beg Duldāi, the son of Sultan Malik Kāshghari, and a younger brother of Ahmed Hāji Beg. After the death of Khuda-berdi Beg, he was appointed Master of the Household, and sent to succeed him. As he was unpopular among the Begs of Andejān, on the death of Sultan Abūsaīd Mirza, he repaired to Samarkand, and entered into the service of Sultan Ahmed Mirza. When the news arrived of the defeat of Sultan Ahmed Mirza in the battle on the Chir, he was governor of Uratippa, and when Omer-Sheikh Mirza had reached Uratippa on his way to attack Samarkand, Hāfiz Beg delivered up the place to the Mirza's people, and himself entered into his service. Omer-Sheikh Mirza again entrusted him with the government of Andejān. He latterly went into the service of Sultan Mahmūd Khan, who gave him the charge of Mirza Khan [A.D. 1504.] with the government of Dizāk. Before I took Kābul he had set out by way of Hind, with the intention of making a pilgrimage to Mekka, but, on the road, he departed to the mercy of God. He was a plain unassuming man, of few words, and not very profound.

Khwājeh Hussein Beg.

Another was Khwājeh Hussein Beg, who was a good-humoured man, of plain, simple manners; he excelled in singing at drinking parties, as was the fashion of the time, what was called *tūiūk*,[a] a sort of Moghul drinking-song.

Sheikh Mazīd Beg.

There was another named Sheikh Mazīd Beg, who was first appointed my governor. His arrangements and discipline were excellent. He had been in the service of

― *Kushuk.*

Bābur Mirza.[1] No man stood higher in the esteem of Omer-Sheikh Mirza than himself. He was, however, of grossly libidinous habits, and addicted to pederasty.

Ali Mazīd Beg Kuchīn was another. He twice rebelled, once in Akhsi and once in Tāshkend. He was a libidinous, treacherous, good-for-nothing hypocrite.

{Ali Mazīd Kuchīn.}

Another was Hassan Yākūb Beg, who was frank,[a] good-tempered, clever, and active. The following verses are his—

{Hassan Yākūb Beg.}

Return again, O Hūma,[2] for without the parrot down of thy cheek
The crow will assuredly soon carry off my bones.

He was a man of courage, an excellent archer, and remarkable for his skill in playing the games of *choughān*[3] and leap-frog. After the death of Omer-Sheikh Mirza, he became Master of my Household. He was, however, narrow-minded, of small capacity, and a promoter of dissension.

Another was Kāsim Beg Kuchīn, who was one of the ancient Begs of the army of Andejān. He succeeded Hassan Beg as Master of the Household. As long as he lived, his

{Kāsim Beg Kuchīn.}

[a] narrow-minded.

---

[1] This Bābur Mirza was the son of Baiesanghar, the son of Shahrokh, one of Taimūr Beg's sons. He was an active prince, was for some time master of Khorasān, and died A. D. 1457.

[2] The *hūma* is a bird much celebrated in oriental poetry. It never alights on the ground, and it is believed that every head which it overshadows will one day wear a crown. The verses here quoted are written in the character of one in adversity, who had formerly indulged better hopes.

[3] [*Chaughān* was a form of polo (from Tibetan *pulu*, a ball) played by horsemen with long curved sticks. The game is said to have originated in Persia 2,000 years ago, whence it reached India through Turkistan, though the game as we know it was introduced from Manipur. There were various ways of playing the game, some of which are described in the *Ayīn i Akbari* (pp. 209-10). In the game that Akbar played the players were divided into six pairs, each couple playing together for twenty-five minutes (one Chakkar), and each trying to trundle the ball into a pit. In a manuscript copy of the Turki *divan* of 'Ali Sher in my possession, there is a fine miniature representing a game of polo as played in Turkistan in Bābur's day. In this two horsemen are seen engaged with a ball and polo sticks just like our own, but the goal is formed by two masonry or stone pillars.]

power and consequence with me went on increasing uninterruptedly. He was a brave man. On one occasion, a party of Uzbeks having ravaged the country round Kāsān, were on their retreat, when he pursued, overtook, engaged, and gave them a severe defeat. He had also distinguished himself by his gallant use of his scimitar in presence of Omer-Sheikh Mirza. In the war of Yāsi-kijet [1] he made some bold forays. During my difficulties, when I proposed going from the hill-country of Masīkha [2] to Sultan Mahmūd Khan, Kāsim Beg separated from me, and went to Khosrou Shah. In the year 910, when I took Khosrou Shah and blockaded Mukīm in Kābul, Kāsim Beg came again and joined me, and I showed him my wonted affection and regard. When I attacked the Tūrkoman Hazāras in the *dereh*, or glen, of Khīsh,[3] as Kāsim Beg, notwithstanding his advanced years, displayed more ardour than many younger men, I gave him the government of the country of Bangash as a reward for his services. Afterwards, on my return to Kābul, I appointed him governor to Humāiūn.[4] He was received into the mercy of God about the time I reduced the Zamīn-dāwer.[5] He was a pious, religious, faithful Moslem, and carefully abstained from all doubtful meats. His judgement and talents were uncommonly good. He was of a facetious turn, and though he could neither read nor write, had an ingenious and elegant vein of wit.

A.D. 1504.

[A.D. 1511.]

Baba Kūli Beg.

Another was Baba Kūli Beg, of the family of Sheikh Ali Bahāder. After the death of Sheikh Mazīd Beg, he was appointed my governor. When Sultan Ahmed Mirza led his army against Andejān, he went over to him and delivered Uratippa into his hands. After Sultan Mahmūd Mirza's death, he fled from Samarkand, and was on his way to join

[1] [The reference is to the battle of Yāsi-Kijet, fought in A. H. 904 (A.D. 1499), in which Bābur's army under Kāsim Beg was defeated by Tambol and the revolted Moghuls (*E. B.*, p. 120).]
[2] [Erskine in his *History of Bābur* states that the territory of Masīkha was a small hill country dependent on Andijān and bordering on Tāshkend. In *T. R.* it is identified with Tarāz.]
[3] [Khush in P. de C.]
[4] Bābur's son, who succeeded him in his dominions.
[5] The district of Zamīn-dāwer lies about ninety miles west of Kandahār, on the right bank of the Helmand, towards the upper part of its course, after it issues from the mountains.

me, when Sultan Ali Mirza, issuing out of Uratippa, encountered, defeated, and slew him. He was remarkable for maintaining his troops in good order, and with excellent equipments. He kept a watchful eye over his servants, but neither prayed nor fasted, and was cruel, and like an infidel in his whole deportment.

Another was Mīr Ali Dost Taghāi, who was of the Begs of the Tumāns of Saghrichi, and related to my maternal grandmother Isān Doulet Begum. I showed him great favour from the time of Omer-Sheikh Mirza. I was told that he would be a useful man; but during all the years that he was with me, I cannot tell what service he ever did. He had been in Sultan Abūsaīd Mirza's service, and pretended to be an enchanter.[1] He was Grand Huntsman, and was a man of disagreeable manners and habits, covetous, mean, seditious, insincere, self-conceited, harsh of speech, and sour of visage.

Mīr Ali Dost Taghāi.

Weis Lāghari was another. He was from Samarkand and of the Tokchi tribe, and was latterly much in the confidence of Omer-Sheikh Mirza. He attended me on my expeditions. He was a man of excellent understanding and talents, but a little disposed to be factious.

Weis Lāghari.

Mīr Ghiās Taghāi, the younger brother of Ali Dost, was another. None of all the young Moghul Amīrs in Sultan Abūsaīd Mirza's court was a greater favourite, and the Great Seal[2] was delivered to his custody by that prince. He was in very great favour with Omer-Sheikh Mirza in his latter years, and was on intimate terms with Weis Lāghari. From the time that Sultan Mahmūd Khan got possession of Kāsān, till the end of his life, he remained in the service of the Khan, by whom he was treated with great consideration. He was an extremely witty and jocose man, but fearless in debauchery.

Mīr Ghiās Taghāi.

[A.D.1494]

---

[1] [i. e. he claimed to produce rain by means of the *sang i yadah* or *yadah* stone.]

[2] *Moher-charsūi*, the square seal. Chardin, in describing the seals used in the Persian court in his time, says, 'Le sçeau carré est le plus considéré, et celui auquel on obeit le plus regulierement ; c'est proprement le sçeau ou le seing du roi, car il le porte a son cou ; et ses ancêtres, depuis Abas le Grand, en ont fait de même.'—See *Voyages de Chardin*, tom. v, p. 461, of the edition of M. Langlès.

Ali Derwīsh.

There was another named Ali Derwīsh, a native of Khorasān, who served in the Khorasān Bands under Sultan Abūsaīd Mirza; for when that prince got possession of Samarkand and Khorasān, he formed such of the young men of these two kingdoms as were fit for service into bands of household troops, which he termed the Bands of Khorasān, and the Bands of Samarkand. He made a gallant charge in my presence in the affair at the gate of Samarkand. He was a brave man. He wrote the *nastālīk* character after a fashion. He was, however, a gross flatterer, and sordidly mean and miserly.

Kamber Ali, Moghul.

Kamber Ali, Moghul, an Akhteji,[1] was another; when his father came to the country, he for some time exercised the trade of a skinner, whence he got the name of Kamber Ali Selākh (or the skinner). He had served Yunis Khan in the capacity of Ewer-bearer, but finally arrived at the rank of Beg. From me he received distinguished favours. Till he had attained high rank, his conduct was exceedingly good; but, after he had gained a certain elevation, he became negligent and perverse. He talked a great deal and very idly; indeed there can be no doubt that a great talker must often talk foolishly. He was a man of contracted capacity, and of a muddy brain.

June 10, 1494.
Bābur attempts Andejān.

At the time when this fatal accident[2] befell Omer-Sheikh Mirza, I was in Andejān, at the Chārbāgh palace. On Tuesday the fifth of Ramzān, the news reached Andejān; I immediately mounted in the greatest haste, and taking with me such of my followers as were at hand, set out to secure the castle. When I had just reached what is called the Mirza's gate, Shīrīm Taghāi seized my horse's bridle and carried me towards the Īd-gāh.[3] The idea had entered his mind that, as Sultan Ahmed Mirza, who was a powerful

---

[1] D'Herbelot informs us that *akhteji*, in the Moghul tongue, signifies a vassal who holds his estates of a liege-lord. See art. Akhtagi, in the *Bibliothèque Orientale*. In the Tūrki it signifies a gelder. [P. de C. translates 'one of the equerries'.]

[2] Bābur now returns to the death of his father, who was killed by falling from the pigeon-house at Akhsi.

[3] The *īd-gāh* or *namāzgāh* is generally an open terrace, with a wall on the side towards the *kibleh*, and on the outside of the town, whither on festival days the people go out in crowds to pray.

prince, was approaching with a great army, the Begs of Andejān might deliver up both the country and me into his hands ; he was therefore for conducting me towards Urkend[1] and the country on the skirt of the hills in that quarter, that if they should deliver up the country, I might not fall into his power, but might join my maternal uncles Ilcheh Khan or Sultan Mahmūd Khan.

Khwājeh Moulāna Kazi, the son of Sultan Ahmed Kazi, was of the race of Sheikh Būrhān-ed-dīn Kilij,[2] and by the mother's side descended of Sultan Ilik Māzi. He was sprung of a religious family that had come to be regarded as the protectors of that country. This family in some sort held the office of Sheikh-ul-Islām [3] by hereditary descent, and will hereafter be often mentioned. The Kazi, and the Begs who were in the castle, on hearing of our proceedings, sent Khwājeh Muhammed Derzi, who was an old and trusty household servant of Omer-Sheikh Mirza, and the *Begatkch* or governor of one of his daughters, to dispel our apprehensions. He overtook us and made me turn, after we had nearly reached the Īd-gāh, and conducted me into the citadel, where I alighted. Khwājeh Moulāna Kazi and the Begs having met in my presence, held a consultation ; and, after having mutually communicated their ideas, and resolved on their plan, applied themselves to put the fortress, with its towers and ramparts, in a state of defence. Hassan Yākūb, Kāsim Kuchīn, and some other Begs, who had been sent on an excursion [4] to Marghinān and that quarter, arrived a day or two after, and entered into my service ; and all of them, with one heart and soul, set themselves zealously to maintain the place.

Is received into the citadel.

Sultan Ahmed Mirza, after having made himself master of Uratippa, Khojend, and Marghinān, advanced to

Sultan Ahmed Mirza approaches Andejān.

[1] Urkend or Uzkent lies towards the Ala-tāgh hills north of Ush. [P. de C. states that it is situated on the left bank of the Seihūn to the east of Andejān.]

[2] [The well-known author of the *Hidāyah*, a celebrated work on Mohammedan jurisprudence (A. D. 1136–97).]

[3] The Sheikh-ul-Islām is the chief judge in all civil and religious causes which are decided by the divine law (*sheriat*). There is generally one in each great city.

[4] [i. e. reconnaisance.]

Kaba,[1] within four farsangs of Andejān, and encamped. At this time one Dervīsh Gau, a man of note in Andejān, was capitally punished on account of some seditious expressions, an example which reduced all the rest of the inhabitants to their duty.

I now sent Khwājeh Kazi, Uzūn Hassan, and Khwājeh Hussain, as ambassadors, to Sultan Ahmed Mirza, with a message to this effect : ' It is plain that you must place some one of your servants in charge of this country ; I am at once your servant and your son ; if you intrust me with this employment, your purpose will be attained in the most satisfactory and easy way.' As Sultan Ahmed Mirza was a mild, weak man, of few words, who was implicitly guided in all his opinions and actions by his Begs ; and as they were not favourably disposed to this proposition, a harsh answer was returned, and he marched forward.—But the Almighty God,[2] who, of his perfect power, has, in his own good time and season, accomplished my designs in the best and most proper manner, without the aid of mortal strength, on this occasion also brought certain events to pass, which reduced the enemy to great difficulties, frustrated the object of their expedition, and made them return without success, heartily repenting of their attempt.

Causes of his failure.

One of these was the following : the Kaba is a black river and extremely slimy, insomuch that it can be only passed by a bridge : as the host was very numerous, there was a great crowding on the bridge, and many horses and camels fell over into the black water and perished. Now as three or four years before this the same troops had suffered a severe defeat at the passage of the river Chir, the present disaster recalled the former to their remembrance, and the soldiers of the army were seized with a panic. Another circumstance was, that, at this time, a disease attacked the horses with such violence that they were taken ill, and began to die in great numbers. A third circumstance was, that

---

[1] Kaba was a small town on the river Kaba, west of Andejān.
[2] Bābur, like all other Turks, uses the word *Tengri* for Deity. It is of pagan origin, and seems originally to have been Moghul. It is now current all over Tartary and in China. It has found its way too into Persian, and is used for the Almighty.

they found my soldiers and subjects so unanimous and resolute, that they perceived clearly that their determination was to fight to the last drop of their blood, and the last gasp of their life, without yielding, and that they would never submit to the government of the invaders. Disconcerted by these circumstances, after they had come within one farsang of Andejān, they on their part sent Derwīsh Muhammed Terkhān,[1] who was met near the Īd-gāh by Hassan Yākūb, from the castle, when they conferred together and patched up a sort of a peace, in consequence of which the invading army retired.

In the meanwhile Sultan Mahmūd Khan had entered the country on the north of the river of Khojend in a hostile manner, and laid siege to Akhsi. Jehāngīr Mirza was in the place, and Ali Derwīsh Beg, Mirza Kuli Gokultāsh, Muhammed Bākir Beg, and Sheikh Abdallah the Chamberlain,[2] were along with him. Weis Lāghari and Mīr Ghiās Taghāi were also there, but, in consequence of some misunderstanding between them and the other Begs, they withdrew to Kāsān, which was Weis Lāghari's government. As Weis Lāghari was *Beg-atkeh* (or governor) to Nāsir Mirza, that prince resided at Kāsān. As soon as the Khan arrived in the neighbourhood of Akhsi, these Begs waited on him, and surrendered Kāsān: Mīr Ghiās continued with the Khan; but Weis Lāghari carried off Nāsir Mirza and delivered him to Sultan Ahmed Mirza, by whom he was given in charge to Muhammed Mazīd Terkhān. The Khan having approached Akhsi, made several assaults on it, but without success; the Begs and youth of Akhsi fought with distinguished valour. At this crisis Sultan Mahmūd Khan fell sick, and being besides disgusted with the war, returned to his own country.

Ababeker Dughlet Kāshghari,[3] who acted as an indepen-

[1] [The title of *Terkhān* was a very ancient rank or order of nobility among the Mongols, and carried with it certain highly esteemed prerogatives (*T. R.*, p. 55).]

[2] *Ishek-Aqha*, lord or keeper of the entrance or door, an officer resembling the chamberlain, or perhaps rather a Prime Minister, and of some consequence in Asiatic courts

[3] [According to the *T. R.* this prince was of the line of the Daghlat Amirs. He lost Kāshghar to Sultan Sa'īd in 1514, and was driven into exile and afterwards murdered.]

Ababeker Kāshghari invades Ferghāna on the east,	dent prince, and had for several years been Hākim of Kāshghar and Khuten, was seized, like the rest, with the desire of conquest, and had advanced to Uzkend, where he constructed a fortress, and employed himself in plundering and laying waste the country. Khwājeh Kazi and a number of Begs were dispatched to expel him. When the army
but is repelled.	approached, the Kāshgharian, who perceived that he was unable to contend with it, applied to Khwājeh Kazi as mediator, and contrived to extricate himself from his situation with great address and cunning.

During these important events, the Begs and younger nobility, who had been about Omer-Sheikh Mirza, united resolutely, and displayed a noble spirit, being eager to devote their lives to the cause. They afterwards conducted the Mirza's mother, Shah Sultan Begum, Jehāngīr Mirza, and the family in the haram, from Akhsi to Andejān, where they performed the ceremonies of mourning for him, and distributed food and victuals to the poor and to religious mendicants.

Bābur's Begs and officers rewarded.

When delivered from these dangers, it became necessary to attend to the administration and improvement of the country, and to placing everything in proper order.[a] The government of Andejān, and the prime authority in the Court, were bestowed on Hassan Yākūb; Ush was given to Kāsim Kuchīn; Akhsi and Marghinān were entrusted to Uzūn Hassan and Ali Dost Taghāi; and each of the Begs and younger nobility of Omer-Sheikh Mirza's court had a district, an estate, or portion of land assigned to him, or received some mark of distinction suited to his rank and consequence.[b]

Death of Sultan Ahmed Mirza.

Middle of July 1494.

Meanwhile Sultan Ahmed Mirza, after having made two or three marches on his return home, fell very ill, and being seized with a burning fever, departed from this transitory world, in the territory of Uratippa, just as he had reached the Aksū[1] (or White river), in the middle of the month Shawāl 899, in the 44th year of his age.

[a] and to supervising the organization of the army.
[b] either an office, high rank, or pension.

[1] The *Habīb-es-seir* makes him die at Armena, a village on the Aksū, which is a considerable river, rising in the Asfera hills, and which falls into the Sirr a little to the west of Khojend.

He was born in 855, the year in which Sultan Abusaīd Mirza came to the throne, and was the eldest of all his sons. His mother was the daughter of Urda Bugha Terkhān, was elder sister of Derwīsh Muhammed Terkhān, and the most respected of the Mirza's wives.

His birth and extraction. A.D. 1451.

He was tall, of a ruddy complexion, and corpulent.[a] He had a beard on the forepart of the chin, but none on the lower part of the cheek. He was a man of extremely pleasant manners. He wore his turban, according to the fashion of the time, in what was termed *chārmāk* (the four-plaited), with the tie or hem brought forward over the eyebrows.

Figure and features.

He was strictly attached to the Hanīfah sect, and was a true and orthodox believer. He unfailingly observed the five stated daily prayers, and did not neglect them even when engaged in drinking parties. He was attached to Khwājeh Obeidullah, who was his religious instructor and guide. He was polite and ceremonious at all times, but particularly in his intercourse with the Khwājeh; insomuch that they say, that, while in company with him, however long they sat, he never changed the position of his knees, by shifting the one over the other, except in one instance, when, contrary to his usual practice, he rested the one knee on the other. After the Mirza rose, the Khwājeh desired them to examine what there was particular in the place in which the Mirza had been seated, when they found a bone lying there.[1]

His manners and religious opinions.

He had never read any, and, though brought up in the city, was illiterate and unrefined. He was a plain honest Tūrk, but not favoured by genius. He was, however, a just man; and as he always consulted the reverend Khwājeh in affairs of importance, he generally acted in conformity to the law. He was true to his promises, and faithful to his compacts or treaties, from which he never swerved. He was brave; and though he never happened to be engaged hand to hand in close combat, yet they say that in several actions he showed proofs of courage. He excelled in archery. He

His character.

[a] with a dark brown beard.

[1] It will be recollected that the Asiatics sit cross-legged on a carpet. The bone of a dead animal being impure, is thought to defile a Musulman, who is obliged, after touching it, to purify himself.

was a good marksman. With his arrows and forked arrows he generally hit the mark;[1] and in riding from one side of the exercise ground to the other, he used to hit the brazen basin several times.[2] Latterly, when he became very corpulent, he took to bringing down pheasants and quails with the goshawks, and seldom failed. He was fond of hawking, and was particularly skilled in flying the hawk, an amusement which he frequently practised. If you except Ulugh Beg Mirza, there was no other king who equalled him in field sports. He was singularly observant of decorum, insomuch that it is said, that even in private, before his own people and nearest relations, he never uncovered his feet.[3] Whenever he took to drinking wine, he would drink without intermission for twenty or thirty days at a stretch, and then he would not taste wine for the next twenty or thirty days. In his social parties he would sometimes sit day and night, and drink profusely; on the days when he did not drink, he ate pungent substances.[a] He was naturally of a penurious disposition, was a simple man, of few words, and entirely guided by his Begs.

His wars. He fought four battles: the first with Sheikh Jemāl

[a] he refrained from conviviality.

---

[1] [P. de C. has 'the duck', which may have been a mark put up to shoot at.]

[2] This refers to an exercise in archery practised by the Tūrks. A brazen basin (*kapak*) is placed on the top of a very lofty pole, to serve as a mark. This is shot at, sometimes from a fixed station, and sometimes while the archer gallops across the ground and past the mark at full speed. Abulghāzi Bahāder, in his account of the festival of Kiun Khan, describes a similar exercise. 'He caused to be erected near these tents two trees, forty fathoms high, and a golden hen to be fixed on the top of the tree, which was planted near the tents on the right hand; and on the top of the tree which was planted near the tents on the left side, a hen of silver; ordering that all who bore the name of Bussick should exercise themselves in shooting at the golden hen, running full speed, and that those of the name of Utz-ock should shoot in the same manner at the silver hen; and he ordered considerable prizes for those who hit the hen.'—*Genealogical History of the Tatars*, vol. i, p. 22. London, 1730. 8vo.

[3] When the Asiatics sit down, they draw in their legs under their bodies. It is regarded as a mark of disrespect, or of great familiarity, to show their feet. Their long and loose dress renders it easy to conceal them.

Arghūn, the younger brother of Niāmet Arghūn, in the territory of Zamīn,[1] at Akār-tūzi, in which he was victorious; the second with Omer-Sheikh Mirza, at Khawās,[2] in which likewise he was victorious; the third affair was with Sultan Mahmūd Khan, in the vicinity of Tāshkend, on the river Chir, in which there was in truth no battle, for as soon as a few scattered plundering Moghuls came up with the army, and seized some baggage, a whole mighty host, without fighting, without resistance, and no man having engaged another, or even seen an enemy, was completely panic-struck and broken up, and numbers of them drowned in their disorderly flight across the Chir.[3] His fourth battle was with Haider Gokaltāsh, in the confines of Yār-ailāk,[4] in which he was victorious.

He possessed the countries of Samarkand and Bokhāra, which his father had given him; and, after the death of Sheikh Jemāl, who was slain by Abdal Kadūs,[5] he got possession of Tāshkend, Shahrokhīa, and Seirām. He afterwards gave Tāshkend and Seirām to his younger brother, Omer-Sheikh Mirza; and also, for some time, occupied Khojend and Uratippa. *His dominions.*

He had two sons, who died young, and five daughters, four of whom were by Kātak Begum. The eldest of them all was Rābia Sultan Begum, whom they called Karagūz (or the Black-eyed) Begum. He gave her in his lifetime to Sultan Mahmūd Khan, by whom she had a son, named Baba Khan, a very promising boy. When the Uzbeks slew the Khan in Khojend, they put to death him and many others like him of tender years.[6] After the death of Sultan *His children.* *1. Rābia Sultan Begum.*

---

[1] [Zamīn, according to P. de C., is the capital of a small district in the district of Samarkand on the road to Ferghāna.] Akār-tūzi signifies the plain of the flowing stream.

[2] Khawās lies between Uratippa and Tāshkend.

[3] [An account of this battle (1469) is given in the *T. R.* (p. 116), in which the Sultan's defeat is attributed to the treachery of Sheibani Khan.]

[4] [This, according to P. de C., is the country which stretches to the north-east of Samarkand on the eastern slope of the Ak Tāgh.]

[5] [An account of this incident, which occurred in 1472, is given in the *T. R.*, p. 95.]

[6] [The murder of Sultan Mahmūd and his five sons by Sheibani's orders in 1508 is fully described in *T. R.*, p. 162.]

Mahmūd Khan, Jāni Beg Sultan married her. The second daughter was Sāliheh Sultan Begum, who was called Ak Begum (or the Fair Lady). After Sultan Ahmed Mirza's death, Sultan Mahmūd Mirza celebrated her marriage with his own eldest son, Sultan Masaūd Mirza, with great festivity. She afterwards fell into the hands of the Kāshgharian at the same time with Shah Begum and Meher Nigār Khanum. The third daughter was Āisha Sultan Begum. When I visited Samarkand, at the age of five years, she was betrothed to me. She afterwards came to Khojend during the troubles, when I married her;[1] and, about the time when I took Samarkand the second time, I had one daughter by her, who lived only a few days. She left my family before the overthrow of Tāshkend, induced by the machinations of her elder sister. The fourth daughter was Sultānim Begum, who was married first to Sultan Ali Mirza, afterwards to Taimūr Sultan, and lastly to Mahdi Sultan. The youngest of all his daughters was Maasūmeh Sultan Begum, whose mother, Habībeh Sultan Begum, was of the tribe of Arghūn, and the daughter of one of Sultan Arghūn's brothers. I saw her when I went to Khorasān, and, being pleased with her, asked her in marriage and carried her to Kābul, where I married her. I had by her one daughter, at the time of whose birth she was taken ill in childbed, and was united to the mercy of God. The daughter whom she bore received her mother's name.

Of his wives and ladies, the principal was Meher Nigār Khanum, the eldest daughter of Yunis Khan, who was betrothed to him by his father, Sultan Abūsaīd Mirza. She was my mother's eldest sister of the full blood.

Another of his wives was of the family of Terkhāns, and named Terkhān Begum.

Another was Kātak Begum, who was the foster-sister of this same Terkhān Begum. Sultan Ahmed Mirza married her for love. He was prodigiously attached to her, and she governed him with absolute sway. She drank wine. During her life, the Sultan durst not venture to frequent any other

---

[1] [Bābur was betrothed to Ayesha in 1488 and married her in 1499 (*E. B.*, p. 128).]

of his ladies. At last, however, he put her to death, and delivered himself from his reproach.

Another of his wives was Khanzādeh Begum, who was sprung of the Khans of Termez. When I went to Samarkand, at the age of five years, to visit Sultan Ahmed Mirza, he had newly married her, and she still kept her face covered with a veil, according to the custom of the Tūrks.[1] He directed me, and I took off her veil. {Khanzādeh Begum.}

Another of them was the daughter of the daughter of Ahmed Hāji Beg, named Latīf Begum, who, after the Mirza's death, was married to Hamzah Sultan, by whom she had three sons. When I defeated the Sultans under the command of Hamzeh Sultan and Taimūr Sultan, and took Hissār,[2] these princes, as well as the children of the other Sultans, fell into my hands, and I set all of them at liberty. {Latīf Begum.}

There was another, named Habībeh Sultan Begum, the brother's daughter of Sultan Arghūn. {Habībeh Sultan Begum.}

Of his Amirs, one was Jāni Beg Duldāi, the younger brother of Sultan Malik of Kāshghar. Sultan Abūsaīd Mirza conferred on him the government of Samarkand, with the prime direction of Sultan Ahmed Mirza's court. He was a man of singular habits and manners, and many strange stories are related of him. Among these it is said, that, when he held the government of Samarkand, an ambassador came from the Uzbeks, who was famous among them for his strength. The Uzbeks call a very stout champion *būkeh*. Jāni Beg asked him, 'Why do they call you *būkeh*? If you are a *būkeh*, come let us have a set-to.' The ambassador, do what he would, was unable to get off. The Hākim grappled with the Uzbek, who was thrown. Jāni Beg was a man of perfect courage. {His Amirs. Jāni Beg Duldāi.}

Another of his nobles was Ahmed Hāji Beg, who was the son of Sultan Malik of Kāshghar. Sultan Abūsaīd Mirza gave him the government of Heri, which he retained for some time. After the death of his paternal uncle, Jāni Beg, {Ahmed Hāji Beg.}

---

[1] It is customary among the Tūrki tribes for the bride to continue veiled, even in her own family, for some time after her marriage. When a few days have elapsed, some child from among her relations is desired to pluck the veil off and run away. This is believed to procure the child so employed success in marriage.

[2] [This occurred in A.D. 1511.]

he was appointed to succeed him in his rank and dignity, and sent to Samarkand. He was of an ingenious [a] and manly character, and in his poetical compositions assumed the name of Wafāi. He was the author of a *diwān*,[1] and was no mean poet. The following is his :

> Let me alone to-day, my good judge, for I am tipsy ;
> Call me to account some other time, when you catch me sober.

Mīr Ali Sher Nawāi accompanied him when he came from Heri to Samarkand ; but when Sultan Hussein Mirza became King, he went to Heri, where he was received with most extraordinary favour. Ahmed Hāji Beg kept excellent horses of the breed termed Tipchāk.[2] He was an admirable horseman, and most of his Tipchāks were of his own breeding. Though a brave man, his generalship was not equal to his courage. He was careless, and left the conduct of his affairs and enterprises to his servants and dependants. When Baiesanghar Mirza attacked Sultan Ali Mirza in Bokhāra,[3] and was defeated, Ahmed Hāji Beg was taken prisoner and shamefully put to death, on the charge of the blood of Derwīsh Muhammed Terkhān.[4]

Derwīsh Muhammed Terkhān.

Another of his officers was Derwīsh Muhammed Terkhān, the son of Urda Bugha Terkhān,[5] and full maternal uncle of

[a] a good natured

---

[1] The composition of a *diwān* is considered as the great trial of skill among the poets of Persia. It is a series of poems, in which the rhyme is taken successively from each letter of the alphabet, beginning with a poem, the rhymes of which terminate with the first letter of the alphabet. and finishing with one rhyming with the last. In these *diwāns* there are generally many poems rhyming in the same letter.

[2] Round-bodied and swift.—*Leyden.* They are taught particular paces.

[3] [In A.D. 1495.]

[4] The Mohammedan law admitting of the doctrine of retaliation, a murderer is frequently given up to the *avengers of blood*, the nearest relations of the person murdered, by whom he is sometimes ransomed, sometimes put to death with circumstances of great cruelty.

[5] The *Terkhān* was originally a rank among the Moghuls and Tūrks, though in the time of Bābur it had come to belong to a particular family or clan. The ancient *Terkhān* was exempt from all duties ; he did not divide his booty even with the prince's collectors ; he could go into the royal presence without asking leave, and was to

Sultan Ahmed Mirza and Sultan Mahmūd Mirza. He stood higher in rank and estimation with the Mirza than any other of the Begs. He was a good Moslem, of religious habits, and simple manners, and was constantly reading the Korān. He was very fond of chess, and played much and well. He was extremely skilful in falconry, and excelled in flying his hawks. In the troubles between Sultan Ali Mirza and Baiesanghar Mirza he died, in bad repute, in the height of his greatness.

Another was Abdal Ali Terkhān, a near relation of Derwīsh Muhammed Terkhān; he married Derwīsh Muhammed Terkhān's younger sister, who was the mother of Bāki Terkhān. Though Derwīsh Muhammed Terkhān was his superior, not only according to the customs and rules of the tribe, but in rank and estimation; yet this haughty Pharaoh pretended to look down upon him. For some years he possessed the government of Bokhāra, when his servants amounted to three thousand. He maintained them well and handsomely. His information and intelligence,[a] his forms of judicial investigation, his court, his suite, his entertainments [1] and levees, were all quite princely. He was a strict disciplinarian, tyrannical, lascivious, and haughty. Sheibāni Khan, though he did not take service with him, lived with him for some time. Many of the smaller and more inconsiderable Sultans were in his service. This Abdal Ali Terkhān was the prime cause of the rise and progress of Sheibāni Khan's fortune, as well as of the downfall and destruction of the family of the ancient Khans.

Abdal Ali Terkhān.

Syed Yūsef Oghlākchi was another. His grandfather was from the horde of Moghuls. Ulugh Beg Mirza had promoted and patronized his father. He was a man of profound

Syed Yūsef Oghlākchi.

---

[a] His gifts and presents, be pardoned nine times, be the fault what it would. Abul-faraj, ap. Petis de la Croix's *Life of Genghis*, p. 49. See also *Vie de Timur*, vol. ii, p. 107. He had perfect liberty of speech, and might say what he pleased in the royal presence.

[1] The *shilān* was an entertainment to dependants, in which food was often distributed, instead of giving a regular dinner; much as the *sportula* was given by the Roman *patroni* to their *clientes*.

reflection and counsel, was brave, and excelled in the exercise of throwing the jerīd.[1] He was one of those who were with me when I first went to Kābul. I showed him great attention, and indeed he was deserving of it. The [A.D. 1505.] first time that I led my army against Hindustān, I left Syed Yūsef Beg behind in Kābul, and he departed into the mercy of God that same year.

Derwīsh Beg.

There was another named Derwīsh Beg, of the race of Aiko Taimūr Beg, who was a favourite of Taimūr Beg's. He was extremely attached to the reverend Khwājeh Obeidullah, was skilled in the science of music, and a good performer. He had a genius for poetry. When Sultan Ahmed Mirza was routed on the banks of the Chir, he perished in the river.[2]

Muhammed Mazīd Terkhān.

Another was Muhammed Mazīd Terkhān, who was the brother of the full blood to Derwīsh Muhammed Terkhān, but younger. He was for some years Hākim or Governor of Turkestān. Sheibāni Khan took Turkestān from him. He had an excellent judgement and understanding, but was impudent and voluptuous.[a] The second and third time that I took Samarkand he came to me, and I gave him a favourable reception. He fell in the battle of Kūl-Malik.[3]

Bāki Terkhān.

Bāki Terkhān was another, the son of Abdal Ali Terkhān, and maternal cousin of Sultan Ahmed Mirza. After his father's death he had the government of Bokhāra. In the time of Sultan Ali Mirza he rose to great consequence, and his retainers amounted to five or six thousand. He was far from being in a proper state of subjection or obedience to Sultan Ali Mirza. He engaged Sheibāni Khan and was defeated at the fort of Dabūsi,[4] when Sheibāni Khan, pursuing his advantage, took Bokhāra. He was very fond of hawking, and is said to have had seven hundred falcons

[a] unscrupulous and vicious.

---

[1] Both Mr. Elphinstone's Tūrki copy and the Persian read, 'He played well on the *kabūz*,' a kind of musical instrument. [This, too, is P. de C.'s reading.]

[2] [Mahmūd Khan defeated Ahmed Mirza on the Chir in 1488 (*E. B.*).]

[3] [This battle was fought in 1512 (*E. B.*).]

[4] [This was a place situated between Samarkand and Bokhāra. The battle was fought in 1500 (*E. B.*).]

at one time. His manners and habits were such as cannot well be described; he was educated and grew up in the midst of magnificence and state. As his father had conferred benefits on Sheibāni Khan, he went over and joined him; but that ungenerous and ungrateful man showed not the least return of favour or kindness for the good which he had received; and Bāki Terkhān departed this life in great wretchedness and misery, in the country of Akhsi.

Another was Sultan Hussain Arghūn. As he for some time held the government of Karakūl, he was thence known by the name of Sultan Hussain Karakūli. He was a man of reflection and sound judgement, and was much with me. Sultan Hussain Arghūn.

Another was Kūl Muhammed Baghdād Kuchīn, a man of courage. Kūl Muhammed Baghdād Kuchīn.

Abdal Kerīm Ashret was another; he was an Yūighūr[1] and chamberlain to Sultan Ahmed Mirza. He was a man of generosity and courage. Abdal Kerīm Ashret.

After the death of Sultan Ahmed Mirza, the Begs, having held a consultation, dispatched a messenger over the hills[2] to Sultan Mahmūd Mirza to invite him to join them. Meanwhile Malik Muhammed Mirza, who was the son of Manucheher Mirza, Sultan Abusaīd Mirza's elder brother, having separated from the camp, set out, attended by some low desperadoes and adventurers, and repaired to Samarkand for the purpose of asserting his pretensions to the sovereignty; but he could accomplish nothing, and was only the cause of his own destruction, and of the death of several innocent princes. Malik Muhammed Mirza's attempt on Samarkand. Unsuccessful.

Sultan Mahmūd Mirza, as soon as he received intelligence of these events, lost no time in repairing to Samarkand, and mounted the throne without any kind of difficulty. He soon, however, by some of his proceedings, disgusted both high and low, soldiery and subjects, who began to fall off from him. The first of these offensive acts regarded the Malik Muhammed Mirza, who has been mentioned, who was his uncle's son, and his own son-in-law: he sent to the Sultan Mahmūd Mirza's reign in Samarkand.

---

[1] [Members of the celebrated Uighur tribe were often chosen as secretaries to the Tartar princes.]

[2] Sultan Mahmūd Mirza was then at Hissār. The messenger, therefore, was obliged to cross the Karatāgh Mountains.

Guk-serai[1] four Mirzas, two of whom he suffered to live, but murdered Malik Muhammed Mirza, and another Mirza.[a] Though Malik Muhammed Mirza was certainly not free from blame, the other prince had been guilty of no kind of fault or crime whatever. Another circumstance which added to his unpopularity was, that though his plan of government and general arrangements were laudable, and though he was naturally just, and qualified to direct the concerns of the revenue, being well versed in the science of arithmetic, yet his temper had something in it tyrannical and profligate. Immediately on his arrival at Samarkand, he began arranging, on a new system, the whole of the regulations of government, including the expenditure and taxes. The dependants of Khwājeh Obeidullah, who, by their influence, had formerly protected many poor defenceless persons from oppression, and delivered them from difficulties, now on the contrary suffered great hardship themselves, and were exposed to much severity and oppression; nay, this severity and harsh treatment were extended even to the family of the Khwājeh himself. What added to these evils was, that, as the Prince himself was tyrannical and debauched, his Begs and servants all faithfully imitated his example. The men of Hissār, and particularly the body of troops that followed Khosrou Shah, were constantly engaged in debauchery and drinking; and to such a length did matters go, that when one of Khosrou Shah's retainers had seized and carried off another man's wife by force, on the husband's coming with a complaint to Khosrou Shah, he received for answer—'You have had her for a great many years; it is certainly but fair that he should now have her for a few days.' Another circumstance which disgusted the inhabitants was, that none of the townsmen or shop-keepers, and not even the Tūrks and soldiers, could leave their houses, from a dread lest their children should

Causes of his un-popularity.

[a] *Add* some of these had not any right to ruling rank, nor did they aspire to it.

[1] The Guk-serai, or Green mansion, was the prison of the Princes of the house of Taimūr, which when they entered, they were never expected to return. The import of the phrase *to send to Guk-serai* is afterwards explained.

be carried off for catamites. The people of Samarkand, who, for twenty-five years, during the reign of Sultan Ahmed Mirza, had lived in ease and tranquillity, and had seen affairs in general managed according to justice and law, in consequence of the influence enjoyed by the reverend Khwājeh, were stung to the soul at the prevalence of such unbridled licentiousness and tyranny; and great and small, rich and poor, lifted up their hands to heaven in supplications for redress, and burst out into curses and imprecations on the Mirza's head.

(*Persian*) Beware of the smoke of internal wounds;
For a wound, though hidden, will at last break out.
Afflict not, if you can, even one heart,
For a single groan is sufficient to confound a world.[1]

From the judgement that attends on such crime, tyranny, and wickedness, he did not reign in Samarkand above five or six months.

EVENTS OF THE YEAR 900.[2]

This year Abdal Kadūs Beg came to me as ambassador from Sultan Mahmūd Mirza, on the occasion of the marriage of his eldest son Sultan Masaūd Mirza to Ak-Begum, the second daughter of his elder brother Sultan Ahmed Mirza, and brought me a marriage present, consisting of almonds and pistachios of gold and silver. This ambassador, on his arrival, while he openly claimed kindred to Hassan Yākūb,[3] yet secretly pursued the object for which he had come, that of diverting him from his duty,[a] and of gaining him over to his master's interest, by tempting offers and flattering promises. Hassan Yākūb returned him a conciliatory answer, and in reality was gained over. When the ceremonial of the congratulations on the marriage was over, the ambas-

Affairs of A. H. 900.

Treasonable views of Hassan Yākūb;

[a] This ambassador, who had ties of relationship with Hasan Yākūb, had only come in reality to divert him from his duty,

---

[1] [These verses are to be found in Sa'dī's *Gulistan*, 1-27.]
[2] This year commenced October 2, A. D. 1494.
[3] [This nobleman joined Bābur in 1494, and was made Master of the Household, and later in the same year was appointed Protector, and governor of Andejān (*E. B.*, pp. 86-91).]

sador took leave. In the course of five or six months the manners of Hassan Yākūb were visibly changed; he began to conduct himself with great impropriety to those who were about me; and it was evident that his ultimate object was to depose me, and to make Jehāngīr Mirza king in my place. His deportment towards the whole of the Begs and soldiers was so highly reprehensible, that nobody could remain ignorant of the design which he had formed. In consequence of this, Khwājeh Kazi, Kāsim Kuchīn, Ali Dost Taghāi, Uzūn Hassan, and several others who were attached to my interests, having met at my grandmother Isān Doulet Begum's, came to the resolution of dismissing Hassan Yākūb, and in that way of putting an end to his treasonable views.

There were few of her sex who equalled my grandmother Isān Doulet Begum[1] in sense and sagacity. She was uncommonly far-sighted and judicious; many affairs and enterprises of importance were conducted by her advice. Hassan Yākūb was at this time in the citadel, and my mother and grandmother in the stone fort.[a] I proceeded straight to the citadel, in execution of the plan which had been concerted. Hassan Yākūb, who had mounted and gone a-hunting, on receiving intelligence of what was going forward, posted off for Samarkand. The Begs and others in his interest were taken prisoners. These were Muhammed Bākir Beg, Sultan Mahmūd Duldai, the father of Sultan Muhammed Duldāi, and some others. The greater part of them I allowed to proceed to Samarkand. Kāsim Kuchīn was appointed Master of the Household,[2] and received the government of Andejān.

who is forced to flee.

Hassan Yākūb, after having proceeded as far as Kandbādām on his way to Samarkand, a few days after, in pursuance of his treacherous intentions, resolved to make an attempt on Akhsi; and, with that view, entered the territory of Khokān.[3] On receiving information of this, I dispatched

[a] the fort of the outer wall.

[1] She was the widow of Yunis Khan, the chief of the Moghuls.
[2] That is to say, prime minister.
[3] Khokān, the Khwākend of the Arabian geographers, is the modern Khokand, which lies on the road from Khojend to Akhsi.

several Begs with a body of troops to fall upon him without loss of time. The Begs having sent on some troops in advance, Hassan Yākūb, who received intelligence of the circumstance, fell by night on this advanced guard, which was separated from the main body, surrounded the quarters they had taken up for the night, and attacked them by discharges of arrows; but, having been wounded in the dark in his hinder parts, by an arrow shot by one of his own men, he was unable to retreat, and fell a sacrifice to his own misdeeds :—(Persian verse)

<small>Is slain.</small>

When thou hast done wrong, hope not to be secure against calamity;
For its appropriate retribution awaits every deed.[1]

This same year I began to abstain from forbidden or dubious meats;[2] and extended my caution to the knife, the spoon, and the table-cloth : I also seldom omitted my midnight prayers.

In the month of the latter Rabīa, Sultan Mahmūd Mirza was seized with a violent disorder, and, after an illness of six days, departed this life, in the forty-third year of his age.

<small>Jan. 1495. Death of Sultan Mahmūd Mirza.</small>

He was born in the year 857, and was the third son of Sultan Abūsaīd Mirza by the same mother as Sultan Ahmed Mirza. He was of short stature, with little beard, corpulent, and a very rough-hewn man in his appearance.

<small>A.D. 1453. His person and features.</small>

As for his manners and habits,[a] he never neglected his prayers, and his arrangements and regulations were excellent; he was well versed in calculation, and not a single *dirhem* or *dinār*[3] of his revenues was expended without his knowledge. He was regular in paying the allowances of his servants; and his banquets, his donatives, the ceremonial of his court, and his entertainment of his dependants, were

<small>Manners.</small>

---

[a] He had good qualities,

[1] [These verses are taken from Nizāmi's *Khusru Shirin*.]

[2] The Musulmans have many observances regarding unlawful meats, and ceremonial defilements. Some of these are not much attended to by soldiers or men in active life.

[3] The *dirhem* and *dinār* are Persian pieces of money the former is now of the value of about fivepence halfpenny; the latter of about nine shillings.

all excellent in their kind, and were conducted by a fixed rule and method. His dress was elegant, and according to the fashion of the day.ᵃ He never permitted either the soldiery or people to deviate in the slightest degree from the orders or regulations which he prescribed. In the earlier part of his life he was much devoted to falconry, and kept a number of hawks; and latterly was very fond of hunting the *nihilam*.[1] He carried his violence and debauchery to a frantic excess; and was constantly drinking wine. He kept a number of catamites; and over the whole extent of his dominions, wherever there was a handsome boy or youth, he used every means to carry him off, in order to gratify his passion. The very sons of his Begs, nay his own foster-brothers,[2] and the children of his foster-brothers, he made catamites and employed in this way. And such currency did this vile practice gain in his time, that every man had his boy; insomuch, that to keep a catamite was thought to be a creditable thing, and not to have one was regarded as rather an imputation on a man's spirit. As a judgement upon him for his tyranny and depravity, all his sons were cut off in their youth.

His genius. He had a turn for versifying, and composed a *diwān*; but his poetry is flat and insipid: and it is surely better not to write at all than to write in that style. He was of an unbelieving disposition, and treated Khwājeh Obeidullah very ill. He was, in short, a man equally devoid of courage and of modesty. He kept about him a number of buffoons and scoundrels, who acted their vile and disgraceful tricks in the face of the court, and even at public audiences.

ᵃ *Omit this sentence.*

[1] [Mr. H. Beveridge in an interesting letter in the *J. R. A. S.* (1900, pp. 137-8) explains the meaning of this obscure word. It is mentioned in the *Akbar-nāmeh* as the Badakshi equivalent of *tasqāwal* = 'a shutter up of the road'. Mr. Beveridge thinks the term may have been applied to an obstacle placed in the path of driven deer to check or turn them, and hence may correspond to our driving of game.]

[2] The connexion formed between foster-brothers is always very strong in rude ages. The Tūrks called them *gokultāsh*, or heart of stone, to denote their unchangeable attachment. Bābur often mentions his *gokultāshes* with great affection.

He spoke ill, and his enunciation was often[a] quite unintelligible.

He fought two battles, both of them with Sultan Hussain Mirza;[1] the first at Asterābād,[2] in which he was defeated; the second in the territory of Andekhūd,[3] at a place named Chekmān,[4] in which likewise he was defeated. He went twice on a religious war against Kaferistān[5] on the south of Badakhshān; on which account he used in the *tughra*[6] of his Firmāns the style of Sultan Mahmūd Ghāzi.[7] His wars.

Sultan Abūsaīd Mirza bestowed on him Asterābād, and, after the unfortunate business of Irāk,[8] he repaired to Khorasān. At that crisis Kamber Ali Beg, the Hākim of Hissār, who, according to orders which he had received from Sultan Abūsaīd Mirza, was conducting the army of Hindustān[9] towards Irāk to the assistance of that prince, had got as far as Khorasān, where he joined Sultan Mahmūd Mirza. The people of Khorasān, immediately on hearing the report of Sultan Hussain Mirza's approach, rose in revolt, and drove Sultan Mahmūd Mirza out of Khorasān; whereupon he repaired to Sultan Ahmed Mirza at Samarkand. A few months after, Syed Beder, Khosrou Shah, and some other officers, under the direction of Ahmed Mushtāk, carried off Sultan Mahmūd Mirza, and fled with him to Hissār, to Kamber Ali Beg. From that time downward, Kolugha, with all the countries to the south of the hill of Kotin,[b][10] such as Termez, Cheghāniān, Hissār, Khutlān, His dominions.

[a] at first
[b] All the country situated to the south of Kohluga and the hill of Kotin,

---

[1] [Hosain Baikara was Sultan of Khorasān, and died in 1506.]
[2] On the south-east corner of the Caspian.
[3] [This town is situated to the south of the Oxus between Balkh and Merv, some 88 miles to the west of the former.]
[4] Mr. Metcalfe's copy has *Chekmān-serāi*.
[5] The country of the Siahposhes.
[6] The *tughra* is the ornamented preamble of public papers containing the prince's titles, &c.
[7] *Ghāzi* means victorious in a holy war.
[8] [The 'calamity of Irāk', in which Abu Sa'īd and his vast host perished, occurred in 1469.]
[9] [Hindustān here probably denotes the districts of Badakhshan, Termiz, and Hissar.]
[10] The hill of Kotin seems to be the mountainous country that

Kunduz, Badakhshān, and the districts as far as the mountain of Hindū-kūsh, remained in the possession of Sultan Mahmūd Mirza. On the death of his elder brother Sultan Ahmed Mirza, that prince's territories also fell into his hands.

<small>His family. Sons. Sultan Masaūd Mirza. Baiesanghar Mirza. Sultan Ali Mirza. Sultan Hussain Mirza.</small>

He had five sons and eleven daughters. The eldest of his sons was Sultan Masaūd Mirza, whose mother was Khanzādeh Begum, a daughter of Mīr Buzūrg of Termez; another of his sons was Baiesanghar Mirza, whose mother was Pasheh Begum; a third was Sultan Ali Mirza, whose mother, Zuhreh Beghi Agha, was an Uzbek and a concubine. Another son was Sultan Hussain Mirza, whose mother was Khanzādeh Begum, the grand-daughter[1] of Mīr Buzūrg. He went to the mercy of the Almighty in his father's life-

<small>Sultan Weis Mirza.</small>

time, at the age of thirteen. The other son was Sultan Weis Mirza, whose mother, Sultan Nigār Khanum, was a daughter of Yunis Khan, and the younger sister of my mother. The transactions of these four Mirzas will be detailed in the succeeding years.

<small>His daughters.</small>

Of the daughters, three were by the same mother with Baiesanghar Mirza; the eldest of whom Sultan Mahmūd Mirza gave in marriage to Malik Muhammed Mirza, the son of his paternal uncle Manucheher Mirza. By Khanzādeh Begum, the grand-daughter of Mīr Buzūrg, he had five daughters, the eldest of whom, after the death of Sultan Mahmūd Mirza, was given to Ababeker Kāshghari. The second daughter was Begeh Begum, whom Sultan Hussain Mirza, when he besieged Hissār, engaged to Haider Mirza, his son by Payandeh Sultan Begum, a daughter of Abūsaīd Mirza; after which he made peace and raised the siege. The third daughter was Ak Begum. When Sultan Hussain Mirza advanced against Kunduz, Omer-Sheikh Mirza sent his son Jehāngīr Mirza with the army of Andejān to succour the place; at which time the fourth princess[2] was betrothed

bounds Karatigīn on the south [a branch apparently of the Karatau range]. Kohlugha, or Kaluga, is the Pass of Derbend (between Hissār and Kesh), where there was probably a fort.

[1] It is to be remembered that Sultan Mahmūd Mirza had two wives of the name of Khanzādeh Begum, the one the daughter, the other the grand-daughter of Mīr Buzūrg.

[2] [The name of this lady is given as Ai Begum by P. de C., and Aq Begum in the *T. R.*, p. 330.]

to Jehāngīr Mirza. In the year 910, when Bāki Cheghāniāni A.D. 1504.
came and met me on the banks of the Amu, these Begums
were with their mothers in Termez, and they all of them
came along with the wife of Bāki Cheghāniāni and accompanied me ; and, on our reaching Kahmerd, Jehāngīr Mirza
married his bride. They had one daughter, who is at present
with her grandmother Khanzādeh Begum in Badakhshān.
The fifth daughter was Zeineb Sultan Begum, whom, when
I took Kābul, I married, at the instance of my mother,
Kūtluk Nigār Khanum. We did not agree very well ; two
or three years after our marriage she was seized with the
small-pox, which carried her off. Another of Sultan
Mahmūd Mirza's daughters was Makhdūm Sultan Begum,
who was the elder sister of Sultan Ali Mirza, by the same
mother. She is now in Badakhshān. His other two
daughters were by concubines ; the name of the one was
Rajeb Sultan, that of the other Muhibb Sultan.

The chief of his wives was Khanzādeh Begum, the His wives.
daughter of Mīr Buzūrg of Termez, to whom the Mirza was Khanzādeh Begum.
strongly attached, and who was the mother of Sultan
Masaūd Mirza. The Mirza was deeply afflicted at her death.
After that event he married the grand-daughter of Mīr Another Khanzādeh Begum.
Buzūrg, the daughter of a brother of Khanzādeh Begum.
She also was called Khanzādeh Begum, and she was the
mother of five daughters and one son. Another of his wives
was Pasheh Begum, the daughter of Ali Sher Beg Behārlu, Pasheh Begum.
one of the Begs of the Turkomān Horde of the Black Sheep.
She had been married before to Muhammed Mirza, the son
of Jehānshāh Mirza Barāni, a Turkomān of the Black
Sheep. At the period when Uzūn Hassan, who was a Turkomān of the White Sheep, took Azarbāijān and Irāk from the
family of Jehānshāh Mirza, the sons of Ali Sher Beg, with
four or five thousand families of the Turkomāns of the Black
Sheep, entered the service of Sultan Abūsaīd Mirza. After
the defeat of the Sultan, they found their way to the
countries north of the Amu : and when Sultan Mahmūd
Mirza went from Samarkand to Hissār, they entered his
service. It was at that time that the Mirza married this
Pasheh Begum, who was the mother of one of his sons and
three of his daughters. Another of his wives was Sultan

Sultan Nigār Khanum. His concubines.

Nigār Khanum, whose extraction has already been mentioned in the account of the Khans.

He had many concubines and handmaids, the principal of whom was Zuhreh Begi Agha, an Uzbek, whom he had taken in the lifetime of Sultan Abūsaīd Mirza. She was the mother of one son and one daughter. By two of his numerous handmaids, he had the two daughters who have already been mentioned.

His Begs. Khosrou Shah.

The first of his Begs was Khosrou Shah,[1] who was from Turkestān, of a tribe of Kipchāk. In his youth he had been in the service of the Terkhān Begs, nay, had been a catamite. He next was in the service of Mazīd Beg Arghūn, who treated him with great favour. He accompanied Sultan Mahmūd Mirza in the disastrous expedition into Irāk; and during the course of the retreat did him such acceptable service, that the Mirza gave him high marks of his regard. He afterwards rose to an exceeding height of power. In the time of Sultan Mahmūd Mirza, his dependants amounted to the number of five or six thousand. From the banks of the Amu to the mountain Hindū-kūsh, the whole country, except Badakhshān, depended on him,[a] and he enjoyed the whole revenues of it. He was remarkable for making a very extensive distribution of victuals,[2] and for his liberality. Though a Tūrk,[b] he applied his attention to the mode of raising his revenues, and he spent them liberally as they were collected. After the death of Sultan Mahmūd Mirza, in the reign of that prince's sons, he reached the highest pitch of greatness, and indeed became independent,[c] and his retainers rose to the number of twenty thousand. Though he prayed regularly, and abstained from forbidden foods, yet he was black-hearted and vicious, of mean understanding, and slender talents, faithless, and a traitor. For

[a] the country of Badakhshān from the banks of the Amu as far as the Hindū-kūsh was dependent on him,
[b] *Omit* though a Turk,
[c] *Omit* and indeed became independent,

[1] This Khosrou Shah acts a considerable part in the course of these Memoirs.
[2] These distributions of victuals were made, as has been remarked, for the purpose of acquiring and retaining followers.

the sake of the short and fleeting pomp of this vain world, he put out the eyes of one, and murdered another of the sons of the benefactor, in whose service he had been, and by whom he had been patronized and protected; rendering himself accursed of God, abhorred of men, and worthy of execration and shame till the day of final retribution. These crimes he perpetrated merely to secure the enjoyment of some poor worldly vanities; yet with all the power of his many and populous territories, in spite of his magazines of warlike stores,[a] and the multitude of his servants, he had not the spirit to face a barn-door chicken. He will be often mentioned again in these memoirs.

Another was Pīr Muhammed Ilchi Būgha, a Kuchīn. In the war of Hazārasp, near the gates of Balkh, he did great execution with his fists by way of bravado, in the presence of Sultan Abūsaīd Mirza. He was a brave man, and always remained in the employment of the Mirza, who was much influenced by his opinions. When Sultan Hussain Mirza besieged Kunduz, Pīr Muhammed, from rivalry to Khosrou Shah, made a night attack on the enemy with a handful of unarmed men, contrary to all rule, but accomplished nothing; and indeed what could be expected from an attempt made on a mighty army with such inferior force? Being hotly pursued by some light-armed horse, he threw himself into the river, and was drowned.

Pīr Muhammed Ilchi Būgha. [A.D. 1453.]

Another was Ayūb, who had served Sultan Abūsaīd Mirza in the band of Khorasān Youths. He was a man of courage, and was *Beg-atkeh* (or governor) to Baiesanghar Mirza. He was moderate[b] in his table and dress, and of a humorous, lively turn. Sultan Mahmūd Mirza having called him *Bīhaya* (or shameless), the epithet stuck to him.

Ayūb.

Wali was another of them, the younger brother of the full blood of Khosrou Shah. He took good care of his servants. It was, however, at the instigation of this man, that Sultan Masaūd Mirza was blinded, and Baiesanghar Mirza put to death. He was in the habit of speaking ill of everybody behind their backs. He was a foul-tongued, scurrilous, self-

Wali.

[a] *Omit this clause.*   [b] particular

conceited, scatter-brained fellow. He never approved of any thing or any person, but himself or his own. When I separated Khosrou Shah from his servants in the country of Kunduz, in the vicinity of Kīlkāi and Dūshi,[a] and dismissed him, Wali, from dread of the Uzbeks, went to Anderāb and Sirāb. The Aimaks of these quarters defeated and plundered him, and he afterwards came to Kābul with my permission. Wali subsequently went to Muhammed Sheibāni Khan, who ordered his head to be struck off in Samarkand.

Sheikh Abdallah Birlās.

Another of his chiefs was Sheikh Abdallah Birlās. He married Shah Sultan Muhammed's daughter,[1] who, by the mother's side, was aunt to Sultan Mahmūd Khan and Ababeker Mirza. He wore his frock very strait and tightened by a belt. He was an upright, unaffected man.

Mahmūd Birlās.

Another was Mahmūd Birlās, who was of the Birlāses of Nundāk. He had attained the rank of Beg in Sultan Abusaīd Mirza's time. When that prince subdued the territories of Irāk, he gave Kermān to this Mahmūd Birlās; and at a later period, when Ababeker Mirza, accompanied by Mazīd Beg Arghūn, and the Begs of the Turkomāns of the Black Sheep, came against Sultan Mahmūd Mirza at Hissār, and the Mirza fled to Samarkand to his elder brother, Mahmūd Birlās refused to surrender Hissār, and manfully held it out. He was a poet, and composed a *diwān*.

Khosrou Shah expelled from Samarkand.

After Sultan Mahmūd Mirza's death, Khosrou Shah wished to conceal the event, and seized upon the treasure. How was it possible that such an event could remain concealed? It was instantly noised about among all the townspeople and inhabitants of Samarkand. That day happened to be a great festival; the soldiery and citizens, rising tumultuously, fell upon Khosrou Shah. Ahmed Hāji Beg and the Terkhān Begs, having allayed the tumult, sent off

[a] When I came from Kunduz, and after separating Khusru Shah from his followers in the neighbourhood of Dūshi,

[1] Shah Sultan Muhammed, King of Badakhshān, has already been mentioned as the father of Shah Begum, who was one of the wives of Yunis Khan, and mother of the Great and Little Khans, and their two sisters.

Khosrou Shah towards Hissār. Sultan Mahmūd Mirza, in his lifetime, had given Hissār to his eldest son Sultan Masaūd Mirza, and Bokhāra to Baiesanghar Mirza, and sent them away to their governments, so that, at this time, neither of them was at hand. After the expulsion of Khosrou Shah, the Begs of Samarkand and Hissār having met and consulted together, sent an express to Baiesanghar Mirza, who was in Bokhāra, and, bringing him to Samarkand, placed him on the throne. When Baiesanghar became king he was only eighteen years of age.

<small>Baiesanghar Mirza is raised to the throne.</small>

At this crisis, Sultan Mahmūd Khàn, at the instigation and by the advice of Sultan Juneid Birlās [1] and some of the chief men of Samarkand, advanced with an army against that capital, as far as Kānbāi, which lies in the territory of Samarkand. Baiesanghar Mirza, with the utmost activity and vigour, led out a strong and well-appointed body of troops, and engaged him not far from Kānbāi. Haider Gokultāsh, who was the great pillar of the Moghul army, and commanded the advanced guard, had dismounted with all his men, who were actively employed in shooting their arrows.[2] The instant that the resolute mailed warriors of Samarkand and Hissār charged keenly on horseback, the whole of Haider Gokultāsh's division, which had dismounted, was ridden down and trampled under the horses' feet. After the discomfiture of this body, the rest of the army no longer made a stand, but were totally defeated. A vast number of Moghuls perished; so many of them were beheaded in the presence of Baiesanghar Mirza, that they were forced three several times to shift his pavilion, in consequence of the heaps of slain that lay before it.[3]

<small>Sultan Mahmūd Khan invades Samarkand,</small>

<small>but is defeated</small>

At this time Ibrahīm Sāru, who was of the tribe of Minkaligh, who had been brought up from his infancy in my mother's[a] service, and had attained the dignity of

<small>Ibrahīm Sāru revolts in Asfera.</small>

[a] father's

[1] [He was the brother of Nizām ud dīn Khalīfah, Bābur's prime minister.]

[2] [*Shibah*, the word used here, means in Persian the shooting of arrows. P. de C. translates it 'a shower (*grêle*) of arrows'.]

[3] The prisoners were brought out one after another, and had their heads struck off before the royal tent.

Beg, but who had afterwards been dismissed on account of some misdemeanour, now entered the fort of Asfera,[1] read the *khutbeh* (or public prayer for the Prince) in the name of Baiesanghar Mirza, and commenced open hostilities against me. In the month of Shābān I made the army mount, and marched to quell the revolt of Ibrāhim Sāru; and in the end of the month I came to my ground and invested the place. The very day of our arrival, the young warriors, in the wantonness of enterprise, immediately on reaching the foot of the walls, mounted a rampart that had been recently built, and entered and took an outwork that had just been finished.[a] Syed Kāsim, the chamberlain, this day acted the most distinguished part, pushed on before the other assailants, and laid about him with his scimitar. Sultan Ahmed Tambol, and Muhammed Dost Taghāi, also wielded their scimitars gallantly; but Syed Kāsim gained the *ulūsh*[2] (or prize of valour). The *ulūsh* (or prize of valour) is an ancient usage that is retained among the Moghuls. In every entertainment and feast, he who has most distinguished himself by the gallant use of his sword, takes the *ulūsh*, or prize of valour. When I went to Shahrokhīa to visit my maternal uncle Sultan Mahmūd Khan, Syed Kāsim claimed and received the *ulūsh*. In this first day's action, Khuda-berdi, my governor, was struck with an arrow from a cross-bow and died. As the troops had rushed into the enterprise without armour, several of them were slain, and a great many wounded. Ibrahīm Sāru had with him a cross-bow man, who shot astonishingly well; I never met with his equal; he wounded a great many of my people. After the surrender of the castle, he entered into my service.

As the siege drew out to some length, orders were given

[a] captured a fortified work which the enemy had recently built on the side of the old citadel.

---

[1] [According to P. de C. this was a town situated to the south of Khokand on the river bearing its name, which is a tributary of the Seihūn.]

[2] [*ulūsh* or *aulush* signifies literally provisions from the royal table.] The honour seems nearly to correspond with the *aristeia* of the Greeks.

to construct, in two or three places, the works called *Sir-kob*,[1] to run mines, and to use every exertion to get ready whatever machines or works were wanted for pushing on the siege. The siege lasted forty days; but, at last, Ibrahīm Sāru, being reduced to the last extremity, made his offers of unlimited submission through the medium of Khwājeh Moulāna Kazi; and, in the month of Shawāl, having come out and presented himself before me with a scimitar[a] suspended from his neck,[2] delivered up the fort. and taken. June, A.D. 1495.

Khojend had, for a long period, belonged to Omer-Sheikh Mirza, but, during the wars at the close of his reign, it had been occupied by Sultan Ahmed Mirza. As I had advanced so near it, I determined, situated as matters were, to proceed against it.[b] Abdal Wahāb Shaghāwel, the father of Mīr Moghul, commanded in the place; and, immediately on my approach, without making any difficulty, surrendered the fortress. Bābur recovers Khojend;

At this period, Sultan Mahmūd Khan happened to be in Shahrokhīa. Some time before, when Sultan Ahmed Mirza advanced into the territory of Andejān, the Khan, on his side, laid siege to Akhsi, as has been mentioned. It occurred to me, that, as we were now so near, and as he stood in the relation of a father and elder brother to me,[3] I ought to go and pay him my respects, and dispel from his mind any misunderstanding that might exist in consequence of past events;[c] a line of conduct which I perceived would be attended with this further advantage, that it would enable me to form a nearer and better idea of the real state of things at his court. and visits Sultan Mahmūd Khan.

[a] *Add* and quiver
[b] As the opportunity offered I marched against it.
[c] which would produce an excellent effect, both far and near, on those who might hear of, or witness it.

---

[1] *Sir-kob* is a framework constructed of carpentry, or a mound of earth, equal in height to the wall, or overtopping it.
[2] This usage is to show that the person so coming surrenders at discretion, and considers himself as ready for execution.
[3] As the remains of the patriarchal system were still strong among the Moghuls and Tūrks, great respect was paid to the father or chief person of the family; and the forms of this respect subsisted, both in language and ceremony, long after the reality had ceased.

Having formed this resolution, I went on, and waited on the Khan in the neighbourhood of Shahrokhīa,[1] in a garden which had been laid out by Haider Beg. The Khan was seated in a pavilion erected in the middle of the garden. Immediately on entering it, I made three low bows. The Khan returned my salutation by rising from his seat and embracing me; after which I went back and again bowed once; when the Khan, inviting me forward, placed me by his side, showing me every mark of affection and kindness. In the course of one or two days afterwards, I set out by way of Kundezlik and Amāni, and [a] proceeded towards Akhsi and Andejān. When I arrived at Akhsi, I went and visited the tomb of my father. Leaving Akhsi, on a Friday, about noon-day prayers, I proceeded towards Andejān, by the route of Bendsālār, and arrived between evening and bed-time prayers. The road by Bendsālār is nine farsangs.

Returns by way of Akhsi.

Among the inhabitants of the wilds of the country of Andejān, there is one tribe, named Jagrag, which is very numerous, consisting of five or six thousand families. They reside in the mountains that lie between Ferghāna and Kāshghar.[2] They have great numbers of horses and sheep; and on these mountains, instead of the common ox, they have the Kutās,[3] or mountain ox, in great numbers; and as they inhabit mountains difficult of access, they will not pay tribute. Having, therefore, given Kāsim Beg the command of a strong force, I dispatched him against the Jagrag, to seize some of their property, that there might be something to give the troops. Kāsim Beg accordingly proceeded against them, and took twenty thousand sheep and fifteen hundred horses, which were divided among the soldiers of the army.

Plunders the Jagrag.

---

[a] marching by the mountain (pass) of Kunderlik

[1] Shahrokhīa, formerly Benāket, stands on the Sirr, between Khojend and Tāshkend.

[2] [According to the *T. R.*, p. 165, the territory of the Jagirak must have been in the mountains west of Karategin, which bound the upper part of the Alai valley on the north, and separate it from the lower country of Ferghāna. The tribe was exterminated about the beginning of the sixteenth century.]

[3] [This was presumably the Yak (*Poephagus Grunniens*).]

After the return of the army from the country of the Jagrag, I proceeded against Uratippa, which had long been subject to Omer-Sheikh Mirza, but had been lost the year of his death. It was at present held for Baiesanghar Mirza by his younger brother, Sultan Ali Mirza. Sultan Ali Mirza, on receiving information of my approach, escaped alone to the hill-country of Masīkha,[1] leaving his governor, Sheikh Zūlnūn, in Uratippa. While on the road, after I had passed Khojend, I dispatched Khalīfeh as my envoy to Sheikh Zūlnūn, to communicate with him; but that wrong-headed man, instead of returning a suitable answer, seized on Khalīfeh, and gave orders that he should be put to death. Such, however, was not the pleasure of God; and Khalīfeh escaped, and, two or three days afterwards, returned back to me, naked and on foot, after having endured a thousand distresses and hardships. I went forward, and entered the territory of Uratippa; but as winter was now near at hand, the inhabitants had taken in all their grain and provender for that season, so that in a few days I was obliged to march back on my return to Andejān. After my departure, the Khan's people attacked Uratippa, and the inhabitants being unable to resist, were obliged to surrender the city. The Khan gave Uratippa to Muhammed Hussain Korkān, in whose hands it remained from that time till the year 908.[2]

Marches against Uratippa.

A.D. 1502.

EVENTS OF THE YEAR 901.[3]

Sultan Hussain Mirza having led an army from Khorasān against Hissār in the winter season, arrived at Termez.[4] Sultan Masaūd Mirza, on his part, also collected an army, advanced towards Termez, and took post in front

Sultan Hussain Mirza marches against Hissār.

---

[1] [This place, according to P. de C., was situated between Samarkand and Khojend on the western slope of the Ak Tāgh range.]

[2] In that year it was taken by Sheibāni Khan. [Hosain Mirza, the eldest son of Haidar Mirza, Amir of Kashghar, was brought up in early life with Sultan Mahmūd Khan, his brother-in-law, who familiarly called him *tāsh* or friend (*E. B.*, p. 90).]

[3] The year of the Hijira 901 commences September 21, A.D. 1495.

[4] Termez is the chief passage over the Amu, between Balkh and Hissār.

of him, to prevent his crossing the Amu.[a] Khosrou Shah, having fortified himself in Kunduz, sent his younger brother, Wali, to join Masaūd's army.[1] Sultan Hussain Mirza spent the greater part of the winter on the banks of the river, without being able to effect a passage. Finally, however, being an experienced and intelligent general, and full of expedients, he marched up the river towards Kunduz; and, after having by this manœuvre put the opposite army off their guard, he dispatched Abdallatīf Bakhshi, who was an excellent officer, with five or six hundred chosen men, down to the passage of Kilif. Before the enemy were apprised of his motions, Abdallatīf Bakhshi had made good his passage with his whole party at the ferry of Kilif,[2] and fortified a position on the opposite bank of the river. When this intelligence reached Sultan Masaūd Mirza, in spite of the warmest instances of Khosrou Shah's brother Wali, who strongly urged an immediate attack on that part of the enemy's army which had passed, the Sultan, either from want of courage, or misled by the advice of Bāki Cheghāniāni,[3] who hated Wali, would not march against them, but, breaking up in terror and confusion, took the road to Hissār. Sultan Hussain Mirza having passed the river, detached Badīa-ez-zemān Mirza, Ibrahīm Hussain Mirza, Muhammed Wali Beg, and Zūlnūn Arghūn, without loss of time, against Khosrou Shah, and sent Muhammed Berenduk Birlās[4] against Khutlān; whilst he himself advanced upon Hissār. On learning the news of his near approach, Sultan Masaūd Mirza no longer thought himself safe even in Hissār; but flying up the river

Sultan Masaūd Mirza retires to Hissār;

and flees thence to Samarkand.

[a] *Omit* to prevent his crossing the Amu.

---

[1] Sultan Masaūd Mirza, it will be recollected, was the eldest son of Sultan Mahmūd Mirza, whom he had nominally succeeded in the sovereignty of Hissār and the adjoining countries. The real authority was in the hands of Khosrou Shah.

[2] Kilif is on the Amu, below Termez. The expression rather imports *ford of Kilif*, but it may be doubted if there is any ford so low down.

[3] [He was Khusru Shah's brother.]

[4] [P. de C. gives the name as Muzaffar Mirza. Possibly both were sent.]

Kamrūd,[1] by way of Siretāk, went to join his younger brother Baiesanghar Mirza, in Samarkand. Wali drew off towards Khutlān; while Bāki Cheghāniāni, Mahmūd Birlās, and Sultan Ahmed, the father of Kūch Beg, fortified themselves in Hissār. Hamzeh Sultan and Mahdi Sultan, who, several years before, had separated themselves from Sheibāni Khan, and had been entertained in the service of Sultan Mahmūd Mirza, with a body of Uzbeks; and Muhammed Dughlet and Sultan Hussain Dughlet, who, with a band of Moghuls, had settled in the country of Hissār, all now, in this general dispersion, retired towards Karatigīn. *His chief nobles disperse.*

Sultan Hussain Mirza being informed of these proceedings, dispatched Abul Muhsin Mirza with a body of troops to the valley of Kamrūd, in pursuit of Sultan Masaūd Mirza. They overtook him at the pass, but were able to effect nothing of importance. Mirza Beg Feringi distinguished himself by his bravery. The Sultan also dispatched Ibrahīm Terkhān and Yākūb Ayūb with a considerable detachment, against Hamzeh Sultan and the Moghuls, who had taken refuge in Karatigīn. The detachment having overtaken them in that country, an engagement ensued, and Sultan Hussain Mirza's troops were defeated. The greater part of the Begs were dismounted and taken prisoners, but afterwards suffered to depart. Hamzeh Sultan, Mahdi Sultan, and Māmak Sultan, the son of Hamzeh Sultan, Muhammed Dughlet, who was afterwards better known by the name of Muhammed Hissāri, Sultan Hussain Dughlet, and such of the Uzbeks as depended on the Sultans, along with the Moghuls who had settled in the country of Hissār, and who had been in the service of Sultan Mahmūd Mirza, after giving me due notice of their approach, came to Andejān, in the month of Ramzān. On this occasion I received them sitting on a *tushak*, according to the custom of the sovereigns of the house of Taimūr. When Hamzeh Sultan with Mahdi Sultan and Māmak Sultan entered, I rose to do them honour, and descending from *and are pursued.* *Several of them join Bābur.* *May or June 1496.*

[1] The Kamrūd river descends from the Kara-tāgh Mountains, flowing south-east towards Hissār.

the *tushak*, embraced them, and placed them on my right hand on a *baghish*.[1] A body of Moghuls, commanded by Muhammed Hissāri, also came and entered into my service.

Sultan Hussain Mirza besieges Hissār.

Sultan Hussain Mirza having invested the fort of Hissār, encamped and busied himself, without rest or intermission, night and day, in running mines, in assaulting the fort, in battering it with shot[2] and planting cannon. Mines were run in four or five places. The mine which advanced towards the city-gate having made great progress; the besieged countermined, discovered it, and from above introduced smoke upon those in the mine :[3] the besiegers, on observing this, instantly closed up the hole of the mine. This was no sooner effected than the smoke was forced back on the besieged, who were obliged to retreat in their turn, nearly suffocated. At length having brought pitchers of water, they poured them into the mine, and drove out the besiegers. On another occasion, a party of active warriors having sallied out from the fort, attacked a party of the besiegers who were stationed at the mine, and drove them off.

On the north side, again, where the Mirza in person was encamped, a battering piece was set a-going, which threw such a multitude of stones, that one of the towers was shaken, and fell about bed-time prayers. A party of warriors, with the greatest alacrity, asked permission to storm, which the Mirza refused to grant, alleging that the night was too dark. Before morning, however, the garrison had repaired the tower, so that then no attack was practicable. For two months, or two months and a half, nothing was attended to except pushing on the work, the running of

---

[1] [*Tūshak* seems to have been a cushion or embroidered quilt stuffed with cotton, placed on a platform which was elevated above the rest of the apartment. *Baghish*, according to P. de C., signifies the action of sitting cross-legged.]

[2] Literally *in casting stones*, that is, *in discharging shot. Sang* means a *bullet* as well as a stone, the first bullets having generally been of stone. [It is not clear when artillery was first introduced into the East. In Europe it is said to have been first employed by the Germans at the siege of Cividale in 1331, and Edward III used guns at the battle of Creçy (1346). In 1453 the Turks had a large park of artillery before Constantinople. Bābur introduced cannon into India, and employed them at the battle of Panipat (1526).]

[3] Probably by throwing in smoke-balls and stink-pots.

mines, the raising of works¹ to overtop the wall, and discharging of stones.² There was no fine fighting.

Badīa-ez-zemān Mirza, with the detachment sent by Sultan Hussain Mirza against Khosrou Shah, having encamped three or four farsangs below Kunduz, Khosrou Shah immediately armed and marched out of that place with such of his troops as he had left with him,ᵃ ³ and next morning came down upon Badīa-ez-zemān Mirza and his army; when that mighty body of Mirzas, and Begs, and Chiefs, who, with their men, if they were not double the number of Khosrou Shah's party, were at least one and a half times the number, consulting only their own comfort and safety, did not dare to leave their trenches. Khosrou Shah's force, good and bad, great and small, might perhaps amount to four or five thousand. And this Khosrou Shah, who, for the sake of this fleeting, unstable world, and for the vanity of being attended by a set of faithless servants, did so many bad actions, earned such a portion of infamy, and was guilty of so much tyranny and injustice; who seized so many extensive countries, and entertained so many adherents and soldiers, that, at last, his army amounted to twenty or thirty thousand men, while the countries and districts which he had occupied, exceeded in extent those of his sovereign and his Mirzas, in the whole course of his life, had only this one exploit to boast of, to entitle him or his adherents to lay claim to the praise of generalship or bravery; while those who did not venture out of their trenches from fear, became notorious for want of spirit, and their cowardice passed into a standing reproach.

Badīa-ez-zemān Mirza, having decamped, halted after some marches at Talikān⁴ in the Ulugh Bāgh.⁵ Khosrou

Badīa-ez-zemān Mirza marches against Kunduz,

but is forced to retreat.

ᵃ *Add* encamped between the town and the enemy,

¹ *Sirkob.*

² *Sāngha*, stones or bullets, that is, either from cannon or *manjāniks* [*balistas*], but probably from the former.

³ A great part of his force had been dispersed on the retreat of Sultan Masaūd Mirza.

⁴ Talikān lies nearly 60 miles higher up the river than Kunduz. [This Talikān must not be confounded with the town of the same name between Balkh and Merv i rūd.]

⁵ That is, ' the Great Garden '.

Shah remained in the fort of Kunduz, and sent his brother Wali with a chosen body of well-appointed troops to Ishkamish,[1] Fūlūl, and the skirts of that hill-country, to hang upon the rear of the enemy, and to harass them in their march. On one occasion Muhibb Ali Korchi, accompanied by a body of well-armed warriors, having fallen in with a party of the enemy on the banks of the river of Khutlān, completely discomfited them. On another occasion he again attacked a party of their troops, and returned, after dismounting some of their men, and cutting off a few heads. In emulation of these exploits, Sīdīm Ali Darbān, and his younger brother Kuli Beg, with Behlūl Ayūb and a party of spirited young men, having overtaken the army of Khorasān at Amberkoh, near Khwājeh Changāl,[2] charged them on their march, but without success; and Sīdīm Ali and Kuli Baba, with a whole body of their followers, were dismounted and made prisoners.

Sultan Hussain Mirza raises the siege of Hissār.

When news of these transactions reached Sultan Hussain Mirza, whose army, besides, was not without apprehensions on account of the spring rains of Hissār, he patched up a peace; in consequence of which Mahmūd Birlās having come out of the fort, and being met on the part of the besiegers by Hāji Pir Bekāwal with a few great lords; and such musicians and singers as were to be got being collected, the eldest daughter of Sultan Mahmūd Mirza by Khanzādeh Begum was given in marriage to Haider Mirza, who was the son of Sultan Hussain Mirza by Payandeh Sultan Begum, and grandson of Sultan Abusaīd Mirza by one of his daughters; after which the Sultan broke up from Hissār and took the route of Kunduz.

Advances to Kunduz and makes peace.

Having reached Kunduz, he drove in all the enemy's parties,[a] and set about making his arrangements for the siege; but Badīa-ez-zemān Mirza having interposed as mediator, a peace was concluded; and, all prisoners made

[a] carried out some preliminary operations,

---

[1] Ishkamish lies higher up the Aksera river than Kunduz, on the Bangi branch of it.

[2] Khwājeh Changāl lies on the Talikān river about fourteen miles below that place.

on both sides being mutually delivered up, the army retired.

The elevation of Khosrou Shah, and all his subsequent doings, so much out of his sphere, were entirely owing to the two expeditions of Sultan Hussain Mirza to reduce him, and to the retreat of that monarch without effecting his purpose.

When Sultan Hussain Mirza reached Balkh, in order the better to watch the potentates of Māweralnaher,[a] he gave Balkh to Badīa-ez-zemān Mirza, and the province of Asterābād[b] to Muzaffer Hussain Mirza; and made them both kneel at the same levee[1] for the grant of these provinces. This arrangement gave great offence to Badīa-ez-zemān,[2] and was the original cause of his engaging in a long series of rebellions and revolts. *Gives Balkh and Asterābād to his two sons*

In the same month of Ramzān, the rebellion of the Terkhāns broke out in Samarkand. It was occasioned by the conduct of Baiesanghar Mirza, who held much greater intercourse with the Begs and soldiers of Hissār, and behaved towards them with much more confidence and familiarity, than he did towards those of Samarkand. Sheikh Abdallah Birlās was a Beg of high rank, and prime minister; such was the intimacy and attachment subsisting between his sons and the prince, that they had all the appearance of standing to each other in the relation of mistress and lover. This gave great offence to the Terkhān Begs, and to several of the nobles of Samarkand, so that in the end Derwīsh Muhammed Terkhān leaving Bokhāra, brought Sultan Ali Mirza from Karshi,[3] proclaimed him king, and advanced along with him to Samarkand to the *May or June 1496. Revolt of the Terkhāns in Samarkand. Baiesanghar Mirza unpopular with them. Sultan Ali Mirza proclaimed king.*

[a] in order that he might devote himself solely to the affairs of Māveralnaher.

[b] *Add* which had been the appanage of Badiuzzemān Mirza,

---

[1] This ceremony of kneeling, or rather bending the knee, to the prince on receiving a grant, was equivalent to an acknowledgement of vassalage.

[2] Badīa-ez-zemān insisted that his father had previously made a grant of Asterābād to Muhammed Mūmin Mirza, a son of Badīa-ez-zemān, and the young Mirza was now in possession of it.

[3] Karshi lies south of Kesh.

New Garden,[1] where Baiesanghar Mirza then resided.[a]
Having seized that prince by stratagem, they separated
him from his servants and retainers, conducted him to the
citadel, and put the two Mirzas in one place. About
afternoon prayers they had a consultation, and came to
the severe resolution of sending the Mirza to Gūk-serāi.
Baiesanghar Mirza, under pretence of a necessary occasion,
entered an edifice on the north-east of the palace gardens.
The Terkhāns waited without at the door, while Muhammed
Kuli Kuchīn and Hassan Sherbetchi entered along with
him. In the back part of this house, into which the Mirza
had gone under the pretence that has been mentioned,
there was a door through which there had formerly been a
passage out, but which had been closed up by bricks on edge.
The young prince contrived to throw down some of the
bricks, got out, effected his escape from the citadel on the
Ghadfer[b] side of the bastion, and, descending by the
Aqueduct, threw himself over the dotihi[2] or parapet wall.
He betook himself to Khwājeh Kafshīr, to the house of
Khwājehka Khwājeh.[3] Those who waited without, after
a certain time, having entered to look after him, found that
the Mirza had escaped.

Next morning the Terkhāns collected round the house
of Khwājehka Khwājeh, demanding the prince; but the
Khwājeh refused to deliver him up;[c] while they, on the
other hand, dared not seize him by force, the Khwājeh's
influence being too great to permit them to make such an
attempt. After one or two days, Khwājeh Abul Makāram,
Ahmed Hāji Beg, and some others of the Begs and soldiers,
with a multitude of the townspeople rising tumultuously,
brought away the Mirza from the Khwājeh's house, and
besieged Sultan Ali Mirza and the Terkhāns in the citadel,
which they were unable to hold out for a single day.

[a] and all proceeded together to the new garden, treating Baisanghar Mirza, who resided there, as a prisoner.
[b] Kafshīr
[c] but he denied that the fugitive was in his house;

[1] *Bagh-e-nou.*
[2] The *dotihi* is a double wall that projects from fortifications in order to enclose and cover a road which generally leads down to water.
[3] [Khwāja Ubeidullah's elder son.]

Muhammed Mazīd Terkhān escaping by the gate of the four roads, proceeded to Bokhāra; while Sultan Ali Mirza, with Derwīsh Muhammed Terkhān, fell into the hands of the assailants.

Baiesanghar Mirza was in Ahmed Hāji Beg's house when Derwīsh Muhammed Terkhān was brought in. One or two questions were put to him, to which he gave no satisfactory answer; and indeed the business in which he had been engaged was not such as admitted of it. He was ordered to be put to death. He showed a want of firmness, and clung to a pillar;[1] but this did not save him, and he received his punishment. Sultan Ali Mirza was ordered to be conducted to Gūk-serāi, and to have the *mīl* or fire-pencil applied to his eyes. The Gūk-serāi is one of the palaces which Taimūr Beg built;[2] it is situated in the citadel of Samarkand. It is remarkable on this account, that every prince of the race of Taimūr who is elevated to the throne, mounts it at this place; and every one who loses his life for aspiring to the throne loses it here. Insomuch, that it has passed into a common expression, that such a prince has been conducted to the Gūk-serai, a hint which is perfectly well understood to mean, that he has been put to death. Sultan Ali Mirza was accordingly carried to Gūk-serāi, and had the fire-pencil applied to his eyes; but whether it happened from the surgeon's want of skill, or from intention, no injury was done to them. Without disclosing this circumstance, he went to Khwājeh Yahya's[3] house, and, after two or three days, fled and joined the Terkhāns at Bokhāra. From this period an enmity

Sultan Ali Mirza sent to Gūk serāi;

but escapes,

---

[1] Probably with a reference to the usage of the Tartars and Arabs, with whom the pole that supports the tent is sacred and considered as a sanctuary; a reverence in some situations transferred to the pillar of a house.

[2] It is curious that though Gūk-serāi, the green palace, is here said to be one of the palaces built by Taimūr Beg, we are told by Petis de la Croix, *Hist. of Genghis Can*, p. 171, that that conqueror put to death Gayer Khan, who made the brave defence of Otrār, *in the palace of Gheucserai*, and the same fact is repeated, p. 227, and said to have taken place in Gheucserai, without the city of Samarkand. Perhaps Taimūr Beg only rebuilt the palace, or the *proverbial saying*, applied by a later historian, may have produced the mistake.

[3] [The younger son of Khwāia Ubeidullah.]

subsisted between the sons of the reverend Khwājeh Obeidullah, for the elder became the spiritual guide of the elder prince, and the younger of the younger. In a few days Khwājeh Yahya followed him to Bokhāra.

and defeats Baiesanghar Mirza. Baiesanghar Mirza, having collected an army, advanced towards Bokhāra against Sultan Ali Mirza; but when he arrived in the vicinity of that city, Sultan Ali Mirza and the Terkhān Begs, having arrayed their force, marched out, and a trifling action ensued, which terminated in favour of Sultan Ali Mirza, Baiesanghar Mirza being defeated. Ahmed Hāji Beg was taken prisoner, with a number of his best troops, the greater part of whom were put to death. The male and female servants and slaves of Derwīsh Muhammed Terkhān, under pretence of revenging the blood of their master, put Ahmed Hāji Beg to a miserable death. Sultan Ali Mirza pursued Baiesanghar Mirza as far as Samarkand.

Bābur marches against Samarkand. This intelligence reached me at Andejān in the month of Shawāl,[1] and in that same month I too mounted and set out with my army to attempt the conquest of Samarkand. As Sultan Hussain Mirza had retired from Hissār and Kunduz, and as Sultan Masaūd Mirza and Khosrou Shah had recovered from their alarm, Sultan Masaūd Mirza now likewise, on his side, advanced by Shehrsebz,[2] in order to assert his pretensions to Samarkand. Khosrou Shah sent his younger brother Wali to accompany the Mirza. For *Samarkand invaded on three sides.* three or four months Samarkand was thus beleaguered on three sides; when Khwājeh Yahya came to me from Sultan Ali Mirza, with proposals for an alliance and confederacy between us, and managed matters so successfully that a personal conference was agreed upon. I therefore moved with my army three or four farsangs,[3] on the Soghd side of Samarkand,[a] and he also came from the opposite direction with his army towards the same place. Sultan Ali Mirza then advancing on his side with four or five persons, and

[a] Marching from Soghd I moved my force to a distance of two or three *igadj cher'i* below Samarkand.

[1] The month of Shawāl A. H. 901, begins June 13, 1496.
[2] Or Kesh, south-east of Samarkand.
[3] [The Persian has *shar'i kos* (about 8 miles).]

I on mine with the same number, we had an interview on horseback in the midst of the river Kohık; and after a short conference,^a he returned towards his own side and I to mine. On that occasion I saw Mulla Banāi and Muhammed Sāliḥ, who were with the Khwājeh. Muhammed Sāliḥ I never saw except on this occasion; but Mulla Banāi¹ was afterwards for some time in my service.

Baber's interview with Sultan Ali Mirza.

After this conference with Sultan Ali Mirza, as the winter season was fast approaching, and great scarcity prevailed in the country of Samarkand, I returned to Andejān, and Sultan Ali Mirza to Bokhāra. Sultan Masaūd Mirza being deeply enamoured of the daughter of Sheikh Abdallah Birlās, married her; and renouncing his schemes of ambition, returned to Hissār. Nay, this was his only object in advancing against Samarkand.

The invaders all retire.

About this time Mahdi Sultan fled from the territory of Shirāz and Kānbāi and went to Samarkand; and Hamzeh Sultan, having received my permission, also went from Zamīn and repaired to the same place.

THE TRANSACTIONS OF THE YEAR 902.²

DURING this winter the affairs of Baiesanghar Mirza had attained their most prosperous situation. Abdal Kerīm Ashret having advanced on the part of Sultan Ali Mirza to Kufīn and its environs, Mahdi Sultan issued from Samarkand with Baiesanghar Mirza's light troops, and attacked him by surprise. Abdal Kerīm Ashret and Mahdi Sultan having met face to face, engaged each other with their scimitars. Abdal Kerīm's horse fell with him, and,^b as he was in the act of rising, Mahdi Sultan struck a blow that

Mahdi Sultan defeats Abdal Kerīm.

^a after making polite enquiries touching each other's welfare,
^b Mahdi Sultan struck Abdul Karīm's horse a blow with his sword, whereupon it immediately fell with him and,

¹ A particular account of Mulla Banāi is afterwards given in describing the eminent men of Sultan Hussain Mirza's Court. He was distinguished as a man of letters and a wit. [Muhammed Sāleh was the author of the *Shaibāni-nāmeh*.]
² The year A. H. 902 begins on September 9, 1496.

severed his wrist; after which he took him prisoner and completely defeated the invaders. These Sultans, however, perceiving that the affairs of Samarkand and the court of the Mirzas were in complete disorder, availed themselves of their foresight and went off to join Sheibāni Khan.[a]

Unsuccessful attempt to surprise Bokhāra.

Elated by the issue of this skirmish, the men of Samarkand assembled and marched out in array to meet Sultan Ali Mirza. Baiesanghar Mirza advanced to Sir-e-pul, and Sultan Ali Mirza to Khwājeh Kārzīn. At this same time, Khwājeh Abul Makāram, with Weis Lāghari, Muhammed Bākir, and Mīr Kāsim Duldāi, who were of the Begs of Andejān, acting on the advice of Khwājeh Murād,[b] set out one night with a party of the household and retainers of Baiesanghar Mirza, intending to surprise Bokhāra. Before they reached the city, however, the people of Bokhāra were alarmed, and the attempt failed; so that they were obliged to return back without effecting anything.

Bābur marches against Samarkand, May 1497.

In my conference with Sultan Ali Mirza, it had been settled that, in the summer, he should advance from Bokhāra, and I from Andejān, to form the siege of Samarkand. According to this agreement, in the month of Ramzān, I mounted, and proceeded from Andejān to Yārailāk, where, having received information that the Mirzas were lying front to front, I dispatched Tūlūn Khwājeh Moghul, with two or three hundred skirmishers, to advance on them with all expedition. By the time that they got near, Baiesanghar Mirza being apprized of our approach, broke up and retreated in great disorder. The detachment, that same night, having overtaken their rear, killed a number of men with their arrows, took a great many prisoners, and acquired much booty. In two days I arrived at the fortress of Shirāz,[1] which at that time belonged to Kāsim Duldāi. The commandant whom he had left in the place not being able to maintain it, delivered up the fortress, which I committed to the charge of Ibrahīm Sāru. Next

June 2, 1497.

[a] retired and went off to the plains to join Sheibāni Khan.
[b] Khwāja Munīr of Aush,

[1] The Shirāz [now in ruins, P. de C.] here spoken of lies about 25 miles north of Samarkand.

morning, after having performed the prayers of the *Īd i fitr*,[1] I proceeded towards Samarkand, and halted in the fields of Abyār.[2] The same day, Kāsim Duldāi, Weis Lāghari, Hassan Nabīreh, Sultan Muhammed Sighel, and Sultan Muhammed Weis, with three or four hundred men, came and entered into my service. Their story was, that, as soon as Baiesanghar Mirza began his retreat, they had left him, and come to offer their services to the king. I afterwards discovered, however, that, at the time of parting from Baiesanghar Mirza, they had undertaken to defend the fortress of Shirāz, and had set out with that intention; but that, on discovering how things stood with regard to Shirāz, they found that there was nothing left for it but to come and join me.

When I halted at Kara-būlāk, many straggling Moghuls, who had been guilty of great excesses in different villages through which they had passed, were seized and brought in. Kāsim Beg ordered two or three of them to be cut to pieces, as an example. Four or five years afterwards, during my difficulties, when I went from Masīkha to the Khan, Kāsim Beg found it necessary to separate from me on account of this very transaction,[3] and went to Hissār. *Kāsim Beg puts some Moghuls to death.*

Marching from Kara-būlāk, I crossed the river, and halted near Yām. The same day, some of my principal Begs attacked a body of Baiesanghar Mirza's troops on the *khiabān*[4] (or public pleasure-ground) of the city. In this skirmish, Sultan Ahmed Tambol was wounded in the neck *Bābur encamps at Yām.*

---

[1] The *Īd-al-fitr* is the festival of the first new moon in Shawāl, when the long fast of Ramzān finishes. The first appearance of the new moon is watched for as the end of the fast, and is instantly announced, as the signal of joy, from the minarets of the mosques.

[2] Fields of Abyār = the *kurūgh* of Abyār. These *kurūgh* are retired fields, in which the Prince in the summer months encamps to enjoy the season, taking the females of his family with him. The outskirts of them are carefully guarded by patrols, to keep off intruders.

[3] From an apprehension that the relations of the Moghuls so punished would prosecute the revenge of blood.

[4] The *khiabān* so often mentioned is a large avenue, planted with several parallel rows of trees, and spreading over a considerable extent of ground, where the townspeople come out in the evening, or on holidays, to divert themselves. The dressed walks of a garden enclosed by low shrubs often receive the same name.

with a spear, but did not fall from his horse. Khwājehka Mullā-i-sadder (or chief judge), who was the elder brother of Khwājeh Kalān, also received an arrow in the neck, and, on the spot, departed to the mercy of God. He was a man of worth. My father had shown him marks of regard, and appointed him keeper of the seal. He was a man of learning, and had great knowledge of language. He excelled in falconry, and was acquainted with magic.[1] While we were in the vicinity of Yām, a number of persons, both traders and others, came from the town to the camp-bazar, and began to traffic, and to buy and sell. One day, about afternoon prayers, there was suddenly a general hubbub, and the whole of those Musulmans were plundered. But such was the discipline of my army, that, on my issuing an order that no person should presume to detain any part of the effects or property that had been so seized, but that the whole should be restored without reserve, before the first watch of the next day was over, there was not a bit of thread or a broken needle that was not restored to the owner.

Moves to Yuret-Khān.

Marching thence, I halted at Yuret-Khān,[2] about three kos to the east of Samarkand. I remained forty or fifty days on this station; and during our stay there many sharp skirmishes took place on the *khiabān* (or pleasure-ground of the city), between our people and the townsmen. In one of these actions, Ibrahīm Begchik received a sabre wound in the face, from whence he was always afterwards called Ibrahīm Chāpuk (or Slashed-face). On a different occasion, in the *khiabān*, at the bridge over the Moghāk,[3] Abul Kāsim Kohbur laid about him with his *piāzi*[4] (or mace) in grand style. At another time, and also in the *khiabān*, in the vicinity of Ternau, there was a skirmish, in which Mīr Shah

---

[1] *Yedehgeri* is properly the art of bringing on rain and snow by means of enchantment and sorcery.

[2] Yuret-Khān means in Tūrki the Khan's mansion or station.

[3] The Moghāk runs a little east of Samarkand. [*Mughāk* means a ditch or ravine.]

[4] The *piāzi* was a sort of mace, which had a set of steel balls fastened to its head by short chains, the whole strongly fixed on a wooden handle. It was a formidable weapon, much used by the warriors in the *Shahnāmeh*.

Kuchīn distinguished himself with his mace, but received such a dreadful wound from a scimitar, that his neck was half cut through; the arteries, however, luckily were not separated.

While we remained at Yuret-Khān, the townspeople treacherously sent a man, who was instructed to tell us, that, if we would come by night on the side next the Lover's Cave, they would deliver the fort into our hands. Seduced by this promise, we mounted at night, and advanced by the bridge over the Moghāk, whence we sent on a small party of chosen horse, with some foot soldiers, to the appointed place. The people of the town seized and carried off four or five of the foot-soldiers, before the rest were aware of the treachery. They were most active men. The name of one of them was Hāji, who had attended me from my infancy. Another was Mahmūd Gundalasang. They were all put to death. Attempt to surprise Samarkand.

While we remained in this station, so many of the townspeople and traders came from Samarkand, that the camp was like a city,[1] and you could find in the camp whatever is procurable in towns. During this interval the inhabitants surrendered to me the whole country, the castles, the high lands and low, except the city of Samarkand. A small body of troops had fortified the castle of Urgut, at the foot of the hill of Shavdār, which obliged me to decamp from the Yuret, and march against them. Being unable to maintain the place, they availed themselves of the mediation of Khwājeh Kazi, and surrendered. I received their submission, and returned to invest Samarkand. Urgut surrenders.

This same year, the misunderstanding that had previously subsisted between Sultan Hussain Mirza and Badīa-ez-zemān came to an open rupture. The circumstances are as follows: In the course of last year, Sultan Hussain Mirza had given Balkh to Badīa-ez-zemān Mirza, and Asterābād to Muzaffer Hussain Mirza, and had received Rupture between Sultan Hussain and Badīa-ez-zemān.

---

[1] This friendly intercourse between enemies bespeaks an advanced state of civilization, and seems to indicate that the long-continued prosperity of Samarkand, from the time of Taimūr Beg downwards, had produced the usual effects of refinement, mildness of manners, and mutual confidence.

their submission¹ on receiving the grant, as has been mentioned. From that time down to the present, a number of ambassadors had been coming and going between them. Ali Sher Beg himself had at last been sent as ambassador, but, with all his endeavours, he could not prevail on Badīa-ez-zemān Mirza to give up Asterābād to his younger brother. That prince asserted, that, at the circumcision of his son Muhammed Mūmin Mirza, the Mirza had made him a grant of it. An incident ᵃ one day occurred between the Mirza and Ali Sher Beg, which equally proves the Mirza's sagacity and presence of mind, and the acute feelings of Ali Sher Beg. Ali Sher Beg had repeated a good many confidential circumstances in a whisper to the Mirza, and, when he concluded, said, 'Now, don't forget what I have mentioned'.ᵇ The Mirza, on the spot, answered, with apparent indifference, 'Pray, what was it you mentioned?' Ali Sher Beg was deeply affected, and cried bitterly.

At last, the discussion between the father and son came to such a pitch, that the father marched against the father, and the son against the son,² towards Balkh and Asterābād.

Sultan Hussain Mirza advancing up the country, and Badīa-ez-zemān Mirza marching down, the two armies encountered below Garzewan,³ in the meadows of Yekchirāgh.

May 3, 1497.

On Wednesday the first of Ramzān, Abul Hassan Mirza, and some of Sultan Hussain Mirza's Begs, having pushed on with a detachment of troops as a plundering party,ᶜ

Badīa-ez-zemān Mirza defeated.

routed Badīa-ez-zemān Mirza after what could hardly be called an action. Many young cavaliers of his party were

ᵃ conversation   ᵇ forget what I have said.   ᶜ reconnaisance,

¹ [i.e homage.]
² That is to say, in consequence of the dispute between Muzaffer Hussain Mirza and Muhammed Mūmin Mirza, matters proceeded to such lengths, that Sultan Hussain Mirza, the father of Muzaffer Hussain Mirza, advanced with an army towards Balkh against Badīa-ez-zemān Mirza, the father of Muhammed Mūmin Mirza; and Muzaffer Hussain Mirza, the son of Sultan Hussain Mirza, led an army towards Asterābād against Muhammed Mūmin Mirza, the son of Badīa-ez-zemān Mirza.—*Persian note.*
³ Garzewān lies between Balkh and Herāt, three or four marches south-west of Balkh.

taken prisoners. Sultan Hussain Mirza ordered the whole of them to have their heads struck off. Nor in this instance alone; on every occasion when any of his sons rebelled and was defeated, he uniformly ordered every one of their adherents who fell into his hands to be beheaded. And why not? he had right on his side. These Mirzas were so extravagantly addicted to vice and pleasure, that, regardless of the approach of their father, a prince of great wisdom and experience, who had come from such a distance,[a] and regardless of the holy and blessed month of Ramzān, of which only a single night had been enjoyed; without any reverence for their father, and laying aside the fear of God, they only thought of drinking wine and revelling in wantonness. But most certain it is that such conduct inevitably leads to destruction; and that they who so demean themselves will inevitably fall before the first attack.[b] Badīa-ez-zemān Mirza had held the government of Asterābād for several years. During all that time, the young cavaliers, both in that place and its environs, were all arrayed in gay and gallant attire.[c] He had many arms and accoutrements[d] of silver and gold, much furniture of rich cloth, with innumerable Tipchāk horses. All these he now gave to the wind. In his flight by the rugged mountain route, he came on a dangerous precipitous road, which they descended with great difficulty. Many of his men perished at this precipice.

After the defeat of his son, Sultan Hussain Mirza advanced to Balkh, which Badīa-ez-zemān Mirza had left in charge of Sheikh Alī Taghāī, who found nothing left for it but to surrender the fortress. Sultan Hussain Mirza having given Balkh to Ibrahīm Hussain Mirza, and left with him Muhammed Wali Beg and Shah Hussain Chihreh, himself returned back to Khorasān.

Loses Balkh.

Badīa-ez-zemān Mirza, after his defeat, being in great

[a] who was within half a day's journey,
[b] and that it does not matter who inflicts it on persons so strangely demeaning themselves.
[c] the members of his suite and immediate circle, as well as his men-at-arms, had lived in affluence and luxury.
[d] utensils

distress, and stripped of everything, accompanied by such of his men old and young,[a] horse and foot, as still adhered to him, proceeded to Kunduz to Khosrou Shah, who gave him a handsome reception, and did him all manner of service. He was so liberal in equipping the Mirza and all that accompanied him with horses, camels, tents, pavilions, and military furnishings of every description, that such as saw them confessed that there was no difference between their former and present arms or accoutrements, excepting that they were not mounted with gold and silver.

Takes refuge with Khosrou Shah.

As some misunderstandings and differences had arisen between Sultan Masaūd Mirza and Khosrou Shah, occasioned by the ungovernable ambition of the latter,[b] he now sent his brothers Wali and Bāki, accompanied by Badiā-ezzemān Mirza, to attack Sultan Masaūd Mirza in Hissār. They were not able to approach the fortress, but, in the environs and vicinity, there was some sharp sword-play on both sides. On one occasion at Kūsh-khāneh,[1] on the north of Hissār, Muhibb Ali Korchi, having pushed forward and advanced in front of the rest of the troops, distinguished himself by his bravery. At the moment when he was unhorsed and taken prisoner, his own party made a push and rescued him. A few days after, a hollow peace was concluded, and the army retired.

Khosrou Shah sends him against Hissār.

Badīa-ez-zemān Mirza soon afterwards set out, by the mountain route, towards Kandahār and Zamīn-dāwer,[2] to Zulnūn Arghūn and his son Shah Shujaa Arghūn. Zulnūn, in spite of his avarice and stinginess, gave the Mirza a good reception.[3] He presented him with forty thousand sheep as a single *peshkesh*.[4] It is a very singular circumstance that

He repairs to Zulnūn Arghūn.

[a] *Omit* old and young,
[b] *Add* and the lack of justice of the former,

---

[1] *Kūsh-khāneh.* The hawk-house.
[2] Zamīn-dāwer lies west of the Helmend below the hills, and on the right bank of the Siahbend river.
[3] [Zu'nnūn was appointed governor of Zamīndāvar in 1483 and afterwards of Kandahar. Badiuzzamān Mirza soon after his revolt was defeated by his father Sultan Hosain Mirza, and fled for refuge to Zu'nnūn in 1497. *E. B.*, p. 268.]
[4] The *peshkesh* is the tribute given to a superior prince.

Muzaffer Hussain Mirza defeated Muhammed Mūmin Mirza at Asterābād on the very Wednesday on which Sultan Hussain Mirza defeated Muhammed Badīa-ez-zemān Mirza ; and what adds to the oddity of the coincidence is, that Chārshembeh (Wednesday) was the name of the person who dismounted and made Muhammed Mūmin Mirza prisoner.

His son Muhammed Mūmin defeated and taken prisoner.

EVENTS OF THE YEAR 903.[1]

WE now encamped behind the Bāgh-e-meidān,[2] in the meadow of Kulbeh.[3] On this occasion the men of Samarkand, both soldiers and townsmen, sallied out in great numbers on the side of Muhammed Chāp's bridge, and came upon us. As my people were off their guard, before they could put themselves in a posture of defence, the enemy dismounted Sultan Ali Baba Kuli and carried him off into the town.

Bābur continues the blockade of Samarkand.

A few days after, we marched and encamped on the hill of Kohik, on the side of Kulbeh.[a] That same day Syed Yūsef Beg came out of Samarkand, and having waited upon me at this station, entered into my service. The men of Samarkand, when they saw us on our march from the one station to the other, fancying that I had taken my departure, rushed out in great numbers, both soldiers and citizens, and advanced as far as the Mirza's bridge ; and poured out by the Sheikhzādeh's gate as far as Muhammed Chāp's bridge. Orders were immediately issued for the cavaliers who were on the spot, to arm without loss of time, and to charge the enemy on the two flanks, both towards the Mirza's bridge, and towards Muhammed Chāp's bridge. God prospered our proceedings—the enemy were defeated. Numbers of Begs and horsemen were dismounted and taken prisoners.

[a] close to Kulbeh behind the hill of Kohik.

---

[1] The year 903 begins on August 30, 1497. It may be worth while to observe, that it was in the end of this year of the Hijira that Vasquez de Gama landed at Calicut.
[2] The garden of the plain.   [3] [Plough.]

Among these were Muhammed Miskīn and Ḥāfiz Duldāi.[1] The latter was wounded with a sabre, and had his forefinger cut off. Muhammed Kāsim Nabīreh, the younger brother of Hassan Nabīreh, was dismounted and taken. Many other officers and fighting men of some note and distinction were also brought in. Of the lower order of townspeople there were taken Diwāneh, a *jāmeh*-weaver,[2] and one nicknamed Kilmasuk, who were notorious as the chief ringleaders of the rabble, in fighting with stones and heading riots.[a] They were directed to be put to death with torture, in retaliation for the foot-soldiers who had been slain at the Lover's Cave.

The defeat of the men of Samarkand was decisive; from that time forward they never sallied out, and matters came to such a pass, that our people advanced right up to the edge of the ditch, and carried off numbers of male and female slaves close under the walls.

The sun had now entered the sign of the Balance,[3] and the cold was becoming severe. I assembled the Begs and held a consultation, when we agreed, that the townspeople were reduced to great distress; that, with the blessing of God, we were likely to take the place in a very few days; but that, as we were exposed to great inconvenience from being encamped in the open country, we should for the present break up from before the city, and construct winter quarters for ourselves in some neighbouring fort; that then, should we finally be obliged to draw off, we might do so without confusion. The fort of Khwājeh Dīdār seemed the fittest for our purpose. We therefore marched from our position, and halted in a plain[b] in front of Khwājeh Dīdār. After visiting the fort, and marking out the ground for the huts and houses, we left workmen and overseers to go on with the work, and returned to our camp. During several days, while the houses for the winter quarters were

Retires to Khwājeh Dīdār.

[a] in riots and disturbances.
[b] meadow

[1] [The two names refer to the same person, the latter being probably the patronymic (P. de C.).]
[2] The *jāmeh* is a gown or tunic.
[3] It was the end of September or beginning of October.

building, we remained encamped on the plain. Meanwhile Baiesanghar Mirza sent repeated messengers into Tūrkestān[1] to Sheibāni Khan, inviting him to come to his assistance. As soon as the erections in the fort were finished, we took up our quarters in it.

The very next morning Sheibāni Khan, who had hastened by forced marches from Tūrkestān, advanced and presented himself before my cantonments. My army was in rather a scattered state, some of my people having gone to Rabāt-Khwājeh-Ameh, some to Kābid, others to Shirāz, for the purpose of securing proper winter quarters. Without being dismayed by these circumstances, however, I put the forces which were with me in array, and marched out to meet the enemy; when Sheibāni Khan did not venture to maintain his ground, but drew off towards Samarkand, and halted in its environs. Baiesanghar Mirza, disappointed on finding that Sheibāni Khan could not render him the effectual assistance which he had hoped for, gave him but an indifferent reception; and, in the course of a few days, Sheibāni Khan, seeing that nothing could be done, returned back in despair to Tūrkestān.

Sheibāni Khan appears before Khwājeh Dīdār

but returns to Tūrkestān.

Baiesanghar Mirza had now sustained the blockade for seven months, and had placed his last hope in this succour. Disappointed in this too, he resigned himself to despair, and, accompanied by two or three hundred hungry and naked wretches, set out for Kunduz to take refuge with Khosrou Shah. In the environs of Termez, while he was passing the river Amu, Syed Hussain Akber, the Hākim or Governor of Termez, who was related to Sultan Masaūd Mirza, and high in his confidence, having received notice of his motions, advanced against him. The Mirza himself had just passed the river, but several of his men and horses that had fallen behind,[a] were taken. Mīrim Terkhān perished in the stream. One Muhammed Tāher, a boy of Baiesanghar Mirza's, was taken prisoner. Baiesanghar Mirza met with a good reception from Khosrou Shah.

Baiesanghar Mirza escapes from Samarkand,

and takes refuge with Khosrou Shah.

[a] *Add* as well as the heavy baggage,

---

[1] This is the Tūrkestān north-west of Tāshkend, north of the Sirr, and east of the Aral, where the head-quarters of the Uzbeks were previous to their conquest of Bokhāra.

76 MEMOIRS OF BĀBUR A. H. 903

Bābur enters Samarkand.

No sooner had Baiesanghar Mirza fled from Samarkand, than I received notice of the event. We instantly mounted and set out from Khwājeh Dīdār, for Samarkand. On the road we were met by the chief men of the city, and by the Begs; and these were followed by the young cavaliers, who all came out to welcome me. Having proceeded to the citadel, I alighted at the Bostān Serai;[1] and, towards the end of the month of the first Rabīa,[a] by the favour of God, I gained complete possession of the city and country of Samarkand.

The end of November 1497.

Description of Samarkand.

In the whole habitable world there are few cities so pleasantly situated as Samarkand. It is situated in the fifth climate, in lat. 39° 37′, and long. 99° 16′.[2] The city is named Samarkand, and the country Māweralnaher.[3] As no enemy has ever stormed or conquered it, it is termed *the protected city*.[4] Samarkand embraced Islām in the reign of Osmān the Commander of the Faithful, through the means of Kāsim-ibn-Abbās, who visited the city. His tomb is close by the Iron-gate, and is at present denominated Mazār-i-Shah, or the Shah's tomb.[5] The city of Samarkand was founded by Sikander.[6] The Moghul and Tūrki hordes term it Samarkand.[7] Taimūr Beg made it his capital. Before Taimūr Beg, no such great monarch had ever made it the seat of his government. I directed its wall to be paced round the rampart, and found that it was ten thousand six hundred paces in circumference.[8] The inhabitants are all orthodox Sūnnis, observant of the law, and religious. From the time of the Holy Prophet, downwards, no other country has produced so many Imāms and excellent

---

[a] *Omit* towards the end of the month of the first Rabīa,

[1] Garden palace.
[2] This is the calculation in Ulugh Beg's tables. The longitude is from Ferro.
[3] That is, the country *beyond the river* Amu. [4] [Shahr-i-mahfūzah.]
[5] [The mosque of Shāhi Zindah (the living king) was built by Timur in A. D. 1323 on the site of the saint's martyrdom.]
[6] Alexander the Great.
[7] [Or rather Simer Kint (P. de C.). Schuyler (*Turkestan*, vol. i, note 2, p. 236) says that *semi* or *semiz* means fat or fertile (*kint* being 'city'), but thinks this may be only an explanatory adaptation.]
[8] This would make it about 5 miles in circumference.

theologians as Māweralnaher. Among these is the great Imām Sheikh Abul Mansūr Materīdi, the eminent scriptural expositor, who was of the quarter of Materīd in the city of Samarkand. There are two sects of scriptural expositors, or *Aimeh Kelāmi*, the one called *Materīdīah*, the other *Ashaarīah*. This Sheikh Abul Mansūr [1] was the founder of the sect of Materīdīah. Another man of eminence was the Sāhib Bokhāri,[2] Khwājeh Ismāel Khertank, who was also of Māweralnaher. The author of the *Hidāyah*,[3] too, a work in jurisprudence, than which according to the sect of Imām Abu Hanīfeh, there is none of greater or of equal authority, was of Marghinān in Ferghāna, which is likewise included in Māweralnaher, though it lies on the farthest bounds of the populous cultivated country.

The eminent theologians of Māweralnaher.

On the east it has Ferghāna and Kāshghar; on the west Bokhāra and Khwārizm; on the north Tāshkend and Shahrokhīa, which are usually written Shāsh and Benāket; and on the south Balkh and Termez. The river Kohik flows to the north of Samarkand, and passes at the distance of two kos from the city. Between the river and the city there is a rising ground called Kohik [4]; and as the river flows close by the base of this hillock, it thence gets the name of the river of Kohik. A great stream, or rather a small river, separating itself from the Kohik, flows on the south

Its boundaries,

rivers,

---

[1] [Abul Mansūr Muhammed bin Mahmūd, known as Imām ul Hudā, was a native of Samarkand, and acquired the surname Matrīdi from the Materīd quarter of that town in which he lived. He died and was buried in Samarkand in A. D. 944. A celebrated philosopher and theologian, he composed several works, including the *Bayān i uahm ul mu'tazalah*, which was directed against the Mu'tazalite sect (d'Herbelot, *Bib. Or.*).].

[2] [This is a mistake for the author of the *Sāhib i Bukhāri*.] Some curious anecdotes of Abu Abdullah Muhammed bin Ismael may be found in D'Herbelot, al Jausi Art. Bokhāri. He passed the latter part of his life in Khertank, a quarter of Samarkand, whence his surname. [He was born A. D. 810 and died A. D. 870.]

[3] This work, written in Arabic by Burhān-ed-din Al Marghināni has been translated into English by Captain Charles Hamilton, in 4 vols. 4to. Bābur does not mention the famous Abu-Ali Sena (or Avicenna), a native of Bokhara.

[4] [It was on this hill (Chaupānāta, or Father of Shepherds) that Ulugh Beg's observatory stood. It was crowned by the tomb of the patron saint of shepherds.]

of Samarkand under the name of the river Derghām. It may be about a sharaa kos from Samarkand, and the gardens and suburbs of Samarkand lie on its banks.[a] The whole country as far as Bokhāra and Kara-kūl, which is an extent of nearly forty farsangs, is covered with population, and the fields cultivated by irrigation from the river Kohik; which, large as it is, barely suffices for the drains made on it for the cultivation of the fields, and for the use of palaces and country houses; insomuch that, for three or four months during the summer heats, the waters do not reach Bokhāra. The fruits of Samarkand of every species, especially the grapes, melons, apples, and pomegranates, are of excellent quality, and produced in great abundance. Samarkand is, however, particularly famous for two kinds of fruit, the apple and a species of grape named *Sāhibi*.[1] Its winter is severe, but less snow falls than at Kābul. It has a fine climate, but its summer does not equal that of Kābul.

fruits,

public buildings.
There are many palaces and gardens that belonged to Taimūr Beg and Ulugh Beg,[2] both in Samarkand and the suburbs. Taimūr Beg built, in the citadel[3] of Samarkand, a stately palace, four stories high, which is famous by the name of Gūk-serāi.[4] There are many other magnificent edifices. One of these is the grand mosque,[5] which is situated near the Iron-gate, within the walls of the city, and built of stone. A number of stone-cutters were brought

[a] It serves to irrigate the gardens and suburbs of the capital as well as several of the districts that appertain to it.

[1] A species of grape named Sāhib is produced at the present day at Aurungabad in the Dekhan, and is in great estimation.

[2] [The grand-son of Timūr and celebrated as an astronomer.]

[3] Sherīfeddīn says (*Hist. de Timur Bec*, vol. i, p. 91), that when the Getes besieged Samarkand, in Taimūr's time, there was then no citadel. Yet Ibn Haukal, p. 253, mentions a citadel as existing in his time; and Petis de la Croix the elder mentions the Gheuk-serai in Gengis-Khan's time.

[4] [Schuyler gives an interesting account of the Gūktāsh, or inauguration stone, which is still to be seen in the verandah of the court (*Turkistan*, vol. i, pp. 254-5).]

[5] [This may be the mosque built by Bībī Khānum, the favourite wife of the great Timur, in A.D. 1385. The building is remarkable for its gigantic dome. (Schuyler's *Turkistan*, vol. i, p. 249.)]

from Hindustān to work on it.¹ In the frontispiece over the portico of the mosque is inscribed the verse of the Korān, *wa iz yarfa'u Ibrahīm al kavāidah*,² &c., in characters of such a size that they may be read nearly a kos off. It is a very grand building. To the east of Samarkand there are two gardens. The one, which is the more distant, is called Bāgh-e-buldi (or the Perfect Garden); the nearer, Bāgh-e-dilkushā (or the Heart-delighting Garden). From the Bāgh-e-dilkushā to the Firozeh gate³ there is a *khiabān* (or public avenue), planted on each side with pine-trees.ª In the garden of Dilkushā, there has also been built a large kiosque or palace, in which is a series of paintings, representing the wars of Taimūr Beg in Hindustān. There is another garden, on the skirts of the hill of Kohik, on the banks of the Āb-e-siāh (black-water) of Ḱanegil, which they call Āb-e-rahmet (or the Water of Mercy), and this is denominated Naksh-e-jehān (the Miniature of the World). When I saw it, it had fallen into decay, and nothing worthy of notice was left. On the south of Samarkand lies the Bāgh-e-chenār (the Plane-Tree Garden), which is in the immediate vicinity of the city.ᵇ Lower down than Samarkand are the Bāgh-e-shimāl (or Northern Garden), and the Bāgh-e-behisht (or Garden of Paradise⁴). Muhammed Sultan Mirza, the son

ª white poplars.
ᵇ near the fortified wall.

[1] The account given by Sherīfeddīn Ali Yezdi of the building of this mosque is curious. See *Hist. de Timur Bec*, vol. iii, pp. 178–81. The stone-cutters, 200 in number, came from Azarbaijān, Fars, and India. There were 480 pillars of hewn stone, each seven cubits high. The Bāgh-e-shimāl, at Samarkand, was built by workmen from Syria and Baghdad, who seem to have excelled in delicate ornaments, in a species of Mosaic, and in the construction of fountains and jets d'eau.—Ibid., vol. iv, p. 179, and vol. ii, p. 409.

[2] These words, *wa iz yarfa'u*, &c., are from the second chapter of the Korān: 'And Ibrahīm and Ismael raised the foundations of the house, saying, Lord! accept it from us, for thou art he who heareth and knoweth: Lord! make us also resigned unto thee, and show us thy holy ceremonies, and be turned unto us, for thou art easy to be reconciled, and merciful.'—Sale's *Korān*, vol. i, p. 24.

[3] Turquoise gate.

[4] [All these buildings and gardens were erected and laid out by Timur.]

of Jehāngīr Mirza, and grandson of Taimūr Beg, founded a college just as you go out of the stone fort[a] of Samarkand. The tomb of Taimūr Beg, and the tombs of all such of the descendants of Taimūr Beg as have reigned in Samarkand, are in that college.

UlughBeg's college, &c. Among the edifices erected by Ulugh Beg Mirza are the college and monastery, or *khānkah*,[1] which stand within the fortifications of Samarkand. The door of the convent is of great magnitude, and, indeed, scarcely to be equalled in the world. In the vicinity of this college and convent there is an excellent set of baths, known by the name of the Mirza's baths. The floor is paved with stones of every sort in chequer-work.[2] There are no baths to equal them in all Khorasān or Samarkand.

On the south of this college is situated a mosque, which is called Mesjid-e-Makatta (or the Carved Mosque), because its timbers are curiously carved[3] with ornaments and flowers of various kinds, and the whole of the walls and roof are adorned in the same manner.[b] The direction of the *kibleh*[4] of this mosque is very different from that of the college; and the probability is, that the *kibleh* of the former was adjusted by astronomical observation.

Another remarkable edifice is the observatory, erected

[a] outer wall
[b] so called because its ceiling and walls are adorned with Chinese designs formed by pieces of wood artistically carved.

---

[1] [*Khāngah* or monastery was an institution for Mahommedan ascetics. Though forbidden by Mahommed, monasticism was widely practised by Moslems in later times, especially in Persia and Turkey.]

[2] This floor seems to have been ornamented with mosaic work.

[3] I am here informed that there is an old mosque at Delhi, in the fort, which goes by the name of Sher Shah, which is said to have furnished the model of this at Samarkand. It is added, that it is easily seen to be ancient by the architecture. It is covered with Arabic inscriptions, and is still a very striking edifice. [The mosque of Sher Shah, which is probably referred to, is not in the fort, but near the Purāna Kila outside the city. Fanshawe in his *Delhi Past and Present* describes it as the most striking bit of coloured decoration in Delhi.]

[4] The *kibleh* is the point to which the Musulmans turn in prayer. The black stone, or *kaaba*, in the temple of Mekka, is their *kibleh*.

on the skirts of the hill of Kohik, which is provided with an astronomical apparatus,[a] and is three stories in height. By means of this observatory, Ulugh Beg Mirza [1] composed the *Zīj-Kurkāni* (or Kurkāni Astronomical Tables), which are followed at the present time, scarcely any other being used. Before they were published, the Ilkhāni Astronomical Tables were in general use, constructed by Khwājeh Nasīr [2] in the time of Hulākū, in an observatory built at Marāgha. Hulākū Khan [3] was also denominated Ilkhāni. Not more than seven or eight observatories have been constructed in the world. Among these, one was erected by the Khalīfeh Māmūn,[4] and in it the astronomical tables entitled *Zīj-Māmūni* were drawn up. Another was built by Batalmiūs.[5] Another was the observatory erected in Hindustān, in the time of Raja Bikermājīt, a Hindū, in Ujein and Dhār, in the kingdom of Mālwa, now known as the kingdom of Māndū. The Hindūs still follow the astronomical tables which were then constructed. Since the building of that

[a] designed for the purpose of preparing astronomical tables,

[1] The illustrious Ulugh Beg Mirza, who governed Samarkand nearly forty years, chiefly in his father's lifetime, devoted much of his leisure to study, and was particularly skilled in the mathematical sciences. The task of composing the astronomical tables which go under his name was first entrusted to Moulāna Selāh-ed-dīn Mūsa, better known by the name of the Kāzızādeh Rūmi. On his death, it devolved on Moulāna Ghiās-ed-dīn Jemshīd; and he having died in the course of the work, they were completed by Ibn Ali Muhammed Koshji, generally called Ali Koshji. Graves pretends that he heard from a Turk worthy of credit, that the radius of the quadrant used by Ulugh Beg in his observations was equal to the height of St. Sophia's. Ulugh Beg is said to have himself assisted in the composition of the Tables. [There is a similar observatory at Jaipūr in Rajpūtāna erected by Maharaja Jai Singh.]

[2] [The celebrated philosopher and astronomer Nasīr ud dīn Tūsi, who was born in A. D. 1201 and died in 1274. He was the prime minister of Hulākū Khan, and the most universal scholar that Persia ever produced. He composed works on geometry, astronomy, philosophy, and theology. He is the author of the *Akhlāq i Nasīri*, and translated Euclid and Al Majisti. (Beale's *O. B.*).]

[3] [The grandson of Chingiz Khan. Died A. D. 1265.]

[4] [The second son of Harūn-ur-Rashīd. He succeeded his eldest brother Amīn in A. D. 813 and died in 833.]

[5] Ptolemy, the geographer.

observatory till the present time[1] is 1,584 years. These tables are, however, more imperfect than any of the others.

At the foot of the hill of Kohik, on the west, there is a garden, named Bāgh-e-meidān (the Garden of the Plain), in the middle of which is a splendid edifice, two stories high, named Chihil-sitūn (the Forty Pillars). The pillars are all of stone. In the four turrets in the corners of this building, they have constructed four Guldestehs,[2] or minarets, the road up to which is by these four towers. In every part of the building are stone pillars curiously wrought; some twisted, others fluted, and some with other peculiarities. The four sides of the upper story consist of open galleries, supported by pillars all of stone; and in the centre is a grand hall or pavilion, likewise of stone. The raised floor of the palace is all paved with stone. Towards the hill of Kohik there is a small garden, wherein is a great open hall, within which is a large throne of a single stone, about fourteen or fifteen gez in length, seven or eight in breadth, and one in height. This huge stone was brought from a great distance. There is a crack in it, which it is said to have received since it was brought to this place. In this garden, there is another state pavilion, the walls of which are overlaid with porcelain of China, whence it is called the Chinese House. It is said that a person was sent to Khitā,[3] for the purpose of bringing it. Within the walls of Samarkand is another ancient building, called the Laklaka (or Echoing) Mosque; because, whenever any person stamps on the ground in the mosque,[a] an echo (*laklaka*) is returned. It is a strange thing, the secret of which is known to nobody.

In the time of Sultan Ahmed Mirza, many of the greater and lesser Begs formed gardens, some large, others smaller

[a] in the centre of its dome,

---

[1] This remark would seem to fix the period when Bābur composed this part of his *Commentaries* at A. H. 934 or A. D. 1527-8, that being the 1,584th year of the era of Vikramaditya, only three years before his death. [The Vikramadıtya era began in 57 B.C.]

[2] The Guldesteh is a minaret, or any high turret-like building; it is generally built with open galleries or corridors, and with a winding staircase to ascend to its summit.

[3] Northern China.

Among these, the Chārbāgh[1] of Derwīsh Muhammed Terkhān, in respect of climate, situation, and beauty, is equalled by few. It is situated lower down than the Bāgh-e-meidān, on a small eminence that rises above the valley [a] of Kulbeh, and commands a view of the whole vale, which stretches out below. In this Chārbāgh there is a variety of different plots laid out one above another, all on a regular plan, and elms, cypresses, and white poplars are planted in the different compartments. It is a very perfect place. Its chief defect is, that it has no great stream of running water.

Samarkand is a wonderfully elegant city. One of its distinguishing peculiarities [b] is, that each trade has its own bazaar; so that different trades are not mixed together in the same place. The established customs and regulations are good. The bakers' shops are excellent, and the cooks are skilful. The best paper in the world comes from Samarkand. The species of paper called *juwāz*[2] comes entirely from Kānegil, which is situated on the banks of the Āb-e-siāh (Black Water), called also the Āb-e-rahmet (or Water of Mercy). Another production of Samarkand is *kermezi*[3] (or crimson velvet), which is exported to all quarters.

Its bazaars

and manufactures.

Around Samarkand are five *aulengs* (or meadows). One of these is famous, under the name of Kānegil. It lies to the east of Samarkand, but a little inclining to the north. It may be about a shiraa kos off. The Āb-e-rahmet (or Water of Mercy) runs through the midst of it, and has volume enough to drive seven or eight mills. The banks of this stream are full of quagmires. Many allege that the original name of this meadow was Auleng i Kān-e-ābgīr (the

The valleys in its vicinity: The Kānegil.

[a] meadow
[b] *Add* not often found in other towns,

[1] *Chehārbāgh*, or *Chārbāgh*, means Four Gardens. It is generally a very large and elegant garden. It perhaps had this name from having been originally laid out in four principal plots, with two avenues crossing each other at right angles in the centre. It is said to have been usual to lay out the different plots or divisions in different styles. Now, however, the term is applied to any large and elegant garden.

[2] [According to Steingass *juwāz* means a pounding or crushing mill.]

[3] Hence the *cramoisy* of our old ballads.

Meadow of Quagmires); but in histories it is always denominated Kān-e-gil (the Clay-Pits).[a][1] The Sultans of Samarkand were accustomed to guard this vale as a *kurūgh*, and were in the habit of taking up their residence for two or three weeks annually in this meadow.

The Yuret-Khan.

Higher up than this meadow, to the south-east, lies another, called the Yuret-Khan (or Khan's halting-place). It is to the east of Samarkand, about one shiraa kos.[2] The Āb-e-siāh (Black Water), after passing through it, proceeds on to Kānegil. The river winds round the Yuret-Khan in such a manner as to leave room within for an army to encamp. The roads leading from it are very narrow. Perceiving the excellence of this position, I encamped here for some time during the siege.

The Kurūgh meadow. The Kūl-e-Maghāk (or deep pool).

Another is the Kurūgh meadow,[3] which lies between the Bāgh-e-dilkushā and Samarkand. Another meadow is that of Kūl-e-Maghāk, which lies to the west of Samarkand, but inclining to the north, at the distance of two shiraa kos. This is also a pleasant valley. On one side of it is a large reservoir or piece of water (Kūl), whence it is called the meadow of Kūl-e-Maghāk. During the siege of Samarkand, when I was encamped at Yuret-Khan, Sultan Ali Mirza took up his station on this plain of Kūl-e-Maghāk.

The Valley of Kulbeh.

Another is the meadow of Kulbeh, which is but small. On the north it has the village of Kulbeh and the river of Kohik; on the south, the Bāgh-e-meidān and the Chārbāgh of Dervīsh Muhammed Terkhān; on the east, the hill of Kohik.

Its Tumāns and provinces. Bokhāra.

Samarkand has many provinces and Tumāns. One of the largest of its provinces, and which comes near to Samarkand, is Bokhāra, lying to the west of Samarkand twenty-five farsangs. Bokhāra is a fine city, and has seven Tumāns or districts, each of them resembling a town. Its fruits are both abundant and of good quality, particularly

[a] *Add* It is a very fine meadow.

---

[1] See *Hist. de Taimur Bec*, vol. i. 96; vol. ii. 133 and 421.

[2] [P. de C. has *igadj* = 4 miles.]

[3] [P. de C. gives the name of the meadow as Budāneh kurūgh, or Quail Reserve.]

its melons, which are exquisite; the melons of Bokhāra are not to be equalled in all Māweralnaher, either for quantity or excellence. Though, at Akhsi, in the country of Ferghāna, there is one extremely sweet and delicate species of melon, which they call Mīr Taimūri, yet, in Bokhāra, there is a profusion of melons of every description, and all good of their kind. The pruin or plum of Bokhāra is also celebrated, and nowhere else is that fruit to be found in equal perfection. They peel off the rind of this fruit and dry it, after which it is carried as a most acceptable rarity to other countries. As a laxative, it is a medicine of approved excellence. The household fowl and goose are here of a good breed. In all Māweralnaher there is no wine superior, in spirit and strength, to that of Bokhāra. When I drank wine at Samarkand, in the days when I had my drinking bouts, I used the wine of Bokhāra.

Another province is Kesh, to the south of Samarkand, at the distance of nine farsangs. Between the cities of Kesh and Samarkand lies a hill, called Amak Dābān, from which all the stones brought to the city are quarried. In the spring, the plains, the town of Kesh, the walls and terraces of the houses, are all green and cheerful, whence it is named *Shahr-i-sabz* (the Green City). As Kesh was the place of Taimūr Beg's nativity, he made incredible exertion to extend and render it his capital. He built a number of magnificent edifices, and, among others, a lofty *tāk*, or arched hall, for holding his court. On the right and left of this great *tāk*, he constructed two smaller *tāks* (or arched halls), for the convenience of the Begs who attended the court. And, for the benefit of those who came to wait the result of their applications, smaller *tāks* and saloons were constructed on all sides of the great hall of audience. There is not in the world any *tāk* or arch that can be compared with the large one, which is said to exceed even the Tāk-e-Kisra.[1] In Kesh there is a college and mausoleum, in which are the tombs of Jehāngīr Mirza and of several of his family. As, however, Kesh was found not to possess the same requisites for becoming a great city as

Kesh.

[1] The Tāk-e-Kisra, below Baghdād on the Tigris, is 105 feet high, 84 feet span, and 150 feet deep.

Samarkand, Taimūr Beg at last fixed on Samarkand as his capital.

Karshi. Another province is Karshi, which they also call Nesef and Nakhsheb. Karshi is a Moghul word, signifying a burial-ground. It probably received this name after the conquest of Chinghiz Khan. It is deficient in water, but is very pleasant in spring. Its apricots [a] and melons are excellent. It is situated south of Samarkand, inclining towards the west, at the distance of eighteen farsangs. There is a small bird resembling the *bāghri kāra* (black-liver [1]), which they call *kilkūirugh* (horse-tails). They are innumerable in the district of Karshi, and, from the quantity of them there found, they get the name of *murghak-karshi* (the small fowl of Karshi).

Khozār. Another district is that of Khozār.

Karmīna. Karmīna is another; it lies between Samarkand and Bokhāra.

Karakūl. There is another district named Karakūl (the black lake), which lies lower down the river than any of the rest. It is seven farsangs to the north-west of Bokhāra, and has some very fine Tumāns.[b]

Soghd. Some of the richest Tumāns are those of Soghd, and the Tumāns connected with Soghd, which commence not far from Bokhāra, and proceed without interruption to their termination at Yār-ailāk. There is not one farsang the whole way that does not contain some populous village. It was in allusion to these Tumāns that Taimūr Beg used to boast that he possessed a garden thirty farsangs in length.

Shādwār. Another Tumān is that of Shādwār, which lies close upon the city and suburbs. It is a very fine Tumān. On one side of it is the hill which lies between Samarkand and Shahr-i-sabz; and the greater part of its villages lie scattered on

---

[a] grain   [b] *Omit* and has some very fine Tumāns.

[1] [Colonel Phillott informs me that the *bāghri kāra* (black-breasted) is the Imperial Sandgrouse (*Pterocles arenarius*). The *kilkuirūgh*, a smaller kind, I am unable to identify. It may be the Pintailed Sandgrouse (*Pterocles alchata*), which breeds in Central and Western Asia, and swarms in such countless numbers in some places s to darken the air (Jerdon's *Birds of India*, vol. ii, p. 500. Calcutta, 1877).]

the skirts of that hill. On the other side it has the river Kohik. The temperature of the air is charming; the appearance of the country beautiful, water abundant, and provisions cheap. Those who have travelled in Misr and Shām [1] acknowledge that nothing there is comparable to it. Though there are other Tumāns dependent on Samarkand, yet they are not equal to those which have been mentioned.[a]

Taimūr Beg conferred the government of Samarkand on his son Jehāngīr; and after the death of Jehāngīr Mirza, he gave it to that prince's eldest son, Muhammed Sultan Jehāngīr. Shahrokh Mirza conferred the government of all the provinces of Māweralnaher on his own eldest son, Ulugh Beg Mirza, from whom it was taken by his son, Abdallatīf Mirza; who, for the sake of the enjoyments of this fleeting and transitory world, murdered his own father, an old man so illustrious for his knowledge. The date of the death of Ulugh Beg Mirza is contained in the following memorial verses:[2]

Succession of princes in Samarkand.

> Ulugh Beg, the ocean of learning and science,
> Who was the protector of this lower world,[b]
> Drank from Abbās the honey of martyrdom,
> And the date of his death is (*Abbās kusht*)—Abbās slew him.

Yet his son did not retain the diadem above five or six months; the following verses were applied to him:

> Ill does sovereignty befit a parricide:
> But should he gain it, let six months be the utmost limit of his reign.

The date of his death is also expressed in memorial verses:

> Abdallatīf, who rivalled the pomp of Khosrou and Jemshīd,
> Who was attended by crowds of courtiers like Ferīdūn and Zerdusht,
> Was slain by Baba Hussain, one Friday night, with an arrow,
> And the date of the event is (*Bābā Hussain kusht*)—Baba Hussain slew him.[3]

[a] *Add* I need not say any more on this subject.
[b] *Add* and of religion,

---

[1] Egypt and Syria.
[2] To commemorate any important event, or to fix the date in the memory, the Persians make much use of memorial verses, in which a certain number of letters have a numerical value, that added together give the required date. Thus *Abbās kusht* gives 853 [A. H. (1449 A.D.). This is called *abjad* in Persian.]
[3] The numerical letters united make 854 [A. H. (1450 A.D.).]

After Abdallatīf Mirza, Abdallah Mirza, the son of Ibrahīm Sultan Mirza, and grandson of Shahrokh Mirza, and the son-in-law of Ulugh Beg Mirza, mounted the throne, and reigned one year and a half, or nearly two years. After [A.D. 1451.] him the government was seized by Sultan Abūsaīd Mirza, who, in his own lifetime, conferred the government on his eldest son Sultan Ahmed Mirza. After the death of Sultan [A.D. 1469.] Abūsaīd Mirza, Sultan Ahmed Mirza continued to exercise the sovereignty. On the death of Sultan Ahmed Mirza, [A.D. 1494.] Sultan Mahmūd Mirza ascended the throne. After Sultan [A.D. 1495.] Mahmūd Mirza, Baiesanghar Mirza was raised to the throne. During the sedition of the Terkhān Begs, Baiesanghar Mirza was seized, and his brother Sultan Ali Mirza placed on the throne for one or two days. Baiesanghar Mirza again recovered it, as has been related. I took it from Baiesanghar Mirza.[1] The events that followed will be mentioned in the course of these Memoirs.

Distressed state of Samarkand.

When I mounted the throne of Samarkand, I showed the same favour and grace to the great lords of Samarkand that they had been accustomed to in times past, and I distinguished the Begs who had accompanied me by rewards proportioned to their situation and merits. I bestowed more eminent rewards on Sultan Ahmed Tambol than on any of my other nobles.[a] Samarkand had been taken after a severe and fatiguing siege of seven months. On getting possession of it, the soldiers of the army acquired considerable booty. All the rest of the country, Samarkand excepted, had voluntarily joined me or Sultan Ali Mirza, and consequently these districts had not been given up to plunder. From a place which had been entirely ruined and sacked, how was it possible to levy anything by taxation?[b] It had all been completely pillaged by the troops.[c] Samarkand when taken was in such a distressed state, that it was absolutely necessary to furnish the inhabitants with seed-

[a] *Add* he had belonged to the corps of Begs attached to my personal household. I treated him with the same honour as the Great Begs.
[b] collect anything?
[c] *Add* the booty acquired by our men was very limited.

[1] [This was in A. D. 1497.]

corn and supplies, to enable them to carry on the cultivation till the harvest. How was it possible to levy anything from a country that was in this exhausted condition? Under these circumstances the soldiers were exposed to considerable distress, and I on my part had nothing to give them. They therefore began to think of home, and to desert by ones and twos. The first man who went off was Khan-Kuli Bayān-Kuli.[1] Ibrahīm Begchik was another. All the Moghuls deserted; and finally, Sultan Ahmed Tambol himself went off, and left me.

Bābur's troops begin to desert.

In order to put a stop to this defection, I sent Khwājeh Kazi to Ūzūn Hassan, who had a great attachment and veneration for the Khwājeh, to prevail upon him to concur in adopting measures to punish some of the fugitives, and send back others to me. But the prime mover of this sedition, and the grand instigator of these desertions and défections was, in reality, the perfidious Ūzūn Hassan himself. After the defection of Sultan Ahmed Tambol, all the fugitives openly and in direct terms professed their hostility.

Though I had never received any kind of assistance or succour from Sultan Mahmūd Khan, during the several years that I had led my army against Samarkand, yet no sooner had I succeeded in conquering that country, than he indicated a desire to occupy Andejān. On the present occasion, when the greater part of my troops, and the whole of the Moghuls, had deserted me and gone to Akhsi and Andejān, Ūzūn Hassan and Tambol expressed a wish that those countries should be placed under Jehāngīr Mirza. It was inexpedient that they should be given up to him, on many accounts. One of these was, that though I never had promised them to the Khan, yet he had demanded them; and if, after such demand, they were bestowed on Jehāngīr Mirza, I must expect to come to an explanation with him. Another reason was, that at this season, when my men had deserted and gone back to their own countries, a request seemed equivalent to a command. Had the request been made before, I might have complied with a good grace; but who could bear a tone of authority? All the Moghuls who had accompanied me, as well as the army of

Tambol asks Andejān and Akhsi for Jehāngīr Mirza.

[1] [i. e. Khan-Kuli, son of Bayān-Kuli.]

Andejān, and some even of the Begs who were near my person, had gone off to Andejān. Only about a thousand men, including Begs, great and small, remained with me in Samarkand.

Excites a rebellion.

When they found that their request was not complied with, they collected all the people who had left me from disappointment, and united them to their party. These deserters, who dreaded the reward of their guilt, stood in such terror of me, that they deemed this revolt an interposition of God in their favour. Having marched from Akhsi against Andejān, they openly raised the standard of rebellion and hostility.

Marches against Andejān.

Tūlūn Khwājeh slain.

One Tūlūn Khwājeh, who was the bravest and most resolute of my skirmishers,[a] had been honourably entertained by my father, Omer-Sheikh Mirza, and I myself had continued to show him distinguished marks of my regard, and raised him to the rank of Beg. He was an extremely gallant soldier, an excellent partisan, and every way worthy of the favour shown him. As Tūlūn Khwājeh was the man of all the Moghuls on whom I had conferred the greatest benefits, and in whom I reposed the most perfect trust, when the Ulūs of Moghuls began to retire, I sent him to confer with them, and to remove from their minds any jealousies or distrusts which they might have conceived, that they might not be led to throw away their lives from any false apprehensions of my resentment;[b] but the traitors had wrought upon them so effectually, that entreaties and promises and threats were tried in vain. The march of Tūlūn Khwājeh was by Miān-Doāb,[1] which is also called Rabātiki-Urchīni.[2] Ūzūn Hassan and Sultan Ahmed Tambol dispatched a body of light troops, who fell by sur-

[a] soldiers,

[b] to drive from their minds distrustful thoughts and prevent them from foolishly giving way to fear.

---

[1] [Miyān-i-dūāb = between two rivers. According to P. de C. the rivers referred to were that of Andejān [Kāra sū] on the west and the Irmich on the east, both being affluents of the Seihūn.]

[2] Or the district of Rebātik (the small caravanserai). It lies to the east of Andejān. *Urchin* in Ferghāna, &c., signifies province or district.

prise on Tūlūn Khwājeh, took him prisoner, carried him off and put him to death.

Ūzūn Hassan and Tambol now carried Jehāngīr Mirza along with them, and laid siege to Andejān. When I set out with the army, I had left Ali Dost Taghāi in command of Andejān, and Ūzūn Hassan in charge of Akhsi. Khwājeh Kazi had also returned back [a] to Andejān. Among those who had deserted from Samarkand were a number of good soldiers. Khwājeh Kazi, immediately on his arrival, with a view of preserving the fort, and induced by his affection and attachment to me, divided eighteen thousand of his own sheep among the troops who were in the town, and among the wives and families of such as were with me. During the siege I received letters from my mothers,[1] as well as from Khwājeh Kazi, mentioning that they were besieged, and so hotly pressed, that if I did not hasten to their relief, things would come to a very bad termination: that I had taken Samarkand with the forces of Andejān, and if I still continued master of Andejān, might once more (should God prosper me) regain possession of Samarkand. Letters of this import followed fast upon each other. At this time I had just somewhat recovered from a severe illness. My circumstances, however, prevented me from nursing myself during my amendment; and my anxiety and exertions brought on such a severe relapse, that for four days I was speechless, and the only nourishment I received was from having my tongue occasionally moistened with cotton. Those who were with me, high and low, Begs, cavaliers, and soldiers, despairing of my life, began each to shift for himself.

The rebels besiege Andejān.

Bābur dangerously ill.

At this very crisis a servant of Ūzūn Hassan's came on an embassy with some seditious propositions. The Begs, very mistakenly, brought him where I was,[b] and then gave him leave to depart. In four or five days I got somewhat better, but still had a little difficulty of speech.[c] A few days

[a] *Add* later [b] showed him the condition I was in,
[c] *Add* After the lapse of a few more days my health was completely restored.

---

[1] i.e. my mother and grandmother.

afterwards I received letters from my mother, my mother's mother Isān Daulat Begum, and from my teacher and spiritual guide Khwājeh Moulāna Kazi, inviting me with so much solicitude to come to their assistance, that I had not the heart to delay. In the month of Rajeb, on a Saturday, I marched out of Samarkand for Andejān. At this time I had reigned just one hundred days in Samarkand. Next Saturday I reached Khojend, and that same day intelligence arrived that, seven days before, on the very Saturday on which I had left Samarkand, Ali Dost Taghāi had surrendered the fortress of Andejān to the enemy.

March 1498.
Marches to the relief of Andejān.
Hears of its surrender.

The truth was, that the servant of Ūzūn Hassan, who had been suffered to depart during my illness, arriving while the enemy were busy with the siege, and relating what he had witnessed, that the king had lost his speech, and received no nourishment except from having his tongue moistened with cotton steeped in a liquid, was made to confirm these circumstances on oath in the presence of Ali Dost Taghāi, who stood at the Khākān Gate. Completely confounded at the news, he commenced a negotiation with the enemy, and having entered into terms of capitulation, surrendered the fort. There was no want of provisions, nor of fighting men in the place. This wretched fellow's conduct, therefore, was the extreme of treachery and cowardice.[a] He merely employed the circumstances that have been mentioned as a cover to his baseness.

Khwājeh Kazi hanged.

After the surrender of Andejān, the enemy having received information of my arrival at Khojend, seized Khwājeh Moulāna Kazi and martyred him, by hanging him in a shameful manner over the gate of the citadel. Khwājeh Moulāna Kazi's real name was Abdallah, but he was better known by the other appellation. By the father's side he was descended of Sheikh Būrhān-ed-dīn Kilij, and by the mother's side from Sultan Ilik Māzi; and his family had for a long time maintained the situation of Muktida (prime religious guide), and of Sheikh-ul-Islām (or chief judge in ecclesiastical law), in the country of Ferghāna. Khwājeh Kazi was the disciple of Khwājeh Obeidullah, by

[a] In short this misfortune was due to the cowardice of that miserable traitor.

whom he was educated. I have no doubt that Khwājeh Kazi was a Wali (or saint). What better proof of it could be required than the single fact that, in a short time, no trace or memorial remained of any one of all those who were concerned in his murder? They were all completely extirpated. Khwājeh Kazi was a wonderfully bold man, which is also no mean proof of sanctity. All mankind, however brave they be, have some little anxiety or trepidation about them. The Khwājeh had not a particle of either.

After the Khwājeh's death they seized and plundered all those who were connected with him as his servants and domestics, his tribe and followers. They sent to me, to Khojend, my grandmother, my mother, and the families of several persons who were with me.[a] For the sake of Andejān, I had lost Samarkand, and found that I had lost the one without preserving the other.[b]

I now became a prey to melancholy and vexation; for since I had been a sovereign prince, I never before had been separated in this manner from my country and followers; and since the day that I had known myself, I had never experienced such grief and suffering. While I was at Khojend, some who envied Khalīfeh could not endure to see his influence in my court; and Muhammed Hussain Mirza and some others exerted themselves with such effect,[c] that I was obliged to allow him to retire to Tāshkend.

Bābur reduced to great distress.

Is obliged to dismiss Khalīfeh.

I had sent Kāsim Beg to Tāshkend to the Khan, to request him to march against Andejān. The Khan, who was my maternal uncle, accordingly, having collected an army, advanced by the Dale of Ahengerān,[1] and I having set out from Khojend, met him by the time he had encamped below Kundezlik and Amāni.[d] Having reduced Kundezlik

Sultan Mahmūd Khan marches to restore Bābur.

[a] *Omit this sentence.*

[b] *Add* I had placed myself undoubtedly in the position of those of whom it is said that 'they advanced on one side while they retired from the other'.

[c] On arriving at Khojend certain hypocrites, adorned with a plausible exterior, who could not endure to see the Khalīfah at my court, wrought to such a degree on Hosain Mirza and others,

[d] the foot of the Kundirlik Pass.

[1] Julgeh-e-ahengerān — Blacksmiths' Dale.

and Amāni, he advanced towards Akhsi and encamped. The enemy too, on their part, having brought together what army they had, came to Akhsi. At this time the fortress of Pāp [1] was held by some of my partisans in hopes of my arrival; but the enemy, gaining courage from a belief of the Khan's retreat,[a] carried it by storm.

But is prevailed on to retreat.

Though the Khan had many valuable qualities and talents, yet he had no talents as a soldier or general. At the very moment when matters were brought to such a pass, that, if we had advanced a single march, the country might have been gained without fighting a battle, he listened to the artful proposals of the enemy, and dispatched Khwājeh Abul Makāram with Tambol's elder brother, Beg Tīlbeh, who at that time was the Khan's chamberlain, on an embassy, with proposals for an accommodation. The cabal, in order to extricate themselves, presented such a mixture of truth and falsehood in their representations, and seasoned their eloquence so well with gratifications and bribes to those who acted as negotiators,[b] that the Khan was prevailed upon to break up and retreat the way he came. As the Begs, captains, and warriors, who were with me, had many of them their wives and families in Andejān; and as they

Bābur abandoned by his army.

now saw no hope of our regaining it, great and small, Beg and common man, to the number of seven or eight hundred men, separated from me entirely. Among the nobles who left me, were Ali Derwish Beg, Ali Mazīd Kuchīn, Muhammed Bākir Beg, Sheikh Abdallah the chamberlain, and Mīram Lāghari. There adhered to me, choosing voluntarily a life of exile and difficulty, of all ranks, good and bad, somewhat more than two hundred, and less than three hundred men. Of the Begs were Kāsim Beg Kuchīn, Weis Lāghari, Ibrahīm Sāru Minkaligh, Shīrīm Taghāi, and Seyad Kārabeg. Of my other officers and courtiers there

[a] but the malcontents taking advantage of the fact that a detachment only of the Khan's cavalry had advanced against them,
[b] the Khan and his intermediaries,

[1] [According to P. de C. this place is situated on the left bank of the Seihūn, between Akhsi and Kāsān.]

were Mīr Shah Kuchīn, Syed Kāsim, the Chamberlain, a Jelāir, Kāsim Ajab, Muhammed Dost, Ali Dost Taghāi, Muhammed Ali Mubashar, Khuda-berdi Tughchi (the Standard-bearer), a Moghul, Yārek Taghāi, Sultan Kuli, Pīr Weis, Sheikh Weis, Yār Ali Belāl, Kāsim, Master of the Horse, Hyder Rikābdār (the Equerry).

I was now reduced to a very distressed condition, and wept a great deal. I returned to Khojend, whither they sent me my mother and my grandmother, with the wives and families of several of those who had continued with me. I spent that Ramzān in Khojend, and afterwards, having sent a person to Sultan Mahmūd Khan to solicit assistance, proceeded against Samarkand. He dispatched his son, Sultan Muhammed Khanekeh, and Ahmed Beg, with four or five thousand men, against Samarkand; and came himself to Uratippa, where I had an interview with him, and then advanced towards Samarkand by way of Yār-ailāk. Sultan Muhammed and Ahmed Beg had reached Yār-ailāk before me by another road. I came by way of Burkeh-ailāk to Sengraz, which is the chief township and seat of the Dārogha[1] of Yār-ailāk; but before my arrival, Sultan Muhammed and Ahmed Beg, having been informed of the approach of Sheibāni Khan, and of his ravaging Shirāz and that vicinity, had retreated back in haste. I too was consequently compelled to retreat, and returned to Khojend.

Marches against Samarkand.

May 1498.

But is forced to return to Khojend.

Inspired as I was with an ambition for conquest and for extensive dominion, I would not, on account of one or two defeats, sit down and look idly around me. I now repaired to Tāshkend to the Khan, in order to gain some assistance in my views on Andejān. This journey also furnished me with a pretext for seeing Shah Begum[2] and my other relations, whom I had not seen for seven or eight years. A few days after my arrival, Syed Muhammed Mirza Dughlet, Ayūb Begchik, and Jān Hassan were appointed to accompany me, with a reinforcement of seven or eight hundred men. With this auxiliary force I set out, and without tarrying in Khojend advanced without loss of

Repairs to Tāshkend.

Gets a reinforcement of Moghuls.

Takes Nasūkh.

---

[1] [Governor.]
[2] Shah Begum was one of Yunis Khan's widows [and Bābur's step-grandmother].

time, and leaving Kandbādām on the left, in the course of the night, reached and applied scaling-ladders to the fortress of Nasūkh, which is ten farsangs from Khojend and three[1] from Kandbādām, and carried the place by surprise. It was the season when the melons were ripe, and at Nasūkh there is a sort of melon termed *Ismāīl sheikhi*, the skin of which is yellow and puckered like shagreen leather; they are in great abundance. The seeds are about the size of those of an apple, and the pulp four fingers thick. It is a remarkably delicate and agreeable melon, and there is none equal to it in that quarter. Next morning the Moghul Begs represented to me that we had only a handful of men, and that no possible benefit could result from keeping possession of a single insulated castle. Indeed there was truth in what they said; so that, not finding it expedient to remain there and garrison the fort, I retired and went back to Khojend.

But abandons it.

Khosrou Shah and Baiesanghar Mirza take Hissār.

This same year Khosrou Shàh, accompanied by Baiesanghar Mirza, marched with an army to Cheghāniān, and, with the most deceitful and treacherous intentions, sent an embassy to Sultan Masaūd Mirza, inviting him to join them in their enterprise against Samarkand; proposing that, if they conquered it, the one Mirza should fix the seat of his government in Samarkand, and the other in Hissār. At this time very general discontents prevailed among the Begs, courtiers, cavaliers, and soldiers of Sultan Masaūd. The reason of their dissatisfaction was, that Sheikh Abdallah Birlās, who had left Sultan Baiesanghar Mirza to join Sultan Masaūd Mirza, and who was the Mirza's father-in-law, had obtained great rank and confidence; and, though Hissār is but a narrow and confined country, Sultan Masaūd Mirza had given him an allowance of a thousand *tumāns*[2] in

---

[1] Forty miles from Khojend and twelve from Kandbādām.

[2] It is extremely difficult to fix the value of money in remote periods. The *tumān*, in Della Valle's time (A. D. 1617), was 10 zecchins *Voyages*, vol. iv, p. 357). Mandelsloe soon after values the zecchin at $8\frac{1}{2}$ or 9 rupees; which would make the *tumān* of that day worth £9 or £10 sterling. In Chardin's time the *tumān* was equal to 45 livres; and Tavernier makes it equal to 46 livres, 1 denier, 1-5th; or, according to his English translator, at the then par of 4s. 6d. for the French crown, £3 9s. and a fraction. The livre, it will be remembered, like the *tumān*, has been sinking in value. Fryer (*Travels*,

money, besides the whole country of Khutlān. Khutlān was the *jagīr*[1] of the Begs and officers about Sultan Masaūd Mirza's person. Sheikh Abdallah Birlās, however, got possession of the whole, and he and his sons gained a complete ascendancy and unlimited direction of affairs at the court. Such as were dissatisfied fled and joined Baiesanghar Mirza. Khosrou Shah and Baiesanghar Mirza having lulled Sultan Masaūd Mirza into a careless security by their deceitful professions, after a sudden march from Cheghāniān, appeared before Hissār about the beat of the morning drum, invested and took it.

At this time Sultan Masaūd Mirza was not within the fortress, but at a palace in the vicinity,[a] which had been built by his father, called the Doulet Serāi. Finding it impossible to throw himself into the fort, he fled towards Khutlān, accompanied by Sheikh Abdallah Birlās; but having separated from him on the road, he proceeded by the Pass of Ubāj[2] and took refuge with Sultan Hussain Mirza.

<small>Sultan Masaūd takes refuge with SultanHussain Mirza.</small>

As soon as Khosrou Shah had taken Hissār, he placed Baiesanghar Mirza in it, and gave Khutlān to his younger brother Wali. A few days after he set out against Balkh. Having dispatched before him one of his principal retainers, named Nazar Bahāder, with four thousand men, to occupy the environs of that place, he himself followed soon afterwards, accompanied by Baiesanghar Mirza, and commenced

<small>Khosrou Shah lays siege to Balkh.</small>

[a] in the suburbs outside the city wall,

---

p. 222) makes the *tumān* £3 and a noble. It was lately worth an English guinea, and from incessant tampering with the coin, is now worth little more than 15 shillings. As the decline has been constant, it was probably, in Bābur's time, worth more than the highest of these sums.

The *shahrukhi* was a silver coin of the value of tenpence or elevenpence English, two and a half *shahrukhis* being equal to a rupee in Akber's time.

The *tang*, or *tankah*, was a small silver coin, of which, in Mandelsloe's time, 14, 15, or 16 went to a *pagoda*. It was of the value of about fivepence, and was formerly more. It has now declined to about a penny. It seems to have been the sixth part of a *dirhem*.

The *dām* was an Indian copper coin, the fortieth part of a rupee.

[1] A *jagīr* is a territorial grant held under a prince, generally for a limited period, often, however, in perpetuity.

[2] Ubāj is a famous pass [i. e. ford] over the Amu, above Kobādiān.

the siege. Ibrahīm Hussain Mirza commanded in Balkh, and had with him a considerable number of Sultan Hussain Mirza's Begs.

Wali sent against Shaberghān.

Khosrou Shah at the same time sent his younger brother Wali with a large detachment to lay siege to Shaberghān,[1] and to ravage and destroy the country around. Wali was not able to approach Shaberghān, but sent out his troops to plunder the Īls and Ulūs (the wandering tribes and hordes) that occupied the desert of Zardek, which they accordingly did, carrying off above one hundred thousand sheep, and nearly three thousand camels. Proceeding thence, he pillaged the district of Sancherik,[a] and having taken prisoners and carried off a number of the inhabitants who had fled for refuge to the hills and there fortified themselves, he returned to Balkh and rejoined his elder brother.

While Khosrou Shah lay before Balkh, he one day sent Nazar Bahāder, who has been mentioned, to destroy the water-courses and spoil the waters in the environs of Balkh. Tengri Berdi Samānchi, an officer who had been brought forward by [b] Sultan Hussain Mirza, issued from the fort with seventy or eighty men, and having fallen in with Nazar Bahāder's party, met him face to face, beat him down from his horse, cut off his head, and returned back with it to the fort, having displayed singular bravery in the whole course of the affair.

Nazar Bahāder slain.

Sultan Hussain Mirza marches against Zulnūn Beg.

This same year Sultan Hussain Mirza levied an army and advanced to the fort of Bost [2] for the purpose of reducing to order Zulnūn Arghūn and Shah Shujaa his son; who,

[a] the districts of San and Jerik (two towns in the territory of Balkh),
[b] most in favour with

---

[1] [Three days' journey west of Balkh.]
[2] Sultan Hussain Mirza had advanced with his army to Zamīndāwer, but found himself forced to retreat into Khorasān. He previously, however, laid siege to Bost, in which were some of Zulnūn's stores. The garrison, by holding out a few days, might have starved the besiegers; but the governor, Abdal Rahmān Arghūn, surrendered after a feeble resistance. Kila Bost lies on the left bank of the Helmend, below Zamīn-dāwer, which lies higher up towards the hills, on the right bank of the Siāhbend river.

having joined Badīa-ez-zemān Mirza, and given him a daughter of Zulnūn's in marriage, were now in a state of rebellion and revolt. On that occasion, when the Sultan could not procure supplies of grain for the army from any quarter, and was on the point of being compelled to raise the siege, and of being reduced to the last extremity from famine, the governor surrendered the fort, and the stores found in the granaries enabled the army to return to Khorasān. Takes Bost.

When a king like Sultan Hussain Mirza, who was attended with such royal equipage, and displayed so much pomp and state, had led his army on several different occasions against Kunduz, Hissār, and Kandahār, and had in every instance returned unsuccessful, his sons and Begs were spirited up to venture on seditions and rebellion. Sultan Hussain Mirza had dispatched Muhammed Wali Beg, with a number of Begs and the bulk of his army,[a] for the purpose of chastising his son Muhammed Hussain Mirza, who was in revolt, and gaining ground at Asterābād,[b] with instructions to advance upon him by rapid marches. He himself, meanwhile, remained encamped in the *auleng* (or meadow) of Nīshīn;[1] when Badīa-ez-zemān Mirza, and Shah Beg the son of Zulnūn, having collected a body of troops, came on him by surprise. By a most fortunate accident, Sultan Masaūd Mirza, who had just lost Hissār, came that very day to join Sultan Hussain Mirza; and, in the course of the same day, the army that had been detached against Asterābād, having returned back, also joined him. When the two armies therefore came to face each other, the enemy found themselves too weak to venture on a battle, and Badīa-ez-zemān Mirza and Shah Beg took to flight. Sultan Hussain Mirza received Sultan Masaūd Mirza in the most gracious manner, gave him one of his daughters in marriage, and distinguished him by every mark of attention and kindness. Seduced, however, by the instigations of Bākī Cheghāniānī, the younger brother of Khosrou Shah, who Sultan Hussain Mirza's sons rebel.

[a] a large army,
[b] and had proclaimed his independence in Asterābād,

[1] Near Herāt.

some time before had entered into the service of Sultan Hussain Mirza, he did not continue in Khorasān, but went off, under some false pretext, without even taking leave of Sultan Hussain Mirza, and joined Khosrou Shah.

Sultan Masaūd Mirza leaves his court.

Khosrou Shah now sent for Baiesanghar Mirza from Hissār. At this time Mirān Shah Mirza, the son of Ulugh Beg Mirza,[1] who had rebelled against his father and taken shelter among the Hazāras, having done something which gave them offence, was obliged to leave them also, and now came to Khosrou Shah. Some evil-minded counsellors advised Khosrou Shah to put all the three princes to death, and to cause the *khutbeh*[2] to be read in his own name. He did not fall into this plan, but yet, for the sake of this fleeting and faithless world, which never was, and never will be, true to any one, this thankless and ungrateful man seized Sultan Masaūd Mirza, a prince whom he himself had reared from infancy to manhood, and whose governor he had been, and blinded him by lancing his eyes. Some of the foster-brothers, clansmen, and playmates [a] of Masaūd Mirza carried him off, with the intention of conducting him to Sultan Ali Mirza in Samarkand, and brought him to Kesh.[3] Here, discovering a plan that had been formed for attacking them, they fled, crossed the river Amu by the passage of Chār-jūi, and took refuge with Sultan Hussain Mirza. Every day until the day of judgement, may a hundred thousand curses light on the head of that man who is guilty of such black treachery, and on his who plans it: let every man who hears of this action of Khosrou Shah, pour out imprecations on him; for he who hears of such a deed and does not curse him, is himself worthy to be accursed.

His eyes put out by Khosrou Shah.

After this abominable transaction, having declared Baiesanghar Mirza King, he sent him off to Hissār; and,

---

[a] foster-brothers, friends, and old servants

[1] This Ulugh Beg Mirza was not the illustrious sovereign of Samarkand, but the king of Kābul, and a brother of Bābur's father.
[2] The prayer for the prince.
[3] [According to P. de C. this was the chief town of a fertile and well-watered district some thirty miles south-east of Samarkand on the road to Karshi. It is generally known as Shah-i-sabz.]

at the same time, sent Mirān Shah Mirza towards Bāmiān, accompanied by Syed Kāmil, who was to lend him his assistance.

TRANSACTIONS OF THE YEAR 904 [1]

HAVING failed in repeated [a] expeditions against Samarkand and Andejān, I once more returned to Khojend. Khojend is but a small place; and it is difficult for one to support two hundred retainers in it. How, then, could a man, ambitious of empire, set himself down contentedly in so insignificant a place?

In order to forward my views against Samarkand, I now sent some persons to Muhammed Hussain Korkān Dughlet, who held Uratippa, to confer with him, and induce him to lend me for one winter Peshāgher, which is one of the villages of Yār-ailāk. It had formerly belonged to the reverend Khwājeh, but, during the confusions, had become dependent on him; and my plan now was, to take up my residence there, and attempt whatever circumstances might suggest against Samarkand. Muhammed Hussain Dughlet gave his consent, and I left Khojend, on my way to Peshāgher.

Bābur gets Peshāgher for one winter.

When I reached Zamīn, I was seized with a fever; notwithstanding which, I mounted, and, having left that place, proceeded with great speed, by the mountain-route against Rabāt-e-Khwājeh,[2] which is the seat of the Dārōgha, or governor of the Tumān of Shādwār, in the hope that we might have been able to come upon it and apply our scaling-ladders unobserved, and so carry the place by surprise. I reached it at daybreak; but, finding the garrison on the alert, retreated, and reached Peshāgher, without halting anywhere. In spite of my fever, I had ridden fourteen farsangs, though with great difficulty, and I suffered much from the exertion.

Attempt to surprise Rabāt-e-Khwājeh.

In a few days, I dispatched Ibrahīm Sāru, Weis Lāghari, and Shīrīm Taghāi, with some Begs of my party, and a body

Reduces the forts of Yār-ailāk;

[a] two successive

[1] This year of the Hijra began August 19, 1498.
[2] It lies west of Samarkand.

of my partisans and adherents, to proceed without loss of time, and reduce, either by negotiation or by force, all the fortresses of Yār-ailāk. At this time, Syed Yūsef Beg was in command of the district of Yār-ailāk. He had remained behind in Samarkand when I abandoned it, and had been well treated by Sultan Ali Mirza.[1] Syed Yūsef Beg had sent his brother and younger son [a] for the purpose of occupying and managing Yār-ailāk. Ahmed Yūsef, who at present has the government of Siālkot,[2] was in charge of the fortresses. My Begs and soldiers set out accordingly; and exerting themselves with uncommon activity during the whole winter, gained possession of the strong places, some by negotiation, some by storm, and others by artifice and stratagem. In consequence of the incursions of the Moghuls and Usbeks, there is not a village in the whole district of Yār-ailāk which is not converted into a fortress. On the occasion in question, suspicions being entertained of Syed Yūsef Beg, his younger brother, and son, on account of their known attachment to me, they were all sent away to Khorasān.

The winter passed in such efforts and attempts as these. In the spring, Sultan Ali Mirza sent Khwājeh Yahya to treat with me, while he himself marched with his army [b] into the neighbourhood of Shirāz and Kābad. My soldiers, though above two hundred in number, did not amount to three hundred; and the enemy was in great force. I had hovered for a while about Andejān, but my star had not prospered. Samarkand, too, had slipped out of my hands.[c] I was now compelled by necessity to make some sort of peace, and returned back from Peshāgher.

but is forced to abandon them.

Khojend is an inconsiderable place, from which a single Beg would have found it difficult to have supported himself.

[a] his younger brother and his son
[b] compelled by his army, marched
[c] The attempted attack on Samarkand had failed.

---

[1] When Bābur abandoned Samarkand to march for Andejān, the former place was occupied by Sultan Ali Mirza from Bokhāra. Indeed that prince was Bābur's ally, and had an army in the neighbourhood when Bābur first entered the place.

[2] In the Panjāb.

There, however, I had remained with my whole family, for a year and a half, or nearly two years. The Musulmans of the place, during all that time, had strained themselves to the utmost extent of their abilities to serve me.[a] With what face, therefore, could I return to Khojend, and, indeed, what benefit could result from it ?

(*Tūrki couplet*) There was no secure place for me to go to,
  And no place of safety for me to stay in.

In this state of irresolution and uncertainty, I went to the Ailāks,[1] to the south of Uratippa, and spent some time in that quarter, perplexed and distracted with the hopeless state of my affairs.[b] *Wanders among the Ailāks.*

One day, while I remained there, Khwājeh Abul Makāram, who, like myself, was an exile and a wanderer, came to visit me. I took the opportunity of consulting him with respect to my situation and concerns—whether it was advisable for me to remain where I was, or to go elsewhere—what I should attempt, and what I should leave untried. He was so much affected with the state in which he found me, that he shed tears, and, after praying over me,[2] took his departure. I myself was also extremely affected. *Visited by Khwājeh Makāram.*

That very day, about afternoon prayers, a horseman was descried at the bottom of the valley. He proved to be a servant of Ali Dost Taghāi, named Yūljūk. He came with a message from his master, to inform me that he had undoubtedly offended deeply, but that he trusted to my clemency for forgiving his past offences; and that, if I would march to join him, he would deliver up Marghinān to me, and would do me such service and duty as would wipe away his past errors, and free him from his disgrace. *Invited to Marghinān.*

Instantly on hearing this news,[c] without delay, I that

[a] *Add* and furnish us with supplies.
[b] *Add* not knowing whether I ought to go or stay, my head in a whirl.
[c] *Add* which reached me when I did not know which way to turn, I hesitated no longer and

---

[1] [i. e. summer encampments.]
[2] [P. de C. has 'recited the *fātihah* over me'. The *fātihah*, or opening chapter of the Qurān, is held in great veneration by Muslims, and is recited, like the Paternoster, over sick or distressed persons.]

very moment (it was then about sunset) set out post for Marghinān. From the place where I then was to Marghinān may be a distance of twenty-four or twenty-five farsangs. That night till morning, and the next day till the time of noon-day prayers, I halted in no place whatsoever. About noon-day prayers, I halted at a village of Khojend, named Tunek-āb;[1] and, after having refreshed our horses, and fed and watered them, we again mounted at midnight, left Tunek-āb, rode all that night till morning, and all next day till sunset, and, just before sunrise the following morning, we came within one farsang of Marghinān. Weis Beg and some others, after considering matters, now represented to me, that Ali Dost Taghāi was one who had stickled at no crimes; that there had been no repeated interchange of messengers between us—no terms or conditions agreed upon; with what confidence, therefore, could we put ourselves in his power[a]? In truth, these reflections had reason on their side. I therefore halted a little, and held a consultation, when it was finally agreed, that, though our reflections were not without foundation, we had been too late of making them. We had now passed three days and three nights without rest; and we had come a distance of twenty-five farsangs without stopping; that neither man nor horse had any strength left; that there was no possibility of retreating, and, even if we could retreat, no place of safety to retire to; that, since we had come so far, we must proceed. Nothing happens but by the will of God. Reposing ourselves on His protection, we went forward.

About the time of the *sunnet*[2] (or morning prayer), we reached the gate of the castle of Marghinān. Ali Dost Taghāi stood over[b] the gateway, without throwing the gate open, and desired conditions. After I had assented to terms, and given him my promise, he caused the gates to

[a] could we advance? [b] behind

[1] [Shallow water.]
[2] The *sunnet* are voluntary devotions, in which the prophet indulged the true believers, to fill up the long interval between the first prayer at *saher*, or morning twilight, and the noon-day prayers. They are exclusive of the five stated times enjoined by the Divinity.

be opened, and paid his respects to me, conducting me to a suitable house within the fort. The men who had accompanied me amounted, great and small, to two hundred and forty.

Ūzūn Hassan and Sultan Ahmed Tambol had, I found, conducted themselves very ill, and behaved with great tyranny to the people of the country. The whole inhabitants now anxiously wished for my restoration. Two or three days after my arrival in Marghinān, therefore, I dispatched Kāsim Beg, with a party of my Peshāgher men, a few others who had recently entered my service, and some of Ali Dost Beg's people, in all rather above a hundred men, with instructions to proceed to the south of Andejān, to the people of the hill country, such as the Ashparis, the Tūrūkshārs, the Jagrags, and others in that quarter, and to attempt to prevail upon them, either by negotiation or force, to make their submission. I also sent Ibrahīm Sāru, Weis Lāghari, and Sayyidī Kāra, with about a hundred men, towards Akhsi, with instructions to pass the river of Khojend, to use all means to gain possession of the forts,[a] and to conciliate and win over the people of the hills.

A few days after, Ūzūn Hassan and Sultan Ahmed Tambol, having taken Jehāngīr Mirza along with them, and collected all the soldiers and Moghuls that they had, and taken from Andejān and Akhsi every man able to bear arms, advanced with the intention of laying siege to Marghinān, and halted at a village named Sapān, which lies about a kos to the eastward of that town. After two or three days, having arrayed and accoutred their host, they came up to the suburbs of Marghinān. Although I had detached Kāsim Beg, Ibrahīm Sāru, Weis Lāghari, and other officers, on service to two different quarters, and only a very few troops remained with me, yet having armed and put in array such as I had, we marched out, and would not permit them to advance beyond the skirts of the suburbs. This day, Khalīl Chihreh Dastār-pech [1] distinguished himself greatly, and fought with singular valour. The enemy could effect

[a] *Omit* to gain possession of the forts, and

[1] [The page whose duty it was to twist his master's turban.]

nothing. Two succeeding attempts were equally frustrated, and they were unable to reach the fortress.

Kāsim Beg gains over the Ashparis, &c.

Kāsim Beg, who had proceeded to the hill country to the south of Andejān, completely brought over the Ashparis, the Tūrūkshārs, the Jagrags, and all the people of that country, both the peasants settled in the hills and plains, and the Aimāks.[1] The enemy's soldiers, too, began to desert by ones and twos, and came and joined me.

Ibrahīm Sāru is put in possession of Pāp, Akhsi, &c.

Ibrahīm Sāru, Weis Lāghari, and the other chiefs who had passed the river towards Akhsi, possessed themselves of the fort of Pāp, and of one or two other forts. Uzūn Hassan and Tambol were tyrannical and debauched, and the peasants and men of the country were disgusted with their proceedings. Hassan Degchi, one of the chief men of Akhsi, with his own followers and a body of the mob and rabble of the place, having armed themselves with sticks and clubs, attacked and drove the garrison of Akhsi out of the place [a] and forced them to take refuge in the citadel. They then invited Ibrahīm Sāru, Weis Lāghari, Sayyidī Kāra, and the chiefs who were along with them,[b] and gave them admittance into the fortified town of Akhsi.

Sultan Mahmūd Khan had dispatched to my assistance Bandeh Ali, Haider, his own foster-brother,[c] with Hāji Ghāzi Monghit,[2] who had fled about this time from Sheibāni Khan, and come over to the Khan, together with the Begs of the Tumān of Bārīn. They arrived at this very crisis, and joined the detachment.

Uzūn Hassan sends a detachment to the relief of the citadel of Akhsi;

Uzūn Hassan was alarmed on receiving this intelligence. He dispatched a party of his most trusty adherents, and of his bravest partisans, to the relief of the citadel of Akhsi. They reached the bank of the river about morning twilight. When notice of this was communicated to my army and to that of the Moghuls, a party was directed to strip their horses of all their furniture, and to be ready to enter the

---

[a] the outer fort   [b] *Omit this clause.*
[c] Haidar Kokultāsh's (son)

[1] The Aimāks were the wandering [pastoral] tribes.
[2] The Monghits are the modern Nogais.

river. The party which was going to relieve the citadel, having, in their confusion and alarm, neglected to pull the boat sufficiently up the stream, dropped down below the place from which they had embarked, and were unable to make the fort, so that the vessel was carried lower down. My troops and the Moghuls, who had stripped their horses, plunged on all sides into the river. The men in the boat, being panic-struck, were unable to defend themselves. Karlughāch Bakhshi [1] having invited one of the sons of Moghul Beg to come to him, laid hold of his hand, and slew him with his sword. What purpose did such an act of treachery serve? Things were now all over; and this cruel deed was the occasion of the death of the greater part of those who were in the boat; for our people, who had rode into the water, dragged them on shore, and put them almost all to death. Of the confidential servants of Ūzūn Hassan, Karlughāch Bakhshi, Khalīl Dīwāneh, and Kazi Gholām were on board. Of these, Kazi Gholām escaped, by pretending to be a slave. Another man of note who escaped was Syed Ali, who is now with me, and high in office. Another was Haider Kuli Kilkeh Kāshghari.[a] Of seventy or eighty experienced and chosen warriors, not more than five or six escaped.

which is cut to pieces.

On receiving information of these occurrences, the enemy, being unable to maintain themselves in the vicinity of Marghinān, moved off in great disorder towards Andejān. They had left in Andejān Nāsir Beg, who had married Ūzūn Hassan's sister, and who, if not next to Ūzūn Hassan in consequence, was, beyond contradiction, in possession of the third place. He was a man of sense and experience, and possessed of courage. Having learned the recent occurrences, and knowing on what an unstable basis the cabal rested, he brought over the garrison of Andejān to my interest,[b] and sent a person to invite me to the city. When the cabal reached Andejān, and found that it had declared

The rebels retire from Marghinān.

Andejān declares for Bābur.

[a] Others were Haidar Kuli and Kilkeh Kāshghari.
[b] and seeing that they were threatened with destruction by my enemies, he fortified Andejān,

[1] [Paymaster.]

for me, and was held on my account, being unable to agree among themselves, and in the greatest confusion, Ūzūn Hassan retired towards the citadel of Akhsi to his family; Sultan Ahmed Tambol drew off to Ush to his own government, while Jehāngīr Mirza was seized by a party of his adherents and followers, who carried him off from Ūzūn Hassan and fled with him to Tambol. They overtook Tambol before he had reached Ush, and accompanied him in his retreat.

Who again enters his capital.

June 1499.

As soon as I received advice that the garrison of Andejān had declared for me, I made no delay, but setting out at sunrise from Marghinān, reached Andejān when the day was on the decline. I saw and conversed with Nāsir Beg and his sons, Dost Beg and Mīram Beg, treated them with every mark of kindness, and gave them reason to expect everything from my favour. And thus, by the grace of the Most High, in the month of Zilkaadeh, and year nine hundred and four, I recovered my paternal kingdom, of which I had been deprived nearly two years.

Tambol expelled from Ush.

Retires to Uzkend.

Sultan Ahmed Tambol, who had proceeded towards Ush, accompanied by Jehāngīr Mirza, no sooner arrived there, than the rabble and common people, arming themselves with sticks and clubs, made a furious attack upon him, drove them fairly out of the town, and sent persons to give me notice that they held the place on my account. Jehāngīr Mirza and Tambol, with a few partisans who still adhered to them, retired in great dismay to Uzkend.

Ūzūn Hassan retires to the citadel of Akhsi,

but surrenders to Bābur,

Ūzūn Hassan, on seeing himself shut out of Andejān, retreated to Akhsi, and information reached me that he had entered the citadel. As he was the very head and ringleader of the rebellion, without staying more than four or five days in Andejān, I marched against Akhsi. No sooner had I arrived there, than, as he had nothing else left for it, he offered to capitulate, asked quarter, and surrendered the fort. After a few days' stay at Akhsi, which I employed in putting the affairs and government of that city and of Kāsān [a] into a proper state of order and arrangement, I dismissed the Moghul Begs who had come to my assistance

---

[a] *Add* and all the country round

on this enterprise, and returned to Andejān, carrying with me Ūzūn Hassan, his family and dependants. Kāsim Ajab, who was of the inferior class of Begs,[a] being raised to a higher rank, was left in the temporary charge of Akhsi.

As I had agreed that Ūzūn Hassan should suffer no injury either in life or property, I allowed him to depart by way [1] of Karatigīn on his road to Hissār. He proceeded towards Hissār with a small retinue, while all the rest of his followers separated from him and remained behind. These were the very men who, during the late disturbances, had pillaged and plundered my adherents and Khwājeh Kazi's men. Several of my Begs united in their representations, telling me,[b] 'This is the very band which has been the cause of all these confusions, and the origin of all the devastations that have afflicted us; these are the men who have plundered so many of the faithful and true believers who adhered to us. What fidelity have they shown to their own chiefs that they should now be faithful to us? What harm would there be if they were seized, or an order given for plundering them? Especially as they are riding our own horses, wearing our garments, and killing and eating our own sheep before our eyes. What patience can possibly endure all this? If from compassion you do not plunder them, or give orders for a general pillage, at least let us, who have adhered to you in all your dangers and difficulties, be permitted to resume whatever part of our property we find in the possession of these men. If they get off on these terms, they ought to be very thankful.' In fine, I agreed to the plan, and an order was issued that such as had accompanied me in my campaigns, might resume possession of whatever part of their property they recognized. Although the order seemed reasonable and just in itself, yet it had been issued with too much precipitation; and, when there was a rival like Jehāngīr Mirza at my elbow, it was a senseless thing to exasperate so many men who had arms in their hands. In war and in affairs of state, though there

and goes to Hissār.

His adherents plundered.

[a] an officer of the household,
[b] After deliberating with several Begs, we came to the following agreement,

[1] That is across the Asfera Hills.

are many things that appear just and reasonable at first sight, yet no matter ought to be finally fixed without being well weighed, and considered in a hundred different lights. From my issuing this single order without sufficient foresight, what commotions and mutinies arose! This inconsiderate order of mine was in reality the ultimate cause of my being a second time expelled from Andejān.

The Moghuls mutiny and revolt from Bābur.

The Moghuls being filled with alarm, mutinied and marched away from Rabātiki-Urchīnī, which they also call Miān-Doāb, towards Uzkend, and sent a person to Tambol to offer him their services. There were with my mother one thousand five hundred or nearly two thousand Moghuls, and about the same number may have come from Hissār along with Hamzeh Sultan, Mahdi Sultan, and Muhammed Dughlet. The horde of Moghuls have uniformly been the authors of every kind of mischief and devastation; down to the present time they have five times rebelled against me. Nor have they mutinied only against me, which might have proceeded from some incompatibility of temper, but they are perpetually guilty of the same offence against their own Khans.

The news of this defection was brought me by Sultan Kuli Chanāk, whose father, Khuda-berdi Bughāk, I had greatly distinguished among the Moghuls. His father had died some time before, and he himself now served along with them. He did me good service by separating himself from his own clan and kin, and bringing me this information; but though, on this occasion, he was useful to me, he was, finally, as will be mentioned, guilty of such villainy as would have wiped away a hundred services like that in question;[1] and the main cause of his future villainy was also his being a Moghul.

Tambol defeats his army.

As soon as I received this information, I assembled the Begs and held a consultation. They were of opinion that it was a trifling occurrence, and that there was no necessity for the King himself to take the field; that Kāsim Beg, with a few of the Begs and a detachment of the army, might proceed on the service. This was accordingly resolved on.

---

[1] [The reference is to the Mutiny of Ghaznah in 1515, in which Sultan Kuli Chanāk took part, and which was crushed by Bābur's forces under Kambar Ali (*T. R.*, p. 357).]

They imagined that it was an easy matter, but were woefully mistaken. That same day Kāsim Beg marched out with his Begs and army, but before they had come to their ground, and while still on their march, Tambol himself arrived and joined the Moghuls. Early next morning, the moment they [1] had passed the river Ailamish at the ford of Yasi-kijet,[2] the two armies met face to face and had a desperate action; Kāsim Beg himself meeting Sultan Muhammed Arghūn, struck him two or three blows one after another with his sword, but did not slay him. Several of my cavaliers made very gallant charges, but they were finally defeated. Kāsim Beg, Ali Dost Taghāi, Ibrahīm Sāru, Weis Lāghari, and Sayyidī Kāra, with three or four others of my Begs and officers, escaped. Most of the other Begs and officers fell into the hands of the enemy. Among these were Ali Derwīsh Beg, Mīram Lāghari, Tūkah Beg, Taghāi Beg, Muhammed Dost, Ali Dost, Mīr Shah Kuchīn, and Mīram Dīwān. In this battle two cavaliers had a gallant combat. On my side was Samad, one of Ibrahīm Sāru's younger brothers, and on the other side was Shah-sawār, one of the Moghuls of Hissār. They met hand to hand, and Shah-sawār urged his blow with such force, that he drove his sabre right through Samad's helmet, and fixed it pretty deep in his skull. In spite of this wound, Samad returned the blow with such fury, that his sword shore clean off a piece of Shah-sawār's skull as big as the palm of the hand. As Shah-sawār had no helmet on, the wound in his head was properly bound up and he recovered; but there being nobody to attend to Samad's wound, he died of it in three or four days.

This defeat came most unseasonably, just at the moment when I had escaped from a scene of petty warfare and disasters, and had again recovered my country. Kamber Ali Moghul, who was one of my great stays, had returned to his own government immediately after I had taken Andejān, and was not at hand. Tambol, following up his success, brought Jehāngīr along with him, and, accompanied by all his forces, advanced within a farsang of Andejān to a plain in face of the rising ground of Aīsh,

[1] [i. e. Bābur's force.]   [2] [Wide-ford.]

Tambol advances to Andejān,

where he encamped.[a] He once or twice put his army in order of battle, and advanced from Chihil-dukhterān[1] to the skirts of Aīsh. My troops, too, moved out and formed on the outside of the suburbs and garden grounds. His advance was checked, and he retreated from the skirts of the hill to another position. It was during this same advance towards the city that he put to death Mīram Lāghari and Tūkah, two of the Begs who had fallen into his hands. After lying nearly a month before the city, and effecting nothing, he returned towards Ush. I had given Ush to Ibrahīm Sāru, whose men were in the place. They held it on my account.

but is obliged to retire.

TRANSACTIONS OF THE YEAR 905 [2]

Bābur assembles his army.

I NOW dispatched commissaries and officers to collect the whole force of my territories, horse and foot, with all possible speed; and, by means of special messengers, I summoned Kamber Ali, and such of the troops as had gone to their own homes, to return without loss of time. I also dispatched commissaries and officers to procure *tūras*,[3] scaling-ladders, shovels, axes, and all kinds of necessaries and stores for the use of the army. I appointed a place where the men, both horse and foot, who came from the different districts to the army, were to assemble.[b] My

[a] and encamped in a meadow which is situated facing the hill of Aīsh (=pleasure) at a distance of a *shar'i kos* (2 miles) from Andejān.

[b] I collected all the men, both horse and foot, who were called up to join the army from the different districts.

---

[1] [Forty daughters.]
[2] This year begins on August 8, 1499.
[3] The *tūra* is often mentioned in the course of these Memoirs, and always on occasion of the siege of some fort, except at the great battle fought with Sultan Ibrahīm above Delhi. I have been able to get no particular account of it. Petis de la Croix describes it as being a large buckler, and probably several of these being joined formed a defence like the Roman *testudo*, under cover of which the besiegers advanced to undermine the wall, or to mount their scaling-ladders. At the siege of Karshi, 'les ennemis pour mieux fuir jetterent leurs grands boucliers nommés Toura, et en se couvrant *la tête* de leurs petits ecus, ils se retirerent dans des retranchements qu'ils avoient faits par precaution.'—*Hist. de Timur Bec*, vol. i, p. 121. [According to P. de C. the *tūra* consisted of pieces of wood and iron fastened together by means of chains and hooks, forming a kind of shield, under cover of which the soldiers advanced to the attack.]

servants and soldiers, who had gone off in different directions, on business or service, were recalled ; and, putting my confidence in God, on the 18th of Muharrem, I marched out and encamped at the Chār-bāgh of Hāfiz Beg. After halting a day or two at the Chār-bāgh in order to get ready such of the arms and stores as had remained incomplete, I marched towards Ush to meet the enemy, having my army divided into right and left wings, centre and advance, with cavalry and infantry all drawn out in regular array. *Aug. 25, 1499.*

When we arrived near Ush, I was informed that the army, finding that they could not maintain themselves in Ush, had retired towards Rabāt-e-Sarhang Urchīni, which lies north of that city. That evening I halted at Lātkend, and, the next morning, as I was passing Ush, learned that the enemy had directed their march on Andejān. We on our part approached Uzkend, and detached forward plundering parties to ravage the country and suburbs. The enemy, arriving at Andejān during the night, instantly entered the ditch ; but while they were planting their scaling-ladders against the ramparts, were discovered by the people within, so that the enterprise failed and they were compelled to retreat. My plundering parties advanced and committed devastations in the suburbs of Uzkend, but came back without acquiring any considerable booty. *And advances towards Uzkend. Tambol attempts to surprise Andejān.*

In one of the forts of Ush, named Mādu, which is distinguished for its superior strength, Tambol had left his younger brother Khalīl with a garrison of two hundred, or two hundred and fifty men. Against this fortress I now marched, and attacked it with great vigour.[a] The castle of Mādu is excessively strong. On the north side, where there is a river, it is very steep and precipitous. If an arrow be discharged from the river, it may perhaps reach the castle wall. Its supply of water is from a conduit on this side. From the bottom of the castle a sort of covered way, having ramparts on each side, reaches down to the river. All round the hillock there is a moat. As the river is near at hand, they had brought from its bed stones about the size of those used for battering cannon, and carried them up into *Bābur besieges Mādu,*

[a] I turned aside from my route to attack it.

the fort. Such a number of huge stones [1] as were launched from the fort of Mādu, in all the storms that I have witnessed, I never saw thrown from any other castle. Abdal Kadūs Kohbur, the elder brother of Kitteh Beg, having climbed up to the foot of the castle-wall, was hit by a large stone discharged from above, which sent him spinning down, heels over head, from that prodigious height, right forward, without touching anywhere till he lighted, tumbling and rolling, at the bottom of the glacis.[2] Yet he received no injury, and immediately mounted his horse and returned back to the camp. At the conduit which had the double wall, Yār Ali Belāl was severely wounded in the head with a stone. The wound was afterwards cut open and dressed. Many of our people suffered[3] from these stones. The morning after the attack, before breakfast time,[4] we had gained possession of the water-course. The action continued till evening, but after losing their water, they could no longer hold out; and next morning they asked for quarter and surrendered the place. Khalīl, the younger brother of Tambol, who was in command, with seventy, eighty, or a hundred of the most active young men, were kept as prisoners, and sent to Andejān to be put in close custody. This was a fortunate occurrence for such of my Begs, officers, and soldiers, as had fallen into the hands of the enemy.

and takes it.

The two armies face each other near Āb-khan.

After taking Mādu, I proceeded to Unjūtūbah, one of the villages of Ush. On the other hand, Tambol, after retreating from Andejān, encamped at a place called Āb-khan, one of the dependencies of Rabāt-e-Sarhang Urchīnī,[5] so that there was only the distance of about one

---

[1] Everything relative to artillery and battering engines, or machines used in sieges, is very indistinctly alluded to in these Memoirs. The Turki *kasan* and Persian *dig* are cannon. It is well known that the Ottomans and other eastern nations, as well as the nations of Europe, on the first invention of cannon, were fond of having them of a very large size, for the purpose of discharging immense stones. They trusted more to the effects of a few discharges than to any regular fire.

[2] The *khākrez* or glacis in Asia, is generally immediately at the foot of the wall, and not separated from it by the ditch.

[3] [i. e. perished.]   [4] *Chāsht gāh*, about 10 o'clock.—*Leyden.*

[5] [i. e. district.]

farsang between the two armies. At this time Kamber Ali, from ill health, was obliged to retire to Ush. For a month or forty days we remained in this posture. There was no general action during that time, but every day there were skirmishes between my foragers and theirs. During this period I paid great attention to support a strict look-out by night, and dug a trench all round the camp; where there was no ditch we placed branches of trees.[1] I made all our soldiers march out and present themselves, accoutred and ready for action, by the side of the ditch; but, notwithstanding all this care, every three or four nights there was an alarm in the camp, and a call to arms. One day Sayyidī Beg Taghāi having gone out to meet and cover the return of the foragers, the enemy came upon him in much superior force, and in the midst of the action that ensued, suddenly made him prisoner.

This year Khosrou Shah, having invited Baiesanghar Mirza to join him, under pretence of proceeding to attack Balkh, carried him to Kunduz, from which place they set out on their march against Balkh. When they had reached Ubāj, Khosrou Shah, the miserable and infidel-like wretch, betrayed by the ambition of usurping the sovereign power—(how is it possible for sovereignty to appertain to such a worthless and contemptible creature, who had neither birth, nor family, nor talents, nor reputation, nor wisdom, nor courage, nor justice, nor right?) yet this reptile seized upon Baiesanghar Mirza and his Begs, strangled him with a bow-string, and thus, on the tenth day of Muharrem, murdered this most accomplished and sweet-tempered prince, who was adorned with whatever endowments rank and birth could bestow. He also put to death a number of his Begs and confidential servants.

Khosrou Shah murders Baiesanghar Mirza.

August 17, 1499.

Baiesanghar Mirza was born in Hissār in the year 882, and was the second son of Sultan Mahmūd Mirza, being younger than Sultan Masaūd Mirza, and older than Sultan Ali Mirza, Sultan Hussain Mirza, and Sultan Weis Mirza, better known by the name of Khan Mirza. His mother was Pasheh Begum.

His birth and extraction. 1477.

He had large eyes, a round face, and was about the

His person and features.

[1] [i.e. palisades made of branches of trees (P. de C.).]

middle size; he had a Turkomān visage, and was an extremely elegant young man.

<small>His disposition and talents.</small>
He was a lover of justice, humane, of a pleasant disposition, and a perfectly accomplished prince. His tutor was Syed Muhammed, a Shīah, whence Baiesanghar himself was tainted with the notions of that sect. It is said, however, that latterly, while at Samarkand, he retracted the errors of that system, and became purely orthodox. He was excessively addicted to wine; but, during the times that he did not drink, was regular in the performance of his prayers. He was sufficiently generous and liberal. He wrote a fine Nastālīk hand, and had considerable skill in painting. He was also a poet, and assumed the poetical name of Aādili. The poems were not so numerous as to be formed into a *diwān*. The following verses are his:—[1] (Persian)

Like an unsubstantial shadow I fall here and there,
And if not supported by the face of a wall, drop flat on the ground.

In Samarkand the Odes (*ghazels*) of Baiesanghar Mirza are so popular, that there is not a house in which a copy of them may not be found.

<small>His wars.</small>
He fought two battles, one of them with Sultan Mahmūd Khan, when he first mounted the throne of Samarkand.[2] Sultan Mahmūd Khan, at the instigation of Sultan Juneid Birlās and some others, had advanced with an army for the purpose of conquering Samarkand, and marched by way of Ak-kūtal[3] as far as Rabāt-e-Soghd and Kānbāi. Baiesanghar Mirza marched from Samarkand to meet him, engaged him at Kānbāi, gave him a severe defeat, and ordered the heads of three or four thousand Moghuls to be struck off. Haider Gokultāsh, who was the Khan's prime adviser, fell in this battle. His second battle was with Sultan Ali Mirza at Bokhāra, in which he was defeated.[4]

<small>His dominions.</small>
His dominions consisted at first only of Bokhāra, which was given him by his father Sultan Mahmūd Mirza. On his father's death the Begs held a consultation, and agreed

---

[1] Bābur quotes the first verses of a well-known ode.
[2] [At Kānbāin, A.D. 1495. *E. B.*, p. 96.]
[3] The White Pass.—*Leyden*. A pass in the Ak-tāgh Mountains.
[4] [In A.D. 1496. *E. B.*, p. 99.]

on making him king of Samarkand also. He continued in possession of Bokhāra as well as Samarkand for some time; but he lost the former after the insurrection of the Terkhāns. [A.D. 1496.] When I took Samarkand, he retired to Khosrou Shah; and [A.D. 1497.] when Khosrou Shah took Hissār, he gave it to Baiesanghar.

He left no offspring. When he first went to Khosrou His family. Shah, he married the daughter of his paternal uncle, Sultan Khalīl Mirza. He had no other wife or concubine.

He never exercised the powers of an independent prince, even so far as to promote any one of the men of consequence about him to the rank of a Beg of the higher class. All his Begs were those of his father and paternal uncle.

After the death of Baiesanghar, Sultan Ahmed Karāwel,[1] Bābur's the father of Kūch Beg, with his brothers and relations, army reinforced. and their families and dependants, came through the country of Karatigīn,[2] and joined me, after giving me notice of their intentions. Kamber Ali, who had been sick in Ush, having recovered from his disorder, now also returned. Hailing as a good omen this unlooked-for arrival of Sultan Ahmed Karāwel and his party to my assistance, I next morning drew out my army in array, and moved against the enemy; who, not finding themselves strong enough to Tambol maintain their position at Āb-khan, marched off from their retreats in disorder, ground. A number of tents and carpets, and a quantity of baggage, fell into the hands of my soldiers. We advanced and occupied the same ground which the enemy had left. That same evening Tambol, taking Jehāngīr with him, passed on my left and entered Khūbān, a village on my and occupies flank, about three farsangs off, towards Andejān. Khūbān.

Early next morning, having drawn up my army in regular Bābur battle array, with right and left wing, centre and advance, offers Tambol and covered the horses with their housings of mail, accoutred battle, my men in their armour, formed them into lines, and sent forward the infantry that carried the *tūras*, we proceeded towards the enemy. Ali Dost Taghāi and his followers formed my right. On the left wing were stationed Ibrahīm Sāru, Weis Lāghari, Sayyidī Kāra, Muhammed Ali Mubasher,

[1] [i. e. scout.]
[2] Karatigīn lies in the hills north of Hissār and Khutlān, and south of Ferghāna.

Kūchik Beg¹ the elder brother of Khwājeh Kalān, and a number of others connected with Sultan Ahmed Karāwel and Kūch Beg, with their followers.ᵃ Kāsim Beg was with me in the centre. Kamber Ali, who had the advanced guard, with several of my adherents and young nobility, had reached Sākeh, a village to the south-east of Khūbān, and about a kos from it, when the enemy marched out of the village of Khūbān in battle array. Upon this we hastened our march as much as was compatible with prudence and the preservation of our order of battle. The *tūras* and infantry had, however, fallen somewhat behind when we engaged. By the divine favour their services were not required in the battle; for, at the instant of closing, the right wing of the enemy and my left having engaged hand to hand, Kūchik Beg, the elder brother of Khwājeh Kalān, smote so lustily that the enemy, unable to maintain their ground, took to flight: and the flankers² and right wing of my army had not an opportunity of coming into action.ᵇ We took a number of prisoners, whose heads I ordered to be struck off. My Begs, such as Kāsim Beg and Ali Dost Beg, but particularly Ali Dost, restrained the pursuit, being apprehensive of some danger from following the fugitives too far, by which means the greater part of them escaped. I halted at the village of Khūbān. This was my first battle,

and defeats him.

ᵃ some officers of my household, Sultan Ahmed, the scout, and Kūch Beg with his elder and younger brothers.

ᵇ *From* Kamber Ali (*line* 4) *to* action (*line* 18) *read*: Kambar Ali and some officers of my household formed the van. We had reached a place called Sākeh, situated some two miles to the south-east of Khūbān just when the enemy came out of the village in battle array. We thereupon hastened our march. The infantry, who were advancing with caution in order to preserve the symmetry of their ramparts of mantelets, and their line of battle, had fallen behind when we engaged. But, thanks to God, its services were not required. Before it came up our left wing was engaged with Tambol's right. Kūchik Beg, the elder brother of Khwāja Kalān Beg, displayed prodigies of valour. Next to him Muhammed 'Ali Munshi carried off the honours of the day. The enemy, being unable to make a stand, took to flight. Our right wing and van did not come into action.

¹ i. e. the little Beg.
² The *harāwel* [or *karāwal*] are properly small guards and pickets pushed on in advance, and along the flanks.

and Almighty God of his bounty and favour vouchsafed me the victory. I accepted it as a favourable omen. The day after we halted in this place my maternal grandmother, Shah Sultan Begum, came from Andejān for the purpose of begging off Jehāngīr Mirza if she had found him a prisoner. As the winter was at hand, and no grain or forage remained in the fields, I did not deem it advisable to advance against Uzkend, but returned to Andejān.

After some days I held a council, in which it was determined that my wintering in Andejān would in no degree tend to the injury of the enemy ; that it was rather to be feared that it would increase their force, by leaving the fields open to their ravages and enterprise ; that it was necessary to hut my troops in winter quarters, that my men might not be distressed for grain or provisions ; and that we might straiten the enemy by keeping them in some measure blocked up. In pursuance of this plan, having proceeded to Rabātiki-Urchīni, which is named Suārasī [1] from being between two rivers, I decamped from Andejān, and moved into the neighbourhood of Armiān and Nūshāb, with the intention of constructing winter cantonments in that vicinity, which we accordingly did. Around these villages there is excellent sporting ground, and good cover for game. Near the river Ilāmish,[a] in the jungle, there are great plenty of mountain-goats, stags, and wild hogs. In the smaller jungle, which is scattered and in clumps, there are abundance of excellent jungle-fowl [b] and hares. The foxes possess more fleetness than those of any other place.[c] While I remained in these winter quarters I rode a-hunting every two or three days. After scouring the larger forests, where we roused and hunted the mountain-goat and stags, we hawked in the smaller jungle for the jungle-fowl, and also shot them with forked arrows.[d] The jungle-fowl are here very fat. While we remained in these winter quarters we had the flesh of jungle-fowl in great abundance.

Huts his army for the winter.

[a] Irmich,   [b] pheasants
[c] On the high ground foxes are numerous. Their coats are of good colour, and they are fleeter than those of any other place.
[d] *Omit* and also shot them with forked arrows.

[1] [*Miyān-i-dūāb* in Persian.]

During my stay in these cantonments, Khuda-berdi the standard-bearer, whom I had lately honoured with the rank of Beg, two or three times fell on Tambol's foragers, routed them and cut off a number of their heads, which he brought back to the camp. The young men of the territory of Andejān and Ush also went out incessantly to plunder the enemy's country, drove away their herds of horses, killed their men, and reduced them to great distress. Had I remained the whole winter in these cantonments, there is every reason to believe that, by the return of spring, the enemy would have been reduced to the last extremity without fighting a battle; but at the moment when I had brought them to this state of distress and embarrassment, Kamber Ali asked leave to go to his government; and, whatever pains I took to impress these views on his mind, and though I forbade him to leave me, the brutal fellow persisted in his resolutions. He was a wonderfully fickle and perverse man. Compelled by necessity, I finally gave him permission to return to his country. His first government was Khojend; and recently when I took Andejān I had given him Asfera and Kandbādām; so that, of all my Begs, Kamber Ali had the greatest number of retainers and the greatest extent of country; no other equalled him in either of these respects. We remained forty or fifty days in these winter quarters. Being obliged to give leave to a number of men to go off, in the same way as I had done to Kamber Ali, in the end I myself found it expedient to return to Andejān.

Kamber Ali returns to his government.

Bābur dismisses his troops.

While I stayed in the winter cantonments,[a] some of Tambol's people were going back and forward without intermission to and from the Khan at Tāshkend. 'Ahmed Beg, who was the Governor [1] of Sultan Muhammed Sultan, the son of Sultan Mahmūd Khan, and who, of all his Begs, had been distinguished by the most conspicuous marks of his favour, was paternal uncle of the full blood to Tambol. Beg Tīlbeh, who was the Khan's Chamberlain,[2] was the

Sultan Mahmūd Khan reinforces Tambol.

[a] *Add* as well as during our sojourn at Andejān.

[1] Beg atkeh [= tutor].
[2] Ishek Agha.

elder brother of Tambol. By coming and going about the Khan, they wrought upon him to send a body of men to Tambol's assistance. Beg Tīlbeh, from his infancy, had been in Moghulistān, and had grown up to manhood among the Moghuls, but had never come into our countries, nor taken service with any of our princes, having always remained in the employment of the Khans. On the present occasion, before this reinforcement was sent, he left his wife and family in Tāshkend, and went and joined his younger brother Tambol.

At this time an awkward incident occurred to Kāsim Ajab, whom I had left in the temporary command of Akhsi. Having gone out with a few men in pursuit of a marauding party, he had followed them rather rashly, and crossed the river of Khojend at Bikhrātā in the pursuit, when he fell in with a large body of Tambol's men, and was taken prisoner.

Kāsim Ajab taken prisoner.

When Tambol learned the disbanding of my army, and had conferred with his elder brother Beg Tīlbeh, who had reached him with advices from the Khan,[a] and given him certain assurances of the coming of reinforcements, he marched from Uzkend to the district termed Suārasī between the two rivers. At the same time I received certain intelligence from Kāsān, that the Khan had sent off[b] his son Sultan Muhammed Khanckeh, who was generally called Sultānim, accompanied by Ahmed Beg, and five or six thousand men, who had passed by the route of Archehkend, and come and laid siege to Kāsān. Without constraining myself by waiting for such of my troops as were at a distance, taking with me only such of my men as were ready at hand, without delay, in the depth of winter, placing my reliance in Almighty God, I marched from Andejān by way of Bendsālār to attack Sultānim and Ahmed Beg. That night we halted nowhere, and next morning we arrived at Akhsi. The cold during the night was extremely intense,[1] insomuch that several of my people were frost-bitten in the hands and

Tambol advances to Suārasī.

Sulten Muhammed Khanckeh besieges Kāsān.

Bābur compels him to raise the siege.

[a] who had conferred with the Khan,
[b] *Add* to the aid of Tambol

[1] The caravans from Tobolsk to Bokhāra generally cross the Sirr below Tāshkend on the ice.

feet, and the ears of some of them were contracted and withered [a] like an apple. We did not tarry at Akhsi, but having placed Yārek Taghāi in charge of that place in the room of Kāsim Ajab, I passed on for Kāsān. When I arrived within one kos of Kāsān, I received intelligence that Ahmed Beg and Sultānim, on being informed of my approach, had broken up in confusion, and retreated in great haste.

Tambol arrives in the neighbourhood; The moment that Tambol knew of my march, he had set out with all speed to the assistance of his elder brother, and now came up. It was about the time between afternoon and evening prayers, when the blackness occasioned by the approach of Tambol's army became visible in the direction of Noukend.[1] Confounded and disconcerted at the sudden *but escapes* and unnecessary retreat of his elder brother, as well as by my *to Arkhiān.* expeditious arrival, he instantly drew up. I said, 'It is God himself that has conducted them hither, and brought them so far to fatigue their horses! Let us come on, and by the favour of God, not one of those who have fallen into our hands shall escape out of them.' Weis Lāghari and some others, however, represented that the day was now far spent; that if we let them alone that day it was out of their power to escape during the night, and that we could afterwards confront them wherever they were found.[b] This advice was followed, and they were not attacked. And thus when, by a piece of rare good fortune, the enemy had come, as if to put themselves in our power, we suffered them to get away without the slightest injury. There is a saying,

(*Tūrki*)—He that does not seize what comes into his grasp,
    Must indulge his regret even to old age, and repine.

Persian)—Occasion must be leaped on when it offers;
    The doings of the indolent, out of season, are utterly worthless.

Regarding the interval granted them till morning as most precious, they rested nowhere all night, but rode on till they

[a] swelled up
[b] 'Even if we do not attack them to-day, where can they go to-morrow? We will meet them in the morning wherever it may be.'

[1] Noukend seems to lie north of the Sirr, between Uzkend and Kāsān.

gained the fortress of Arkhiān. When morning came we went against the enemy, but they were not to be found. We pursued them, and as we did not judge it advisable to lay close siege to Arkhiān, encamped a kos from it in a village of Nemengān.[1] We continued thirty or forty days in this station, while Tambol remained in the fortress of Arkhiān. Small parties sometimes advanced from my army, and were met by parties from the fort, when skirmishes ensued in the ground between us. One night they made a sally to surprise us, but stopped on the outside of the camp, and retired, after discharging a few arrows. We drew a trench around the camp, and fenced it with branches of trees, so that they could do us no injury.

Bābur pursues him.

While we remained in this encampment, Kamber Ali, who had taken umbrage, was two or three times on the point of returning to his own government; he once actually mounted, and had set out, but several Begs being sent after him, with a great deal of difficulty prevailed on him to come back.

Kamber Ali discontented.

About the same time Syed Yūsef Machemi sent a person to Sultan Ahmed Tambol to inform him of his wish to enter his service, and finally joined him. Among the districts along the bottom of the hills of Andejān, there are two called Oīghūr and Machem. Syed Yūsef was the *kalān*[2] or Head-man of Machem. He had lately become known to me, by sight, among my courtiers, had taken it into his head to shake off the *kalāntar*, and affected the airs of a Beg, though nobody had ever made him a Beg. He was a wonderfully sly, treacherous, unsettled sort of a creature. From the period when I took Andejān[3] until the present occasion, he had two or three times joined me against Tambol, and two or three times gone over and joined Tambol against me. This, however, was the last time that

Defection of Syed Machemi.

[1] Ghazneh Nemengān.—*Tūrki.* A marginal note on the Tūrki manuscript says, that it is the name of a Tumān (or district). Leyden explains it as *the bound of arrow-mark.* [According to P. de C., Nemengān is a village situated to the north of Nukent. He adds that for Ghaznah the Persian version reads *qaryah* (village).]

[2] The *kalān*, or rather *kalāntar*, is a sort of mayor of the towns of Persia.

[3] [A. D. 1499.]

he ever rebelled. He had with him a number of Īls, Ulūses, and Aimāks.[1] 'They must be prevented from uniting with Tambol,' we exclaimed, 'and we must catch him on the road.' So saying, we took to horse. On the third day we reached the vicinity of Bishkhārān, but Tambol had arrived and entered the fort. Of the Begs who accompanied me on this expedition, Ali Derwīsh Beg, Kūch Beg, and their brothers, advanced close up to the gates of Bishkhārān and had some gallant skirmishes with the enemy. Kūch Beg and his brothers particularly distinguished themselves. Some of them fought with great intrepidity and success.

Bābur marches to Bishkhārān.

I halted on an eminence at the distance of one kos from Bishkhārān. Tambol, bringing Jehāngīr along with him, came and encamped, resting on the fort of Bishkhārān. In the course of three or four days, several Begs, who were by no means friendly to my interests, such as Ali Dost and Kamber Ali the skinner, with their dependants and adherents began to talk of peace and an accommodation. Those who were really attached to me were kept entirely in the dark as to the intended treaty, and we were altogether averse to it. But, as the two personages who have been named were the Begs of chief authority, it was to be apprehended that, if we did not listen to their wishes, and refused to make peace, more serious consequences might follow. It was necessary therefore to comply, and a peace was concluded on the following terms : That the country lying on the Akhsi side of the river of Khojend should belong to Jehāngīr Mirza ; that on the Andejān side to me: that Uzkend,[2] too, should be given up to me, when they had withdrawn their wives and families from it : that after we had settled our territories, I and Jehāngīr Mirza should unite and proceed in concert against Samarkand ; and that, as soon as I had conquered and gained complete possession of Samarkand, I should resign Andejān to Jehāngīr Mirza. The day after these conditions were agreed on, it being towards the end of Rajeb,[3] Jehāngīr Mirza and Tambol came and paid me

A peace concluded. The terms.

---

[1] These were the wandering tribes of the country.

[2] [Uzkend is situated on the right bank of the Kāra affluent of the Seihūn, to the east of Andejān and beyond the Miyān-i-dūāb.]

[3] The end of February A.D. 1500.

their respects. We ratified everything that had been arranged; Jehāngīr Mirza having taken leave, proceeded to Akhsi, while I returned to Andejān. On my arrival there, I ordered Khalīl, the younger brother of Tambol, and a number of other prisoners, to be brought out, and having given them dresses of honour, dismissed them. The enemy on their part released such of my Begs and officers as had been taken prisoners, as Taghāi Beg, Muhammed Dost, Mīr Shah Kuchīn, Sayyidī Beg, Kāsim Ajab, Pīr Weis, and Mīram Dīwān, and sent them to me.

After our return to Andejān, the manners and deportment of Ali Dost Beg underwent a complete change. He began to conduct himself with great hostility towards those who had adhered to me in all my dangers and difficulties. He first of all dismissed Khalīfeh. He then imprisoned and plundered Ibrahīm Sāru and Weis Lāghari without fault or pretext; and dismissed them, after stripping them of their governments. He next fell upon Kāsim Beg, and got quit of him. He published a proclamation, that Khalīfeh and Ibrahīm Sāru were staunch friends of Khwājeh Kazi, and had intended to murder him in revenge for the Kazi's blood. His son Muhammed Dost began to assume the state of a sovereign. His style of intercourse,[a] his entertainments, his levee, his furniture, were all those of a king. The father and son ventured on such doings, relying on the support of Tambol. Nor did I retain sufficient authority or power to be able to check them in their outrageous proceedings; for, while I had close at hand an enemy so powerful as Tambol, who was always eager to afford them his aid, and to bear them out in any act, however violent, they might safely do whatever their hearts desired. My situation was singularly delicate, and I was forced to be silent. Many were the indignities which I suffered at that time, both from the father and son.

Tyrannical proceedings of Ali Dost Beg.

Āisha Sultan Begum, the daughter of Sultan Ahmed Mirza, to whom I had been betrothed in the lifetime of my father and uncle, having arrived in Khojend, I now married her, in the month of Shābān. In the first period of my being a married man, though I had no small affection for her,

Bābur marries Āisha Sultan Begum. March 1500.

[a] receptions,

yet, from modesty and bashfulness, I went to her only once in ten, fifteen, or twenty days. My affection afterwards declined, and my shyness increased; insomuch, that my mother the Khanum, used to fall upon me and scold me with great fury, sending me off like a criminal to visit her once in a month or forty days.

His attachment to Bāburi. At this time there happened to be a lad belonging to the camp-bazaar, named Bāburi. There was an odd sort of coincidence in our names:—

> (*Tūrki verse*)—I became wonderfully fond of him;
> Nay, to speak the truth, mad and distracted after him.

Before this I never had conceived a passion for any one; and indeed had never been so circumstanced as either to hear or witness any words spoken expressive of love or amorous passion.[a][1] In this situation I composed a few verses in Persian,[b] of which the following is a couplet:

> Never was lover so wretched, so enamoured, so dishonoured as I;
> And may fair never be found so pitiless, so disdainful as thou!

Sometimes it happened that Bāburi came to visit me; when, from shame and modesty, I found myself unable to look him direct in the face. How then is it to be supposed that I could amuse him with conversation or a disclosure of my passion? From intoxication and confusion of mind

---

[a] I did not know even by hearsay what love was.
[b] *Add* in single lines or couplets.

---

[1] The whole of this is very curious. Bābur, following the ideas of his age and country, talks of this as his first love, considering his marriage, as marriages in Asia are considered, merely as a contract of convenience, with which affection has nothing to do. This is inevitable, from the state of seclusion in which women are kept, and from the tender age at which the children of respectable families are always betrothed to each other. The levity with which he speaks of his passion for Bāburi is no less characteristic. The prevalence of the vice in question, in Muhammedan countries, results from the degraded situation of women in society. We must not look for refined moral excellence in man, while woman is a slave, or occupies an inferior place in the scale of social life. We may regret that Bābur did not rise higher above the moral level of his country; but it is useful to see how even the most powerful minds may be influenced by education. With these remarks, I take leave of this passage in Bābur's life, to which I shall not again recur.

I was unable to thank him for his visit ; it is not therefore to be imagined that I had power to reproach him with his departure. I had not even self-command enough to receive him with the common forms of politeness. One day while this affection and attachment lasted, I was by chance passing through a narrow lane with only a few attendants, when, of a sudden, I met Bāburi face to face. Such was the impression produced on me by this rencounter. that I almost fell to pieces. I had not the power to meet his eyes, or to articulate a single word. With great confusion and shame I passed on and left him, remembering the verses of Muhammed Sālih :

> I am abashed whenever I see my love ;
> My companions look to me, and I look another way.

The verses were wonderfully suited to my situation. From the violence of my passion and the effervescence of youth and madness, I used to stroll bare-headed and barefoot through lane and street, garden and orchard, neglecting the attentions due to friend and stranger ; and the respect due to myself and others :

> (*Tūrki verse*)—During the fit of passion, I was mad and deranged ;
> nor did I know
> That such is his state who is enamoured of a fairy face.

Sometimes, like a distracted man, I roamed alone over the mountains and deserts ; sometimes I went wandering about from street to street in search of mansions [a] and gardens. I could neither sit nor go ; I could neither stand nor walk.

> (*Tūrki verse*)—I had neither strength to go nor power to stay ;
> To such a state did you reduce me, O my heart !

This same year a quarrel broke out between Sultan Ali Mirza [1] and Muhammed Mazīd Terkhān, originating in the high state and overbearing influence attained by the Terkhāns. They [2] had taken complete possession of the

Rupture between Sultan Ali Mirza and the Terkhāns.

[a] suburbs

---

[1] Sultan Ali Mirza, it will be remembered, was still king of Bokhāra and of Samarkand, which he had entered when it was abandoned by Bābur.

[2] [i. e. Bākī (Terkhān), P. de C.]

whole of Bokhāra, and did not give any one a single *dang*[1] from its revenues. Muhammed Mazīd Terkhān had in like manner gained unbounded influence in Samarkand, and conferred all the districts belonging to it on his own sons, his followers, and adherents: and, excepting a small provision settled on him from the revenue of the city, not a *fils*[2] from any other quarter reached Sultan Ali Mirza. The Sultan had now grown up to man's estate, and it was not to be expected that he could continue to submit to such treatment. In conjunction with some of his most attached servants, he formed a design against Muhammed Mazīd Terkhān, who, having got notice of the plot, left the city with his domestics and servants, his adherents and retainers, along with such of the Begs as were intimately connected with him, such as Sultan Hussain Arghūn, Pīr Ahmed, Khwajeh Hussain, the younger brother of Ūzūn Hassan, Kāra Birlās, Sālih Muhammed, and several other Begs and cavaliers.

<small>Muhammed Mazīd Terkhān flies from Samarkand.</small>

At this period, Sultan Mahmūd Khan dispatched Khan Mirza,[3] accompanied by Muhammed Hussain Dughlet, Ahmed Beg, and a number of his Moghuls,[4] against Samarkand. Hāfiz Beg Duldāi, with his son, Tāhir Beg, were the governors of Khan Mirza. Hassan Nabīreh, Hindū Beg, and a great many cavaliers, from attachment to Hāfiz Beg and Tāhir Beg, deserted from Sultan Ali Mirza and joined Mirza Khan. Muhammed Mazīd Terkhān sent messengers to invite Khan Mirza and the Moghul army; and himself, advancing to the territory of Shādwār, had a conference with Mirza Khan and the Moghul Begs. The Moghul Begs, however, agreed so ill with Muhammed Beg and the others, that they even formed the design of seizing upon him; but he and his Begs having discovered the plot, made their escape from the Moghul army by stratagem. After the

<small>Khan Mirza marches against Samarkand;</small>

---

[1] A small silver coin, the sixth part of a *dirhem*; at the present day of the value of about a penny.

[2] A small copper coin.

[3] Khan Mirza was Weis Mirza, the youngest son of Sultan Mahmūd Mirza. On his father's death, his mother had him conveyed to Tāshkend to her brother's court.

[4] [i. e. Moghul Begs. P. de C.

defection of this force, the Moghuls found themselves unable to maintain their ground alone. Sultan Ali Mirza, accompanied by a small force which he had with him at the time, pushed on by rapid marches from Samarkand, and overtook and fell upon Khan Mirza and the Moghul army, as they reached their ground at Yār-ailāk. The Moghuls were unable to sustain the attack, and fled in confusion. Thus, towards the close of his life, Sultan Ali Mirza performed one tolerably fair achievement. *but is defeated by Sultan Ali Mirza.*

Muhammed· Mazīd Terkhān, and the rest of his party, seeing that they had now nothing to expect from Sultan Ali Mirza, or the Mirzas his brothers,[a] dispatched Abdal Wahāb (a Moghul, who had formerly been in my service, and who, at the siege of Andejān, had gallantly exerted himself, and freely hazarded his life to support Khwājeh Kazi), for the purpose of inviting me to their assistance. I was at that time in the sad condition which has been mentioned. I was fully resolved to attempt Samarkand, and, in making peace, this had been the view held out to me. I now, therefore, immediately sent the Moghul to Akhsi to Jehāngīr Mirza, post, with relays of horses, while I myself set out against Samarkand with such troops as were along with me. It was the month of Zilkaadeh when I marched on the expedition. On the fourth day I reached Kaba,[b][1] and halted. About the time of afternoon prayers, I received intelligence that Khalīl, Sultan Ahmed Tambol's younger brother, had surprised the fortress of Ush. *Babur invited to Samarkand, June 1500. Hears of the loss of Ush.*

The affair happened in this way: At the peace, the prisoners, the chief of whom was Khalīl, the younger brother of Tambol, had been set at liberty, as has been mentioned. Tambol had sent Khalīl, in order to remove his family and effects from Uzkend. Having entered Uzkend under pretence of carrying away the family, day after day he promised to carry them off; but, under one pretext or another, never left the place. When I had set out on my

[a] *Omit this clause.*
[b] I made two halts before reaching Kaba.

[1] [According to P. de C. this was a village situated near Shāsh, on the right bank of the river Seihūn.]

expedition, availing himself of the opportunity, and perceiving Ush to be destitute of troops, he made an attack in the night, and took it by surprise.

Continues his march. When this news reached me, I judged it inexpedient, on several accounts, either to halt or turn back against him; I therefore continued to advance on Samarkand. One of the reasons which influenced me was, that all my soldiers of note had gone off different ways, each to his own home, to make ready their accoutrements and arms, and, relying on the peace, we had never suspected any craft or treachery from our enemy. Another was, that the intrigues and cabals of Kamber Ali and Ali Dost, two of my Begs of the first eminence, now began to be very evident, so that all confidence in them was at an end, as I have already given to understand. A farther motive was, that as the party of the nobles of Samarkand, at the head of whom was Muhammed Mazīd Terkhān, had sent to invite me, it would have been most absurd, on account of a small place like Andejān, to lose time, and perhaps such a noble capital as Samarkand. From Kaba we advanced to Marghinān, which I had bestowed on Sultan Ahmed Beg, the father of Kūch Beg. He was himself prevented by his situation and connexions from accompanying me, and remained in Marghinān; but his son, Kūch Beg, with one or two of his brothers, went along with me. We proceeded by way of Aspera, and halted on reaching Mahen, a village belonging to that district. By a fortunate coincidence, Kāsim Beg, with his troops, Ali Dost, with his men, Syed Kāsim, and a very considerable number of good soldiers, that very night arrived in Mahen, as if they had come post by assignation, and all joined me. Leaving Mahen, and passing by the route of the plain Yasān, we reached Uratippa, crossing the bridge of Chupān. Kamber Ali, confiding in Tambol, had gone from his own government of Khojend to Akhsi, in order to consult with him regarding the arrangements of the army; no sooner had he reached that place, than he was taken into custody, and Tambol advanced to seize his districts; verifying the Tūrki proverb:

Kamber Ali seized by Tambol.

> To trust a friend will show you raw;
> Your friend will stuff your hide with straw.

While they were conducting him from one place to another, however, he effected his escape by the way, and, barefooted and bareheaded,[a] after encountering a multitude of hardships, came and joined me while I was at Uratippa.

Effects his escape.

At Uratippa I received intelligence that Sheibāni Khan had defeated Bāki Terkhān, at the fort of Dabūsi,[1] and was advancing against Bokhāra. From Uratippa, by the route of Ilāk-burkeh, I reached Sangrāz,[2] the commandant of which surrendered the place. As Kamber Ali had joined me in a ruined state, and completely plundered, I left him behind in Sangrāz, and advanced forward. When we had reached Yuret-Khan, the Begs of Samarkand, at the head of whom was Muhammed Mazīd Khan, came to meet me, and tendered me their duty. I consulted with them about the taking of Samarkand. They assured me that Khwājeh Yahya was attached to me; and that if he could be prevailed upon heartily to co-operate, Samarkand might be taken with the greatest facility, without combat or struggle. I therefore several times sent persons to confer with Khwājeh Yahya. The Khwājeh did not send me any message, but silently used every exertion to facilitate my entrance into Samarkand; at the same time, he did not say a word to make me despair of success.[b]

Bābur reaches Yuret-Khan.

Marching from Yuret-Khan, I advanced to the Derghām. From the banks of the Derghām I sent Khwājeh Muhammed Ali, my librarian, to Khwājeh Yahya. He brought me back instructions to advance, and that the city should be given up to me. Mounting just at nightfall, we left the Derghām, and rode towards the city. But Sultan Mahmūd Duldāi, the father of Sultan Muhammed Duldāi, having deserted from me at Yuret-Khan, and gone over to the enemy, had

---

[a] As Kambar Ali was being conducted to the place of confinement he escaped on foot, and,

[b] As he had resolved to make me come to Samarkand, he sent me no message. In spite of my desperate efforts I was unable to extract a word out of him.

[1] [According to P. de C. this is a town in Soghd to the west of Samarkand, between that city and Bokhāra.]

[2] [Or Sangzār (P. de C.). It was the capital of Yār-ailāk.]

[3] [A tributary, according to P. de C., of the Kohik to the south of Samarkand.]

informed them of our proceedings; so that, our motions being discovered, the design did not succeed. I therefore returned back to the banks of the Derghām.

Many of his Begs return to his service.

While I remained encamped there,[a] Ibrahīm Sāru Minkaligh, who had received many favours from me, but whom Ali Dost had plundered and driven from my service while we were at Yār-ailāk, returned, accompanied by Muhammed Yūsef, the son of Syed Yūsef Beg, and again entered into my service. The greater part of my Begs and most attached servants, whom Ali Dost Beg, from jealousy, had treated ill, banishing some of them, plundering others, and ruining the rest by heavy contributions,[b] all returned to me at this period, one after another. The power of Ali Dost was now gone. He had placed his entire reliance on Tambol, and had harassed and persecuted me and all my friends. I had conceived a rooted dislike to the man. Partly from shame and partly from apprehension, he could no longer remain with me, and asked leave to retire, which I granted with great pleasure. Ali Dost and Muhammed Dost, on leaving me, went and joined Tambol, by whom they were received and treated with much distinction; and I afterwards had many proofs of the mutinous incendiary temper of both father and son. A year or two after, Ali Dost was seized with a cancerous sore [1] in the hands, of which he died. Muhammed Dost went among the Uzbeks, where he did not succeed badly; but there, also, having been guilty of some piece of treachery to those whose salt he ate, he was obliged to flee, and came to the hilly districts of Andejān, where he spirited up some disturbances; but falling at last into the hands of the Uzbeks, they put out his eyes, and thus was verified the saying, 'the salt has seized his eyes'.[2]

Ali Dost and his son allowed to retire.

Their future history.

[a] *Omit and substitute from below*, while we were at Yār-ailāk,
[b] and imprisoning others,

[1] [P. de C. has 'ulcer', and remarks that the word in Turki means guinea worm.]

[2] In the East, it is looked upon as the greatest crime to betray one in whose family or service a man has lived, or even with whom he has eaten. Hence the epithet *nimak harām*, or *treacherous to his salt*, is one of the severest of reproaches.

After they had taken leave, I dispatched Ghūri Birlās with a party of horse towards Bokhāra, in quest of intelligence. He brought me back information that Sheibāni Khan had taken Bokhāra, and was marching on Samarkand. Not thinking my stay in that neighbourhood advisable, I proceeded towards Kesh,[1] in which place were the families of many of the Begs of Samarkand. A week or two after my arrival there, information was brought that Sultan Ali Mirza had delivered up Samarkand to Sheibāni Khan.

Sheibāni Khan takes Bokhāra

and Samarkand.

The circumstances of this event are as follows: The mother of Sultan Ali Mirza, named Zuhreh Beghi Agha, was led by her stupidity and folly to send a messenger privately to Sheibāni Khan, proposing that, if he would marry her, her son should surrender Samarkand into his hands, on condition that, when Sheibāni recovered his own paternal dominions, he should restore Samarkand to Sultan Ali Mirza. Abū Yūsef Arghūn was let into the secret of this plan; nay, that traitor may be fairly regarded as the original projector of it.

Particulars of this event.

TRANSACTIONS OF THE YEAR 9)6 [2]

Sheibāni Khan, advancing as had been arranged with the princess, halted at the Bāgh-e-meidān.[3] About noon, Sultan Ali Mirza, without acquainting any of his Begs, officers, cavaliers, or servants with his intention, and without holding any consultation, left the town by the Chārrāheh gate,[4] accompanied only by a few insignificant individuals of his personal attendants, and went to Sheibāni Khan at the Bāgh-e-meidān. Sheibāni did not give him a very flattering reception; and, as soon as the ceremonies of meeting were over, made him sit down lower than himself. Khwājeh Yahya, on learning that the Mirza had gone out, was filled with alarm; but, seeing no remedy left, also went out of the town, and waited on Sheibāni Khan, who received him without rising, and said some severe things to him. On his rising to go away, however, Sheibāni Khan behaved

Sheibāni Khan arrives before Samarkand.

Sultan Ali Mirza goes out and meets him.

Universal submission.

---

[1] South of Samarkand, beyond the hills.
[2] This year commenced on July 28, 1500.
[3] Garden of the plain.   [4] [i. e. gate of the four roads.]

more courteously, and rose from his seat. Jān Ali, the son of Khwājeh Ali Bai, who was in Rabāt-e-Khwājeh, as soon as he heard that the Mirza had gone out, likewise went and presented himself to Sheibāni Khan; so that the wretched and weak woman, for the sake of getting herself a husband, gave the family and honour of her son to the winds. Nor did Sheibāni Khan mind her a bit, or value her even so much as his other handmaids, concubines, or women. Sultan Ali Mirza was confounded at the condition in which he now found himself, and deeply regretted the step which he had taken. Several young cavaliers about him, perceiving this, formed a plan for escaping with him; but he would not consent. As the hour of fate was at hand, he could not shun it. He had quarters assigned him near Taimūr Sultan. Three or four days afterwards, they put him to death in the meadow of Kulbeh. From his over-anxiety to preserve this transitory and mortal life, he left a name of infamy behind him; and, from following the suggestions of a woman, struck himself out of the list of those who have earned for themselves a glorious name. It is impossible to write any more of the transactions of such a personage, and impossible to listen any farther to the recital of such base and dastardly proceedings.

Sultan Ali Mirza put to death.

After the murder of Sultan Ali Mirza, the Khan sent Jān Ali after his prince; and as he entertained suspicions of Khwājeh Yahya, banished him, and sent him off for Khorasān, with his two sons, Khwājeh Muhammed Zakeriā and Khwājeh Bāki. They were followed by a party of Uzbeks, who martyred the Khwājeh and both his young sons, in the neighbourhood of Khwājeh Kārzīn. Sheibāni Khan denied all participation in the Khwājeh's death, alleging that it was the act of Kamber Bī and Kūpek Bī.[1] This is only making the matter worse, according to the saying, 'the excuse is worse than the fault'; for when Begs presume to perpetrate such deeds without being authorized

Murder of Khwājeh Yahya and his sons.

---

[1] The Uzbeks, down to the present time, distinguish the richer and more substantial men of property by the title of *Bī*, which corresponds very much with *master*. The Uzbeks were composed of the four tribes of Uigurs, Naimans, Durmans, and Kankerats.—See *Astley's Voyages*, vol. iv, p. 483.

by their Khan or King, what confidence can be reposed in such a government?

No sooner had the Uzbeks taken Samarkand, than we moved away from Kesh towards Hissār.[1] Muhammed Mazīd Terkhān, and some of the other Begs of Samarkand, accompanied me, along with their wives, children, and families. On halting at the Valley[2] of the district of Cheghāniān, Muhammed Mazīd Terkhān, and the Samarkand nobles, separating from me, went and took service with Khosrou Shah, while I, without town or territory, without any spot to which I could go, or in which I could remain, in spite of the miseries which Khosrou Shah had inflicted on my house and family, saw myself compelled to pass through the midst of his territories. I once had a fancy that I might go by way of the country of Karatigīn[3] to join my younger maternal uncle Ilcheh Khan, but I did not. We resolved to go up by the Kāmrūd and to cross over the mountain of Sir-e-tāk.[4] By the time we reached the confines of Nowendāk, a servant of Khosrou Shah came to me, and, in his master's name, presented me with nine horses, and nine pieces of cloth.[5] When I reached the gorge of Kāmrūd, Sher Ali Chihreh[6] deserted from me and joined Wali, the younger brother of Khosrou Shah. The next morning Kūch Beg separated from me and went to Hissār. Having entered the Valley of Kāmrūd, we went up the river. In these roads, which are extremely dangerous, often

Bābur leaves Kesh.

Passes through Khosrou Shah's territories.

[1] They probably proceeded through the hills of the Derbend or the Kaluga Pass

[2] *Auleng*, a valley, meadow, or pasture-ground. [P. de C. has the 'meadow of Chaltu in the Cheghāniān district'.]

[3] In that case he would probably have passed the hills into the Kāshgar territory, and then proceeded to the east of the Ala-tāgh mountains, which separated Kāshgar and the country of the Moghuls from Ush, Kāsān, &c. The Persian copies read *Karatigīn and Alāi*.

[4] The valley of Kāmrūd leads up from the low country of Hissār to Sir-e-tāk, which seems to be on the summit of the Kara-tāgh mountains. On getting across these mountains, Bābur came on the country near the source of the Kohik, and on one skirt of Yār-ailāk.

[5] The Moghuls and Tūrks have a superstitious reverence for the number nine, and presents are generally made by nine or thrice nine pieces of each kind.

[6] [i. e. page.]

overhanging precipices, and in the steep and narrow hill passes and straits which we were obliged to ascend, numbers of our horses and camels failed, and were unable to proceed.

Surmounts the Pass of Sir-e-tāk. After four or five days' march, we reached the mountain pass of Sir-e-tāk. It is a pass, and such a pass! Never did I see one so narrow and steep; never were paths so narrow and precipitous traversed by me. We travelled on with incredible fatigue and difficulty, amid dangerous narrows and tremendous gulfs. Having, after a hundred sufferings and losses, at length surmounted these murderous, steep,

Reaches Kān. and narrow defiles, we came down on the confines of Kān. Among the mountains of Kān [a] there is a large lake, which may be about a kos in circumference, and is very beautiful.[b]

Ibrahīm Terkhān occupies Yār-ailāk. Here I received information that Ibrahīm Terkhān had thrown himself into the fortress of Shirāz, which he had put in a state of defence, and that Kamber Ali and Abul Kāsim Kohbur, who had been in the fort of Khwājeh Dīdār, when the Uzbeks took Samarkand, not believing themselves able to hold out in the place, had repaired to Yār-ailāk, the fortresses of which district [c] they had occupied and put in a state of defence, and established themselves there.

Bābur is ill received by the Malik of Kān. Leaving Kān on the right, we marched towards Keshtūd. The Malik[1] of Kān was renowned for his hospitality, generosity, politeness, and humanity. When Sultan Hussain Mirza came against Hissār, Sultan Masaūd Mirza fled to his younger brother Baiesanghar Mirza at Samarkand, by this road. The Malik of Kān presented him with seventy or eighty horses as a *peshkesh*, and did him many other services of the like nature. To me he presented a single worthless horse, but did not come himself to greet me: Yet so it was, that those who were famed for generosity, proved niggards when they had to do with me; and those who were so celebrated for their hospitality, quite forgot it when I was concerned. Khosrou Shah, too, was one who possessed a high reputation for liberality and generosity,

---

[a] or Jān
[b] *Add* and which presents a very wonderful sight.
[c] of the lower part of which district

[1] [i. e. Chief or Headman.]

and the services which he rendered to Badīa-ez-zemān Mirza have already been mentioned. He certainly received Bāki Terkhān and the other Begs with unbounded kindness and liberality. I twice passed through his country. Let it not be told to my peers that the humanity and politeness, which he showed to my lowest servants, were not vouchsafed to me; nay that he did not even treat me with so much respect as he did them:

(*Turki*)—O, my soul! who has ever experienced good treatment from worldlings?
Hope not that those in whom there is no good, can show it to others?

Advances to Keshtūd. Immediately on leaving Kān, it occurred to me that Keshtūd must certainly be in the possession of the Uzbeks, I made a rapid push towards it, but found the place ruined and desolate, not a man being there. Leaving it behind, I advanced, and halted on the banks of the Kohik. I passed this river by a bridge towards its bend at Yāri, and dispatched Kāsim Beg and some other Begs for the purpose of surprising the fortress of Rabāt-e-Khwājeh. Passing Yāri and the hill of Shankar-khāneh,[1] we arrived in Yār-ailāk. *Reaches Yār-ailāk.* The Begs who were sent against Rabāt-e-Khwājeh, at the instant of applying their scaling-ladders, perceiving that the garrison had taken the alarm, and that the attempt had failed, mounted their horses and abandoned the enterprise. Kamber Ali, who was in Sangrāz, came and waited on me. Abūl Kāsim Kohbur and Ibrahīm Terkhān sent some of their confidential servants to pay me their respects, and assure me of their attachment.[a]

From the villages of Yār-ailāk we came to Asfendek.[2] At that time Sheibāni Khan was in the vicinity of Khwājeh-Dīdār, accompanied by three or four thousand Uzbeks, and about as many more soldiers who had been collected from various quarters. He had bestowed the Dāroghaship[3] of Samarkand on Jān Wafā Mirza, who occupied the place

[a] placed at my service the pick of their men, and gave me clear proof of their devotion and loyalty.

---

[1] Hawk-house. [2] [A dependency of Yār-ailāk.]
[3] [i. e. Government.]

with five or six hundred men. Hamzeh Sultan and Mahdi Sultan, with their adherents and followers, were encamped near Samarkand in the Kurūgh-budīneh.[1] My men, good and bad, amounted only to two hundred and forty. Having consulted with the whole of my Begs and officers, we finally were agreed in opinion, that as Sheibāni Khan had taken Samarkand so recently, the men of the place had probably formed no attachment to him, nor he to them; that if anything was ever to be done, this was the crisis; that could we succeed in scaling the fort by surprise, and making ourselves masters of it, the inhabitants of Samarkand would certainly declare in our favour; they had nothing else for it; that if they did not assist me, at least they would not fight for the Uzbeks. At all events, after the city was once taken, whatever God's will might be, be it done. Having come to these conclusions, we mounted and left Yār-ailāk after noon-tide prayers, and rode rapidly the greater part of the night. By midnight we reached Yuret-Khan. That night, learning that the garrison were on the alert, we did not venture to approach the place, but returned from Yuret-Khan: and as the morning dawned, we passed the river Kohik a little below Rabāt-i-Khwājeh, and regained Yār-ailāk.

One day I happened to be in the castle of Asfendek with some of my inferior nobles and officers, such as Dost Nāsir, Nuyān Gokultāsh, Kāsim Gokultāsh, Khan Kuli Kerīmdād, Sheikh Dervīsh, Khosrou Gokultāsh, and Mīram Nāsir, who were sitting and conversing around me. The conversation turned at random on a variety of subjects. I happened to say, 'Come! let us hit on a lucky guess, and may God accomplish it! When shall we take Samarkand?' Some said, 'We shall take it in the spring'[a] (it was then the harvest); some said in a month, some in forty days, some in twenty days. Nuyān Gokultāsh said, 'We shall take it within a fortnight'; and Almighty God verified his words, for we did take it within the fortnight.

About this time I had a remarkable dream. I thought

[a] summer

[1] [Quail reserve.]

that the reverend Khwājeh Obeidullah[1] had come to visit me. I went out to receive him, and the Khwājeh came in and sat down. It appeared to me that a table was spread for him, but perhaps not with sufficient attention to neatness, on which account the holy man seemed to be somewhat displeased. Mulla Bāba observing this, made me a sign. I answered him likewise by signs, that the fault was not mine, but the person's who had spread the table-cloth. The Khwājeh perceived what passed, and was satisfied with my excuse. When he rose to depart I attended him out. In the hall of the house, however, he seemed to seize me by the right or left arm, and lifted me up so high that one of my feet was raised from the ground, while he said to me in Tūrki, *Sheikh Maslehet berdi*, ' Your religious instructor has counselled you.'[2] A few days after this I took Samarkand.

One or two days after seeing this dream, I went from the fort of Asfendek to that of Wasmand. Although I had once already set out to surprise Samarkand, and, after reaching the very suburbs, had been obliged to return, from finding the garrison on the alert ; nevertheless, placing my confidence in the Almighty, I once more set out from Wasmand on the same enterprise, after mid-day prayers, and pushed on for Samarkand with the greatest expedition. Khwājeh Abdal Makāram was along with me. At midnight we reached the bridge of the Maghak at the *khiabān* (or public pleasure-ground), whence I detached forward seventy or eighty of my best men, with instructions to fix their scaling-ladders on the wall opposite to the Lovers' Cave, to mount by them and enter the fort ; after which they were to proceed immediately against the party who were stationed at the Firōzch-gate,[3] to take possession of it, and then to apprise me of their success by a messenger. They accordingly went, scaled the walls opposite to the Lovers' Cave, and entered the place without giving the least alarm.

Makes another attempt

and enters Samarkand by surprise.

[1] ['Ubaidullah Ahrār Naqshband was a famous saint of Khorasān, who counted the poet Jāmi among his disciples. He died in 1491 and is buried in Samarkand. (Beale's *O. B.*, p. 406.)]
[2] Or rather, perhaps, ' Sheikh Maslehet has given it '.
[3] [Turquoise Gate.]

Thence they proceeded to the Firōzeh-gate, where they found Fāzil Terkhān, who was not of the Terkhān Begs, but a Terkhān merchant of Tūrkestān, that had served under Sheibāni Khan in Tūrkestān, and had been promoted by him. They instantly fell upon Fāzil Terkhān and put him and a number of his retainers to the sword, broke the lock of the gate with axes, and threw it open. At that very moment I came up to the gate and instantly entered. Abul Kāsim Kohbur did not himself come on this enterprise, but he sent his younger brother Ahmed Kāsim with thirty or forty of his followers. There was no person with me on the part of Ibrahīm Terkhān ; but, after I had entered the city, and while I was sitting in the Khānkāh[1] (or monastery), Ahmed Terkhān, his younger brother, arrived with a party of his retainers. The citizens in general were fast asleep, but the shopkeepers, peeping out of their shops, and discovering what had happened,[a] offered up prayers of thanksgiving. In a short time the rest of the citizens were apprised of the event, when they manifested great joy, and most hearty congratulations passed on both sides between them and my followers. They pursued the Uzbeks in every street and corner with sticks and stones, hunting them down and killing them like mad dogs : they put to death about four or five hundred Uzbeks in this manner. The Governor of the city, Jān Wafā, was in Khwājeh Yahya's house, but contrived to make his escape, and rejoined Sheibāni Khan.

And expels the Uzbeks.

Received with joy by the inhabitants.

On entering the gate, I had instantly proceeded towards the college and Khānkāh, and, on reaching the latter, I took my seat under the grand *tāk* (or arched hall). Till morning the tumult and war-shouts were heard on every side. Some of the chief people and shopkeepers, on learning what had passed, came with much joy to bid me welcome, bringing me such offerings of food ready dressed as they had at hand, and breathed out prayers for my success.

[a] having recognized me,

---

[1] The Khānkāh was a monastery, with which was connected a caravanserai for travellers, an endowment for charitable purposes, and sometimes an establishment for lectures. The extent of the buildings made it convenient for head-quarters.

When it was morning, information was brought that the Uzbeks were in possession of the Iron Gate,[a] and were maintaining themselves in it. I immediately mounted my horse, and galloped to the place, accompanied only by fifteen or twenty men; but the rabble of the town, who were prowling about in every lane and corner,[b] had driven the Uzbeks from the Iron Gate before I could come up.

Sheibāni Khan, on learning what was passing, set out hurriedly, and about sunrise appeared before the Iron Gate, with a hundred or a hundred and fifty horse. It was a noble opportunity; but I had a mere handful of men with me, as has been mentioned. Sheibāni Khan, soon discovering that he could effect nothing, did not stop, but turned back and retired.

I now left the town, and encamped at the Bostān-serai.[1] The men of rank and consequence, and all such as were in office in the city, now came out and waited on me, offering me their congratulations. For nearly a hundred and forty years, Samarkand had been the capital of my family. A foreign robber,[c] one knew not whence he came, had seized the kingdom, which dropped from our hands. Almighty God now restored it to me, and gave me back my plundered and pillaged country. Sultan Hussain Mirza had also surprised Heri,[2] much in the same way in which I had now taken Samarkand. But to persons of judgement and discrimination it is evident, and it is clear to every man of candour, that there was a very great difference between the two occurrences. The first distinction is, that Sultan Hussain Mirza was a mighty and powerful sovereign, of great experience, and in the maturity of his years and understanding. The second is, that his opponent, Yādgār Muhammed Mirza, was an inexperienced lad of seventeen or eighteen years of age. A third distinction is, that Mīr Ali, the master of horse, who was perfectly acquainted with the whole conduct and proceedings of the enemy, was in his interest, and sent messengers to give him notice of them, and

Encamps without the town.

Compares the surprise of Samarkand with that of Heri.

[a] had fortified the place between the two (outer and inner) gates
[b] *Add* to loot the houses,   [c] An Uzbek enemy,

[1] The Garden Palace.   [2] [A. D. 1470.]

to bring him in an unguarded hour on his foe. A fourth difference is, that his opponent was not in a fortress, but at the Raven Garden, and when Sultan Hussain Mirza took the place, Yādgār Muhammed Mirza, with his attendants, had drunk so deeply of wine, that the only three persons on watch at Yādgār Muhammed Mirza's door were all drunk, as well as himself. The fifth distinction is, that he came and took it at the very first attempt, while the enemy were in the state of unsuspecting negligence that has been described.[a] On the other hand, when I took Samarkand, I was only nineteen, and had neither seen much action nor been improved by great experience. In the next place, I had opposed to me an enemy like Sheibāni Khan, a man full of talents, of deep experience, and in the meridian of life. In the third place, no person came from Samarkand to give me any information; for though the townspeople were well inclined to me, yet, from dread of Sheibāni Khan, none of them dared to think of such a step. In the fourth place, my enemies were in a fortified place, and I had both to take the place and to rout the enemy. Fifthly, I had once before come for the purpose of surprising Samarkand, and thereby put the enemy on their guard; yet, on a second attempt, by the favour of God, I succeeded and gained the city. In these observations, I have no wish to detract from any man's merit; the facts were exactly as has been mentioned. Nor, in what I have said, is it my wish to exalt the merits of my own enterprise beyond the truth; I have merely detailed the circumstances precisely as they stood.

Some poets amused themselves in making memorial verses expressive of the date of the transaction. I still recollect a couplet of one of them:

> Tell me, then, my soul! what is its date?
> Know, that it is ' *The Victory of Bābur Bahāder* '.[b][1]

Shādwār, Soghd, &c., declare for Bābur.

After the conquest of Samarkand, Shādwār, Soghd, and the people who were in the forts in the Tumāns,[c] began to

[a] *Omit this clause.*

[b] My spirit told me that the date of this exploit was contained in the words 'The Victory of Bābur, the Hero'.

[c] and the forts situated in the vicinity of these districts,

---

[1] [This chronogram gives the date A. H. 906 (A. D. 1500).]

come over to me one after another. The Uzbeks abandoned, from terror, some of the forts which they held, and made their escape. In others, the inhabitants attacked the Uzbeks, drove them out, and declared for me. Many seized on their Däroghas, and put their towns in a state of defence on my account. At this time, Sheibāni Khan's wife and family, with his heavy baggage, as well as that of the other Uzbeks, arrived from Tūrkestān. Sheibāni Khan had remained till now in the vicinity of Khwājeh-Dīdār and Ali-ābād; but, perceiving such a disposition in the garrisons to surrender the forts, and in the inhabitants to come over spontaneously to my side, he marched off from his encampment towards Bokhāra. By the divine favour, before the end of three or four months, most of the fortified places of Soghd and Miānkār [1] had come under my allegiance. Bāki Terkhān, too, seized a favourable opportunity, and entered the fort of Karshi. Khozār and Karshi [2] were both lost to the Uzbeks. Karakūl was also taken by Abul Hassan Mirza's men, who came from Merv. My affairs succeeded everywhere prosperously.

Sheibāni Khan retreats to Bokhāra.

After my departure from Andejān, my mother and grand-mother,[3] with my family and household,[a] had set out after me, and with great difficulty, and after enduring many hardships, had reached Uratippa. I now sent and brought them to Samarkand. About this time I had a daughter by Āisha Sultan Begum, the daughter of Sultan Ahmed Mizra, the first wife whom I had married. She received the name of Fakher-al-nissa (the Ornament of Women). This was my first child, and at this time I was just nineteen. In a month or forty days she went to share the mercy of God.

Bābur's family arrive in Samarkand.

No sooner had I got possession of Samarkand, than I repeatedly dispatched ambassadors and messengers, one after another, to all the Khans and Sultans, Amirs and

He sends to the neighbouring princes to solicit assistance.

[a] my wife and relations,

---

[1] Miānkār, or Miānkāl, is the country on both sides of the Kohik, near Dabūsi.
[2] Khozār and Karshi lie south-west from Shahr-i-sabz; Karakūl south-west from Bokhāra.
[3] *Wālidhā* may mean my mothers, i.e. my father's widows.

chiefs,[1] on every hand round about, to request their aid and assistance. These messengers I kept going back and forward without intermission. Some of the neighbouring princes, although men of experience, gave me an unceremonious refusal. Others, who had been guilty of insults and injuries to my family, remained inactive out of apprehension; while the few that did send me assistance, did not afford me such as the occasion demanded, as will be particularly mentioned in its place.

Corresponds with Ali Sher Beg.

At the time when I took Samarkand this second time, Ali Sher Beg [2] was still alive. I had a letter from him, which I answered. On the back of the letter which I addressed to him, I wrote a couplet that I had composed in the Tūrki language; but before his reply could arrive, the commotions and troubles had begun.

Mulla Bināi in Samarkand.

Sheibāni Khan, after taking Samarkand, had received Mulla Bināi into his service, since which time the Mulla had attended him. A few days after I took the place, the Mulla came to Samarkand. Kāsim Beg having suspicions of him, ordered him to retire to Shahr-i-sabz; but soon after, as he was a man of great knowledge, and as the charges against him were not established, I invited him to return to the capital. He was constantly composing *kasīdehs* and *ghazels*.[3] He addressed to me a *ghazel* adapted to a musical air, in the Nawa measure; and about the same time composed and sent me the following quatrain:

> I neither possess *grain* to eat,
> Nor *the perversion of grain* [4] to put on;
> Without food nor raiment,
> How can one display his learning and genius?

---

[1] [Wardens of the Marches (P. de C.).]

[2] A more particular account of this eminent man, who was the greatest patron of literature and the arts of the age in which he lived, is afterwards given in the account of Herāt.

[3] [*Ghazal* is an ode and *qasīdah* a 'purpose poem' (elegy or panegyric).]

[4] The merit of these verses depends upon an untranslatable play of words in the original. The Persians and Hindustānis are accustomed to divert themselves by ringing changes on their words. *Ghaleh, maleh, roti, boti,* &c. The perverted word the Persians call the *muhmal* of the proper term. The *muhmal,* or perversion of *ghaleh,* grain, is *maleh,* which happens to signify a sort of reddish-

About this period, I sometimes amused myself with composing a couplet or two, but did not venture on the perfect *ghazel*, or ode. I composed and sent him a *rubái* (or quatrain), in the Tūrki language:

Your affairs *shall* all succeed to your heart's content,
Presents and a settled allowance *shall be* ordered for your reward.
I comprehend your allusion to the grain and its perversion;
Your person shall fill the cloth, and the grain *shall* fill your house.

Mulla Bināi composed and sent me a *rubái,* in which he assumed the rhyme of my quatrain for the *redīf* [1] of his own, and gave it another rhyme:

My Mirza, who *shall be* sovereign by sea and land,
Shall be distinguished in the world for his genius;
If my reward was such for a single unmeaning word,[2]
What would it have been had I spoken with understanding! [3]

At this time Khwājeh Abul-barka, surnamed Ferāki, came from Shahr-i-sabz.[4] He said, 'You [5] should have kept the same rhyme'; and recited the following *rubái*:

This tyranny which the sphere exercises *shall be* inquired into;
This generous Sultan *shall* redress her misdeeds;
O cup-bearer! if hitherto thou hast not brimmed my cup,
At this turn (or reign) *shall* it *be* filled to the brim.

This winter my affairs were in the most prosperous state, while those of Sheibāni Khan were at a low ebb. At this very period, however, one or two rather unfortunate incidents occurred. The party from Merv, that had taken

<small>Bābur's affairs prosperous.</small>

coloured cotton, of which cloth is manufactured. The poet, therefore, by saying that he has not *ghaleh* (grain), nor its *muhmal, maleh* (cotton), gives to understand that he has neither food nor clothing. [*Muhmal* signifies a letter without diacritical points, or an obsolete or meaningless word (opposed to *musta'mal*) as here.]

[1] The *kāfia* is the rhyme; the *redīf* consists of a few syllables, like a running chorus, that close the line. The *redīf* here is the Tūrki word *bulghūsidur* = *shall be*, which served as the rhyme to Bābur's verses. In the subsequent verses of Khwājeh Abul-barka, the original rhyme is resumed. It is to be observed that the third line of a quatrain requires no rhyme.

[2] In most instances the *muhmal* of a word has no sense whatever.

[3] [i. e. words with a meaning.]

[4] [P. de C. adds ' to Samarkand '.]

[5] [P. de C. has ' He ', i. e. Bināi.]

possession of Karakūl, proved unable to maintain it, so that it fell again into the hands of the Uzbeks. Ahmed Terkhān, the younger brother of Ibrahīm Terkhān, held the fortress of Dabūsi. Sheibāni Khan came and invested it; and before I could collect my army and march to its relief, took it by storm, and made an indiscriminate massacre of the garrison. At the taking of Samarkand, I had with me in all only two hundred and forty men. In the course of five or six months, by the favour of God, they had so much increased, that I could venture to engage so powerful a chief as Sheibāni Khan in a pitched battle at Sir-e-pul, as shall be mentioned. Of all the princes in my vicinity, from whom I had asked assistance, none afforded me any except the Khan, who sent Ayūb Begchik and Kashkeh Mahmūd, with about four or five hundred men. From Jehāngīr Mirza, Tambol's younger brother [1] brought a hundred men to my assistance. From Sultan Hussain Mirza, a prince of power and talent, a monarch of experience, and than whom none was better acquainted with the temper and views of Sheibāni Khan, not a man appeared; nor did I receive a single man from Badīa-ez-zemān Mirza. Khosrou Shah, from terror, did not send any; for, as my family had suffered much from his unprincipled conduct, as has been mentioned, he entertained great apprehensions of me.

He receives no reinforcements from his neighbours.

In the month of Shawāl [2] I marched out of the city to meet Sheibāni Khan, and fixed my head-quarters in the Bāgh-e-nou,[3] where I halted five or six days for the purpose of collecting the troops, and getting ready all the necessaries of war. Setting out from the Bāgh-e-nou, I proceeded by successive marches to Sir-e-pul,[4] after passing which I halted and encamped, strongly fortifying our camp with a palisade and ditch. Sheibāni Khan moved forward from the opposite direction to meet us, and encamped near the town of Khwājeh Kārzīn. There was about a farsang between his camp and mine.

Bābur marches against Sheibāni Khan.

They meet near Kārzīn.

We remained four or five days in this position, and every day parties of my men fell in with the enemy, and skirmished

Skirmishes ensue.

---
[1] [P. de C. adds 'Khalīl'.]
[2] Shawāl 906 begins April 20, 1501.
[3] New garden.   [4] [Bridgehead.]

with them. One day, a larger body of the enemy than usual advanced, and there was a very sharp fight, without any marked advantage on either side. Of my troops, one who had a standard behaved ill, ran off, and got into the trench. There were persons who pretended to say that the standard was Sayyidī Kāra Beg's; and, in truth, Sayyidī Kāra, though most valiant in speech, by no means made the same figure with his sword. One night Sheibāni Khan attempted to surprise us, but we were so well defended by our ditch and chevaux-de-frise, that he could effect nothing. After raising the war-shout on the edge of our ditch, and giving us a few discharges of arrows, they drew off.

I now turned my whole attention and solicitude to the approaching battle. Kamber Ali assisted me. Bāki Terk-khān, with a thousand or two thousand men, had arrived in Kesh, and would have joined me in two days. Syed Muhammed Dughlet, the Mir's son, too, was advancing with a thousand or fifteen hundred men, who had been sent to my assistance by the Khan my maternal uncle; they had reached Dabūl,[1] only four farsangs from my camp, and would have joined me next morning. Such was our situation, when I precipitated matters, and hurried on the battle:

Bābur resolves to engage.

> He who with impatient haste lays his hand on his sword,
> Will afterwards gnaw that hand with his teeth from regret.[2]

The cause of my eagerness to engage was, that the stars called the <i>Sakzyaldāz</i> (or eight stars)[3] were on that day exactly between the two armies; and if I had suffered that day to elapse, they would have continued favourable to the enemy [a] for the space of thirteen or fourteen days. These observances were all nonsense, and my precipitation was without the least solid excuse.

In the morning, having made the troops array themselves in their armour, and caparison and cover their horses with cloth of mail, we marched out and moved towards the enemy, having drawn out the army in order of battle, with

Arrangements for battle.

[a] behind the enemy

---

[1] [Or 'Dayal' according to P. de C.]
[2] [This couplet is taken from Sa'di's <i>Bustān</i>, book i, p. 246.]
[3] [Possibly the Great Bear.]

right and left wing, centre and advance. On the right wing were posted Ibrahīm Sāru, Ibrahīm Jāni, Abul Kāsim Kohbur, with several other Begs. On the left wing were stationed Ibrahīm Terkhān, Muhammed Mazīd Terkhān, with the other Begs of Samarkand, Sultan Hussain Arghūn, Kara Birlās, Pīr Ahmed, and Khwājeh Hussain. In the centre were Kāsim Beg and some of my inferior nobility and attached adherents.[a] In the advance were Kamber Ali Salākh (the skinner), Bandeh Ali, Khwājeh Ali, Mīr Shah Kuchīn, Syed Kāsim the chamberlain, Khāldār the younger brother of Bandeh Ali, Kūch Beg, Haider Kāsim the son of Kāsim Beg,[1] with a number of my best armed men and most faithful partisans. We marched right forward to the enemy, and they, on their part, appeared ready drawn up to receive us. On their right wing were Mahmūd Sultan, Jāni Beg Sultan, and Taimūr Sultan; and on their left Hamzeh Sultan, and Mahdi Sultan, with a number of other Sultans. When the lines of the two opposite armies approached each other, the extremity of their right wing turned my left flank, and wheeled upon my rear. I changed my position to meet them. By this movement the advance, which contained most of my experienced and veteran warriors and officers, was thrown to the right; and scarcely any of them were left with me.[b] In spite of this, however, we charged and beat off the troops that came on to attack us in front, driving them back on their centre; and things even came to such a pass, that several of his oldest and most experienced officers represented to Sheibāni Khan, that it was necessary immediately to retreat, and that all was over. He, however, remained firm and kept his ground. The enemy's right having, meanwhile, routed my left, now attacked me in the rear. As my advance had been thrown to the right on the change of our position, my front[2] was left defenceless. The enemy now began to charge us both

Bābur's left wing turned.

[a] officers of my household.
[b] our front was left entirely uncovered.

---

[1] [Kūch Haidar, the son of Kāsim Beg, according to P. de C.]
[2] That is, the centre.

in front and rear, pouring in showers of arrows. The Moghul troops which had come to my assistance, did not attempt to fight, but, instead of fighting, betook themselves to dismounting and plundering my own people. Nor is this a solitary instance, such is the uniform practice of these wretches the Moghuls; if they defeat the enemy they instantly seize the booty; if they are defeated, they plunder and dismount their own allies, and, betide what may, carry off the spoil. The enemy who were in front, made several furious attacks on me, but were worsted and driven back; they, however, rallied again and charged; the division of the enemy that had gained our rear coming up at the same time, and discharging showers of arrows on our troops. Being thus surrounded and attacked both before and behind, my men were driven from their ground. In battle, the great reliance of the Uzbeks is on the *tulughmeh*[1] (or turning the enemy's flank). They never engage without using the *tulughmeh*. Another of their practices is to advance and charge in front and rear, discharging their arrows at full gallop, pell-mell, chiefs and common soldiers, and, if repulsed, they in like manner retire full gallop. Only ten or fifteen persons were now left with me. The river Kohik was near at hand, the extremity of my right wing having rested upon it. We made the best of our way to it, and no sooner gained its banks than we plunged in, armed at all points both horse and man. For more than half of the ford we had a firm footing, but after that we sank beyond our depths, and were forced, for upward of a bowshot, to swim our horses, loaded as they were with their riders in armour and their own trappings. Yet they plunged through it. On getting out of the water on the other side, we cut off our horses' heavy furniture and threw it away. When we had reached the north side of the river, we were separated from the enemy. Of all others, the wretches of Moghuls were the most active in unhorsing and stripping the stragglers. Ibrahīm Terkhān, and a great number of excellent

Bābur routed.

Crosses the Kohik.

[1] [Lane Poole describes this tactic of the Uzbegs (*tulugh-ma*) as 'first turning the enemy's flank, then charging simultaneously on front and rear, letting fly their arrows at a break-neck gallop, and, if repulsed, retiring at top speed'.—(*Bábar*, p. 57.)]

soldiers, were unhorsed, stripped, and put to death by them.

> If the Moghul race were a race of angels, it is a bad race;
> And were the name Moghul written in gold, it would be odious.
> Take care not to pluck one ear of corn from a Moghul's harvest;
> The Moghul seed is such that whatever is sowed with it is execrable.

Reaches Samarkand. Advancing up the north side of the river Kohik, I recrossed it in the vicinity of Kulbeh. Between the time of afternoon and evening prayers, I reached the Sheikh-zādeh's gate and entered the citadel[1]

Bābur's loss in the battle. Many Begs of the highest rank, many admirable soldiers and many men of every description perished in this fight. Ibrahīm Terkhān, Ibrahīm Sāru, and Ibrahīm Jāni, were among the slain. It is rather an extraordinary coincidence that three men of such rank and distinction, and all of the name of Ibrahīm, should have fallen in the same battle. Abul Kāsim Kohbur, the eldest son of Haider Kāsim Beg, Khuda-berdi the standard-bearer, Khalīl, the younger brother of Sultan Ahmed Tāmbol, who has been frequently mentioned, all perished in this action. The greater part of *He is deserted by many of his nobles.* the rest dispersed and fled in every direction. Of these, Muhammed Mazīd Terkhān fled towards Kunduz and Hissār, to Khosrou Shah. Kamber Ali the skinner, the Moghul, whom among all my Begs I had distinguished by the highest marks of favour, in despite of all these benefits, at this season of need did not stand by me; but having first removed his family from Samarkand, afterwards went himself and joined Khosrou Shah. Several others of my officers and men, such as Kerīmdād, Khudadād the Turkoman, Jānikeh Gokultāsh, and Mulla Bābā Peshāgheri, fled towards Uratippa. Mulla Bābā was not at that time in my service, but was entertained as a guest. Others, again, acted like Shīrīm Taghāi, who returned to me indeed in Samarkand along with his men, and joined me in a consultation, in which it was resolved to defend the place to the last drop of our blood, and to exert ourselves to the utmost to put it in a state of defence; yet did he, though my mother and sisters remained in the fortress, send off his family with his effects and people to Uratippa, he himself alone staying behind with a small party, unencumbered, and ready to move off in any direction. Nor is this the only instance in which he so acted ; for in every case of difficulty or danger, he uniformly displayed the same want of steadiness and attachment.

Next day I called together Khwājeh Abul Makāram, Kāsim Beg, and the rest of the Begs and officers, with such of my adherents and cavaliers as were best qualified to offer advice, and held a general consultation. We came to a resolution to put the place in the best possible state of defence, and to maintain ourselves in it for life or for death. I and Kāsim Beg, with my most trusty and faithful adherents, formed a body of reserve. I had a public tent [1] pitched for me on the Arched Portal of Ulugh Beg's College, in the midst of the city, in which I established my head-quarters. I distributed the other Begs and cavaliers at the different gates, and around the works, on the ramparts and defences. *Resolves to defend Samarkand.*

After two or three days Sheibāni Khan approached, and took a station at some distance from the city. The idle and worthless rabble, assembling from every district and street of Samarkand, came in large bodies to the gate of the College, shouting aloud, ' Glory to the Prophet ! ' [a] and clamorously marched out for battle. Sheibāni Khan, who, at the moment, had mounted, and was preparing to make an assault, did not venture to approach the place. Some days passed in this manner. The ignorant mob, who had never experienced the wound of arrow or sabre, nor witnessed the press of onset, or the tumult of battle, plucked up courage from these incidents, and ventured to advance to a very considerable distance [b] from the works. When the old and experienced veterans remonstrated with them on such improvident and useless advances, they were only answered with reproach and abuse. *Sheibāni Khan appears before Samarkand.*

One day Sheibāni Khan made an attack near the Iron gate. The rabble, who had become very courageous, had advanced most valiantly a great way from the city, accord- *Drives the townspeople into the place.*

[a] shouting out prayers on my behalf
[b] farther and farther

---

[1] The *chāder sefīd* (= white tent) was a sort of public tent at head-quarters.

ing to their custom. I made a party of horse follow them, to cover their retreat. A body of Gokultāshes,[1] with some inferior nobility, and a few of my domestic troops,[a] such as Nuyān Gokultāsh, Kūl Nazer Taghāi, and Mazīd, with some others, marched out towards the Camel's-neck.[2] From the other side two or three Uzbeks galloped up to charge them and assaulted Kūl Nazer, sabre in hand. The whole of the Uzbeks dismounting, fought on foot, swept back the city-rabble, and drove them in through the Iron gate. Kūch Beg and Mīr Shah Kuchīn remained behind, and took post close by Khwājeh Khizer's mosque. After the field was pretty well cleared of those who fought on foot, the cavalry of the enemy moved up towards the mosque of Khwājeh Khizer, in order to attack them. Upon this Kūch Beg, sallying forth on the Uzbeks who first came up, attacked them sabre in hand, and made a gallant and distinguished figure, in the sight of all the inhabitants, who stood looking on. The fugitives, occupied solely with their flight, had ceased to shoot arrows, or to think of fighting for their ground. I shot from the top of the gateway with a cross-bow, and those who were along with me also kept up a discharge. This shower of arrows from above prevented the enemy from advancing up to [b] Khwājeh Khizer's mosque, and they were forced to retire from the field.

Besieges the city.

During the continuance of the siege, the rounds of the rampart were regularly gone, once every night,[c] sometimes by Kāsim Beg, and sometimes by other Begs and captains. From the Firozeh gate to the Sheikh-zādeh gate, we were able to go along the ramparts on horseback; everywhere else we were obliged to go on foot. Setting out in the beginning of the night, it was morning before we had completed our rounds.[d]

[a] my foster-brothers with some officers of my household,
[b] beyond
[c] *Add* sometimes by myself,
[d] Those who made the entire round on foot did not complete it before dawn.

---

[1] [i. e. foster-brothers.]
[2] *Shuter gerden*, a subterraneous watercourse issuing in a flowing well.

One day Sheibāni Khan made an attack between the Iron gate and that of the Sheikh-zādeh. As I was with the reserve, I immediately led them to the quarter that was attacked, without attending to the Washing-green gate [1] or the Needlemakers' gate. That same day, from the top of the Sheikh-zādeh's gateway, I struck a palish white-coloured horse [a] an excellent shot with my cross-bow: it fell dead the moment the arrow touched it: but in the meanwhile they had made such a vigorous attack, near the Camel's-Neck, that they effected a lodgement close under the rampart. Being hotly engaged in repelling the enemy where I was, I had entertained no apprehensions of danger on the other side, where they had prepared and brought with them twenty-five or twenty-six scaling-ladders, each of them so broad, that two and three men could mount a-breast. He had placed in ambush opposite to the city-wall, seven or eight hundred chosen men with these ladders, between the Iron-smiths' [b] and Needlemakers' gates, while he himself moved to the other side, and made a false attack. Our attention was entirely drawn off to this attack; and the men in ambush no sooner saw the works opposite to them empty of defenders, by the watch having left them, than they rose from the place where they had lain in ambush, advanced with extreme speed, and applied their scaling-ladders all at once between the two gates that have been mentioned, exactly opposite to Muhammed Mazīd Terkhān's house. The quarters of Kūch Beg, Muhammed Kuli Kuchīn, and of the party of warriors who had the duty of guarding this post, were then in Muhammed Mazīd Terkhān's house. Kara Birlās was stationed at the Needlemakers' gate; the station of the Washing-green gate was allotted to Shīrīm Taghāi and his brothers, with Kūtluk Khwājeh Gokultāsh. As there was fighting on the other side, the persons in charge of these works were not apprehensive of any danger at their posts, and the men on these stations had dispersed on their own business to their houses or to the markets. The Begs who were on guard had only

Attempts to enter it by escalade,

[a] centurion's horse. [b] Bleaching-green

[1] [*Gāzeristān* means bleaching-ground in Persian.]

two or three of their servants and attendants about them.—Nevertheless Kūch Beg, Muhammed Kuli Kuchīn, Shah Sūfi, and another brave cavalier, boldly assailed them, and displayed signal heroism. Some of the enemy had already mounted the wall, and several others were in the act of scaling it, when the four persons who have been mentioned arrived on the spot, fell upon them sword in hand, with the greatest bravery, and dealing out furious blows around them, drove the assailants back over the wall and put them to flight. Kūch Beg distinguished himself above all the rest; and this was an exploit for ever to be cited to his honour. He twice during this siege performed excellent service by his valour. Kara Birlās, too, who was almost alone in the works at the Needlemakers' gate, made a good stand. Kūtluk Khwājeh Gokultāsh and Kūl Nazer Mirza, who were in their stations at the Washerman's gate, made a stout resistance with a few men, and attacking them in the rear, made a desperate charge. The attempt was completely defeated.[a]

<small>but is repulsed.</small>

On another occasion Kāsim Beg sallied out, with a small body of men, by the Needlemakers' gate, and having beat the Uzbeks back as far as Khwājeh Kafshīr, he dismounted several of them, and returned, bringing back their heads.

<small>Distress of Samarkand.</small>

It was now the season of the ripening of the grain, and nobody had brought in any new corn. As the siege had drawn out to great length, the inhabitants were reduced to extreme distress, and things came to such a pass, that the poor and meaner sort were forced to feed on dogs' and asses' flesh. Grain for the horses becoming scarce, they were obliged to be fed on the leaves of trees; and it was ascertained from experience that the leaves of the mulberry and blackwood [1] answered best. Many used the shavings and raspings of wood, which they soaked in water, and gave to their horses. For three or four months Sheibāni Khan did not approach the fortress, but blockaded it at some distance on all sides, changing his ground from time to time.

[a] *This sentence is omitted.*

[1] *Kara-ighaj* [the elm, according to P. de C.].

One night when everybody was gone to rest, towards midnight, he approached the Firōzeh gate, beating his large kettle-drums, and raising the shout for an assault. I was then in the College, and was in considerable uneasiness and terror. After this they returned every night beating their kettle-drums, and shouting, and making an alarm. Although I had sent ambassadors and messengers to all the princes and chiefs round about, no help came from any of them. Indeed, when I was in the height of my power, and had yet suffered neither discomfiture nor loss, I had received none, and had therefore no reason to expect it now, that I was reduced to such a state of distress. To draw out the siege in hopes of any succour from them was evidently needless. The ancients have said, that in order to maintain a fortress, a head, two hands, and two feet are necessary. The head is a captain, the two hands are two friendly forces that must advance from opposite sides; the two feet are water and stores of provision within the fort. I looked for aid and assistance from the princes my neighbours; but each of them had his attention fixed on some other object. For example, Sultan Hussain Mirza was undoubtedly a brave and experienced monarch, yet neither did he give me assistance, nor even send an ambassador to encourage me; although during the siege he sent Kemāl-ed-dīn Hussain Gāzargāhi on an embassy to Sheibāni Khan.

Tambol having advanced from Andejān as far as Bishkent,[1] Ahmed Beg and a party of men brought out the Khan to take the field against him. They met in the vicinity of Laklakān and Chārbāgh-e-turāk, but separated and retired without any action, and without even confronting each other.[a] Sultan Mahmūd Khan was not a fighting man, and was totally ignorant of the art of war. When he went to oppose Tambol on this occasion, he showed pretty plain indications of want of heart, both in his words and actions. Ahmed Beg, who was a plain rough man, but sincere in his master's service and brave, said in his harsh way, 'What

Tambol marches against Sultan Mahmūd Khan.

---

[a] *This clause is omitted.*

[1] [According to P. de C. this is a district of Shāsh, about 4 marches from Khujend.]

kind of a fellow is this Tambol, that he occasions you so much consternation and alarm? If your eyes are afraid, why, bind them up, and then let us engage him.'

EVENTS OF THE YEAR 907 [1]

Distress of Samarkand.

THE blockade drawing out to a great length, provisions and supplies coming in from no quarter, and no succours or reinforcements appearing on any hand, the soldiers and inhabitants at length began to lose all hope, went off by ones and twos, escaped from the city [a] and deserted. Sheibāni Khan, who knew the distress of the inhabitants, came and encamped at the Lovers' Cave. I also moved my headquarters and came to Kūe payān (Low Street) to Malik Muhammed Mirza's house.[b] At this crisis, Ūzūn Hassan, the son of Khwājeh Hussain, who had been the chief ringleader in the rebellion of Jehāngīr Mirza, by which I had formerly been obliged to leave Samarkand; and who had afterwards been the prime mover of much rebellion and sedition, as has been related, entered the town with ten or fifteen followers. The famine and distress of the town's-people and soldiers had now reached the greatest excess. Even men who were about my person, and others high in my confidence, began to let themselves down over the walls and make their escape. Of the chiefs, Weis Sheikh and Weis Bāburi [2] deserted and fled. I now despaired of assistance or relief from any quarter. There was no side to which I could look with hope. Our provisions and stores, which from the first had been scanty, were now totally exhausted, and no new supplies could enter the city. In these circumstances, Sheibāni Khan proposed terms. Had I had the slightest hopes of relief, or had any stores remained within the place, never would I have listened to him. Compelled, however, by necessity, a sort of capitulation

[a] let themselves down from the walls of the city
[b] *Add* facing Shaibani Khan.

[1] This year of the Hijira commenced July 17, 1501.
[2] ['Lāghari,' according to P. de C., who adds: 'two of my old adherents.']

was agreed upon, and about midnight I left the place by Sheikh-zādeh's gate, accompanied by my mother the Khanum. Two other ladies escaped with us, the one of them Bechega Khalīfeh, the other Mingelık Gokultāsh : my eldest sister Khanzādeh Begum was intercepted, and fell into the hands of Sheıbānı Khan, as we left the place on this occasion. Having entangled ourselves among the great branches of the canals of the Soghd, during the darkness of the night, we lost our way, and after encountering many difficulties, we passed Khwājeh Dīdār about dawn. By the time of early morning prayers, we arrived at the hillock of Kārbūgh, and passing it on the north below the village of Khardek [1] we made for Ilān-ūtī. On the road, I had a race with Kamber Ali and Kāsim Beg. My horse got the lead. As I turned round on my seat to see how far I had left them behind, my saddle-girth being slack, the saddle turned round, and I came to the ground right on my head. Although I immediately sprang up and mounted, yet I did not recover the full possession of my faculties till the evening, and the world, and all that occurred at the time, passed before my eyes and apprehension like a dream, or a phantasy, and disappeared. The time of afternoon prayers was past ere we reached Ilān-ūtī, where we alighted, and, having killed a horse, cut him up, and dressed slices of his flesh ; we stayed a little time to rest our horses, then mounting again, before daybreak we alighted at the village of Khalīleh. From Khalīleh we proceeded to Dizak.[2] At that time Tāher Duldāi, the son of Hāfiz Muhammed Beg Duldāi, was governor of Dizak. Here we found nice fat flesh, bread of fine flour well baked, sweet melons, and excellent grapes in great abundance ; thus passing from the extreme of famine to plenty, and from an estate of danger and calamity to peace and ease :

(*Tūrki*)—From famine and distress we have escaped to repose
We have gained fresh life, and a fresh world.

(*Persian*)—The fear of death was removed from the heart
The torments of hunger were removed away.

In my whole life, I never enjoyed myself so much, nor at

[1] ['Khūb kint,' according to P. de C.]   [2] [Jizakh on the map.]

any period of it felt so sensibly the pleasures of peace and plenty. Enjoyment after suffering, abundance after want, come with increased relish, and afford more exquisite delight. I have four or five times,[1] in the course of my life, passed in a similar manner from distress to ease, and from a state of suffering to enjoyment : but this was the first time that I had ever been delivered from the injuries of my enemy, and the pressure of hunger, and passed from them to the ease of security, and the pleasures of plenty. Having rested and enjoyed ourselves two or three days in Dizak, we proceeded on to Uratippa.

Visits Peshāgher. Peshāgher is a little out of the road, yet as I had formerly passed some time there, I turned aside and visited it again. In the fortress of Peshāgher I unexpectedly fell in with an *atūn* (or governess), who had long been in the service of the Khanum, my mother, but whom, on the present occasion, for want of horses, we had been compelled to leave behind in Samarkand. On accosting her, we found that she had travelled all the way from Samarkand on foot. My mother's younger sister, Khub Nigār Khanum,[2] had departed from this transitory life ; information of the event was communicated to my mother and me at Uratippa. My father's mother had also paid the debt of mortality at Andejān, and the news was communicated here. My mother,[3] since the death of my maternal grandfather,[4] had never seen her mothers,[5] nor her younger brother and sisters, Shah Begum, Sultan Muhammed Khan, Sultan Nigār Khanum,[6] and Doulet Sultan Khanum,[7] and had been separated from them thirteen or fourteen years. She now set out for Tāshkend,

---

[1] [The three subsequent occasions were in 1502 (after his expulsion from Akhsi) ; in 1508 (after quelling the Moghul revolt) ; and in 1512 (after his defeat by Obeidullah at Ghazhdivān (*E. B.*, pp. 172, 285, 325).]

[2] The wife of Sultan Muhammed Hussain Korkān Dughlet, who held Uratippa at this time.

[3] Kūtluk Nigār Khanum.

[4] Yunis Khan.

[5] That is, Yunis Khan's other wives.

[6] The widow of Sultan Mahmūd Mirza, and daughter of Shah Begum.

[7] Shah Begum's youngest daughter,

for the purpose of seeing them. After consulting with Muhammed Hussain Mirza, it was arranged that I should take up my winter-quarters in the village of Dehkat, which belongs to Uratippa. I therefore went thither with my baggage, which I deposited there, and in the course of a few days afterwards, I, too, went to Tāshkend to see Shah Begum, my maternal uncle, and my other friends and relations. I waited on Shah Begum and my uncle accordingly, and remained with them for some days. My mother's eldest sister of the full-blood, Meher Nigār Khanum,[1] also arrived from Samarkand. My mother the Khanum fell sick, became desperately ill, and was reduced to the point of death. The reverend Khwājehka Khwājeh had left Samarkand, and now arrived at Farket. I went to Farket and paid the Khwājeh a visit. I had entertained hopes that the Khan my uncle, from affection and regard, might give me some country or district; and he did give me Uratippa, but Mahmūd Hussain Mirza refused to deliver it up. Whether he did this of himself, or acted on a hint from higher authority, I cannot tell; however that be, in a few days I returned to Dehkat.

Dehkat is one of the hill-districts of Uratippa.[a] It lies on the skirts of a very high mountain, immediately on passing which, you come on the country of Masīkha. The inhabitants, though Sarts,[2] have large flocks of sheep, and herds of mares, like the Tūrks. The sheep belonging to Dehkat may amount to forty thousand. We took up our lodgings in the peasants' houses. I lived at the house of one of the head men of the place. He was an aged man, seventy or eighty years old. His mother was still alive, and had attained an extreme old age, being at this time a hundred and eleven years old. One of this lady's relations had accompanied the army of Taimūr Beg, when it invaded Hindustān.[3]

[a] *Add* situated in the Malik Tāgh [north-west of Uratippa].

---

[1] The widow of Sultan Ahmed Mirza of Samarkand.
[2] Or Tājiks, husbandmen or villagers, who speak the Persian tongue They are the remains of those who inhabited that country before the later Tartar invasions.
[3] [Delhi fell to Timur in A. D. 1398.]

The circumstances remained fresh in her memory, and she often told us stories on that subject. In the district of Dehkat alone, there still were of this lady's children, grandchildren, great-grandchildren, and great-great-grandchildren, to the number of ninety-six persons; and including those deceased, the whole amounted to two hundred. One of her great-grandchildren was at this time a young man of twenty-five or twenty-six years of age, with a fine black beard. While I remained in Dehkat, I was accustomed to walk on foot all about the hills in the neighbourhood. I generally went out barefoot, and, from this habit of walking barefoot, I soon found that our feet became so hardened that we did not mind rock or stone in the least. In one of these walks, between afternoon and evening prayers, we met a man who was going with a cow in a narrow road. I asked him the way. He answered, 'Keep your eye fixed on the cow; and do not lose sight of her till you come to the issue of the road, when you will know your ground.' Khwājeh Asadullah, who was with me, enjoyed the joke, observing, 'What would become of us wise men were the cow to lose her way?'

This winter many of my soldiers, principally because we could not go out in plundering parties, asked leave to go to Andejān. Kāsim Beg strongly advised me that, as these men were going that way, I should send some article of my dress as a present to Jehāngīr Mirza. I accordingly sent him a cap of ermine. Kāsim Beg then added, 'What great harm would there be in sending some present to Tambol?' Though I did not altogether approve of this, yet, induced by the pressing instances of Kāsim Beg, I sent Tambol a large sword, which had been made in Samarkand for Nuyān Gokultāsh,[1] from whom I took it.[a] This was the very sword that afterwards came down on my own head, as shall be mentioned in the events of the ensuing year.

Bābur's grandmother joins him.

A few days after, my grandmother Isān Doulet Begum,[2]

[a] who gave it to me.

[1] Nuyān Gokultāsh was at that time with Bābur.
[2] She was Bābur's maternal grandmother and a widow of Yunis Khan.

who had remained behind in Samarkand when I left it, arrived with the family and heavy baggage, and a few lean and hungry followers.

This same winter Sheibāni Khan, having passed the river of Khojend on the ice, ravaged the territory of Shahrokhīa and Bishkent. As soon as I heard the intelligence, without regarding the smallness of my numbers, I mounted and set out for the districts below Khojend, opposite to Hasht-yek. It was wonderfully cold, and the wind of Hā-derwīsh had here lost none of its violence, and blew keen. So excessive was the cold, that in the course of two or three days we lost two or three persons from its severity. I required to bathe on account of my religious purifications, and went down for that purpose to a rivulet, which was frozen on the banks, but not in the middle, from the rapidity of the current. I plunged myself into the water, and dived sixteen times. The extreme chillness of the water quite penetrated me. Next morning I passed the river of Khojend on the ice, opposite to Khaslār, and the day after arrived at Bishkent; but Sheibāni Khan had gone off, after plundering the environs of Shahrokhīa. At this time Abdal Minān, the son of Mulla Haider, held Shahrokhīa. A son younger than Abdal Minān, one Mūmin, a worthless and dissipated young man, had come to me while I was in Samarkand, and I had shown him every kindness. I do not know what bad turn Nuyăn Gokultāsh had done him at that time; however, the young catamite treasured up a deadly enmity against him.

Sheibāni Khan passes the Sirr, and ravages the Khan's territories.

Bābur also passes the river to meet him.

When I received certain accounts that the plundering party of the Uzbeks was retired, I dispatched a messenger with the intelligence to the Khan, and leaving Bishkent tarried three or four days in the village of Ahengerān.[1] Mūmin, the son of Mulla Haider, on the plea of their previous acquaintance in Samarkand, invited Nuyan Gokultāsh, Ahmed Kāsim, and some others, to an entertainment; and, when I left Bishkent, this party stayed behind. The entertainment was given on the top of a precipice. I went on to the village of Sām-sīrek, which is one of the

Death of Nuyăn Gokultāsh.

---

[1] [P. de C. has 'district of Ahengerān (Blacksmiths)', and further on Bābur calls it the Valley of Blacksmiths.]

dependencies of Ahengerān, and there halted. Next morning, I was informed that Nuyān Gokultāsh had fallen over the precipice while intoxicated, and was killed. I dispatched Hak Nazar, the maternal uncle of Nuyān Gokultāsh, with a detachment, who went, examined the place from which he had fallen, and, after interring him in Bishkent, returned back to me. They found Nuyān's corpse at the distance of a bowshot from the spot where the entertainment had been given, at the bottom of a steep precipice. Many suspected that Mūmin, cherishing in his heart the grudge against Nuyān, which he had contracted at Samarkand, was the cause of his death. The truth no man can know. His death affected me deeply. There are few persons for whose loss I have felt so much. I wept incessantly for a week or ten days. I discovered the date of his death in *fout-shud Nuyān* [1] (Nuyān is dead). A few days afterwards, I set out from this place, and returned to Dehkat.

Bābur's grief.

It was now spring, and intelligence was brought that Sheibāni Khan was advancing against Uratippa. As Dehkat was in the low country, I passed by Āb-burden and Amāni, and came to the hill-country of Masīkha. Āb-burden is a village which lies at the foot of Masīkha.[a] Beneath Āb-burden is a spring, and close by the spring is a tomb. From this spring, towards the upland, the country belongs to Masīkha, but downwards from the spring it depends on Yelghar. On a stone which is on the brink of this spring, on one of its sides, I caused the following verses [2] to be inscribed:

He goes to Masīkha.

> I have heard that the exalted Jemshīd
> Inscribed on a stone beside a fountain,
> ' Many a man like us has rested by this fountain,
> And disappeared in the twinkling of an eye.
> Should we conquer the whole world by our manhood and strength,
> Yet could we not carry it with us to the grave.'

In this hill-country, the practice of cutting verses and other inscriptions on the rocks is extremely common.

[a] the lowest (= last) village in the district of Masīkha.

---

[1] [The words give the year A. H. 907 = A. D. 1501.]
[2] These verses occur in Sa'di's *Būstān*, Book I, pp. 292-4.

While I was in Masīkha, I had a visit from Mulla Hijari, the poet, who came from Hissār. At this time I composed the following *matla*[1]:

> (*Tūrki*)—Whatever skill the painter employs in portraying your features, you exceed his art;
> They call you Soul; but of a truth you are more admirable than the soul.

Sheibāni Khan advanced into the neighbourhood of Uratippa, and retired after committing some devastations. While he was in the territory of Uratippa, without regarding the fewness of my men, or their bad equipment, leaving my household and baggage in Masīkha, I marched rapidly over the hills, passing Āb-burden and Amāni, and came into the vicinity of Dehkat, about the time when the night mingles with the morning, resolved to lose no opportunity, and to be in the way of seizing every chance that might present itself.[a] Sheibāni Khan, however, had retired hastily, so that I measured back my way over the hills, and returned to Masīkha.

I now began to reflect, that to ramble in this way from hill to hill, without house and without home, without country and without resting-place, could serve no good purpose, and that it was better to go to Tāshkend to the Khan. Kāsim Beg was very averse to this journey. He had put to death three or four Moghuls at Kara-būlāk, as an example and punishment for marauding, as has been mentioned, and on that account he had considerable apprehensions of going among their countrymen. Whatever remonstrances we could use were of no avail. He separated from me, and moved off towards Hissār, with his elder and younger brothers, their adherents and dependants ; while I proceeded by the pass of Āb-burden, and advanced towards Tāshkend, to join the Khan.

Bābur resolves to go to Tāshkend.

[a] I wished to take advantage of the night to concentrate my forces in order to attempt an attack at dawn.

---

[1] This is the opening couplet (*matla*) of one of Bābur's poems. The same observation will apply to most of the other couplets which he quotes. They are used for reference to those who are acquainted with the poems themselves.

164　　　MEMOIRS OF BĀBUR　　　A. H. 907

Conspiracy in Tambol's army.

At this same time, Tambol, having collected an army, advanced to the dale of Ahengerān. In the very heart of his army a conspiracy was formed against him by Muhammed Dughlet, known by the name of Muhammed Hissāri, in concert with his younger brother, Sultan Hussain Dughlet, and Kamber Ali, the skinner. On Tambol's discovering the plot, being unable longer to remain in his camp, they fled, and came to the Khan. I passed the Īd-e-kurbān[1] in Shahrokhīa, but, without tarrying there, I went to Tāshkend to the Khan.

10th Zilhijeh.
June 16, 1502.

Bābur's verses.

I had composed the following *rubāi* in a well-known measure, and was dubious about the correctness of its rhymes, as, at that time, I had not studied with much attention the style and phraseology of poetry. The Khan had pretensions to taste, and, moreover, wrote verses; though his odes, to be sure, were rather deficient both in manner and substance. I presented my *rubāi*, however, to the Khan, and expressed to him my apprehensions, but did not get such an explicit or satisfactory answer as to remove my doubts. Indeed, it was pretty clear that he had no great skill in poetic diction. The following is the *rubāi* or quatrain in question:

> (*Tūrki*)—No one remembers him who is in adversity;
> A banished man cannot indulge his heart in happiness;
> My heart is far from joy in this exile;
> However brave, an exile has no pleasures.

I afterwards learned, however, that, in the Tūrki language, *te* and *dāl*, as well as *ghain*, *kāf* and *qāf*, by a poetical licence, are frequently interchanged[2] for each other, for the sake of the rhyme.

Tambol advances to Uratippa.

A short time afterwards, Tambol advanced against Uratippa. As soon as this information arrived, the Khan led out his army from Tāshkend, and between Bishkent and Sām-sīrek, having drawn it up in regular array, with right

---

[1] [The Feast of Sacrifice, the greatest of Muhammedan festivals, which is celebrated on the tenth of the month Zu'l Hijjah in commemoration of Abraham's willingness to offer up his son as a sacrifice.]

[2] That is, that the *te* is changed for *dāl*, and that *ghain*, *kāf*, and *qāf* are used for each other. This refers to the rhyme in the original.

and left wings, he formed the *ivīm* (or circle [1]). The Moghuls blew horns according to their custom.[a] The Khan having alighted, they brought nine horsetail standards,[2] and placed them by him. One Moghul stood by, holding in his hand an ox's shank-bone, to which he tied a long white cotton cloth. Another having fastened three long slips of white cloth beneath the horsetail of the standard, passed them under the banner-staff of the ensigns.[3] One corner of one of the cloths the Khan took, and, putting it beneath his feet, stood upon it. I stood on one corner of another of the long slips, which was in like manner tied under one of the horsetail standards; while Sultan Muhammed Khanekeh [4] took the third, and, placing the cloth under his feet, in like manner stood on a corner of it. Then the Moghul that had tied on these cloths, taking the ox-shank in his hand, made a speech in the Moghul tongue, looking often to the standards, and pointing and making signs towards them. The Khan and all the men around took *kumīz* [5] in their hands, and sprinkled it towards the standards. All the trumpets and drums struck up at once, and the whole soldiers who were drawn up raised the war-shout. These ceremonies they repeated three times. After that, they leaped on horseback, raised the battle-shout, and put their horses to the speed. Among the Moghuls, the Institutions [6] established by Chingiz Khan have continued to be strictly observed down to the present time. Every man

Ceremonies of a Moghul review.

[a] The ceremony of the display of the standards was celebrated according to the custom of the Mongols.

[1] [Later on this term is explained as signifying the muster of the army.]

[2] These standards are made of the *kutās*, which is properly the tail of the mountain-cow, or ox [yak], placed above a triangular flag or pennant. The mountain-ox [yak] has a tail like the horse, with long shaggy hair on its back and belly. The tail is sometimes hung on the neck of a riding-horse for ornament, and as a mark of rank. The animal is very powerful, and the natives of the hill-countries often pass mountain torrents holding by the tail.

[3] [This is not very clear. Bābur apparently means that three pieces of white cloth were attached to the poles of the standards below the horse-tails.]

[4] The son of Sultan Mahmūd Khan.
[5] A spirit made from mare's milk.   [6] *Tūzak*.

has his appointed station; those appointed to the right wing, the left wing, or the centre, have their allotted places, which are handed down to them from father to son. Those of most trust and consequence are stationed on the extremities or flanks of the two wings. Among those who compose the right wing there is a dispute between the tribes [1] of the Chirās and Begchik, which of them should occupy the extremity of the line. At this time, the chief of the tribe [2] of Chirās was Kāshkeh Mahmūd, a very brave young man. The chief of the tribe of Begchik, which is noted among the Tumāns, was Ayūb Yakūb. They had a dispute which of them was to occupy the flank, which came to such lengths, that swords were drawn. Finally, an apparently friendly compromise was made, that the one of them should stand highest at great hunting-matches,[3] and that the other should occupy the flank when the army was in battle array.

Next morning, the army forming the large hunting circle, they hunted in the vicinity of Sām-sīrek, and, advancing forward, at length halted at the Chārbagh of Burāk. The first *ghazel* that I ever composed was finished that day at this station. The *ghazel* was the following:[4]

I have found no faithful friend in the world but my soul;
Except my own heart I have no trusty confidant.

The *ghazel* consists of six couplets, and all the *ghazels* that I afterwards wrote were composed in the same measure as this.

From hence, march by march, we proceeded till we reached the banks of the river of Khojend. One day, having passed the river, and ridden out on a pleasure party, I got ready a dinner, and made all the officers and young people of the army [a] merry. That same day, the golden clasp of my

---

[a] their attendants

[1] *Urugh*, subdivisions of greater tribes.
[2] *Tumān* [i. e. a body nominally of ten thousand men].
[3] These hunting-matches were often conducted with great pomp. The hunting circle sometimes enclosed many miles. Accounts of them may be found in Petis de la Croix's Life of Genghiscan, and in the life of Taimūr Beg.
[4] [i. e. the opening lines of the Ode were as follows.]

girdle was stolen. Next morning, Khānkuli, Biānkuli, and Sultan Mahmūd Weis deserted, and went over to Tambol. The general suspicion was, that they were the guilty persons, though it was not established. Ahmed Kāsim Kohbur also asked leave and went to Uratippa, but he never came back, and he too went and joined Tambol.

TRANSACTIONS OF THE YEAR 908 [1]

This expedition of the Khan's was rather a useless sort of expedition. He took no fort, he beat no enemy, he went and came back again.

While I remained at Tāshkend at this time, I endured great distress and misery. I had no country, nor hopes of a country. Most of my servants had left me from absolute want; the few who still remained with me were unable to accompany me on my journeys from sheer poverty. When I went to my uncle the Khan's Divān,[2] I was attended sometimes by one person, sometimes by two; but I was fortunate in one respect, that this did not happen among strangers, but with my own kinsmen. After having paid my compliments to the Khan my uncle, I went in to wait on Shah Begum,[3] bare-headed and bare-foot, with as much freedom as a person would do at home in his own house. *Bābur's distress.*

At length, however, I was worn out with this unsettled state, and with having no house nor home, and became tired of living. I said to myself, rather than pass my life in such wretchedness and misery, it were better to take my way and retire into some corner where I might live unknown and undistinguished; and rather than exhibit myself in this distress and debasement, far better were it to flee away from the sight of man, as far as my feet can carry me. I thought of going to Khitā,[4] and resolved to shape my course in that direction; as from my infancy I had always had a strong desire to visit Khitā, but had never been able to accomplish my wish, from my being a King, and from my *He resolves to go to China.*

---

[1] This year commences July 7, 1502. [2] [Court.]
[3] The widow of Yunis Khan, and the mother of Sultan Mahmūd Khan.
[4] Northern China.

duty to my relations and connexions. Now my kingship was gone, my mother was safe with her mother and younger brother; in short, every obstacle to my journey was removed, and all my difficulties were at an end.[a] By means of Khwājeh Abul Makāram, I made some ideas to be suggested,[b] that when an enemy so formidable as Sheibāni Khan had started up, from whom Tūrks and Moghuls had equal cause of apprehension, it was but prudent to watch with jealousy his progress at this moment, before he had completely subjected the Ulūses,[1] and while he was not yet grown too powerful to be restrained ; as it is said,

> Extinguish to-day the flame while yet you can ;
> For when it blazes forth, it will consume the world.
> Let not your foe apply his arrow to the bowstring,
> When you can pierce him with your shaft.[2]

Besides that it was twenty-four or twenty-five years since the Khan had seen my younger uncle,[3] and I had never seen him at all ; that it would be well if I went and visited my younger uncle, and acted as mediator, using my endeavours to procure an interview between them. My purpose was to escape from my relations[c] under these pretexts ; and I had now fully made up my mind to visit Moghulistān and Tarfān, after which the reins were in my own hand. I, however, acquainted no person with my plan, nor could I impart it to any one, not only because my mother could not have supported the mention of such a proposition; but also because I had about me a number of persons who had attached themselves to me with very different hopes, and supported by them had shared with me my wanderings and distresses. It was unpleasant to communicate such a project to them. Khwājeh Abul Makāram started the subject to Shah Begum and my uncle the Khan, and gained their

---

[a] *This clause is omitted.*
[b] I made a confidant of Khwāja Abul Mukāram, and the result of our deliberations was
[c] entourage

---

[1] The wandering Tartar tribes.
[2] [Sa'di's *Gulistān*, chap. 8.]
[3] [i.e. Sultan Ahmed Khan.]

acquiescence; but it afterwards came into their head, that I had asked permission to go in consequence of the poor reception they had given me; and this suspicion made them delay some time before granting me liberty to depart. At this very crisis, a messenger came from the Khan, my younger maternal uncle, bringing certain information that he was himself coming. My plan, therefore, was totally disconcerted. A second messenger followed immediately after, with news that he was close at hand. Shah Begum, with the younger Khan's younger sisters, Sultan Nigār Khanum, Doulet Sultan Khanum, myself, Sultan Muhammed Khanekeh, and Mirza Khan, all of us set out to meet my uncle.

Sultan Ahmed Khan visits his elder brother.

Between Tāshkend and Seirām there is a village named Yaghma, as well as some other small villages, where are the tombs of Ibrahīm Ātā and Ishāk Ātā. We advanced as far as these villages, and not knowing precisely the time that the younger Khan would arrive, I had ridden out carelessly to see the country, when all at once I found myself face to face with him. I immediately alighted and advanced to meet him; at the moment I dismounted the Khan knew me, and was greatly disturbed; for he had intended to alight somewhere, and having seated himself, to receive and embrace me with great form and decorum: but I came too quick upon him, and dismounted so rapidly, that there was no time for ceremony; as, the moment I sprang from my horse, I kneeled down and then embraced. He was a good deal agitated and disconcerted. At length he ordered Sultan Saīd Khan and Baba Khan Sultan to alight, kneel, and embrace me. Of the Khan's children, these two Sultans alone accompanied him, and might be of the age of thirteen or fourteen years. After embracing these two Sultans I mounted, and we proceeded to join Shah Begum. The Little Khan my uncle soon after met, and embraced Shah Begum and the other Khanums, after which they sat down, and continued talking about past occurrences and old stories till after midnight.

Is met by Bābur.

On the morrow, my uncle the younger Khan, according to the custom of the Moghuls, presented me with a dress complete from head to foot, and one of his own horses ready saddled. The dress consisted of a Moghul cap, embroidered with gold thread; a long frock of satin of Khitā,[1] ornamented with flowered needle-work; a cuirass of Khitā of the old fashion, with a whetstone and a purse-pocket; from this purse-pocket were suspended three or four things like the trinkets which women wear at their necks, such as an *abīrdān* (or box for holding perfumed earth [2]), and its little bag. On the left hand in like manner three or four things dangled. From this place we returned towards Tāshkend. My uncle the elder Khan came three or four farsangs out from Tāshkend, and having erected an awning, seated himself under it. The younger Khan advanced straight up, and on coming near him in front, turned to the left of the elder Khan, fetching a circle round him, till he again presented himself in front, when he alighted; and when he came to the distance at which the *kornish*[3] is performed, he knelt nine times, and then came up and embraced him. The elder Khan, immediately on the younger Khan's coming near, stood up and embraced him; they stood a long time clasping each other in their arms. The younger Khan, while retiring, again knelt nine times, and when he presented his *peshkesh* (or tributary offering), he again knelt many times; after which he went and sat down. All the younger Khan's men had dressed themselves out after the Moghul fashion. They had Moghul caps, frocks of Khitā satin, embroidered with flowers after the same fashion, quivers and saddles of

Interview of the two Khans.

[1] i. e. China satin.

[2] [*Abīr* is a compound perfume composed of musk, sandal-wood, and rose-water.]

[3] The *kornish* is a Moghul ceremony used in saluting the Supreme Prince, which has been introduced into India. Originally, the person who performed it knelt nine times, and touched the earth with his brow each time. The ceremony, as enjoined by Akbar, differs extremely from this. 'His Majesty has enjoined the palm of the right hand to be placed upon the forehead, and the head to be bent forwards. This kind of salutation is called *kornish*, i.e. the head being placed in the hand of supplication, becomes an offering to the holy assembly.'—*Ayeen e Akberī*, vol. i, p. 162. As now practised, it is merely bowing, and at the same time sliding the hands down the thighs, till they reach the knees. It is understood to be offering the neck to the sword. People sometimes only slide one hand down, laying the other on their dagger.

green shagreen, and Moghul horses dressed up and adorned in a singular style.

The younger Khan came with but few followers; they might be more than one thousand, and less than two. He was a man of singular manners. He was a stout, courageous man, and powerful with the sabre, and of all his weapons he relied most on it. He used to say that the *shashper* (or mace with six divisions), the rugged mace, the javelin, the battle-axe, or broad axe, if they hit, could only be relied on for a single blow.[a] His trusty keen sword he never allowed to be away from him; it was always either at his waist, or in his hand. As he had been educated, and had grown up, in a remote and out of the way country, he had something of rudeness in his manner, and of harshness in his speech. When I returned back with my uncle the younger Khan, tricked out in all the Moghul finery that has been mentioned, Khwājeh Abdal Makāram, who was along with the elder Khan, did not know me, and asked what Sultan that was, and it was not till I spoke that he recognized me.

Having come to Tāshkend, they speedily marched against Sultan Ahmed Tambol.[b] They advanced by way of Bānī.[1] On reaching the dale of Ahengerān, the little Khan and myself were sent [2] on in advance. After having crossed the hill-pass of Dābān, the two Khans met again in the neighbourhood of Zarkān and Karnān. In the vicinity of Karnān they one day had the *vīm*[3] or muster of the army, and found it amount to about thirty thousand horse. Reports reached us from the country in our front, that Tambol had also collected his forces and advanced to Akhsi. The Khans, after consultation, determined to give me a detachment of the army, with which I should pass the

The two Khans advance against Akhsi.

Bābur detached against Usb and Uzkend.

[a] could only produce an effect on one place at a time while the sword cuts the body from head to foot.
[b] *Add* who was at Andejān.

---

[1] The Persian has Kundirlik and Amāni.
[2] The author of the Rauzet-es-sefā says, that the two Khans left Tāshkend on the 15th Muharrem (July 21, 1502), to restore Bābur and expel Ahmed Tambol.
[3] This is the same as the *īvīm* that has been mentioned. I know not which is the right name.

river of Khojend, advance towards Ush and Uzkend, and take him in rear. This being arranged, they sent with me Ayūb Begchik with his *tumān* (or tribe), Jān Hassan Bārīn with his Bārīns, as well as Muhammed Hissāri Dughlet, Sultan Hussain Dughlet, and Sultan Ahmed Mirza Dughlet, but the Tumān of the Dughlets did not accompany them; Kamber Ali Sārīk-bāsh[1] Mirza, the Steward,[2] was made the Dārogha or Commander of the Army.[a] Having separated from the Khans at Karnān, I passed the river of Khojend at Sakan on rafts, and proceeding by the Rabāt[3] of Khukān, and having reduced Kaba, advanced upon Ush by a rapid march by the route of Rabāt-e-Alā-balūk. At sunrise I came upon the fort of Ush while the garrison were off their guard, being totally ignorant of our approach; seeing no remedy, they were forced to surrender. The inhabitants of the country, who were warmly attached to me, had longed much for my arrival: but, partly from dread of Tambol, partly from the distance at which I had been, had no means of doing anything; no sooner, however, had I arrived in Ush, than all the Īls and Ulūses poured in from the east and south of Andejān, from the hills and plains. The inhabitants of Uzkend, a fortress of great strength, which had formerly been the capital of Ferghāna, and lay on the frontier, declared for me, and sent a person to tender their allegiance. A few days after, the people of Marghinān having attacked and driven out their Governor, joined my party. The whole population on the Andejān side of the river of Khojend, with all the fortified places, except Andejān itself, declared for me. All this time, although so many forts were falling into my hands, and though such a spirit of insurrection and revolt had overrun the country, Tambol, without being in the least disconcerted, lay with his cavalry and infantry facing the Khans, between Akhsi and Karnān,[4] where he encamped and fortified his position

Takes Ush,

Uzkend and Marghinān.

Tambol maintains his post.

[a] Kambar Ali and Sārīk-bāsh Mirza, who was made commander of the army.

[1] *Sārīk-bāsh* = yellow-head.—*Leyden.*   [2] *Ambārchi.*
[3] The *rabāt* is a large enclosed caravanserai, built for the reception of travellers and their cattle.
[4] [Karnān lies north-west of Akhsi.]

with a trench guarded by a chevaux-de-frise. A number
of skirmishes and affairs took place, but without any visible
advantage on either side.

Most of the clans and tribes, with the fortresses and country all around Andejān, had now submitted to me, and the men of Andejān were no less eager to declare in my favour, but could not find a safe opportunity. It came into my head to advance one night to the vicinity of Andejān, to send in a man to confer with the Khwājeh and chief inhabitants of the place, and, if they fell in with my views, to concert with them about introducing me, some way or other, into the fortress. With this plan, I one evening set out from Ush, and having about midnight arrived within a kos of Andejān, opposite to Jild-Khizān,[1] sent forward Kamber Alı Beg, and several other Begs, with instructions to introduce secretly into the place some person who might confer with the Khwājeh and leading men. I and my party remained on horseback where they had left us, awaiting the return of the Begs. It might be about the end of the third watch of the night,[2] some of us were nodding, others fast asleep, when all at once saddle-drums struck up, accompanied with martial shouts and hubbub. My men being off their guard, and oppressed with drowsiness, without knowing how many or few the enemy might be, were seized with a panic, and took to flight, no one trying to keep near another. I had not even time to rally them, but advanced towards the enemy, accompanied by Mīr Shah Kuchīn, Baba Sherzād, and Dost Nāsir. Except us four, all the rest ran off to a man. We had advanced but a little way, when the enemy, after discharging a flight of arrows, raised the war-shout, and charged towards us. One cavalier, mounted on a white-faced[a] horse, came near me. I let fly an arrow, which hit the horse, and he instantly fell dead. They pulled up their bridles a little. My three companions said, 'The night is dark, and it is impossible to ascertain the number and force of the enemy; all the troops which

[a] with a white star on its forehead

[1] The Persian translation has *Chihıl-dukhterān* [which is P. de C.'s reading]. [2] Three o'clock in the morning.

we had with us have fled. We are only four men, and with so small a number, what injury can we hope to do the enemy? Let us follow our party, rally them, and lead them back into action.' Having galloped up and overtaken our men, we horsewhipped some of them; but all our exertions were ineffectual to make them stand. Again we four turned, and gave the pursuers a discharge of arrows. They halted a little; but when, after one or two discharges, they perceived that we were only four in number, they again set off in pursuit of our men, to strike them down and dismount them. In this way, we three or four times covered and protected our people, and, as they would not be rallied, I repeatedly turned along with my three companions, when we kept the enemy in check, and brought them up with our arrows. They kept pursuing us for the space of two or three kos, till they came over against the hillock of Kharabūk and Shibamūn. On reaching the hillock, Muhammed Ali Mubashar met us. I said, 'These people are few in number; come, let us charge them.' When we turned and put our horses to speed to charge them, they stood still. The scattered fugitives now began to collect and come in from different quarters; but there were many good soldiers who did not recover from their alarm, but went on straight to Ush. The business had happened in the following manner: Some Moghuls of Ayūb Begchik's division had gone out prowling round Andejān on a pillaging party. On hearing the noise made by my detachment, they came secretly upon us, when a mistake occurred regarding the watchword. The watchword is of two kinds. One of these is the word of the tribe: for example, some take *Durdāneh*, others *Tūkkai*, others *Lūlū*, as their distinguishing watchword. The other is the watchword given out to the whole army in time of war, and consists of two words; so that, in time of action, if two parties meet, and one person gives the first word, one of the other party answers by the other word, as preconcerted, by which means, they can distinguish their own men from the enemy, and friends from foes. On the night of this occurrence, the word was *Tāshkend*, and the countersign *Seirām*, r if *Seirām* was given as the word, the answer was to be *Tāshkend*. When they fell in with us, Khwājeh

Muhammed Ali was on my advance; and when the Moghuls came on, calling out 'Tāshkend! Tāshkend!' Khwājeh Muhammed Ali, who was a Tājik, in his confusion blundered out, 'Tāshkend! Tāshkend!' in reply. The Moghuls, taking him for an enemy, set up the war-shout, beat their horse-drums, and let fly their arrows. In this manner, from a false alarm, we were dispersed and scattered; the plan which I had conceived failed, and I returned back to Ush, after a fruitless journey.

After five or six days, Tambol and his adherents became disheartened and depressed on learning that the people of the hills, with the low country and forts, had returned to their obedience; and his men and soldiers began to desert and flee to the hills and deserts. Some of those who left his army reported, that Tambol's affairs were on the verge of ruin, and that, in three or four days, he would be compelled to break up from absolute necessity. Immediately on receiving this intelligence, I mounted and marched against Andejān. Sultan Muhammed Gulbeg, the younger brother of Tambol, was in the fortress of Andejān. Advancing by way of Tūtluk,[1] I sent on a foraging party from Khākān, on the south of Andejān, about the time of midday prayers. I myself followed in the rear of the foragers, till I reached the skirts of the heights of Aīsh, on the Khākān side, when we received information from our advanced guards that Sultan Muhammed Gulbeg, with all his force, had advanced out beyond the suburbs and gardens, and was now on the skirts of the heights of Aīsh. The foragers had not yet collected, but without waiting for them, I advanced without delay against the enemy. Gulbeg's force exceeded five hundred in number; though my men were much more numerous, yet a great proportion of them were on the foraging party, and were now scattered. When I met him, perhaps I might have with me about the same number with himself. Without minding array or order, we advanced on the enemy at full gallop. When we came to the charge, they could not stand us, but fled without exchanging a blow. My people followed them close up to the Khākān gate, dismounting and making prisoners all the way.

Bābur marches against Andejān.

Skirmish at the suburbs.

[1] The mulberry grove.

Having routed the enemy, we reached the outskirts of the suburbs at Khwājeh Kitteh, about the time of evening prayers. It was my wish to have ridden right up to the gates, and made a push to enter them. But the old and experienced Begs of rank, such as Nasīr Beg, the father of Dost Beg, Kamber Ali Beg, and other aged veterans, represented to me, that it was now late, and that to approach[a] the fortress in the dark was not a wise measure; that it was better to retire a little and alight; that in the morning they would have nothing left for it but to surrender the fortress. Having acquiesced in the opinion of these experienced officers, we retired from the suburbs. Had we advanced up to the gates of the fortress, there is not a shadow of doubt that the place would have fallen into our hands.

Passes the Khākān. It was about the hour of bed-time prayers when we passed the river Khākān, and encamped close by the village of Rabāt-e-zourek. Although we had received intelligence of the breaking up of Tambol, and his retreat towards Andejān, yet my inexperience made me guilty of a gross oversight; for, instead of occupying the ground along the banks of the river Khākān, which was naturally strong, and encamping there, we passed the river and halted beside the village of Rabāt-e-zourek, in a level plain, where we went to sleep in negligent security, without advanced guard[b] and without videttes. Just before the dawn, while our men were still enjoying themselves in sleep, Kamber Ali Beg *Surprised by Tambol.* galloped up, exclaiming, 'The enemy are upon us—rouse up!' Having spoken these words, without halting a moment, he passed on. I had gone to sleep, as was my custom even in times of security, without taking off my *jāmeh*, or frock, and instantly arose, girt on my sabre and quiver, and mounted my horse. My standard-bearer seized the standard, but without having time to tie on the horse-tail and colours;[c] but, taking the banner-staff in his hand just as it was, leaped on horseback, and we proceeded towards the quarter in which the enemy were advancing. When I first mounted, there were ten or fifteen men with

[a] enter [b] rear guard [c] *Omit* and colours;

me. By the time I had advanced a bowshot, we fell in with
the enemy's skirmishers. At this moment there might
be about ten men with me. Riding quick up to them, and
giving a discharge of our arrows, we came upon the most
advanced of them, attacked and drove them back, and
continued to advance, pursuing them for the distance of
another bowshot, when we fell in with the main body of the
enemy. Sultan Ahmed Tambol was standing, with about
a hundred men. Tambol was speaking with another person *Advances*
in front of the line, and in the act of saying, ' Smite them ! *on Tambol.*
Smite them ! ' but his men were sidling in a hesitating
way, as if saying, ' Shall we flee ? Let us flee ! ' but yet
standing still. At this instant there were left with me only
three persons : one of these was Dost Nāsir, another Mirza
Kuli Gokultāsh, and Kerīmdād Khudāidad, the Turkomān,
the third. One arrow, which was then on the notch, I discharged on the helmet of Tambol, and again applied my
hand to my quiver, and brought out a green-tipped barbed
arrow,[1] which my uncle, the Khan, had given me. Unwilling
to throw it away, I returned it to the quiver, and thus lost
as much time as would have allowed of shooting two arrows.
I then placed another arrow on the string and advanced,
while the other three lagged a little behind me. Two
persons came on right to meet me ; one of them was Tambol,
who preceded the other. There was a highway between us.
He mounting on one side of it as I mounted on the other, we
encountered on it in such a manner that my right hand
was towards my enemy, and Tambol's right hand towards
me. Except the mail for his horse, Tambol had all his
armour and accoutrements complete. I had only my sabre
and bow and arrows.[a] I drew up to my ear and sent right
for him the arrow which I had in my hand. At that very *Wounded.*
moment an arrow of the kind called *shībah* struck me on
the right thigh, and pierced through and through. I had
a steel cap [2] on my head. Tambol, rushing on, smote me

[a] Quiver.

[1] Or perhaps a green [new] finger-guard—*goshehgīr sar i sebz.*—Pers.
[2] [Apparently a mistake for a cloth cap, as Bābur expressly states he was bare of armour, and, farther on, he says that not a thread of his cap was penetrated.]

such a blow on it with his sword as to stun me; though not a thread of the cap was penetrated, yet my head was severely wounded. I had neglected to clean my sword, so that it was rusty, and I lost time in drawing it. I was alone and single in the midst of a multitude of enemies. It was no season for standing still; so I turned my bridle round, receiving another sabre stroke on the arrows in my quiver. I had gone back seven or eight paces, when three foot-soldiers [1] came up and joined us. Tambol[a] now attacked Dost Nāsir sword in hand. They followed us about a bow-shot. Arigh-Khākān-shah [2] is a large and deep stream, which is not fordable everywhere; but God directed us aright, so that we came exactly upon one of the fords of the river. Immediately on crossing the river the horse of Dost Nāsir fell from weakness. We halted to remount him, and, passing among the hillocks that are between Kharabūk and Feraghīneh, and going from one hillock to another,[b] we proceeded by by-roads [c] towards Ush. When we were leaving these hillocks, Mazīd Taghāi met and joined us. He had been wounded by an arrow in the right leg, below the knee; though it had not pierced through and through, yet he reached Ush with much difficulty. The enemy slew many of my best men. Nāsir Beg, Muhammed Ali Mubashar, Khwājeh Muhammed Ali, Khosroū Gokultāsh, and Naamān Chihreh, fell on that day. A great many cavaliers and soldiers also fell at the same time.

Escapes to Ush.

The Khans having followed close after Tambol, took post in the vicinity of Andejān. The elder Khan had his quarters on the edge of the *kurūgh* (or Park) in the garden of my grandmother Isān Doulet Begum, which is known by the name of Kūshtigirmān.[3] The younger Khan had his quarters near the *langer* [4] or monastery of Bāba Tawakkel. After two days I came from Ush, and waited on the elder

Joins the Khans near Andejān.

---

[a] *Add* after striking me,   [b] *Omit this clause.*
[c] we proceeded along the slopes of the mountain

[1] [i. e. his three companions mentioned previously, but the context shows that they were mounted.]
[2] [i. e. the river Khākān referred to before.]
[3] Bird's mill.—*Leyden.*   [4] [Almshouse.]

Khan at Kūshtigirmān. On this first visit he made over to the younger Khan all the places which I had gained possession of, giving me for an excuse, that as an enemy so formidable as Sheibāni Khan had taken the city of Samarkand, and was daily increasing in power, it had become necessary to summon the younger Khan from a great distance; that he had no possessions in this quarter; that it was therefore expedient to give him the country south of the river of Khojend, including Andejān, that he might have a convenient station and place in which to fix himself. The districts to the north of the river of Khojend, along with Akhsi, were promised to me; and after settling this country they were to proceed against Samarkand, which was to be conferred on me; when the whole of Ferghāna was to be ceded to the younger Khan. It is probable that all this talk was merely to over-reach me; and that in case of success they would have forgot their promises. However, there was no help for it. Willing or not, I was obliged to appear contented with this arrangement. On leaving the elder Khan, I mounted and went to visit the younger Khan. On the road, Kamber Ali, who was known by the name of the Skinner, came up alongside of me, and said, 'Do you observe? they are taking away from you the countries which you possess. Depend upon it, you will never gain anything at their hands. Now that you have Ush, and Marghinān, Uzkend, and the country of the Īls and Ulūses, set out at once for Ush, fortify all your castles, dispatch some person to Sultan Ahmed Tambol, to conclude a peace, join in attacking and driving out the Moghuls, and then make a division of the country as between yourself and a younger brother.' I answered, 'It is more satisfactory to me, as the Khans are my own family and kinsmen, to be a vassal of theirs, than a Sovereign along with Tambol.' Perceiving that I did not approve of his suggestion, he seemed to regret having mentioned it, and drew off. I went on and saw my uncle the younger Khan. In my first interview with him I had come upon him unexpectedly, and gone up to him at once, so that he had not even time to dismount from his horse, and our meeting took place without ceremony. On this occasion, however, when I had approached near, he

The southern districts of Ferghāna given to the younger Khan.

Kamber Ali's advice.

Bābur visits the younger Khan.

came out hastily, beyond the range of his tent ropes, and as I walked with considerable pain, and with a staff in my hand, from the arrow-wound in my thigh, he ran up and embraced me, saying, 'Brother, you have behaved like a hero!' and taking me by the arm, led me into the tent. His tent was but small. As he had been brought up in a rude and remote country, the place in which he sat was far from being distinguished for neatness, and had much of the air of a marauder's. Melons, grapes, and stable furniture were all lying huddled about in the same tent in which he was sitting.

The Khan's Moghul surgeon.

After getting up from the Little Khan's I came to my own camp, when he sent me his own Yakhshi [a] or Surgeon to examine my wound. The Moghuls term a surgeon Yakhshi. He was wonderfully skilful in surgery. If a man's brains had come out he could cure him by medicine; and even where the arteries were cut he healed them with the utmost facility. To some wounds he applied a kind of plaster; and to some wounded persons he gave a medicine to be swallowed. To the wound in my thigh he applied the skin of some fruits which he had prepared and dried,[b] and did not insert a seton. He also once gave me something like a root to eat, and said, 'A man had once the bone of his leg broken in such a manner that a part of the bone, of the size of the hand, was completely shattered to pieces. I cut open the integuments, extracted the whole of the shattered bones, and inserted in their place a pulverized preparation; the preparation grew in the place of the bone, and became bone itself, and the leg was perfectly cured.' He told me many similar strange and wonderful stories of cures, such as the surgeons of our countries are totally unable to accomplish. Three or four days afterwards, Kamber Ali, being apprehensive of evil consequences from the conversation which he had had with me, fled to Andejān.

Bābur goes against Kāsān and Akhsi.

After a few days, the Khans, having held a consultation, sent Ayūb Begchik, with his *tumān*, Jān Hassan Bārīn, with the *tumān* of Bārīns, and Sārīk-bāsh Mirza, as commander of the detachment, with a thousand or two

[a] Bakshi   [b] applied a bandage,

thousand men to attend me, and dispatched us towards Akhsi. Sheikh Bayezīd, Tambol's younger brother, held Akhsi, and Shahbāz Kārlūk held Kāsān. On this occasion, Shahbāz came out and took post in advance of the fortress of Noukend. Having passed the river of Khojend unobserved, opposite to Ata, I hastened by a rapid march towards Noukend to surprise Shahbāz. Just before morning, when we were hard upon Noukend, my Begs represented to me that in all probability Shahbāz had got notice of our approach; that therefore it was better not to advance in disorder, but slowly and in regular array. We therefore advanced deliberately, and, as we approached, Shahbāz, who had in reality been off his guard, and ignorant of our motions, on being apprised of our coming, fled away and took shelter in the fortress. Things very often turn out just as they did on this occasion. On its being suggested that the enemy must be acquainted with our motions, enterprises are easily given up, and the moment for action is lost. The result of my experience on these matters is, that after we have formed our plan, and are in the moment of execution, we ought to admit of no remission of activity or exertion in carrying it through; for afterwards what do regret and repining avail? When it was morning, there was some fighting around the fort, but I made no serious attack. *Advances to Noukend.*

From Noukend we proceeded towards the hills near Bishkhārān, for the purpose of plundering. Shahbāz Kārlūk availing himself of the opportunity, abandoned Noukend and threw himself into Kāsān. On my return I took up my quarters in Noukend. During the interval that followed, my troops made various excursions in different directions. On one occasion they fell upon the villages of Akhsi; on another they plundered those of Kāsān. Shahbāz, with the adopted son of Ūzūn Hassan, one Mīram, came out to fight, and did engage; but they were defeated, and Mīram fell in the action.

One of the strongest fortresses of Akhsi is Pāp, the garrison of which declared for me, put it in a state of defence, and sent a messenger to call me in; when I dispatched Syed Kāsim with a detachment, who passed the *Pāp declares for him.*

river[1] opposite to some villages above Akhsi, and marching on, entered the castle of Pāp.

<small>Attempt to surprise Pāp</small>

A few days after this, an event worthy of notice occurred. At this time, Ibrahīm Chāpuk Taghāi, Ahmed Kāsim Kohbur, and Kāsim Jangeh Arghūn, with Sheikh Bayezīd, were in Akhsi. Tambol one night sent these officers with about two hundred chosen men to surprise Pāp. Syed Kāsim had gone to sleep without taking the proper precautions for guarding the place. The enemy having reached the fort, applied their scaling-ladders, mounted the walls, seized the gate, let down the drawbridge, and introduced seventy or eighty of their men, before Syed Kāsim received intelligence of what was passing. Half awakened from his sleep, he rushed out just as he was, in his vest, and with five or six others, began to discharge arrows upon them, and molested them so effectually by dint of repeated

<small>fails.</small>

attacks that he drove them out of the fort and cut off the heads of some of them, which he sent me. Though it was very unworthy of a captain to go to sleep in this negligent manner, yet, with a few men, to drive out such a number of brave soldiers clad in mail, merely by hard fighting and the edge of the sword, was a most gallant exploit.

All this time the Khans were engaged in the siege of the fortress of Andejān. The garrison, however, would not suffer them to approach it, and parties of horse frequently sallied out and skirmished with the besiegers.

<small>Sheikh Bayezīd invites Bābur to Akhsi.</small>

Sheikh Bayezīd, who was in Akhsi, now made a show of being devoted to my interests, and sent a confidential messenger earnestly inviting me to repair to that city. The motive of this invitation was a wish to detach me, by any device, from the Khans, being persuaded that after I left them they could no longer maintain themselves in the country. It was done by him on an understanding with his elder brother Tambol. But to separate myself from the Khans, and to unite myself with them, was a thing to me altogether impossible. I let the Khans understand the invitation I had received. The Khans advised me by all means to go, and to seize Sheikh Bayezīd one way or

Probably the river of Kāsān.

another; but such artifice and underhand dealing were totally abhorrent from my habits and disposition, especially as there must have been a treaty, and I never could bring myself to violate my faith. But I was anxious by one method or another to get into Akhsi, that Sheikh Bayezīd might be detached from his brother Tambol, and unite with me, till some plan should offer, of which I could avail myself with honour. I therefore sent a person to Akhsi, who concluded an agreement with him, when he invited me to the place, and I accordingly went. He came out to meet me, bringing my youngest brother Nāsir Mirza along with him, and conducted me into the fort,[a] where he left me. I alighted at the apartments which had been prepared for me in my father's palace in the stone fort.[1] *Bābur repairs thither.*

Tambol had sent his elder brother, Beg Tilbeh, to Sheibāni Khan, proffering him his allegiance, and summoning him to his assistance. At this very time he received letters from Sheibāni Khan, by which he was informed that the Khan was about to come to join him. As soon as the Khans received this intelligence they were disconcerted and broke up from before Andejān in great alarm. The Little Khan himself had a high character for justice and piety; but the Moghuls whom he had left in Ush, in Marghinān, and the other fortresses of which I had gained possession, instead of protecting, had set about oppressing and tyrannizing over the inhabitants. As soon, therefore, as the Khans raised the siege of Andejān, the men of Ush, Marghinān, and the other fortresses, rose on the Moghuls who were in garrison, seized and plundered them, and drove them out of the towns. The Khans did not immediately cross the river of Khojend, but retreated by way of Marghinān and Kandbādām, and passed the river at Khojend. Tambol followed them as far as Marghinān. I was now greatly distracted; I had no great confidence in their adhering staunchly to me, but I did not like to fly off from them without evident necessity. *Tambol calls in Sheibān Khan.* *The two Khans retire by Khojend.*

One morning Jehāngīr Mirza came and joined me, having fled from Tambol, whom he had left at Marghinān. I was *Jehāngīr Miraz flies*

[a] Town,

---

[1] [This is called the 'outer fort' farther on.]

in the bath when the Mirza arrived, but immediately received and embraced him. At this time Sheikh Bayezīd was in great perturbation, quite unsettled what line of conduct to pursue. The Mirza and Ibrahīm Beg insisted that it was necessary to seize him, and to take possession of the citadel. In truth the proposition was a judicious one. I answered, 'I have made an agreement, and how can I violate it?' Sheikh Bayezīd meanwhile entered the citadel. We ought to have placed a guard at the bridge, yet we did not station a single man to defend it. These blunders were the effects of our inexperience. Before the dawn, Tambol arrived with two or three thousand mailed warriors, passed by the bridge, and entered the citadel. I had but very few men with me from the first, and after I came to Akhsi I had dispatched many of them on different services; some to garrison forts, others to take charge of districts, and others to collect the revenue, so that, at this crisis, I had not with me in Akhsi many more than a hundred. However, having taken to horse with those that remained, I was busy posting them in the entrances to the different streets, and in preparing supplies of warlike stores for their use,[a] when Sheikh Bayezīd, Kamber Ali, and Muhammed Dost, came galloping from Tambol to propose a pacification. Having ordered such of my men as had stations assigned them to remain steadily at their posts, I went and alighted at my father's tomb, to hold a conference with them. I also sent to call Jehāngīr Mirza to the meeting. Muhammed Dost returned back, while Sheikh Bayezīd and Kamber Ali remained with me. We were sitting in the southern portico of the Mausoleum, engaged in conversation, when Jehāngīr Mirza and Ibrahīm Chāpuk, after consulting together, had come to a resolution to seize them. Jehāngīr Mirza whispered in my ear, 'It is necessary to seize them.' I answered him, 'Do nothing in a hurry: the time for seizing them is gone by. Let us try if we can get anything by negotiation, which is much more feasible, for at present they are very numerous, and we are extremely few: besides, their superior force is in possession of the citadel, while our inconsiderable

---

[a] in making preparations for the fight,

strength only occupies the outer fort.' Sheikh Bayezīd and Kamber Ali were present while this passed. Jehāngīr Mirza, looking towards Ibrahīm Chāpuk, made a sign to him to desist. I know not whether he misunderstood it, or whether from perversity he acted knowingly; however that may be, he seized Sheikh Bayezīd. The men who were around closed in on every side, and, in an instant, dragged away and rifled these two noblemen. There was now an end of all treaty. We, therefore, delivered them both into custody and mounted for battle.

I entrusted one side of the town to Jehāngīr Mirza; as the Mirza's followers were very few in number I attached some of my own to him. I first of all went and put his quarter of the town in order, visiting all the posts and assigning each man his station; after which I proceeded to the other quarters.[1] In the midst of the town there was an open level green, in which I had posted a body of my men, and passed on. They were soon attacked by a much superior number of horse and foot, who drove them from their ground and forced them into a narrow lane. At this instant I arrived, and immediately pushed on my horse to the charge. The enemy did not maintain their ground, but fled. We had driven them out of the narrow lane and were pushing them over the green, sword in hand, when my horse was wounded in the leg by an arrow. He bolted, and springing aside, threw me on the ground in the midst of the enemy. I started up instantly and discharged one arrow. Kāhil, one of my attendants, who was on a sorry sort of steed, dismounted and presented it to me. I got on it, and having posted a party there, proceeded to the foot of another street. Sultan Muhammed Weis, observing what a bad horse I had got, dismounted and gave me his own, which I mounted. At this very instant Kamber Ali Beg, the son of Kāsim Beg, came to me wounded, from Jehāngīr Mirza, with notice that Jehāngīr Mirza had been attacked for some time past in such force that he was reduced to the last extremity, and had been compelled to retreat out of the town and take to flight. While still disconcerted by this accident, Syed

Bābur attempts to defend Akhsi.

[1] It would appear that the town was open and without walls on the side of the citadel.

Kāsim, who had held the fort of Pāp, arrived. This was a strangely unseasonable time for coming; for, at such an extremity, had I retained possession of a fortress of such strength as Pāp, there had still been some resource. I said to Ibrahīm Beg, 'What is to be done now?' He was a little wounded, and I know not whether it was from the irritation of his wound, or from his heart failing him, but he did not give me a very distinct answer. An idea struck me, which was to retreat by the bridge, and breaking it down behind us, to advance towards Andejān. Baba Sherzād behaved extremely well in this exigency. He said, 'Let us attack and force a passage through this nearest gateway.' According to this suggestion we proceeded towards the gate. Khwājeh Mīr Mirān also spoke and comported himself in a manly manner, in this extremity. While we were entering the street, Syed Kāsim and Dost Nāsir, with Bāki Khīz, maintained the action, and covered our retreat; I and Ibrahīm Beg, and Mirza Kuli Gokultāsh, had rode on before them. We had no sooner come opposite the gate than we saw Sheikh Bayezīd, with a quilted corslet over his vest, who just then entered the gateway with three or four horsemen, and was proceeding into the town. In the morning, when, contrary to my wish, he was seized along with those who were with him, they had been left with Jehāngīr's men, who, when forced to retreat, carried off Sheikh Bayezīd with them. They once thought of putting him to death, but fortunately they did not, but set him at liberty. He had just been released, and was entering the gate when I met him. I immediately drew to the head the arrow which was on my notch, and discharged it full at him. It only grazed his neck, but it was a fine shot. The moment he had entered the gate he turned short to the right, and fled by a narrow street in great perturbation. I pursued him. Mirza Kuli Gokultāsh struck down one foot-soldier with his mace, and had passed another, when the fellow aimed an arrow at Ibrahīm Beg, who startled him by exclaiming, '*hāī! hāī!*' and went forward; after which the man, being about as far off as the porch of a house is from the hall, let fly at me an arrow, which struck me under the arm. I had on a Kalmuk mail; two plates of it were pierced and broken

Retreats towards the gate;

from the blow. After shooting the arrow he fled, and
I discharged an arrow after him. At that very moment
a foot-soldier happened to be flying along the rampart, and
my arrow pinned his cap to the wall, where it remained
shot through and through and dangling from the parapet.
He took his turban, which he twisted round his arm, and ran
away. A man on horseback passed close by me, fleeing up
the narrow lane by which Sheikh Bayezīd had escaped.
I struck him such a blow on the temples with the point of
my sword that he bent over as if ready to fall from his horse,
but supporting himself on the wall of the lane he did not lose
his seat, but escaped with the utmost hazard. Having
dispersed all the horse and foot that were at the gate we
took possession of it. There was now no reasonable chance which he
of success; for they had two or three thousand well-armed gains,
men in the citadel, while I had only a hundred, or two
hundred at most, in the outer stone fort: and, besides,
Jehāngīr Mirza, about as long before as milk takes to boil,
had been beaten and driven out, and half of my men were
with him. In spite of all this, such was my inexperience
that, posting myself in the gateway, I dispatched a man
to Jehāngīr Mirza to request him to join me if he was near,
and that we might make another effort. But, in truth, the
business was over. Whether it was that Ibrahīm Beg's
horse was really weak, or whether the Beg was fretful from
his wound, I cannot tell; but he said to me, 'My horse is
useless.' Immediately, Sulemān, a servant of Muhammed
Ali Mubashar, dismounted and gave him his horse of his own
accord, without anybody suggesting such a thing to him.
It was a fine trait of character in the man. While we
remained waiting at the gate, Kūchik Ali, who is now
collector [1] of Koel, displayed great bravery. He was then
in the service of Sultan Muhammed Weis. He, on another
occasion, performed good service at Ush. We continued at
the gate, waiting for the return of the messenger whom I had
sent to call the Mirza. He did return, and informed us that
Jehāngīr Mirza had already been gone some time in his

[1] [i. e. Governor. Coel is a village in the Aligarh district of the
United Provinces. Bābur must have written or revised this portion
of his Memoirs in India many years after the incident referred to.]

and retreats.

retreat. It was no longer a season to tarry, and we also set off. Indeed, my halting so long was very ill advised. Not above twenty or thirty men now remained with me. The moment we moved off in our retreat a great band of the enemy's troops came smartly after us. We had just passed the drawbridge when they reached the town side of it. Bandeh Ali Beg, the son of Kāsim Beg, who was the maternal grandfather of Hamzah Beg, called aloud to Ibrahīm Beg, 'You are always boasting and bragging: stop and let us exchange a few sword-cuts.' Ibrahīm Beg, who was close by me, answered, 'Come away, then: What hinders us?' The senseless madcaps! in such a moment of peril and discomfiture, to think of adjusting their rival claims. It was no time for a trial of skill, nor for delay nor loss of time. We retreated with all speed, the enemy being in full pursuit of us. They brought down man after man as they overtook us.

Is warmly pursued.

Within a kos of Akhsi there is place called *Gumbaz-e-chaman* (or the Garden-dome). We had just passed it, when Ibrahīm Beg called out to me for assistance. I looked round and perceived him engaged with a home-bred slave [a] of Sheikh Bayezīd. I instantly turned my bridle to go back. Jān Kuli Bayān Kuli,[1] who was by me, exclaimed, 'What time is this for turning back?' seized my bridle-reins, and hurried me on. Before we reached Sang they had unhorsed the greater part of my adherents. Sang may be about two kos from Akhsi. After passing Sang we saw no more of the enemy in pursuit. We proceeded up the river of Sang, being at this time only eight in all—Dost Nāsir, Kamber Ali Kāsim Beg, Jān Kuli Bayān Kuli, Mirza Kuli Gokultāsh, Shahim Nāsir, Abdal Kadūs Sayyidī Kāra, and Khwājeh Hussaini; I myself was the eighth. A sort of path leads up the river amidst broken glens, remote from the beaten road. By this unfrequented and retired path we proceeded up the river, till, leaving the river on the right, we struck into another narrow [b] path. It was about afternoon prayers

[a] page   [b] arid

---

[1] [P. de C. has 'Jān Kuli' *and* 'Bayān Kuli'. The correct reading may be: 'Jān Kuli son of Bayān Kuli'; and the same remark applies to the other double names found here.]

when we emerged from the broken grounds into the level country. A blackness was discernible afar off in the plain. Having placed my men under cover, I myself, on foot, ascended an eminence to spy what it might be; when suddenly a number of horsemen galloped up the hillock behind us. We could not ascertain precisely how many or how few they were, but took to our horses and continued our flight. The horsemen who followed us were not in all above twenty or twenty-five; and we were eight, as has been mentioned. Had we but known their number when they first came up we should have given them warm play; but we imagined that they were certainly followed by a detachment sent in pursuit of the fugitives. Impressed with this notion, we continued our flight. The fact is, that the fliers, even though the most numerous, can never contend with the pursuers, though the inferior number. As it is said,

(*Persian verse*)—The shout of *hāī* is sufficient for vanquished bands.

Jān Kuli said, 'We must not go on in this way or they will take us all. Let you and Mirza Kuli Gokultāsh, therefore, select the two best horses of the party,[1] and galloping off together keep one another's horses at speed; perhaps you may escape.' The advice was not a bad one; for, since we could not engage them, this presented a possibility of escape; but I could not consent in such circumstances to leave any of my followers dismounted in the midst of the enemy. At length, however, the party began to separate and fall behind each other. The horse on which I was mounted began to lag. Jān Kuli dismounted and gave me his horse. I leaped from my own and mounted his, while he mounted mine. At this very instant Shahim Nāsir, with Abdal Kadūs Sayyidī Kāra, who had fallen behind, were dismounted by the enemy. Jān Kuli also fell behind; but it was no season for trying to shield or assist him. We, therefore, pushed our horses to their utmost speed, but they gradually flagged and fell off. The horse of Dost Beg

His followers taken one after another.

[1] He seems to have wished them to take each a spare horse, as is usual in the forays of the Tūrks.

too began to flag, and fell behind; and the horse which I rode likewise began to be worn out. Kamber Ali dismounting, gave me his own horse. He mounted mine, and presently dropped behind. Khwājeh Hūssaini, who was lame, turned off towards the heights. I now remained alone with Mirza Kuli Gokultāsh. Our horses were too weak to admit of being put to the gallop; we went on at a canter, but the horse of Mirza Kuli began to move slower and slower. I said to him, 'If deprived of you, whither can I go? Come, then, and be it death or life, let us meet it together.'—I kept on, turning from time to time, to see Mirza Kuli. At last, Mirza Kuli said, 'My horse is completely blown, and it is impossible for you to escape if you encumber yourself with me. Push on, and shift for yourself. Perhaps you may still escape.' I was in a singularly distressful situation. Mirza Kuli also fell behind, and I was left alone. Two of the enemy were in sight; the name of the one was Baba Seirāmi, that of the other Bandeh Ali; they gained upon me; my horse began to flag. There was a hill about a kos off, and I came up to a heap of stones. I reflected with myself that my horse was knocked up, and the hill still a considerable way off. What was to be done? I had about twenty arrows left in my quiver. Should I dismount at this heap of stones, and keep my ground as long as my arrows lasted? But it occurred to me again, that perhaps I might be able to gain the hill, and that if I did I might stick a few arrows in my belt and succeed in climbing it. I had great reliance on my own nimbleness. Impelled by this idea I kept on my course. My horse was unable to make any speed, and my pursuers got within arrow's reach of me; I was sparing of my arrows, however, and did not shoot. They also were somewhat chary and did not come nearer than a bowshot, but kept on tracking me.

About sunset I got near the hill, when they suddenly called out to me, 'Where do you intend going that you flee in this manner? Jehāngīr Mirza has been taken and brought in; Nāsir Mirza, too, has been seized.' I was greatly alarmed at these words; because, if all of us[1] fell nto their hands, we had everything to dread. I made no

[1] Jehāngīr and Nāsir Mirza were Bābur's only two brothers.

reply but kept on for the hill. When we had gone a certain way farther they again called out to me. This time they spoke to me in a more gracious style than at first. They dismounted from their horses and began to address me. I did not attend to what they said, but proceeded in my course and, entering a glen, I began to ascend it, and went on till about bedtime prayers, when I reached a large rock about the size of a house. I went behind it and came to an ascent of steep ledges, where the horse could not keep his feet. They also dismounted and began to address me in a still more courteous and respectful style, expostulating with me, and saying, ' What end can it serve to go on in this manner, in a dark night, and where there is no road ? Where can you possibly go ? ' Both of them, with a solemn oath, asserted, ' Sultan Ahmed Beg wishes to place you on the throne.' 'I cannot', I replied, 'confide in anything of the sort ; and to join him is for me impossible. If you are serious in your wish to do me an important service you have now such an opportunity as may not occur for years. Point out to me a road by which I may rejoin the Khans, and I will show you kindness and favour even beyond your highest wishes. If you refuse this, return by the way you came, and leave me to fulfil my destiny—even that will be no mean service.' ' Would to God ', they replied, ' that we had never come ; but, since we have come, how can we desert you in this desolate situation ? Since you will not accompany us we shall follow you and serve you, go where you will.' I answered, ' Swear then unto me by the Holy Book that you are sincere in your offer.' And they swore the heavy and awful oath. They swear to be true to him.

I now began to have a certain degree of confidence in them, and said to them, ' An open road was formerly pointed out to me near this same valley ; do you proceed by it.' Though they had sworn to me, yet still I could not perfectly confide in them ; I therefore made them go on before and followed them. We had advanced a kos or two, when we reached a rivulet. I said, ' This cannot be the road by the open valley that I spoke of.' They hesitated, and said, ' That road is still a considerable way forward.' The truth is, that we then really were on the very road of the open valley and they were deceiving me and concealing the truth. We went on till midnight, when we again came to a stream. They now said, 'We have not been sufficiently attentive, and have certainly left behind the road in the open valley.' I said, 'What then is to be done?' They said, 'The road to Ghava lies a little farther on, and by it you may go to Farket.' We kept on in our way, therefore, and continued travelling forward till the end of the third watch of the night,[1] when we reached the river of Karnān, which comes down from Ghava. Baba Seirāmi then said, 'Stop here, while I go on before, and I will return after reconnoitring the road to Ghava.' He did return in a short time and told us, 'A good many men are passing over the plain along the road; it will be impossible for us to go this way.' I was alarmed at this information. I was in the midst of an enemy's country, the morning was near at hand, and I was far from the place to which I had wished to go. 'Show me, then,' I said, 'some spot where we may remain concealed during the day, and, when it is night, we can get something for our horses, pass the river of Khojend, and then proceed straight for Khojend by the other side of the river.' They answered, 'Hard by there is a hillock, in which we may hide ourselves.' Bandeh Ali was the Dārogha of Karnān. He said, 'Neither we nor our horses can long stand out unless we get something to eat. I will go to Karnān, and will bring out whatever I can procure.' We therefore passed on, and took the road for Karnān. We stopped about a kos from Karnān, while Bandeh Ali went on, and stayed away for a long time. The morning had dawned, yet there was no appearance of our man. I began to be greatly alarmed. Just as it was day, Bandeh Ali came cantering back, bringing three loaves, but no grain for the horses. Each of us taking a loaf under his arm we went off without loss of time, reached the hillock where we wished to remain in concealment, and, having tied our horses in the low marshy broken grounds, we all mounted the eminence and sat keeping watch on different sides.

Bābur compelled to conceal himself.

It was now near mid-day, when we spied Ahmed Kūshchi (the falconer), with four horsemen, coming from Ghava

[1] Three o'clock in the morning.

towards Akhsi. I once thought of sending for the falconer, and getting possession of their horses by fair words and promises; for our horses were quite worn out, having been in constant exercise and on the stretch for a day and night, without having got a grain of anything to eat. But my heart immediately began to waver again, and I could not make up my mind to put confidence in them. I and my companions arranged, however, that as these people were likely to stay all night at Karnān, we should secretly enter the town, carry off their horses, and so make our escape to some place of safety.

It was about noon, when, as far off as the sight could reach, we perceived something that glittered on a horse. For some time we could not distinguish what it was. It was, in truth, Muhammed Bākir Beg. He had been in Akhsi along with me; and in the dispersion that followed our leaving the place, when every one was scattered here and there, Muhammed Bākir Beg had come in this direction, and was now wandering about and concealing himself. Bandeh Ali and Baba Seirāmi said, 'For two days past our horses have had neither grain nor fodder. Let us go down into the valley, and suffer them to graze.' We accordingly mounted, and, having descended into the valley, set them a-grazing. It was about the time of afternoon prayers, when we descried a horseman passing along over the very height on which we had been hiding. I recognized him to be Kādir Berdi, the head-man of Ghava. I said to them, 'Let us call Kādir Berdi.' We called him, and he came and joined us. Having greeted him, asked him some questions, spoken obligingly and with kindness to him, made him promises, and disposed him favourably towards me by every means in my power, I sent him to bring a rope, a grass-hook, an axe, apparatus for crossing a river, provender for the horses and food for ourselves, and, if possible, a horse likewise; and we made an appointment to meet him on this same spot at bedtime prayers.

Evening prayers were over, when a horseman was seen passing from Karnān towards Ghava. We called out, 'Who goes there?' He answered us. This was, in truth, the same Muhammed Bākir Beg, whom we had observed at noon. He had, in the course of the day,[1] moved from the place in which he had lain concealed, to another lurking-place; and now so thoroughly changed his voice, that, although he had lived for years with me, I did not discover him. Had I known him, and kept him with me, it had been well for me. I was rendered very uneasy by this man's passing us, and durst not adhere to the assignation we had made with Kādir Berdi of Ghava by waiting till the specified time. Bandeh Ali said, 'There are many retired gardens among the suburbs of Karnān, where nobody will suspect us of lurking. Let us go thither, and send a person to conduct Kādir Berdi to us.' With this intention we mounted and proceeded to the suburbs of Karnān. It was winter, and excessively cold. They brought me an old mantle of year-old lambskin, with the wool on the inside, and of coarse woven cloth without, which I put on. They also procured and brought me a dish of pottage of boiled millet-flour, which I ate, and found wonderfully comfortable. I asked Bandeh Ali, 'Have you sent anybody to Kādir Berdi?' He answered, 'Yes, I have.' These unlucky perfidious clowns had in reality met Kādir Berdi, and had dispatched him to Tambol at Akhsi.

Hides himself in Karnān.

Having gone into a house that had stone walls, and kindled a fire, I closed my eyes for a moment in sleep. These crafty fellows, pretending an extreme anxiety to serve me, 'We must not stir from this neighbourhood,' said they, 'till we have news of Kādir Berdi. The house where we are, however, is in the very middle of the suburbs. There is a place in the outskirts of the suburbs where we might be quite unsuspected, could we but reach it.' We mounted our horses, therefore, about midnight, and proceeded to a garden on the outskirts of the suburbs. Baba Seirāmi watched on the terrace-roof of the house, keeping a sharp look-out in every direction. It was near noon when he came down from the terrace and said to me, 'Here comes Yūsef, the Dārogha.' I was seized with prodigious alarm and said, 'Learn if he comes in consequence of knowing that I am here.' Baba went out, and, after some conversation, returned and said, 'Yūsef, the Dārogha, says, that, at the

[1] Literally *yesterday*, a new day commencing from sunset.

gate of Akhsi, he met a man on foot, who told him that the King was in Karnān, at such a place ; that, without communicating this intelligence to any one, he had put the man into close custody, along with Wali, the treasurer, who had fallen into his hands in the action ; after which he hastened to you full speed ; and that the Begs are not[a] informed of the circumstance.' I asked him, 'What do you think of the matter ?' He answered, 'They are all your servants ; there is nothing left for it but to join them. They will undoubtedly make you king.' 'But after such wars and quarrels,' I replied, 'with what confidence can I place myself in their power ?' I was still speaking, when Yūsef suddenly presented himself, and throwing himself on both his knees before me, exclaimed, 'Why should I conceal anything from you ? Sultan Ahmed Beg knows nothing of the matter ; but Sheikh Bayezīd Beg has got information where you are, and has sent me hither.'

On hearing these words I was thrown into a dreadful state of agitation. There is nothing in the world which affects a man with more painful feelings than the near prospect of death. 'Tell me the truth,' I exclaimed, 'if indeed things are about to go with me contrary to my wishes, that I may at least perform my last ablutions.' Yūsef swore again and again, but I did not heed his oaths. I felt my strength gone. I rose and went to a corner of the garden. I meditated with myself, and said, 'Should a man live a hundred, nay a thousand years, yet at last he [1]——.' Bāburin imminent danger.

[The copyist adds, 'The remaining transactions of this year, viz. 908, may God grant that they come to hand.' In this wish I most heartily join.—*Leyden.*]

[a] no one was

---

[1] [P. de C. fills the gap with the words 'must die'.]

NOTE.—[In P. de C.'s French translation the gap in the Memoirs is filled by a short account of Bābur's rescue from his critical position, the authenticity of which, however, is open to doubt (see Appendix B).]

SUPPLEMENT

CONTAINING

A SHORT ACCOUNT OF THE EVENTS THAT OCCURRED IN THE END OF A. H. 908 AND IN A. H. 909 [1]

THE narrative of Bābur is here broken off, at one of the most interesting moments of his history. Whether this defect be owing to the imperfection of the copies or to design in the author, it is not easy to decide; though, from a similar interruption at the beginning of the year 914 of the Hijira, when Bābur appears to be on the point of falling into the hands of a desperate band of conspirators, it seems probable that it was intentional; and, we may be almost tempted to believe, that the Imperial author derived a sort of dramatic pleasure from working up to a very high pitch the curiosity of his reader or hearer, and leaving the mind in a state of awakened suspense by a sudden break in the narrative. All the three copies which I have had an opportunity of comparing, break off precisely at the same period in both instances. This holds in the original Tūrki as well as in the translation; and it is hardly conceivable that a translator would have deserted his hero in the most memorable passages of his life. The copy which Dr. Leyden followed was evidently, in this respect, exactly like the others. The blank which Bābur has left in his own Memoirs it is difficult to supply, in spite of the great number of authors who have written the details of his reign; as they have in general confined themselves to the grand military and political actions of his times, and give us little assistance where Bābur, who is his own best biographer, happens to fail in detailing the earlier, which are by no means the least interesting events of his life.

A.D. 1508.

The Khans defeated by Sheibāni Khan.

The Memoirs break off in A. H. 908, and are resumed in A. H. 910.[2] Whether Bābur was delivered into the hands of Sheikh Bayezīd, or whether he effected his escape from

[1] From the end of A. D. 1502 to June 1504.
[2] Leaving a blank from the end of A. D. 1502 to June 1504.

the painful custody in which he was held at Karnān, I have not been able to discover. The narrative of Abul-Fazel [1] is here very imperfect. It would appear, however, from the brief account of Ferishta,[2] and of Khāfi Khan,[3] that Bābur had succeeded in rejoining his maternal uncles the two Khans; but, if this was the case, the advantage derived from this junction was of short continuance. Sheibāni Khan, whom Ahmed Tambol had invited to his assistance, arrived soon after with an army more in number than the rain-drops, says Mīr Khāwend Shah,[4] attacked the Moghuls, defeated them in a bloody battle,[5] made both the brothers prisoners, and compelled Bābur to fly into Moghulistān. Immediately after the battle, Sheibāni Khan dispatched a messenger to Tāshkend, to communicate information that the two Khans were in his hands, and that Bābur had been obliged to abandon the country; and with instructions to add that, if the inhabitants had any wish to save their princes, they must prevent the escape of Khwājeh Abul Makāram and detain him in custody. Sheibāni Khan, after having kept the Khans a few days as his prisoners, dismissed them to go where they would; 'and they came by their end', continues Mīr Khāwend Shah, 'in the way mentioned in the Account of the family of Chaghatāi Khan.' The particulars of their death I have not been able to ascertain, and there is some disagreement among historians on the subject.[6] By some, Sheibāni Khan [7] is represented

---

[1] In the account of Bābur's reign in the first volume of the *Akbernāmeh* [translated by Beveridge, 1907].

[2] See his *General History of Hindustān*, Dow's Translation, vol. ii, p. 182 [London, 1770].

[3] In his valuable and amusing History of the House of Taimūr in India. [Muntakhab ul lubāb.]

[4] *Tārīkh e Rauzet-es-sefā*, vol. vii, folio MS. containing the History of Sultan Hussain Mirza [translated by Shea, 1832].

[5] [The disaster of Tāshkend occurred in A. H. 908 (A. D. 1503). *E.B*, p. 184.]

[6] [Ahmed Alacha, the younger Khan, died a natural death in A. H. 909 (A. D. 1504). The elder Khan, Sultan Mahmūd Khan, and his five sons were put to death by Shaibāni Khan's orders in A. H. 914 (A. D. 1508). *E. B.*, pp. 190-2.]

[7] See *Tārīkh e Khāfi Khan*, vol. i, and the *Akbernāmeh* of Abul-Fazel, vol. i.

as having used his victory with considerable lenity. He is said to have set the brothers at liberty, prompted by the recollection that he had formerly been in their service, and that he had been received and kindly treated by Yunis Khan, their father. We are told by Ferishta that Sultan Mahmūd Khan, the elder brother, fell into a deep melancholy; when advised by one of his friends to use a famous antidote brought from China, for the purpose of averting the effects of poison, which it was suggested might have been administered by Sheibāni Khan, he is said to have replied, 'Yes; Sheibāni has indeed poisoned me! He has taken away my kingdom, which your antidote cannot restore.'[1] But these accounts are not very consistent with the narrative of Bābur himself, who informs us that Sheibāni Khan put Sultan Mahmūd Khan to death in Khojend, with his son Baba Khan, and many other princes of his family. It is not improbable that Sheibāni Khan affected to set the Khan at liberty a few days after the battle, as is mentioned by Mīr Khāwend Shah, and that he gave orders to pursue, and put him to death privately, along with his family; a policy which he appears to have followed on other occasions, in order to avoid part of the odium likely to arise from an unpopular act.

Fate of Khwājeh Abul Mukāram.
Khwājeh Abul Mukāram was thrown into prison at Tāshkend, but in two or three days effected his escape and set out from that city on foot. That he might not be recognized, he submitted to the mortification of cutting off his beard: but being unable, from his age and infirmities, to reach any place of safety, he was compelled to take refuge with a man who lived in a neighbouring village. This person concealed him for a day or two, but having afterwards informed against him, he was seized and carried before Sheibāni Khan. The Khan, on seeing him, inquired, 'What have you done with your beard?' to which the Khwājeh answered in two Persian verses, the sense of which is, that he who puffs at the lamp which God has lighted, singes his beard. But the felicity of this allusion did not avail him,

[1] [This story is told of the younger Khan, and Ferishtah erroneously attributes it to Sultan Mahmūd Khan. *E. B.*, p. 191 and note.]

and he [1] was put to death. Sheibāni Khan, following up the advantages which he had gained, took possession of Tāshkend, Shahrokhīa, and all the dominions of Sultan Mahmūd Khan, as well probably as of the territories of his younger brother Alacheh Khan, so that his territories now extended along both sides of the Sirr or Jaxartes, and stretched southward to the banks of the Amu. He fixed the seat of his government at Samarkand, and gave his brother Mahmūd Sultan the charge of Bokhāra. Tāshkend, with the dominions of the two Khans, he gave to his paternal uncles, Gujenjeh Khan and Sanjek Sultan, whose mother was the daughter of the celebrated Mirza Ulugh Beg Gurgān. The office of Dārogha of Shahrokhīa he bestowed on Amīr Yākub, who was one of the chief of his nobles.

Bābur is said to have taken refuge after this disaster in Moghulistān, an incident to which he himself never refers. This at least is certain, that he was soon after fortunate enough to escape from the north side of the Sirr, and to gain the hill country of Sūkh and Hūshiār, villages which lie in the district of Asfera, among the mountains that separate Ferghāna from Hissār and Karatigīn, where he wandered for nearly a year as a fugitive, often reduced to the greatest difficulties.[2] Finding his partisans completely dispersed, however, and all hopes gone of recovering his hereditary kingdom, after consulting with his few remaining adherents, he resolved to try his fortune in Khorasān, which was at that time held by Sultan Hussain Mirza, a sovereign of great power and reputation, and beyond comparison the most distinguished prince then living of the family of Taimūr.

Bābur flies to Asfera, A. D. 1503.

A. D. 1503-4.

When Bābur bade adieu for the last time to his native country, which he appears to have regarded during all the future years of his life with the fondness which a man of warm attachments feels for the scenes of his early affections, he crossed the high range of hills to the south of Ferghāna, and came down west of Karatigīn on the country of Cheghāniān and Hissār, territories at that time belonging to

Bābur leaves Ferghāna.

---

[1] See *Tārīkh e Rauzet-es-sefā*, vol. vii.
[2] [According to the *T. R.*, p. 175, Bābur was accompanied by his mother and family in these wanderings.]

Khosrou Shah, to whom Bábur always professes a deep-rooted hatred. The murder of Baiesanghar Mirza, and the blinding of Sultan Masaúd Mirza, both cousins of Bábur, and the latter the full brother of one of his wives, were certainly sufficient to justify the terms of strong detestation in which that prince always speaks of him; but Ferishta seems to insinuate that he hated the man whom he had injured; and that Bábur, though treated by Khosrou Shah with great hospitality, stirred up a faction in his court, seduced the affections of his army, and by his intrigues forced him to abandon his troops, his treasure, and his dominions. Whether or not Bábur was aware that such charges had been made, or were likely to be brought against him, is uncertain; but the narrative in his Memoirs is certainly fitted to meet accusations of this nature; and he appears throughout to show uncommon solicitude to justify himself in regard to Khosrou Shah, whose general character for hospitality and generosity to others he acknowledges, while he pointedly accuses him of niggardliness and want of common civility to himself, in the two different instances in which he was obliged to pass through the country of that chieftain. That he intrigued with the army of Khosrou Shah, particularly with the Moghul troops, Bábur boldly avows, but appears to regard his conduct in that respect as only an act of fair hostility towards an inveterate foe.

Ulugh Beg Mirza, Bábur's paternal uncle, the King of Kábul and Ghazni, had died in the year A. H. 907, leaving his territories to his son Abdal Razák Mirza, who was still young. The whole power was usurped by one of his ministers, Shírím Ziker, who soon rendered himself odious to the chief men of the country. A conspiracy, headed by Muhammed Kásim Beg and Yunis Ali, was formed against the minister, in consequence of which the conspirators, entering Kábul with a formidable band of adherents, put Ziker to death while sitting in state at a grand festival, which was held for celebrating the Íd.[1] The kingdom for some time was a prey to disorder and tumult. Muhammed Mukím Beg, the son of Zúlnún Arghún and brother of Shah

---

[1] The feast on the conclusion of Ramzán. [The murder took place on June 6, 1503. *E. B.*, p. 215.]

Beg, names which often occur in the following pages, availing himself of this situation of things, marched without orders from the Garmsīr,[1] which he held for his father, and appeared suddenly before Kābul, which opened its gates. Zūlnūn Beg, without professing to approve of the proceedings of Mukīm, sanctioned his retaining possession of his conquest. Abdal Razāk Mirza had retired among the hills, and was still making ineffectual efforts for the recovery of his capital, when Bābur entered the territories of Khosrou Shah.[2]

A. H. 908.
A. D. 1502–3.

A. H. 910.
A. D. 1504.

It is necessary then to recollect that, at this period, when Bābur resumes the history of his own adventures, Sheibāni Khan had conquered Samarkand and Bokhāra, Ferghāna and Uratippa, Tāshkend and Shahrokhīa; Sultan Hussain Mirza governed Khorasān; Khosrou Shah still held Hissār, Khutlān, Kunduz, and Badakhshān; and Zūlnūn Beg, though he acknowledged Sultan Hussain Mirza, had the chief and almost independent power in Kandahār and Zamīn-dāwer, the country of the Hazāras[3] and Nukderis[4], the Garmsīr, and great part of Sīstān, and the country south of Kandahār.

[1] The Garmsīr, as afterwards mentioned by Bābur, is the country east of the Pass of Bādām-cheshmeh.
[2] See Khāfi Khan, Ferishta, &c.
[3] [The Hazāras held the tract stretching from Zamīndāwer up the Helmand to the Mountain of Koh i Baba, west of Kabul, with the hills immediately to the south of that line. E. B., p. 220.]
[4] [The Nukdaris occupied the mountains between Zamīndāwer and Herāt. E. B., p. 220.]

MEMOIRS OF BĀBUR

EVENTS OF THE YEAR 910

Bābur sets out for Khorasān.

IN the month of Muharrem,[1] I set out from the vicinity of Ferghāna, intending to proceed to Khorasān, and halted at the summer-cots of Ilāk,[2] one of the summer pasturing districts belonging to the country of Hissār. I here entered my twenty-third year, and began to apply the razor to my face.[3] The followers who still adhered to my fortunes, great and small, exceeded two hundred, and fell short of three hundred. The greater part of them were on foot, with brogues on their feet, clubs in their hands, and long frocks[4] over their shoulders. Such was our distress, that among us all we had only two tents. My own tent was pitched for my mother, and they erected for me at each stage a felt-tent of cross-poles,[5] in which I used to take up my quarters. Although I was on my way for Khorasān, yet, in the present state of things, I was not quite without hopes of still effecting something here among the territories and servants of Khosrou Shah. Scarce a day passed in which somebody did not join me, bringing such reports regarding the country and wandering tribes as served to feed my expectation.

At this very time, Mulla Baba Peshāgheri, whom I had sent on a mission to Khosrou Shah, came back. From Khosrou Shah he brought me no message that could cheer

---

[1] Muharrem, 910, began on June 14, 1504, the year when Ferdinand the Catholic drove the French out of Naples.

[2] There is still a place called Ilāk to the north-west of Darbend, which may be in the district here alluded to.

[3] Among the Tūrki tribes, the time of first applying the razor to the face is celebrated by a great entertainment. Bābur's miserable circumstances did not admit of this.

[4] *Chāpān.*

[5] The *alāchack* is a sort of tent formed of flexible poles, covered with felt, and easily folded up.

my mind; but he brought me favourable accounts of the disposition of the Īls and Ulūses (the wandering Tūrki and Moghul tribes of the country).

From Ilāk, in three or four journeys, I reached Khwājeh Imād, a place in the territory of Hissār. In this station, Muhibb Ali Korchi waited on me as ambassador from Khosrou Shah. Twice did my course lie through the country of this Khosrou Shah, so far-famed for his liberal conduct and generosity; and that humanity which he displayed to the meanest of men, he never showed to me. As I had expectations from the Īls and Ulūses of these districts, I halted a day at each stage. Shīrīm Taghai, than whom I had not with me a man of more eminence, from a dislike to the plan of going to Khorasān, began to think of leaving me. At the time when I had been defeated at Sir-e-pul,[1] and was forced to retire, he had sent away the whole of his family, and had remained with me in the fort (of Samarkand) alone, and without any encumbrance to impede his going off. He was rather unmanly, and had several times played the same game.

When I arrived at Kabādiān,[2] Bāki Cheghāniāni, the younger brother of Khosrou Shah, who held Cheghānian,[3] with the towns of Safa and Termez, sent the Khatīb[4] of Karshi, to express to me his wishes for my prosperity, and his desire to be permitted to join and accompany me as his prince; and, as I crossed the Amu, at the ferry of Ubāj, he himself came and paid his respects to me. At the desire of Bāki Cheghāniāni, I moved down towards Termez, when he brought his whole family and effects across the river and joined me, after which we proceeded towards Kahmerd and Bamiān (places at this time held by the son of Ahmed Kāsim,[5] the sister's son of Khosrou Shah), intending to place our families in the fortress of

Joined by Bāki Cheghāniāni.

---

[1] In the neighbourhood of Samarkand. [This defeat by Shaibāni Khan occurred in 1500.]

[2] Kabādiān stands on the Amu, somewhat higher up than Termez.

[3] Cheghāniān, or Saghāniān, whence the whole country of Hissār formerly took its name, lies north of Termez.

[4] The *khatīb* is the preacher by whom the Khutbeh, or prayers for the prince, are repeated in the mosque.

[5] [Or rather 'his son, Ahmed Kāsim'. P. de C.]

Ajer, one of the towns of Kahmerd,[1] and, after having put it in a posture of defence, to follow whatever plan seemed best to promise success. When we reached Aibek,[2] Yār Ali Belāl, who had formerly been in my service, and had conducted himself with bravery, but who had been separated from me during the commotions, and was now in the employment of Khosrou Shah, deserted with several young cavaliers, and came and joined me, bringing assurances from the Moghuls in Khosrou Shah's service that they were all attached to my interests. On reaching the valley of Zindān,[3] Kamber Ali Beg, surnamed Salākh (or the skinner), fled and came to me. In three or four marches we reached Kahmerd, having left our wives and families in the fortress of Ajer.

Reaches Kahmerd.

While we remained in the fort of Ajer, the marriage of Jehāngīr Mirza with the daughter of Sultan Mahmūd Mirza by Khanzādeh Begum was consummated. They had been engaged during the lifetime of the Mirzas, their fathers.

Bāki advises him to send away Jehāngīr Mirza.

At this same period, Bāki Beg repeatedly, and with much earnestness, urged his sentiments, that to have two sovereigns in one country, and two generals in one army, was an unfailing source of confusion and ruin, and inevitably productive of rebellion, mutiny, and finally of dissolution; as the poet says,

> (*Persian*)—Ten dervīshes may repose on one cloak,
>   But two sovereigns cannot be contained in the same climate.
> The man of God, when he eats half a loaf,
> Divides the other half among the poor and needy.
> If a king subdues a whole kingdom, nay a climate,
> Still, as before, he covets yet another.[4]

That there was every reason to expect that, in a few days, all the chiefs and servants of Khosrou Shah would come in and make their submission to the King; that among them there were many seditious and turbulent men, such

---

[1] Kahmerd, or Kohmerd, lies between Balkh and Kābul, in the hill country. Ajer is about twelve miles west from Kahmerd.
[2] This is Aibek on the Khulm river.
[3] The Dareh Zindān lies about seven miles to the south of Aibek on the road to Sarbāgh.
[4] From the *Gulistān* of Sa'di (Chap. I, story 3).

as the sons of Ayūb Beg and some others, who had always been the movers and exciters of discord and enmity among the Mirzas; that it was best, at the present moment, to send away Jehāngīr Mirza for Khorasān on good and friendly terms, that he might not, by and by, occasion me regret and repentance. As it was not in my nature to treat my brothers or any of my relations with disrespect or harshness, however instant he was in his representations, I could not be prevailed on to assent to them. For although great heart-burning and difference had formerly existed between Jehāngīr Mirza and me, arising from our rivalry in authority, and from our both aiming at the possession of the sovereignty,[a] yet, at this time, he had left his country to accompany me, he was my brother and my dependant, and, in addition to this, had not at this time done anything which could be the ground of dissatisfaction. Afterwards, however, these very exciters of sedition who had been pointed out, Yūsef Ayūb and Behlūl Ayūb, deserted from me, went over to Jehāngīr Mirza, and were so successful in their seditious schemes and machinations, that they alienated his mind from me, and carried him into Khorasān, exactly as Bāki Beg had predicted.

He refuses.

At this time there came strange long-winded letters from Sultan Hussain Mirza to Badīa-ez-zemān, to me, to Khosrou Shah, and to Zūlnūn Beg. These letters are still by me. The purport of them was as follows: When the three brothers, Sultan Ahmed Mirza, Sultan Mahmūd Mirza, and Ulugh Beg Mirza, united their forces and advanced against me, I guarded the banks of the river Murghāb,[1] and the Mirzas, after having come close up to me, were compelled to retreat, without effecting anything. Should the Uzbeks now advance, I will again defend the banks of the Murghāb. Badīa-ez-zemān Mirza, after having put the fortresses of Balkh, Shaberghān, and Andckhūd,[2] in a state of defence, and confided them to

Sultan Hussain Mirza's letters.

---

[a] *For this clause substitute* and disputes about adherents,

[1] The river Murghāb, rising in the hills of Hazāra, flows down by Merv.

[2] These were the three chief fortresses between the hills and the desert to the north of the Paropamisan mountains.

trusty officers, must himself proceed to Garzewān, the Dareh-e-Zang,[1] and the rest of that hill-country. He also wrote to me to this effect [a] : Do you defend Kahmerd, Ajer, and the tract of hill-country in that neighbourhood. Khosrou Shah, after leaving trusty men in Hissār and Kunduz, is to proceed, accompanied by his brother Wali, to the defence of the hilly tracts of Badakhshān and Khutlān, so that the Uzbeks will be forced to retreat without effecting anything.

These letters of Sultan Hussain Mirza threw us into despair; for, at that time, of the whole house of Taimūr Beg, there was no sovereign so respectable, either in regard to age, dominions, or military force; and it was expected that envoys and agents would have been treading hard on each other's heels, and assiduously giving orders to collect so many vessels at the passes of Termez, Kilif, and Kirki,[2] and so many materials for constructing bridges; and that commands would have been issued for guarding carefully the upper passes [3] of Togūzūlūm, that the inhabitants, whose spirit for some years had been quite broken down by the incursions of the Uzbeks, might have time to recover heart.. But when a mighty prince, like Sultan Hussain Mirza, who occupied the throne of Taimūr Beg, instead of proposing to march against the enemy, only issued directions to strengthen a few posts, what hopes could people entertain?

Meanwhile, having left in Ajer such of the men and horses that had accompanied me as had been worn out with hunger and fatigue, together with the family, women, effects, and baggage of Bāki Cheghāniāni, of Ahmed Kāsim's son, of the troops that accompanied them, and of the Aimāks who adhered to them, as well as everything on which they set a value, we marched out and took the field.

[a] *Add* knowing that I was in that neighbourhood:

[1] Garzewān and the valley of Zang were the chief passes into the hill country between Balkh and Herāt.
[2] These are the three chief ferries over the river Amu or Jeihūn, between Kabādiān and Chārjū.
[3] [ferries.]

Persons now arrived in uninterrupted succession from the Moghuls in Khosrou Shah's service, announcing that the whole Moghul tribes, desirous of professing their allegiance to the King, were on their march from Taikhān,[1] towards Ishkamish and Felūl; that it was necessary, therefore, that his Majesty should move with the utmost speed to join them; that many of Khosrou Shah's followers were much distracted,[a] and would embrace the King's service.

The Moghuls in Khosrou Shah's service declare for Bābur.

At this very period, information arrived that Sheibāni Khan had taken Andejān, and was advancing against Hissār and Kunduz. On hearing this news, Khosrou Shah, unable to support himself in Kunduz, took the route of Kābul with his whole force. No sooner had he left Kunduz, than Mulla Muhammed Tūrkestāni, one of his old and confidential servants, occupied that fortress, and declared for Sheibāni Khan. Just as I reached the Kizilsū[2] (the Red River), by the route of Shamtū, three or four thousand heads of houses of the Moghul clans, who had been dependent on Khosrou Shah, and who had been in Hissār and Kunduz, came and joined me, with their whole families. Here, in order to gratify Bāki Beg, I was obliged to discharge Kamber Ali, the Moghul, who has been so often mentioned. He was a thoughtless and rude talker; and Bāki Beg could not put up with his manners. From this time forward, his son Abdal Shakūr continued in the service of Jehāngīr Mirza.

When Khosrou Shah learned that the Moghul tribes had joined me, he felt his own helplessness; and, seeing no remedy left, sent his son-in-law, Yākūb Ayūb, as his envoy, to make professions of submission and allegiance, and to assure me that, if I would enter into terms with him, he would come and submit himself. As Bāki Cheg-

Khosrou Shah submits,

---

[a] would disband,

[1] Mr. Metcalfe's copy has Tālikhān. Ishkemish is about fifteen miles from Kunduz to the south-east, and thirty miles west of Tālikhān, which lies on the river of Kunduz.

[2] It is properly called the Surkhāb, which has the same signification. It is the river that flows by Surkh-kilaa (Red-castle), from near Kahmerd on the west, and falls into the river of Anderāb, below Dūshi.

hāniāni, a man of much weight, though steadily attached to my service, yet was not without a natural bias in favour of his brother, he recommended a compromise to be made, on condition that Khosrou's life should be spared, and his property left entirely to his own disposal. A treaty was accordingly concluded on these terms. After Yākūb had taken leave, we marched down the Kizil-sū, and encamped near its conflux with the river of Anderāb.

<small>and visits Bābur.</small>

Next morning (it was about the middle of the first Rabīa [1]) I passed the Anderāb with a few attendants, and took my seat under the shade of a lofty palm-tree,[a] in the territory of Dūshi.[2] From the opposite quarter Khosrou Shah advanced with great pomp and retinue; according to the custom and usage, he dismounted at a considerable distance, and walked up on foot. In approaching to salute, he bowed three times, and as often when he retired back. He also bowed once on the usual inquiries being made, and when he presented his offering; and he showed the same marks of respect to Jehāngīr Mirza, and Mirza Khan. This pompous man,[b] who for years had acted according to his own will and pleasure, and who wanted nothing of royalty, except that he had not caused the Khutbeh to be read in his own name, now bent himself for twenty-five or twenty-six times successively, and went and came back and forward, till he was so tired that he nearly fell right forward. The visions of empire and authority in which for years he had indulged, vanished from his view. After he had saluted me and presented his tributary offering, I desired him to be seated. He sat down and for one or two *garis*[3] we conversed on various subjects and incidents. Besides being of an unmanly and perfidious character, he showed also great want of propriety, and a sneering turn in his conversation.[c] He

[a] plane tree,
[b] This broken down, good for nothing, mannikin,
[c] dull and stupid conversation.

---

[1] The end of August 1504.
[2] Dūshi lies above Ghuri, on the river Anderāb, at its conflux with the Surkhāb.
[3] A *gari* is twenty-four minutes

made two remarks, in particular, which appeared singular as coming from him, at the moment when his most trusty and confidential servants were going over in troops before his eyes, and taking service with me ; and when his affairs had arrived at such a pass, that though a man who in his day had enacted the sovereign, he yet was compelled, sore against his will, to come in this wretched and miserable way, and submit himself in a very paltry manner. One of these was when I was consoling him for the desertion of his servants ; he replied, 'These fellows have already left me four times, and always come back again.' The other was on my asking after his younger brother, Wali : when he would come, and by what ford he would cross the Amu ? he answered, ' If he can find a ford he will come over speedily ; but when a river comes down in flood, the fords change ; as the proverb runs, " the river has carried down its fords." ' At the very moment of the change of his fortune and of the desertion of his servants, Almighty God brought these words out of his own mouth. After one or two *garis*, I mounted and returned back to the camp, and he also returned to his encampment. That same day, great and small, good and bad, officers and servants, began to forsake him, and came and joined me with their families and effects ; so that, on the morrow, between mid-day and afternoon prayers, not a man remained with him. (*Arabic*) 'Say, O my Lord ! Thou art the King of kings ! Thou givest empire unto whom thou pleasest, and takest empire from whom thou pleasest ; and increasest whom thou pleasest, and reducest whom thou pleasest : Beneficence is in thy hand ; for, verily, thou art powerful over all things.'[1] The Lord is wonderful in his might ! A man who was master of twenty or thirty thousand retainers, and who possessed the whole tract of country formerly subject to Sultan Mahmūd Mirza, extending from Kalūgheh,[2] which is also termed *Derbend-e-āheni* (the Iron-gate), as far as the Hindū-kūsh mountains,

---

[1] [This is a quotation from the Qurān III, 25.]
[2] This pass, generally called *Kalūgha*, is famous in the history of Taimūr Beg and Chingiz Khan. It leads through the chain of the Kara-tāgh hills that lies between Khozār and Hissār.

and one of whose tax-gatherers, named Hassan Birlās, an aged man, had conducted me, in the surliest manner, from Ilāk to Ubāj, giving me orders how far I was to march, and where I was to encamp; that this very person, in the space of half a day, without battle, without contest, should be reduced to appear in such a state of distress and wretchedness before a needy and reduced fugitive like me, who had only two hundred or two hundred and fifty tatterdemalions, all in the greatest want; that he should no longer have any power over his own servants, nor over his wealth, nor even his life, was a wonderful dispensation of the Omnipotent!

He is charged with murder by Mirza Khan,

The evening of the same day in which I returned from the interview with Khosrou Shah, Mirza Khan[1] came into my presence and accused him of[a] the murder of his brothers. Many among us were for receiving the charge; and, indeed, it was conformable to every law, human and divine, that such a man should meet with condign punishment; but as an agreement had been entered into with Khosrou Shah, he was left free and unmolested, and orders were given that he might carry off as much of his property as he chose. He accordingly loaded three or four strings[2] of mules, and as many camels as he had, with jewels, gold and silver utensils, and other valuables, and set out with them. I directed Shīrīm Taghāi to conduct Khosrou Shah by the route of Ghūri[3] and Dehāneh towards Khorasān, and then to proceed himself to Kahmerd and bring my family after me to Kābul.

but suffered to depart.

Bābur marches against Kābul;

I now left my encampment and marched against Kābul. I halted at Khwājeh zaid. That same day, as Hamzah-bī Mangfat, who headed a plundering party of Uzbeks, had made an incursion, and was ravaging the territory of

[a] demanded vengeance for

---

[1] Mirza Khan was Sultan Weis Mirza, youngest son of Sultan Mahmūd Mirza, Bābur's uncle. One of his brothers, Baiesanghar Mirza, had been murdered, and Sultan Masaūd Mirza, another of them, had been blinded by Khosrou Shah, as has been already related in these Memoirs.

[2] Seven to a string.—*Leyden.*

[3] Ghūri lies north-east from Kahmerd.

Dūshi,[1] I dispatched Syed Kāsim, the chamberlain, and Ahmed Kāsim Kohbur, with a party of horse, who fell upon the pillagers, completely routed them, and brought in a number of their heads. At this station the arms and armour which were left in the stores of Khosrou Shah were divided among the troops. There were about seven or eight hundred coats of mail, and suits of horse furniture. These were one part of the articles which Khosrou Shah left behind [a]; there were many others beside, but nothing of consequence.

From Khwājeh zaid, by three or four marches, we reached Ghūrbend.[2] On coming to our ground at Ushter-sheher, we got intelligence that Sherkeh Arghūn, the Beg in whom Mukīm reposed the greatest confidence, still ignorant of my approach, had advanced with an army, and taken post on the river Bārān, for the purpose of intercepting any who might attempt, by the route of Penjhīr,[3] to join Abdal Razāk Mirza,[4] who had fled at that time from Kābul, and was then among the Turkolāni Afghans in the territory of Lamghān. The instant I received this information, which was between mid-day and afternoon prayers, we set out, and marching all night, ascended the hill-pass of Hupiān.[b][5]

[a] *Add* besides a great many pieces of Chinese porcelain.
[b] *Add* at dawn.

---

[1] Dūshi lies ten or twelve miles south-east of Ghūri.
[2] Ghūr-bend, or the Pass of Ghūr, which lies to the south of the high hills of Hindū-kūsh, is one of the chief passes from Balkh to Kābul, across that great range.   [3] Now Penjshīr.
[4] Abdal Razāk Mirza was the son of Ulugh Beg Mirza, one of Bābur's uncles, the King of Kābul and Ghazni. Ulugh Beg died in 907 of the Hijira, about three years before Bābur's invasion. He was succeeded by his son Abdal Razāk Mirza; but that prince being very young, Shīrīm Ziker, one of his nobles, usurped the supreme direction of affairs. The other Begs, disgusted with Shīrīm's conduct, formed a conspiracy and put him to death. During the confusions that ensued, Muhammed Mukīm, a son of Zūlnūn Beg, surprised Kābul in 908, and married a sister of Abdal Razāk Mirza. Affairs were still in confusion when Bābur entered the country in 910.
[5] Hupiān, or Upiān, is a few miles north of Chārikār, on the way to Parwān. Sanjed Dareh lies west, or north-west of Ghūrbend. [Professor H. H. Wilson identified this place with the *Hu-pi-an* of Hiouen Tsang, and the *Alexandria opiana* of Stephanus of Byzantium, but Raverty dissents from this view. Raverty's *Notes*, p. 694.]

Till this time I had never seen the star Soheil[1] (Canopus), but on reaching the top of a hill, Soheil appeared below,[a] bright to the south. I said, 'This cannot be Soheil!' They answered, 'It is indeed Soheil.' Bāki Cheghāniāni recited the following verse:

O Soheil, how far dost thou shine, and where dost thou rise ?
Thine eye is an omen of good fortune to him on whom it falls.

The sun was a spear's length high when we reached the foot of the valley of Sanjed and alighted. The party whom we had sent on in advance to reconnoitre, with a number of enterprising young warriors, fell in with Sherkeh below Karabāgh,[2] in the territory of Aikeri-yār, and instantly attacked him; they kept harassing him for some time in a skirmishing fight, till reinforcements came up, when they made a vigorous charge, and completely routed his troops. Sherkeh himself was dismounted and made prisoner, with seventy, eighty, or a hundred of his best men. I spared his life, and he entered into my service.

is joined by some Hazāras.

When Khosrou Shah abandoned Kunduz, and set out for Kābul, without troubling himself about his Īls and Ulūses (the wandering Tūrki and Moghul tribes), the troops in his service, including the Īls and Ulūses, formed five or six bodies. One of these bodies was composed of the men from the hill-country of Badakhshān. Sīdīm Ali Darbān,[3] with the Hazāras of the desert,[b] having passed the straits of Penjhīr,[4] joined me at this stage, and entered into my service. Another of these bodies, under Yūsef Ayūb and Behlūl Ayūb, joined me in like manner at the same place. Other two of these bodies, the one from Khutlān, under the command of Wali, the brother of Khosrou; the other from Īlānchuk, Nūkderi, and Kākshāl, with the Aimāks[5] that had settled in Kunduz, advanced

Wali defeated, and put to death.

[a] low and   [b] of Rustak,

[1] *Soheil* is a most conspicuous star in Afghanistān. It gives its name to the south, which is never called *junūb*, but *soheil*. The rising of *Soheil* marks one of their seasons.
[2] Black-garden.   [3] [Door-keeper.]
[4] The Pass of Penjhīr, or Penjshīr, is in the Hindū-kūsh range, to the east of that of Kipchāk, by which Bābur had come.
[5] [Pastoral tribes.]

by the route of Anderāb and Seirāb,¹ with an intention of passing by the straits of Penjhīr. The Aimāks reached Seirab first; and as Wali was advancing in their rear, they took possession of the road, engaged and defeated him. Wali himself, after his discomfiture, fled for refuge to the Uzbeks; but his head was struck off in the public market ² of Samarkand by the orders of Sheibāni Khan; all the rest of his servants and officers, being discomfited, plundered, and destitute, came and joined me, along with the Aimāks, at this same stage. Syed Yūsef Beg Oghlākchi also came along with the Aimāks to this place.

Marching thence, we halted in the *auleng*, or meadow, of Āk-serāi,³ which is situated close upon Karabāgh: Khosrou Shah's men, who had long been inured to the practice of violence, and to disregard of discipline, now began to oppress the people of the country. At last an active retainer of Sīdīm Ali Darbān having carried off a jar of oil from some person by force, I ordered him to be brought out ᵃ and beaten with sticks. He expired under the punishment. This example put an end to such practices.

We here held a consultation whether or not it was advisable to proceed against Kābul. Syed Yūsef Beg and others were of opinion that, as the winter was at hand, we should proceed to Lamghān, and there act as circumstances might require. Bāki Cheghāniāni and several others were for marching directly on Kābul; and that plan being finally adopted, we marched off from our station, and stopped at the *kūrūgh* (or Park) of Āma. I was here joined by my mother the Khanum, and the rest of the household that had been left behind at Kahmerd. They had endured great hardships in their march to meet me. The incidents were as follows: I had sent Shīrīm Taghāi to conduct Khosrou Shah on the route to Khorasān, and directed him afterwards to bring on my household. By the time, however, that they reached Dehāneh, Shīrīm Taghāi found

Khosrou Shah expelled from Kahmerd.

ᵃ *Add* before the door of my tent

¹ [*Sar i āb* = waterhead.]   ² *Chārsū* [square].
³ White-house. It is about twelve or fourteen miles north-west from Kābul.

that he was not his own master, and Khosrou Shah took the resolution of accompanying him to Kahmerd. Ahmed Kāsim, the sister's son of Khosrou Shah, was then in Kahmerd. Khosrou Shah prevailed upon Ahmed Kāsim to behave very ill to the families left in the place. Many of the Moghul retainers of Bāki Cheghāniāni were in Kahmerd along with these families. They privately, in concert with Shīrīm Taghāi, prepared to seize both Khosrou Shah and Ahmed Kāsim, who, however, taking the alarm, fled away by the road which leads by the skirts of the valley of Ajer, and took the route of Khorasān. The effect of this firmness of the Moghuls having been to rid themselves of these enemies, the guard which was with the families being now freed from any danger from Khosrou Shah, left Ajer. By the time they reached Kahmerd, however, the Saghānchi clan were up in arms, seized the passes on the road, and plundered a number of the families, and of the Īls and Ulūses (or wandering clans), who had followed the fortunes of Bāki Beg. The son of Kūl Bayezīd Tūrk,[1] who was young, was made a prisoner by them. He came to Kābul three or four years after. The families which had been plundered and dispersed came on by way of the pass of Kipchāk, the same by which I had come, and joined me in the *kūrūgh* of Āma.

Bābur resolves to besiege Kābul.

Leaving this station, the second march brought us to the *auleng* (or pasture grounds)[a] of Chālāk, where we halted. Having held a consultation, in which the siege of Kābul was determined on, we marched forward. I, with the main body, halted between Haider Tāki's garden and the tomb of Kūl Bayezīd, the cup-bearer. Jehāngīr Mirza, with the right wing, took his station at my great Chārbāgh.[2] Nāsir Mirza, with the left wing, took post in an *auleng* (or meadow) behind the tomb of Kūtluk Kadem. I repeatedly sent persons to confer with Mukīm; they sometimes brought

[a] meadow

[1] [P. de C. has 'The son of Kūl i Bayazīd, Tīzak'.]
[2] That is, the ground which Bābur afterwards laid out as a grand garden or Chār-bāgh. [Kūtluk kadam was alive at this time and fought at Kānwāhā in A. H. 933.]

back insincere excuses, sometimes conciliatory answers.
But his real object, all the while, was to gain time; for,
when I took Sherkeh prisoner, he had dispatched expresses
to his father and elder brother, and he now attempted to
create delays, in hopes of getting succour from them.

One day I ordered that the whole host, main body, right
wing, and left, after arraying themselves in complete
armour, and clothing their horses in mail, should advance
close up to the city, display their arms, and inflict a little
chastisement on the town's people. Jehāngīr Mirza, with
the right wing, marched forward towards the Kūcheh
bāgh.[1] As there was a river in front of the main body,
I proceeded by the tomb of Kūtluk kadem, and stationed
myself on an eminence in front of a rising ground. The
advanced body spread themselves out above Kūtluk
kadem's bridge; at that time, however, there was no
bridge there. Our troops galloped insultingly close up
to the Currier's[2] gate. The men who had advanced out of
the town, being few in number, could not stand their
ground, but took to flight, and sought shelter in the city.
A number of the town's people of Kābul had gone out on
the glacis of the citadel, on the side of an eminence, in order
to witness the sight. As they fled, a great dust arose, and
many of them were thrown down. Between the gate and
the bridge, on a rising ground, and in the high road, pits
had been dug, in which pointed stakes had been fixed,[a] and
then the whole covered over with grass. Sultan Kulī
Chanāk, and several other cavaliers, fell into these pits
as they pushed on at full speed. On the right wing, one
or two cavaliers exchanged a few sabre blows with a part
of the garrison who sallied out on the side of the Kūcheh
bāgh, but soon returned, as they had no orders to engage.

The men in the town were now greatly alarmed and dejected, when Mukīm, through some of the Begs, offered to submit, and agreed to surrender Kābul; on which he

Mukīm surrenders it.

[a] *Omit this clause.*

[1] Suburb Garden. The Kūcheh bāgh is still a garden about four miles from Kābul, on the north-west, and divided from it by a low kotal or pass. There is still a bridge on the way.

[2] *Darwāzeh charmgerān.*

was introduced by the mediation of Bāki Beg Cheghāniāni, and tendered his allegiance. I did all that I could to dispel his apprehensions, and received him with affability and kindness. It was arranged that he should next day march out with all his soldiers, adherents, effects, and property, and surrender the fortress. As the retainers of Khosrou Shah had not, for a long period, been subjected to discipline, but, on the contrary, had indulged in all kind of injustice and rapine, I appointed Jehāngīr Mirza, and Nāsir Mirza, with some of the principal Begs, and my most trusty servants,[a] to guard the family of Mukīm, as well as Mukīm himself and his dependants, while they left Kābul with their goods and property; and I appointed Tībah [1] as his place of residence. Next morning the Mirzas and Begs who had gone to the gate, observing an uproar and mobbing of people, dispatched a man to inform me of the circumstance; adding, 'Until you come, we shall not be able to put a stop to the commotion.' I mounted, and having repaired to the spot, allayed the tumult, but not until I had ordered three or four of the rioters to be shot with arrows, and one or two to be cut to pieces. Mukīm and his train then set out, and reached Tībah in quiet and safety.

In the latter end of the month of the latter Rabīa,[2] by the blessing of Almighty God, I gained possession of Kābul and Ghazni, with the country and provinces dependent on them, without battle or contest.

Description of Kābul and Ghazni. The country of Kābul is situate in the fourth climate, in the midst of the inhabited part of the world. On the east it has the Lamghānāt,[3] Pershāwer, Hashnaghar,[4] and some of the countries of Hind. On the west it has the mountain districts, in which are situated Karnūd and Ghūr. This mountainous tract is at present occupied and inhabited

[a] officers of the household,

---

[1] Tībah [or Tīpa] is about three miles south of Ākserāi, and to the left of the road from that place to Kābul.
[2] About the beginning of October 1504.
[3] [According to P. de C., Lamghānāt denotes the district of which Lamghān is the chief place.]
[4] [i. e. Peshāwar and Hashtnagar.]

by the Hazāra and Nūkderi tribes. On the north are the countries of Kunduz and Anderāb, from which it is separated by the mountain of Hindū-kūsh. On the south are Fermūl and Naghz,[1] and Bannu and Afghanistān.[2] It is a narrow country, but stretching to a considerable extent. Its length is in the direction of east and west. It is surrounded on all sides by hills. The walls of the town extend up a hill. To the south-west of the town there is a small hill, which is called Shah-Kābul,[3] from the circumstance of a King of Kābul's having built a palace on its summit. This hill begins at the defile of Deveren,[4] and reaches all the way to that of Deh-Yākūb. It may be about a farsang[5] in circumference. The skirts of this hill are entirely covered

City of Kābul.

[1] [Or Naghr.]
[2] Bābur confines the term Afghanistān to the countries inhabited by the Afghan tribes. These were chiefly the hill tracts to the south of the road from Kābul to Pershāwer. Kābul, Ghazni, the low country of Lamghān, and in general all the plains and lower grounds, with the towns, were inhabited by Tājiks, or men of a different race. Forster, vol. ii, p. 79, describes Kābul 'as a walled town of about a mile and a half in circumference, and situated on the eastern side of a range of two united hills, describing generally the figure of a semi-circle'. 'Balausir [Bālāhisār],' he adds (p. 80), 'the name of the Shah's palace, where also the household servants, guards, and the slaves are lodged, stands on a rising ground in the eastern quarter of the city, and exhibits but a slender testimony of the dignity of its master.'—' Kābul stands near the foot of two conjoined hills, whose length has nearly an east and west direction. Towards the base of the eastern, stands, on a flat projection, a fortified palace, which was formerly the habitation of the governors of the city; but it has been converted by Timur Shah into a state prison, where the brothers of this prince, and other branches of his family, are kept in confinement. Above this building is seen a small tower on a peak, whence the ground rises to a considerable height, and is united by a neck of lower land to the other hill. From the peak a stone wall extends over the summit of the two hills, and is terminated at the bottom of the westernmost by an ordinary redoubt.' (pp. 83, 84.)
[3] There is a hill south of Kābul, on which Kābul (Cain, the son of Adam), the founder of the city, is said to be buried; but the only hill south-west is that where Bābur himself is interred. It is now known by no name but that of Bābur Bādshāh, and is the great holiday resort of the people of the city.
[4] [The Gorge of Durīn, through which the Kābul river flows, separates the ranges of rocky hills rising immediately westwards of the city of Kābul, known as Asa Mai and Takht i Shah. Raverty's *Notes on Afghanistan*, p. 689.]
[5] Nearly four miles.

with gardens. In the time of my paternal uncle Ulugh Beg Mirza, Weis Ātkeh [a] conducted a stream of water along the bottom of it; and all the gardens about the hill are cultivated by means of this stream. Lower down [b] the river there is a place called Kulkīneh,[1] in a retired, hidden situation. Much debauchery has gone on at that place. The verse of Khwājeh Hāfiz may be parodied and applied to it—

O for the happy times, when, free and uncontroll'd,
We lived in Kulkīneh with no very good fame.

Southward from the town, and to the east of Shah-Kābul, there is a lake [2] nearly a farsang in circumference. Three springs of water issue from Shah-Kābul, and flow towards the city; two of them are in the vicinity of Kulkīneh. One of these runs by the tomb of Khwājeh Shams, and the other by the Kademgāh [3] (place of the footsteps) of Khwājeh Khizer. These two places are the favourite resorts of the people of Kābul. The third fountain is opposite to Khwājeh Abd-al-samad, and bears the name of Khwājeh Roushenāi. There is a small ridge which runs out from the hill of Shah-Kābul, and is called Ukābein; [4] and there is besides another small hill, on which stands the citadel of Kābul. The fortified town lies on the north of the citadel. The citadel is of surprising height, and enjoys an excellent climate, overlooking the large lake, and the three *aulengs* (or meadows) called *Siāh-sang*, *Sung-kurghān*, and *Chālāk*, which stretch below it. These *aulengs* present a very beautiful prospect when the plains

[a] *Add* his guardian
[b] at the end of

[1] Or Gulkīnah. [The *Ayīn i akbari* refers to this place 'as a delightful spot in the neighbourhood of *Pul i mastān*'.]

[2] This lake is now called Kheirābād. It is about three miles round.

[3] The spot on which a Musulman saint lived, or on which he is supposed to have stood while he performed any celebrated act, becomes his *kademgāh*, the place of his footsteps, and is visited and circumambulated by the pious Mahommedan with great veneration.

[4] The hill called Ukābein [two eagles] seems to be that now called Āshikān Ārifān, which connects with Bābur Bādshāh. The Bāla Hissār, or citadel, is on the same ridge, farther east, and south-east of the town.

are green. In the spring,[a] the north wind blows incessantly; they call it *bād e Parwān* (the pleasant breeze).[1] In the north part of the citadel there are houses with windows, which enjoy a delightful atmosphere. Mulla Muhammed Tālib Maamāi[2] composed the following distich in praise of the citadel of Kābul, under the character of Badia-ez-zemān Mirza[3]:

> (*Persian*)—Drink wine in the citadel of Kābul, and send round the cup without stopping;
> For it is at once a mountain and a sea, a town and a desert.

The people of Hindustān call every country beyond their own Khorasān, in the same manner as the Arabs term all except Arabia, Ajem. On the road between Hindustān and Khorasān, there are two great marts: the one Kābul, the other Kandahār. Caravans, from Ferghāna, Tūrkestān, Samarkand, Balkh, Bokhāra, Hissār, and Badakhshān, all resort to Kābul; while those from Khorasān repair to Kandahār. This country lies between Hindustān and Khorasān. It is an excellent and profitable market for commodities. Were the merchants to carry their goods as far as Khitā or Rūm,[4] they would scarcely get the same profit on them. Every year, seven, eight, or ten thousand horses arrive in Kābul. From Hindustān, every year, fifteen or twenty thousand pieces of cloth are brought by caravans. The commodities of Hindustān are slaves,[b] white clothes, sugar-candy, refined and common sugar, drugs, and spices. There are many merchants that are not satisfied with getting thirty or forty for ten.[5] The

Its trade.

[a] summer,
[b] The caravans of India, consisting of 10, 15, or 20,000 persons, bring with them slaves,

---

[1] Or rather the breeze of Parwān, from the pass of that name which lies north from Kābul. [Parwāndarah.]
[2] [The riddle maker.]
[3] [Badī'uzzamān = the Marvel of the Age, and the meaning seems to be that Kābul, like Badī'uzzamān Mirza, was the Wonder of the World.]
[4] Khitā is Northern China, and its dependent provinces. Rūm is Turkey, particularly the provinces about Trebizond.
[5] Three or four hundred per cent.

productions of Khorasān, Rūm, Irāk, and Chīn,[1] may all be found in Kābul, which is the very emporium of Hindustān. Its warm and cold districts are close by each other. From Kābul you may in a single day go to a place where snow never falls, and in the space of two astronomical hours, you may reach a spot where snow lies always, except now and then when the summer happens to be peculiarly hot. In the districts dependent on Kābul, there is great abundance of the fruits both of hot and cold climates, and they are found in its immediate vicinity. The fruits of the cold districts in Kābul are grapes, pomegranates, apricots, peaches, pears, apples, quinces, jujubes,[2] damsons, almonds, and walnuts; all of which are found in great abundance. I caused the sour-cherry-tree[3] to be brought here and planted; it produced excellent fruit, and continues thriving. The fruits it possesses peculiar to a warm climate are the orange, citron, the *amlūk*,[4] and sugar-cane, which are brought from the Lamghānāt. I caused the sugar-cane to be brought, and planted it here. They bring the *jilghūzek*[5] from Nijrau. They have numbers of bee-hives, but honey is brought only from the hill-country on the west.[a] The *rawāsh*[6] of Kābul is of excellent quality; its quinces and damask plums are

Climate of Kābul.

Produce.

[a] Honey comes in great quantities from the hilly tracts situated at the extreme limits of the Province of Kābul, where bees are kept. But none comes from the mountains of Ghazni.

---

[1] Chīn is China.
[2] [The *Zizyphus jujuba* or Indian *Ber*. The fruit, which resembles the crab-apple in flavour, is about the size of a gooseberry. Watts's *Dict.*, p. Z. 247.]
[3] [Ālu bālu (*Prunus cerasus*). Watts's *Dictionary of Economic Products of India*, p. P. 1303. The *Shah ālu* is the common sweet cherry.] [4] [*Diospyrus lotus*.]
[5] The *jilghūzek* is the seed of a kind of pine, the cones of which are as big as a man's two fists. [This is the edible pine (*Pinus gerardiana*), the seeds of which are largely exported from Afghanistan to India, where they are much appreciated for food. Each cone is said to contain 100 seeds. The oil extracted from the seeds is also highly esteemed for medical purposes. Watts's *Dict.*, p. P. 753.]
[6] The *rawāsh* [or *rawand* = rhubarb] is described as a root something like beet-root, but much larger—white and red in colour, with large leaves, that rise little from the ground. It has a pleasant mixture of sweet and acid. [The *rawāsh* or *rawand* is the Rhubarb (*Rheum*

excellent, as well as its *bādrengs*.¹ There is a species of grape which they call the water-grape, that is very delicious; its wines are strong and intoxicating. That produced on the skirt of the mountain of Khwājeh Khan-Saīd is celebrated for its potency, though I describe it only from what I have heard;

> The drinker knows the flavour of the wine; how should the sober know it?

Kābul is not fertile in grain; a return of four or five to one is reckoned favourable. The melons too are not good, but those raised from seed brought from Khorasān are tolerable. The climate is extremely delightful, and in this respect there is no such place in the known world. In the nights of summer you cannot sleep without a *postīn* (or lambskin cloak). Though the snow falls very deep in the winter, yet the cold is never excessively intense. Samarkand and Tabrīz are celebrated for their fine climate, but the cold there is extreme beyond measure.

In the neighbourhood of Kābul there are four fine *aulengs* or meadows. On the north-east is the *auleng* of Sung-Kurghān, at the distance of about two kos. It is a fine plain, and the grass agrees well with horses; there are few mosquitoes in it. To the north-west lies the *auleng* of Chālāk, about one kos from Kābul. It is extensive; but in the summer the mosquitoes greatly annoy the horses. On the west is the *auleng* of Deveren,² which consists properly of two plains, the one the *auleng* of Tībah, the other that of Kūsh-nāder, which would make the *aulengs*

The aulengs of Kābul.

emodi), a species that grows wild in Central Asia and the Himalayas, and is said to be the chief source of the Rhubarb of commerce. Watts's *Dict.*, p. R. 215.]

¹ The *bādreng* is a large green fruit, in shape somewhat like a citron. The name is also applied to a large sort of cucumber. [According to Vuller's *Persian Lexicon* (Bonn, 1855), the term *badrang* is applied to (1) a species of cucumber, and (2) a kind of citron (*turunj*), which would appear to be the meaning here.]

² [The defile of Durīn leads to the *ulang* or *jalgah* of Durīn, about three-quarters of a mile from which is situated Bābur's tomb. The *ulang* of Durīn is now known as the Plain of the Four Villages (*Maidān i chahārdih*). This extensive plain, which is densely cultivated, is surrounded by mountains on all sides, and the view over it is unequalled for beauty. Raverty's *Notes on Afghanistan*, p. 689.]

of Kābul five in number. Each of these two *aulengs* lies about a farsang from Kābul. Though but of small extent, they afford excellent pasture for horses, and are not pestered with gnats. There is not in all Kābul any *auleng* equal to these. The *auleng* of Siāh-Sang lies on the east of Kābul. Between this last *auleng* and the Currier's-gate stands the tomb of Kūtluk kadem. This *auleng* being much infested with mosquitoes in the hot weather, is not in such high estimation as the others. Adjoining to this last valley is that of Kamri. By this computation it appears that there are six *aulengs* about Kābul, but we hear only of the four *aulengs*.

Passes over Hindū-kūsh.

The country of Kābul is very strong, and of difficult access, whether to foreigners or enemies. Between Balkh, Kunduz, and Badakhshān on the one side, and Kābul on the other, is interposed the mountain of Hindū-kūsh, the passes over which are seven in number. Three of these are by Penjhīr;[1] the uppermost[2] of which is Khawāk;[3] lower down is that of Tūl;[4] and still lower that of Bazārak. Of these three passes, the best is that of Tūl, but the way is somewhat longer, whence it probably got its name of Tūl (or the long). The most direct pass is that of Bazārak. Both of these passes lead over to Sirāb.[5] As the pass of Bazārak terminates at a village named Parendi, the people of Sarāb call it the pass of Parendi. Another route is that of Parwān. Between Parwān and the high mountain[a] there are seven minor passes, which

[a] main pass

---

[1] Now Penjshīr.

[2] In this enumeration Bābur begins from the east.

[3] There is a pass over the Hindū-kūsh range, at the head of the valley of Penjshīr, which is called the Kurindah Pass.

[4] Bazārak must be the straight road from Seifābād to Chārmaghzār. The Parwān route is that by Parwān to Chārmaghzār, which passes between Seifābād and the head of the valley of Sauleh *auleng*. Yangi-yūli is that by Dushākh direct upon Khinjān. The Kipchāk route runs up the valley of Ghūrbend, and then over the mountains to the junction of the two rivers at Kila Beiza. The Shibertu Pass is by Shiber. There seems to have been a direct road from that to Mader in dry weather; but in wet, people went round by Bāmiān, Saighān, and the pass of Dandān-shikan.

[5] [Sar i āb.]

they call *Haft-bacheh* (the Seven Younglings). As you come from the Anderāb side, two roads unite below the main pass, and lead down on Parwān by way of the Seven Younglings. This is a very difficult road. There are besides three roads in [a] Ghūrbend. That which is nearest to Parwān is the pass of Yangi-yuli (the new road), which descends by Waliān and Khinjān. Another route is that of Kipchāk, which leads by the junction of the rivers of Surkhāb and Anderāb. This is a good pass. Another route is by the pass of Shibertu. During the summer, when the waters are up, you can go by this pass only by taking the route of Bāmiān and Sıkān ;[1] but in the winter season, they travel by way of Ābdareh. In winter, all the roads are shut up for four or five months, except this alone ;[b] such as then proceed to Shibertu through this pass, travel by way of Ābdareh. In the season of spring,[c] when the waters are in flood, it is as difficult to pass these roads as in winter; for it is impossible to cross the water-courses, on account of the flooding of the torrents, so that the road by the water-courses is not passable ; and as for passing along the mountains, the mountain track is so difficult, that it is only for three or four months in autumn, when the snow and the waters decrease, that it is practicable. The Kafir robbers also issue from the mountains and narrow paths, and infest this passage.

The road from Khorasān leads by way of Kandahār. It is a straight level road, and does not go through any hill-passes.

From Hindustān there are four roads which lead up to Kābul. One of these is by way of the Lamghānāt,[2] and comes by the hill of Kheiber, in which there is one short hill-pass. Another road leads by Bangash ; a third by Naghz,[3] and the fourth by Fermūl.[4] In all of these roads

The Passes to India.

---

[a] leading out of
[b] except that across the Shibertu Pass ;
[c] summer,

---

[1] Or Seighān.
[2] The Lamghān road is the great road from Kābul to Peshāwar.
[3] [Naghz, according to Raverty (*Notes*, pp. 68 and 318), is Baghzan, the chief place in Iri-āb, 35 miles SSW. of Kābul.]
[4] [Fermūl is the district of Urghūn.]

there are passes of more or less difficulty.[a] Those who come by them cross the river Sind at three different places.[1] Those who go by the Nilāb passage,[2] take the road of Lamghānāt. In the winter season, however, they cross the river Sind, the river of Sawād, and the river of Kābul, above the conflux of this last river with the Sind. In most of the expeditions which I made into Hindustān, I forded [A.D. 1525.] these rivers in this way; but the last time, when I invaded that country, defeated Sultan Ibrahīm and conquered Hindustān, I crossed at the Nilāb passage in boats. Except at the place that has been mentioned, the river Sind can nowhere be passed unless in boats. Those again who cross at Dīnkŏt[3] take the Bangash road; while those who cross at Choupāreh[4] take the road of Fermūl, if proceeding to Ghazni, and the road of the dasht or plains if they are going to Kandahār.

In the country of Kābul there are many and various tribes. Its valleys and plains are inhabited by Tūrks, Aimāks, and Arabs. In the city and the greater part of the villages, the population consists of Tājiks.[b] Many other of the villages and districts are occupied by Pashāis, Parāchis, Tājiks, Berekis, and Afghans. In the hill-country to the west, reside the Hazāras and Nukderis. Among the Hazāra and Nukderi tribes, there are some who speak the Moghul language. In the hill-country to the north-east

[a] comparatively low. [b] Sarts.

---

[1] [i.e. ferries (P. de C.).]

[2] Nilāb stands somewhat lower down the Sind than Attok. The present Nilāb is about fifteen miles below Attok. I may remark, that I have not been able to discover any Indian authority previous to the time of Abulfazl for the Sind being called Nilāb, though it would help to explain an ancient geographical difficulty.

[3] [Erskine in a subsequent note expressed the opinion that Dīnkot was situated near Kālabāgh, though it is marked on Major Rennell's map as lying much lower down the Indus on the east bank. Fermūl was a district of which Urghūn is the chief town.]

[4] The road from Choupāreh to Fermūl was probably the direct road through Kāneguram to Urghūn. The road of the *dasht* or plain was no doubt that through Dāmān, the flat part of which Bābur always calls *Dasht*. [Chaupārah is marked on Rennell's map as a town and district lying in the fork formed by the rivers Indus and Sohān, due south of Dīnkot.]

lies Kaferistān, such as Kattor¹ and Gebrek. To the south is Afghanistān. There are eleven or twelve different languages spoken in Kābul: Arabic, Persian, Tūrki, Moghuli, Hindi, Afghani, Pashāi, Parāchi, Geberi, Bereki, and Lamghāni.² It is dubious whether so many distinct races, and different languages, could be found in any other country.

The country of Kābul is divided into fourteen Tumāns. In Samarkand, Bokhāra, and those quarters, the smaller districts into which a country is divided are called Tumān: in Andejān, Kāshghar, and the neighbouring countries they get the name of Urchīn, and in Hindustān they call them Perganah. Although Bajour, Sawād, Pershāwer, and Hashnaghar³ originally belonged to Kābul; yet at the present date some of these districts have been desolated, and others of them entirely occupied by the tribes of Afghans, so that they can no longer be properly regarded as provinces.ᵃ

Divisions of Kābul.

On the east lies the Lamghānāt,⁴ which comprehends five Tumāns and two Bulūks.⁵ The largest of the Tumāns of

Lamghānāt.

ᵃ are no longer the seat of any government.

---

¹ Kattor [which roughly corresponds to the modern Chitrāl] is a place of note in Kaferistān. Gebrek also lies in the Kafer country.

² [I am indebted to the kindness of Sir George Grierson for the following note:
Pashai and Laghmāni are Pisāchah languages, in fact Laghmāni is Pashai, the difference, if any, being one of dialect. Prāchi is the general name given to the languages of East India by those living in the west As a specific language it often denotes the tongue of Oudh (Purbi), and might have got to Kābul through the Purbyas, who were and are great travellers. Geberi or Gabri is the language of the Parsees of Yezd and Kirmān. It is a very interesting dialect of Persian (see *Grundriss der iranischen Philologie*, vol. i (2, p. 381). Bereki or Baraki is the language generally known as Urmuri, though by its speakers it is called Bragistah. It is spoken by a tribe living mainly at Kāniguram in Wazīristan, and gets its name of Baraki from Barak in the Logar Valley, where some of them lived. Urmuri is a curious linguistic island, and presents an interesting ethnological problem, as it is an Eranian language having no connexion whatever with Pushtu or Baluchi, being most nearly allied to Kurdish.]

³ [Peshāwar and Hashtnagar.]

⁴ A singular proof of the imperfect state in which the geography of those countries long remained is, that Petis de la Croix place Lamghān in Kashmīr.—*Hist. de Timur Bec*, vol. ii, p. 18.   [Sub-districts.]

Lamgān is Nangenhār,[1] which, in many histories, is written Nagarhār. The residence of the Dārogha, or commandant of this district, is Adīnapūr. Nangenhār lies to the east of Kābul, thirteen farsangs of very difficult road. In three or four places there are some very short *kotals* or steep hill-passes, and in two or three places there are narrows or straits. The Khirilchi and other robber Afghan tribes infest this road with their depredations.[a] There was no population along this road till I settled Karatū below the Kurūk-sāi,[2] which rendered the road safe. The Garmsīl (or region of warm temperature) is divided from the Sardsīl (or region of cold temperature) only by the steep pass of Bādām-chashmeh.[3] Snow falls on the Kābul side of this pass, but not on the Kurūk-sāi and Lamghānāt side. The moment you descend this hill-pass, you see quite another world. Its timber is different, its grains [b] are of another sort, its animals of a different species, and the manners and customs of the inhabitants are of a different kind. Nangenhār has nine streams.[4] Its rice and wheat are excellent. Oranges, citrons, and pomegranates are very abundant, and of good quality. Opposite to the fort of Adīnapūr,[5] to the south, on a rising

[a] infested this tract as long as it was unpopulated.
[b] plants

---

[1] Nangenhār lies along the Kābul river on the south. [According to Raverty (*Notes*, p. 49), Nangrahār is a corruption of Nīkanhār (or good streams), and was in former times also called Juī Shāhī. It consisted of nine separate valleys, and extended from Bhati Kot on the east to the Surkhāb Kotal on the west, and from the mountain of Darunthah on the Kābul river on the north to Kaja on the south.]
[2] The dry water channel.—*Leyden*. Perhaps the Park river.
[3] i.e. Almond-spring. The Pass of Bādām-chashmeh lies south of the Kābul river, between Little Kābul and Barīk-āb.
[4] Whence it is said to derive its name, which in Afghani means *nine streams*.
[5] The fort of Adīnapūr is to the south of the Kābul river. ['The town of Adīnapūr was the ancient seat of government in Ningrahār, but as it was situated in broken, uneven ground, and distant from the river Kābul, a new town was founded half a kos to the north of the old one, adjoining the river, which was named Jelālābād after the Emperor Jalāluddīn Muhammed Akbar, its founder' (Raverty's *Notes*, p. 49).]

ground, I formed a chārbāgh (or great garden), in the year nine hundred and fourteen.¹ It is called Bāgh e wafā (the Garden of Fidelity). It overlooks the river, which flows between the fort and the palace.ª In the year in which I defeated Behār Khan and conquered Lahore and Dipālpūr, I brought plantains and planted them here. They grew and thrived. The year before I had also planted the sugar-cane in it, which throve remarkably well. I sent some of them to Badakhshān and Bokhāra. It is on an elevated site, enjoys running water, and the climate in the winter season is temperate. In the garden there is a small hillock, from which a stream of water, sufficient to drive a mill, incessantly flows into the garden below. The fourfold field-plot² of this garden is situated on this eminence. On the south-west part of this garden is a reservoir of water ten gaz square, which is wholly planted round with orange trees; there are likewise pomegranates. All around the piece of water the ground is quite covered with clover. This spot is the very eye of the beauty of the garden. At the time when the orange becomes yellow, the prospect is delightful. Indeed the garden is charmingly laid out. To the south of this garden lies the Koh-e-sefīd (the White Mountain) of Nangenhār, which separates Bangash from Nangenhār. There is no road by which one can pass it on horseback. Nine streams descend from this mountain. The snow on its summit never diminishes, whence probably comes the name of Koh-e-sefīd³ (the White Mountain). No snow ever falls in the dales at its foot. Between the mountain and the garden there may be as much interval as would serve a party to encamp on.ᵇ On the skirts of this hill there are many airy and beautiful situations. The water which descends from it is naturally so cold, that it does not require

A. H. 930.
A. D. 1524.

ª *Add* It produces an abundance of oranges, citrons, and pomegranates.

ᵇ The distance between the mountain and the garden is half a day's journey.

¹ About A.D. 1508.
² It is usual for the Persians to divide their gardens into four plots by two roads which cross each other.
³ The Koh-e-sefīd is a remarkable position in the geography of Afghanistān. It is seen from Peshāwer.

ice to cool it. On the south of the fort of Adīnapūr is the Surkh-rūd[1] (the Red Rivulet). The fort is situated on an eminence, which, towards the river, is forty or fifty gaz in perpendicular height. On the north there is a detached mass of mountain. The fortress is very strong. This last mountain forms the division between Nangenhār and the Lamghānāt. Whenever it snows at Kābul, the snow falls also on the top of this mountain, by which means the people of the Lamghānāt can tell, from the appearance of its top, when it snows at Kābul. In travelling from Kābul to Lamghān,[2] there is one road by which, after passing Kurūk-sāi, you proceed through the steep pass of Dibri, and reach the Lamghānāt by way of Būlān.[a] There is another road,[3] by which, crossing Kurūk-sāi lower down than Karabūk, and passing the river Bārān[4] at Uluk-Nūr,[5] and thence proceeding by the hill-pass of Badij,[6] you come down upon Lamghān. If one travel by the road of Nijrau he passes on by Bedrau, and, proceeding by Karabankerik,[b] falls into the hill-pass of Badij. Though Nangenhār be

[a] after crossing the Bārān river at Būlān.
[b] Haranaīgerik,

---

[1] The Surkh-rūd rises in the Sefīd Koh, and runs into the Kābul river between Jagdalak and Gandamak.

[2] A friend to whose observations on Bābur's geography of Afghanistān I have been much indebted, remarks, 'The change of names here is astonishing. I know many routes in Lamghān, one in particular, by the way of Nijrau here referred to, and yet I cannot discover one place of those here mentioned, unless the *kotal* of Badij be allowed any resemblance to Bādpash (by changing the diacritical points). Bādpash is a steep *kotal*, half a day's journey to the north of Undroor on the Kābul river, and about 16 or 18 miles west of Turgurree, where the streams of Alingār and Alisheng join.'

[3] In this route they proceed by the north side of the Kābul or Bārān river.

[4] Rain river.—*Leyden*. [The Bārān river, or Āb i Bārān, as it is also called, is a tributary of the Lohgar, which with several other streams unite to form the Kābul river. The name Bārān is often applied to the united streams until after their junction with the Surkh-rūd above Gandamak. Raverty's *Notes*, p. 101.]

[5] Uluk-Nūr.—The Great Light.—*Leyden*. [Or the Great Rock.]

[6] [According to Raverty this is a corruption for Bādfaj, or Windy Pass.]

spoken of as one of the *five* Tumāns of Lamghān,[1] yet there are only *three* Tumāns which properly bear the name of Lamghān.

The first of these three is the Tumān of Alisheng,[2] which, on the north, consists of rugged snowy hills that join the mountain of Hindū-kūsh. That mountainous country is entirely in Kaferistān. The part of Kaferistān nearest to Alisheng is Mīl; and the river of Alisheng comes down from Mīl.[3] The tomb of the holy Lām, the father of Nūh,[4] is in the Tumān of Alisheng. In some histories, the holy Lām is denominated Lāmek and Lāmekān. The people of that country have a general practice of changing the letter *Kāf* into *Ghain*, and it seems very probable that the name Lamghān originated from that circumstance.

Tumān of Alisheng.

The second Tumān is Alingār. The part of Kaferistān that is nearest to Alingār is Gawār, and the river of Alingār comes down from Gawār. These two rivers,[5] after passing through Alisheng and Alingār, unite with each other, and afterwards fall into the river Bārān,[6] below the third Tumān, which is called Mandrāwar.

Alingār.

Of the two Bulūks which have been mentioned, one is Dareh-Nūr[7] (the Valley of Light), which is an uncommonly fine tract. The fort is situated at the entrance of the valley, on the projecting point of a mountain, and washed by a river on both of its sides. The grounds are chiefly laid out in rice-fields, and can be passed only by the high road. It has the orange, the citron, and the fruits of a warm climate. It has likewise a few date trees. The banks of the river, which flows on the two sides of the fort, are quite covered with trees; the most abundant of which is the *chob-amlūk*,

Dareh-Nūr.

[1] Lamghān is now always called Laghmān.
[2] The two streams which form the glens of Alisheng and Alingār, coming from the north, unite above Mandrāwar, and fall into the Kābul river below that place. [A full account of the valleys of Lamghān, Nijrau, Alisheng, Alingār, Wālā Sā'ū (Alah saī), and Mandrāwar is given in Raverty's *Notes*, pp. 100-4.]
[3] Now called Kila i Akheri.
[4] i.e. Lamech, the father of Noah.
[5] [i.e. the Alisheng and Alingār rivers.]
[6] The Bārān and Kābul rivers unite above this junction.
[7] [There is a description of this valley in Raverty's *Notes*, pp. 108 and 135. It lies on the Kashkar, or Chitral river.]

which the Tūrks generally name *karayemūsh*.[1] This fruit is very abundant in the Dareh-Nūr, but is found nowhere else. It has also grapes, all of which they grow upon trees.[2] The wine of Dareh-Nūr is famous over all the Lamghānāt. It is of two kinds, which they term *areh-tāshi* (the stone-saw), and *suhān-tāshi* (the stone file). The stone-saw is of a yellowish colour; the stone-file, of a fine red. The stone-saw, however, is the better wine of the two, though neither of them equals their reputation. Higher up, at the head of the glens, in this mountain, there are some apes to be met with. Apes are found lower down towards Hindustān, but none higher up than this hill. The inhabitants used formerly to keep hogs,[3] but in my time they have renounced the practice.

Kūner and Nūrgil.

Kūner and Nūrgil form another Tumān, which lies out of the way, and at some distance from Lamghān. It is situated in the midst of Kaferistān, which forms its boundary. Although it is equal in extent to the other Tumāns, yet, from this circumstance, it yields less revenue, and the inhabitants pay less. The river of Cheghānserāi,[4] after passing through Kaferistān from the north-east, and dividing this country, unites with the river Bārān, in the Bulūk of Kāmeh, and

---

[1] It is very singular that the Amlūk should now be called in Laghmān, Karamūsh, which is evidently mentioned here as a contrast to the Laghmāni name. [The Amlūk (*Diospyrus Lotus*), according to Watts (*Dict. Economic Products of India*), is a fruit, which is sweetish when ripe, and is eaten by Afghan and other tribes. It is supposed by some to be one of the fruits eaten by the Lotophagi.]

[2] On this passage Captain John Briggs, of the Madras Establishment, who is well versed in oriental usages, remarks, 'Bābur means in this place, I imagine, that the vines are not standards, but allowed to creep and spread. Standing vines are, however, very common in Persia. The plant is kept about three feet only in height, by lopping, and it is found to be a much more productive plan, though it sooner exhausts the soil.'

[3] This practice Bābur viewed with disgust, the hog being an impure animal in the Muhammedan law.

[4] This is the river which rises at Pūshtekhar, near the Pamir, and which is called by Mr. Elphinstone the Kashkar, or Kāmeh river. [The Cheghānserāi (white caravanserai) river is a tributary of the Kashkar, or Chitral river. This valley is described in Raverty's *Notes*, p. 107.]

then passes onward to the east. Nūrgil¹ lies on the west, and Kuner on the east of this river. Amīr Syed Ali Hamadāni departed this life in a spot one farsang higher up than Kuner.ᵃ His disciples carried him hence to Khutlān. A mausoleum is erected on the place where he died. In the year 920, when I came and took Cheghānseräi, I circumambulated his tomb²; the orange, citron, and *karenj*³ abound there. They get a strong and heady wine from Kaferistān. The inhabitants relate a strange circumstance, which appears to be impossible, but which is, however, constantly told. The lower part of this Tumān is called Milteh-Kandi, below which the country belongs to the Dareh-Nūr and Ater.⁴ Higher up than this Milteh-Kandi, in the whole of this hill country, comprehending Kuner, Nūrgil, Bajour, Sawād, and all that neighbourhood, it is the custom, when a woman dies, to place her on a bier, which they lift up by the four sides. If the woman has lived virtuously, she shakes the bearers to such a degree, that, even when they are upon their guard, and attempting to prevent it, the corpse falls from the bier. If, however, she has done anything amiss, no motion takes place. It is not solely from the people of this place that I have had information of the practice, but the men of Bajour, Sawād, and the whole of the hill-country, agree in their accounts. Haider Ali Bajouri, who was Sultan of Bajour, and who governed that country with much justice, when his mother died, neither made lamentation, nor expressed sorrow, nor arrayed himself in black, but only said, 'Go and place her on the bier; if she does not move, I will burn her.'⁵ They placed her on the bier, and the corpse had the desired motion. On hearing this he put on black, and gave vent to his sorrow.

A. D. 1514.

ᵃ coming here on a journey died a *shar'î kos* (two miles) above Kunar.

¹ Nūrgil lies in the hills west of Kūner.
² It is usual for pious Muhammedans to circumambulate the tomb of a saint or holy man seven times, as a mark of veneration. [The saint died at Pakhli on his return to Persia from Kashmir in A. D. 1384 (Beale).]
³ [The *karenj* is the coreander seed (*Coriandrum sativum*), which the Persians mix with their bread.]
⁴ Ater is five or six kos north of Jalālābād.
⁵ That is, treat the corpse as that of an infidel.

Cheghān-serāi.

Another Bulūk is Cheghānserāi, which contains one village only, and is of limited extent, lying in the very jaws or entrance of Kaferistān. As its inhabitants, though Musulmans, are mingled with the Kafers, they live according to the customs of that race. The large river, known by the name of the River of Cheghānserāi, comes from the north-east of Cheghānserāi, behind Bajour. Another smaller stream,[1] coming from the west, after flowing down through the midst of Pīch, a district of Kaferistān, falls into it, The wine of Cheghānserāi is strong and yellowish ; but bears no sort of comparison with that of the Dareh-Nūr. In Cheghānserāi there are neither grapes nor vineyards ; but they bring the wines down the river from Kaferistān and Kaferistān-Pīch. When I took Cheghānserāi, the Kafers of Pīch came to their assistance. So prevalent is the use of wine among them, that every Kafer has a *khīg*, or leathern bottle of wine about his neck ; they drink wine instead of water.

Kāmeh.

Kāmeh,[2] though not a distinct district, but under Nangenhār, yet gets the name of a Bulūk.

Nijrau.

Another Tumān is Nijrau, which lies north-east from Kābul, in the hill-country. Behind it, in the hill-country, all the inhabitants are Kafers, and the country is Kaferistān, It is a sort of sequestered corner. Grapes and fruits are extremely abundant in this district ; and it produces a great quantity of wine, but in making they boil it. In the winter season they fatten a number of fowls. The inhabitants are wine-bibbers, never pray, fear neither God nor man, and are heathenish in their usages. In the hills of this district they have the pine, the *jilgūzeh*,[3] the oak, and the mastic tree [4] in abundance. The fir, pine, and oak trees grow beneath Nijrau, but are not met with higher up ; they are among the trees of Hindustān. The people of this hill-country burn

[1] This is probably the river on which Kandi stands.

[2] Kāmeh lies to the east of the Cheghānserāi river, at its junction with that of Kābul.

[3] The *jilgūzeh*, as has already been remarked, is a kind of pine, which has cones larger than artichokes, containing seeds resembling pistachio nuts.

[4] [The mastic tree is the *Mastica terebintha var. mutica*, which yields a valuable resin. By the oak is meant the Holm oak (*Quercus bilūt*) so common in the Himalayas.]

the fir instead of lamps; it gives light, and burns like
a candle. It has a very singular appearance. In the
mountain districts of Nijrau, the flying-fox[1] is found. It is
an animal larger than a squirrel, with a kind of leathern
web stretching between its fore and hind feet, like a bat's
wing. They frequently brought them to me. It is said that
they can fly a bowshot from a higher tree to a lower one. I
myself have never seen them fly, but have let one go beside
a tree, which it quickly clung to and ascended; and, when
driven away, expanded its wings like a bird, and came to
the ground without injury. In these mountains is found
the bird *lūkheh*,[2] which is also termed the *būkalamūn*, or
Chameleon-bird, and which has, between its head and its
tail, five or six different colours. It has a brilliant changeable
colour, like the neck of a dove, and is larger than the beautiful
partridge, named *kibk-i-dari*. It is probable that this
bird is that which in Hindustān passes for the *kibk-i-dari*.
The people of the country relate a singular circumstance
concerning it. In the winter season these birds come down
to the skirts of the hills; and if in their flight they happen
to pass over a vineyard, they are no longer able to fly, and
are caught.[3] In Nijrau there is also a species of rat, which
is named the musk-rat, and has scent of musk, but I have
not seen it.[4]

Penjhīr[5] is another Tumān. It lies upon the road, and

[1] [(*Pteromys petaurista*) the flying squirrel, which is so common in the Hazāra district of the N.W. Frontier.]

[2] The hill chikōr. [More probably the Manāl pheasant (*Lophophorus impeyanus*). The *kibk i dari* is the snow-cock (*Tetragallus caspius*), which is allied to the *T. himalayensis*, or *ramchikor* of Kashmir.]

[3] A similar story is told of some fields near Whitby: 'These wild geese, which in the winter fly in great flocks to the lakes and rivers unfrozen in the southern parts, to the great amazement of every one, fall suddenly down upon the ground, when they are in their flight over certain neighbouring fields thereabouts; a relation I should not have made, if I had not received it from several credible men.'—See Notes to *Marmion*, p. xlvi.

[4] Are we entitled to infer from this, that the musk-rat was not so common in Hindustān in the age of Bābur as it has since become? Bābur was not a careless observer.

[5] Penjhīr, now always called Panjshīr, lies on the upper part of the Panjshīr river, above Parwān, nearly north of Kābul.

is in the immediate vicinity of Kaferistān. The thoroughfare and inroads of the robbers of Kaferistān are through Penjhīr. In consequence of their vicinity to the Kafers, the inhabitants of this district are happy to pay them a fixed contribution. Since I last invaded Hindustān, and subdued it, the Kafers have descended into Penjhīr, and returned, after slaying a great number of people, and committing extensive ravages.

Ghūrbend.   There is another Tumān, named Ghūrbend.[1] In this country they call a steep hill-pass *bend*; and as they cross over to Ghūr by this pass, the district, from that circumstance, has acquired the name of Ghūrbend. The Hazāras have got possession of the tops of its valleys. It contains a few villages, but yields little revenue. It is said, that on the mountains of Ghūrbend there are mines of silver and of lapis-lazuli. On the skirts of the hills there are some districts; in the upper part are Mīteh, Kacheh, and Parwān; and lower down are twelve or thirteen villages. All of them abound in fruits, and their wines come from this tract; the strongest wine comes from Khwājeh Khan-Saīd. As all these villages lie on the skirts of the mountain, or on the mountain itself, although they pay something as revenue, yet they are not regularly rated in the revenue rolls. Lower down than these villages, along the skirts of the mountains, and between them and the river Bārān, lie two detached spots of level ground; the one called the *Kurrah-e-Tāziān*, the other the *Dasht-e-Sheikh*.[2] In the warm season they are covered with the *chekīn-taleh* grass in a very beautiful manner,[a] and the Aimāks and Tūrks resort to them. In the skirts of these mountains the ground is richly diversified by various kinds of tulips. I once directed them to be counted, and they brought in thirty-two or thirty-three different sorts of tulips. There is one species which has a scent in some degree like the rose, and which I termed *lāleh-gulbūi* (the rose-scented tulip). This species is found only in the *dasht-e-Sheikh* (the Sheikh's plain), in a small spot of

[a] in abundance,

---

[1] Ghūrbend lies north-west of Kābul; its river runs into the Bārān.
[2] *The Arab's encampment*, and *the Sheikh's plain*.

ground, and nowhere else. In the skirts of the same hills, below Parwān, is produced the *lāleh-sad barg*[1] (or hundred-leaved tulip), which is likewise found only in one narrow spot of ground, as we emerge from the straits of Ghūrbend. Between these two plains there is a small hill, on which there is a line of sandy ground, reaching from the top to the bottom of the hill. They called it Khwājeh reg i rawān.[2] They say that in the summer season the sound of drums and nagarets issues from this sand.

There are a number of other districts [a] belonging to Kābul. On the south-west of Kābul, is a high snowy [3] mountain, on which the snow of one year generally falls on the snow of another. It happens very rarely that the old snow has disappeared before the new falls. When the ice-houses of Kābul are exhausted, they fetch ice from this mountain to cool their water. It is three farsangs from Kābul. This hill and that of Bāmiān are both exceedingly lofty. The Hirmand,[4] the Sind, the Dūghābeh of Kunduz, and the river of Balkh, all take their rise in this mountain; and it is said, that in the same day a person may drink from the streams of all these four rivers. The districts [b] which I mentioned are chiefly on the skirts of this mountain. Their gardens are numerous,[c] and their grapes, as well as every other kind of fruit, abundant. Among these villages there are none to be compared with Istālīf and Isterghach,[5]

[a] villages   [b] villages   [c] *This clause is omitted.*

---

[1] This is the double poppy.

[2] i.e. Khwājeh moving-sand

[3] By this high snowy mountain, Bābur evidently means the Koh i Bāba, which, by an inaccuracy in the points of the compass not unusual with him, he places SW. of Kābul, instead of NW. The Helmand and river of Kābul both rise there. The river of Balkh rises in the NW. of the same mountain. The river of Eibak, and the Surkhrūd, which descends by Kunduz, rise at no great distance.

[4] The Hirmand or Helmand, which rises to the west of the mountains not far from Kābul, after passing Girishk, falls into the lake of Sistān; the Sind, I presume, is the Kābul river, which finally falls into the Sind. The other two fall into the Amu, or Jeihūn, which discharges itself into the sea of Aral.

[5] These districts lie on the river of Karabāgh, north-west of Kābul. It falls into the Bārān. Isterghach is now termed Sırghach by the Afghans. Pamghān is called Paghmān.

which were termed by Ulugh Beg Mirza, Khorasān and Samarkand. Pamghān is also within the range of these districts [a]; and though it cannot be compared with those just mentioned, in respect to grapes and fruits, is beyond all comparison superior to them in respect to climate. The mountain of Pamghān [1] always keeps its snow. Few quarters possess a district [b] that can rival Istālīf. A large river runs through it, and on either side of it are gardens,[c] green, gay, and beautiful. Its water is so cold, that there is no need of icing it; and it is particularly pure. In this district is a garden, called Bāgh-e-kalān (or the Great Garden), which Ulugh Beg Mirza [2] seized upon. I paid the price of the garden to the proprietors, and received from them a grant of it. On the outside of the garden are large and beautiful spreading plane-trees, under the shade of which there are agreeable spots finely sheltered. A perennial stream, large enough to turn a mill, runs through the garden; and on its banks are planted planes [d] and other trees. Formerly this stream flowed in a winding and crooked course, but I ordered its course to be altered [e] according to a regular plan, which added greatly to the beauty of the place. Lower down than these villages, and about a kos or a kos and a half above the level plain, on the lower skirts of the hills, is a fountain, named Khwājeh sih-yārān (Khwājeh three-friends), around which there are three species of trees; above the fountain are many beautiful plane-trees, which yield a pleasant shade. On the two sides of the fountain, on small eminences at the bottom of the hills, there are a number of oak-trees; except on these two spots where there are groves of oak, there is not an oak to be met with on the hills to the west of Kābul. In front of this fountain, towards the plain, there are many spots, covered with the flowering *arghwān* [3] tree, and besides these *arghwān* plots,

[a] villages;   [b] village   [c] *Add* and vineyards,
[d] poplars   [e] made straight

[1] The four *tappahs*, or districts, now dependent on Kābul are Pamghān, or Paghmān, Kohdāmen, Būtkhāk, and Logar.
[2] This Ulugh Beg Mirza was the paternal uncle of Bābur.
[3] The name *arghwān* is generally applied to the anemone; but in Afghanistān it is given to a beautiful flowering shrub, which grows

there are none else in the whole country. It is said that
these three kinds of trees were bestowed on it by the power
of these three holy men, beloved of God ; and that this is
the origin of the name Sih yārān.[1] I directed this fountain
to be built round with stone, and formed a cistern of lime
and mortar ten gaz by ten. On the four sides of the fountain,
a fine level platform for resting was constructed on a very
neat plan.[a] At the time when the *arghwān* flowers begin to
blow, I do not know that any place in the world is to be
compared to it. The yellow *arghwān* is here very abundant,
and the yellow *arghwān's* blossom mingles with the red.
On the south-west of this fountain there is a valley, in which
is a rivulet, containing half as much water as would suffice
to turn a mill. This rivulet I confined within artificial banks,
and caused a channel to be dug for it over one of the heights
on the south-west of Sih yārān. On the top of this height
I formed a circular platform for sitting on.[b] The date of
my forming this rivulet was found in the words, *Jūi khush* [2]
(a charming stream).

Lohūger[3] is another Tumān, the largest town of which is Chirkh. Moulāna Yākūb, on whom be mercy, was of
Chirkh; the Mulla zādeh Mulla Osmān is also from Chirkh.
Sajāwend[4] is also one of the towns of Lohūger, whence
are Khwājeh Ahmed and Khwājeh Yunis. Chirkh has
numerous gardens, but there are none in any of the other
villages of Lohūger. The men are *Aughān-shāl*, a term
well known in Kābul ; it is probable, that the phrase

[margin: Logar.]

---

[a] *Add* so as to overlook the grove of Judas trees.
[b] round which willow trees were planted.

---

nearly the size of a tree. [The Judas tree (*Cercis siliquastrum*) is
common in Persia, and flourishes in Greece The specimen in my
garden, however, is not doing very well.]

[1] Three Friends. A note on the margin of Mr. Elphinstone's
Tūrki copy informs us, that these three friends were Khwājeh
Moudūd-e-Chīsti, Khwājeh Khāwand Saīd, and Khwājeh Regi-rawān.

[2] The numerical letters of these words give 925 [A. H. (A.D. 1519)].

[3] Lohgar, or Logar, is situated SE. from Kābul about seventeen
miles.

[4] Sajāwan lies between Chirkh and Spīga.

Afghān-shaār (or Afghanlike) has been converted into *Aughān-shāl*.

Ghazni.   There is also the country of Ghazni,[1] which is often denominated a Tumān. Ghazni was the capital of Sabuktegīn, of Sultan Mahmūd, and of the dynasty sprung from them. Many call it Ghaznīn. This was also the capital of Shāhāb-ed-dīn Ghūri,[2] who, in the *Tabakāt-e-Nāsiri*, and many of the histories of Hind, is called Muizzeddīn. It is situated in the third climate. It is also named Zābul, and it is to this country that the term Zābulistān relates; many include Kandahār in Zābulistān. It lies to the west of Kābul,[3] at the distance of fourteen farsangs. A person setting out from Ghazni at early dawn may reach Kābul between noonday and afternoon prayers. Adīnapūr is only thirteen farsangs distant; but, from the badness of the road, it is never travelled in one day. Ghazni is a country of small extent. Its river[4] may be large enough to drive four or five mills. The city of Ghazni, and four or five other districts,[a] are supplied from this river, while as many more are fertilized by subterraneous water-courses.[5] The grapes of Ghazni are superior to those of Kābul, and its melons more abundant. Its apples too are excellent, and are carried into Hindustān. Cultivation is carried on with great difficulty and labour, and whatever ground is cultivated is obliged to have a new dressing of mould every year; but the produce of the crops exceeds that of Kābul. The madder is chiefly cultivated here, and is carried over all Hindustān.[b] It is the most profitable crop in this district. The inhabitants of the open country are Hazāras and Afghans. Ghazni is a cheap place compared with Kābul. The inhabitants are Moslems of the sect of Hanīfah, and orthodox in their faith.

[a] villages,
[b] the whole crop of which was exported to India.

[1] This country is famous in history as the seat of government of Sultan Mahmūd Ghaznevi, and of the Ghaznevi dynasty. [Sabuktegīn died in A.D. 997 and his son Mahmūd in A.D. 1030.]
[2] [Shahābuddīn Ghūri, A.D. 1202-6.]
[3] Ghazni is rather south than west of Kābul.
[4] The river of Ghazni runs north to Lohgar, and joins the Kābul river.   [5] *Kāriz*.

Many of them fast for three months [1] in the year, and their wives and children live in a correct and sequestered manner. Mulla Abdal Rahmān was one of the eminent men of Ghazni. He was a man of learning, and always taught a class.[a] He was a holy, pious, and virtuous person. He took his departure from this world the same year with Nāsir Mirza. The tomb of Sultan Mahmūd is in one of the suburbs of Ghazni, which, from that circumstance, is termed Rauzeh.[2] The best grapes in Ghazni are from Rauzeh. The tombs of his descendants, Sultan Māsaūd and Sultan Ibrahīm, are in Ghazni. There are many holy tombs at that city. In the year in which I took Kābul, after ravaging Kohat, the plain of Bannu, and Afghanistān with great slaughter, I proceeded by Dūki, and having come on to Ghazni, along the banks of Āb-istādeh,[3] I was told, that in one of the villages of Ghazni there was a mausoleum, in which the tomb moved itself whenever the benediction on the Prophet was pronounced over it. I went and viewed it, and there certainly seemed to be a motion of the tomb. In the end, however, I discovered that the whole was an imposture, practised by the attendants of the mausoleum. They had erected over the tomb a kind of scaffolding; contrived that it could be set in motion when any of them stood upon it, so that a looker-on imagined that it was the tomb that had moved; just as to a person sailing in a boat, it is the bank which appears to be in motion. I directed the persons who attended the tomb to come down from the scaffolding; after which, let them pronounce as many benedictions as they would, no motion whatever took place. I ordered the scaffolding to be removed, and a dome to be erected over the tomb, and strictly enjoined the servants of the tomb not to dare to repeat this imposture.

[A.D. 1515.]

[A.D. 1504-5.]

[a] and devoted himself without intermission to study.

---

[1] Some very pious Musulmans fast all the months of Rajeb, Shābān, and Ramzān. The Muhammedan fasts only by day. The night is often given to feasting.

[2] The garden. The tombs of the more eminent Musulmans are generally in gardens, and surrounded by elegant parterres.

[3] Āb-istādeh, a lake south from Ghazni. [For a description of Lohgar, Chirkh, and Sajāwand, see Raverty's *Notes*, pp. 677-9.]

Ghazni is but a poor, mean place, and I have always wondered how its princes, who possessed also Hindustān and Khorasān, could have chosen such a wretched country for the seat of their government, in preference to Khorasān. In the time of the Sultan, there were three or four mounds for collecting water.[1] One of these, which is of great dimensions, was formed by the Sultan of Ghazni, on the river of Ghazni, about three farsangs up the river, on the north-west of the town. The height of this mound is about forty or fifty gaz, and its length may be about three hundred gaz. The water is here collected, and drawn off according as it is wanted for cultivation. Alāeddīn Jehānsōz[2] Ghūri, when he subdued this country, broke down the mound, burned and destroyed many of the tombs of the royal family of the Sultan, ruined and burned the city of Ghazni, and plundered and massacred the inhabitants. In short, there was no act of desolation and destruction from which he refrained. Ever since that time, the mound had remained in a state of ruin. In the year[3] in which I conquered Hindustān, I sent by Khwājeh Kalān a sum of money for the purpose of rebuilding it, and I entertain hopes that, by the mercy of God, this mound may once more be repaired. Another mound is that of Sakhen, which lies to the east of Ghazni at the distance of three or four farsangs from that city. This also has long been in a state of ruin, and is not reparable. Another mound is that of Sardeh,[4] which is in good repair. Some books mention, that in Ghazni there is a fountain, into which, if any filth or ordure be thrown, immediately there rises a tempest and hurricane, with snow and rain. I have seen in another history, that, when the Rai of Hind

---

[1] [i.e. dams.] In the East, where the success of cultivation depends chiefly on the supply of water, it is usual to dam up the bottoms of narrow valleys, or of low meadows, so as to collect all the water into one body, whence it is afterwards distributed for the supply of the country below. These artificial lakes in India are sometimes several miles in circumference, and are perhaps the most useful works in the country.

[2] Jehānsōz, the burner or desolator of the world. He is said to have got this name from his horrible massacre at Ghazni. [A.D. 1152.]

[3] A. H. 932.—A.D. 1526.   [4] Sardeh lies SE. from Ghazni.

besieged Sabuktegīn in Ghazni, Sabuktegīn ordered dead flesh and other impurities to be thrown into this fountain, when there instantly arose a tempest and hurricane, with rain and snow, and by this device he drove away the enemy.[1] I made strict inquiry in Ghazni for this well, but nobody could give me the slightest information about it. In these countries, Ghazni and Khwārizm are celebrated for their cold, in the same manner as Sultanīah and Tabrīz are in the Irāks and Azarbāijān.

Another Tumān is that of Zurmet,[2] which lies on the south of Kābul, and south-east of Ghazni. It is distant twelve or thirteen farsangs from Kābul, and seven or eight from Ghazni. It contains seven or eight districts or villages, and the residence of the Dārogha is at Gerdez. In the walled town of Gerdez, the greater part of the houses are three or four stories in height. Gerdez is of considerable strength; and when the inhabitants were in a state of hostility to Nāsir Mirza, occasioned the Mirza no small trouble. The inhabitants of Zurmet are *Aughān-shāl* (Afghans in their manners). They apply to agriculture, and the raising of corn, but not to orchards or gardening. On the south of this Tumān, there is a mountain which is termed the Hill of Tūrkestān;[3] on the skirts of which, on a rising ground, is a fountain, near which is the tomb of Sheikh Muhammed Muselmān.

Zurmet.

Another Tumān is that of Fermūl,[4] which is of small extent, and little importance; but its apples are tolerable, and they are carried even to Multān and Hindustān. The Sheikh zādehs (descendants of Sheikhs), who were treated with such distinguished favour in Hindustān during the time of the Afghans, were all of Fermūl, and descended of Sheikh Muhammed Musalmān.

Fermūl.

[1] Bābur has here reversed the situation of Sabuktegīn and the Hindu Raja [Jaipāl]. Sabuktegīn besieged the Raja, and, after being repelled, was informed in a vision of the quality of the well.—*Leyden.*
[2] Zurmet lies east of Ghazni, on the sources of the Kurram river.
[3] [Barkistān according to Leyden and P. de C.]
[4] [Fermūl is a district lying south-east from Ghazni, of which Urghūn was the capital. It is marked on Rennell's map as situated to the west of Kurram river.]

Bangash.

Bangash [1] is another Tumān. It is entirely surrounded by hills inhabited by Afghan robbers, such as the Khugiāni, the Khirilchi, the Tūri, and the Lander, who, lying out of the way, do not willingly pay taxes. Being occupied by many affairs of superior importance, such as the conquest of Kandahār, Balkh, Badakhshān, and Hindustān, I never found leisure to apply myself to the settlement of Bangash. But if Almighty God prosper my wishes, my first moments of leisure shall be devoted to the settlement of that district, and of its plundering neighbours.

Alah-sāi.

One of the Bulūks of Kābul is Alah-sāi,[2] which lies two or three farsangs to the east of Nijrau, from which you advance in a straight level direction towards Alah-sāi. On reaching a place named Kūrah, you proceed by a small *kotal*, or hill-pass, towards Alah-sāi. In this quarter, the space between the warm climate (*garmsīl*) and the cold (*sardsīl*) is merely the extent of this hill-pass of Kūrah. By this hill-pass, at the beginning of the spring, the birds take their flight from the one to the other. The people of Pīchghān, a place dependent on Nijrau, catch a great number of birds in their passage. In the ascent of the pass they build from distance to distance cots of stone, in which the fowlers sit and conceal themselves. They fasten one side of a net strongly, at the distance of five or six gaz;[3] one side of it is fixed down to the ground by stones, the other end, as far as half its length, three or four gaz, they fix to a stick, one end of which is held by the fowler, who is concealed, and sits on the watch, looking through holes left in the cot for the purpose, and waiting for the approach of the game from below. As soon as the birds come close up, he elevates one end of the net, and they rush into it by their own impulse. By this device, they take a great quantity of fowl; they boast, that sometimes they take

---

[1] Bangash occupies the lower grounds from Gerdez to Kohat. [According to Raverty (*Notes*, p. 75) Bangash was divided into two parts, Upper and Lower, the chief town being Kohat. It consisted of six main valleys, Khost, Dāwar, Maidān, Sibri, Bakr Khel, and Kohat.]

[2] Alah-sāi, now called Tagau. Bābur reckons it in the *garmsīl*. The great difference of climate, however, takes place farther east, between Alisheng and Uzbīn.

[3] [i. e. to a stick that was three or four yards long.]

such a number, that they have not time to kill them in the mode commanded by the law.[1] In this country, the pomegranates of Alah-sāi are famous: for, although they are not very excellent, yet there are none better in the country. They carry them all to Hindustān. Its grapes too are pretty good. The wines of Alah-sāi are not stronger, but are pleasanter than those of Nijrau.[a]

Bedrau[2] is another Bulūk, which lies close by Alah-sāi. Here there are no fruits, and the cultivators are all Kafers. They raise corn.

Bedrau.

As in Khorasān and Samarkand the possessors of the Wolds[3] are the Tūrks and Aimāks, so, in this country, the inhabitants of the Waste are Hazāras and Afghans. The most powerful of the Hazāras in this territory are the Sultan Masaūdi Hazāras, and the most powerful of the Afghans are the Mahmend Afghans.

Inhabitants.

The amount of the revenue of Kābul, whether arising from settled lands, or raised from the inhabitants of the wastes, is eight laks of shahrokhis.[4]

Revenue.

The mountainous country on the east frontier of Kābul is broken and of two kinds, and the mountainous country on the west of Kābul is also of two sorts, in which it differs from the hilly countries in the direction of Anderāb, Khost, and the Badakhshānāt, which are all covered with the *archeh*, or mountain pine, well watered with springs, and abounding with soft and smooth heights; the vegetation on these last, whether on the hills, the gentle heights and eminences, or the valleys, is all of one sort, and is of good quality. It abounds with the grass named *kāh-būtkeh*,

Pasture. Eastern hills.

---

[a] stronger and finer than those of Nijrau.

---

[1] That is, by repeating the Musulman confession of faith, and cutting their throats. It is usual to say only *bismillah* (*in the name of God*).

[2] Bedrau is perhaps the upper part of Tagau, now called Bāhāghāi. It is evidently higher up, by its having no fruits, and belonging to the Kafers.

[3] [By wolds and wastes are meant the uncultivated pasture lands inhabited by the nomad tribes.]

[4] The rupee being equal to two shahrokhis and a half, the shahrokhis may be taken at tenpence, thus making the revenue only £33,333 6s. 8d.—See *Ayeen e Akberi*, vol. ii, p. 169.

which is excellent for horses. In the country of Andejān, they also call this grass *būtkeh-aūti*,[1] but I was not acquainted with the origin of the name. In this country I learned that it is so called because it grows in *būteh*, knots, or patches.[2] The *yāilāks*, or summer residences of Hissār, Khutlān, Samarkand, Ferghāna, and Moghulistān, are all the same kind of *yāilāks* and pasturages as these; and though the summer retreats of Ferghāna and Moghulistān are not to be compared with the others, yet the hills and pastures are of the same sort. Nijrau again, and the hill country of Lamghānāt, Bajour, and Sawād, are of another kind, having many forests of pine, fir,[a] oak, olive, and mastic, but the grass is by no means equal to that of the hill country just mentioned. It is abundant enough and likewise tall enough, but good for nothing, and not kindly either for horses or sheep. Though these mountains are not nearly so elevated as those that compose the other hill-country, and appear diminutive in comparison, yet they are singularly hard[3] hills; there are indeed slopes and hillocks which have a smooth, level surface; yet hillocks and hills are equally hard, are covered with rocks, and inaccessible to horses. In these mountains there are many of the birds and animals of Hindustān, such as the parrot, the *shārak*,[4] the peacock, the *lūkheh*, the ape, the *nil-gau*,[5] and the *koteh-pāi* (short-foot[6]), and besides these, many other kinds of birds and animals, exceeding in number what I have heard of even in Hindustān.[b]

The mountainous country which lies to the west is composed of the hills that form the valley of Zindān,[7] the

Western hills.

[a] *Omit* pine, fir,
[b] which I never heard of in India.

---

[1] [*Kāh* in Persian and *auti* in Tūrki both mean grass.]
[2] [Or rather, according to P. de C., 'shoots' or 'tufts'.]
[3] [i. e. difficult.]
[4] [A species of Myna (*Acridotheres*).]   [5] [*Portax pictus*.]
[6] [A species of deer, probably the Hog deer (*Axis porcinus*).]
[7] This valley seems to run east and west, or north-east and southwest, across the road from Sārbāgh to Eibak. The Dareh-sūf, often mentioned by the Arabian writers, seems to lie west of Bāmiān; Garzewān stretches west from the river of Balkh, north

vale of Sūf, with Garzewān and Gharjestān, which hills are all of the same description. Their grazing grounds are all in the valleys ; the hills, or hillocks, have not a single handful of grass such as is to be found on the mountains to the north, nor do they even abound much with the *archeh* pine. The grass in the grazing grounds is very fit for both horses and sheep. Above these hills, the whole country is good riding ground, and level, and there all the cultivated ground lies. The deer are very numerous in these mountains. The courses of the streams are generally profound glens, often quite perpendicular, and incapable of being descended. It is a singular circumstance, that, while in all other mountainous tracts, the strengths,[1] and steep and rugged places, are at the top of the hills, in these mountains the strong places are all towards the bottom. The hill-countries of Ghūr, Karbū,[2] and Hazāra are all of the kind that has been described. Their pasture-grass is in the valleys and plains. They have few trees, and even the *archeh* pine does not grow in them. The grass is nutritive to horses and sheep. The deer are numerous ; and the rugged and precipitous places, and strengths of these hills, are also near the bottom.[a]

This hill-country, however, bears no resemblance to the hill-countries of Khwājeh Ismāel, Dasht,[3] Dūki, and Afghanistān, which have all a uniformity of aspect, being very low, having little grass, bad water, and not a tree, and which are an ugly and worthless country. At the same time, the mountains are worthy of the men ; as the proverb says, 'A narrow place is large to the narrow-minded.' There are perhaps scarcely in the whole world such dismal-looking hill-countries as these.

Southern hills.

[a] These mountains in contradistinction to those last mentioned have their strongholds on the top.

of Chārkend, to the head of the Murghāb. Gharjistān seems to have had Herāt on the west, Farrah on the south, and Ghor on the east.—*Mines de l'Orient*, vol. i, p. 325.

[1] [i. e. strongholds.]
[2] In my Persian MS. it is sometimes called Karnūd.
[3] Dasht [plain] is Damān [foot-hills]; Dūki is the Hindi for a hill Bābur always uses it for the south-eastern hills of Afghanistān.

Fuel.

In Kābul, although the cold is intense, and much snow falls in winter, yet there is plenty of firewood, and near at hand. They can go and fetch it in one day. The fuel consists chiefly of mastic, oak, bitter almond, and the *karkend*. The best of these is the mastic, which burns with a bright light, and has also a sweet perfume; it retains its heat long, and burns even when green. The oak, too, is an excellent firewood, though it burns with a duller light; yet it affords much heat and light; its embers last a long time, and it yields a pleasant smell in burning. It has one singular property: if its green branches and leaves are set fire to, they blaze up and burn from the bottom to the top briskly and with a crackling noise, and catch fire all at once. It is a fine sight to see this tree burn. The bitter almond is the most abundant and common of all, but it does not last. The *karkend* is a low, prickly thorn, that burns alike whether green or dry; it constitutes the only fuel of the inhabitants of Ghazni.

Animals.

The different districts of Kābul lie amid mountains which extend like so many mounds,[1] with the vales and level plains expanding between them. The greater part of the villages and population is found on these intermediate spaces. Deer and game are scarce. In the autumn and spring, the red deer, which is the *arkārghalcheh*, always has a stated track which it follows, in going from its winter to its summer range. Those who are fond of hunting, and who have hounds, preoccupy this track, and, remaining on the watch, catch the deer. The red deer[2] and [a] wild ass[3] are also found near the Surkhāb,[4] and Little Kābul, but the white deer[5] is never found there. In Ghazni, they have both the white deer and wild ass, and the white

[a] *Omit* red deer and

[1] [i. e. dams.]   [2] [Probably the *Ovis ammoni.*]
[3] *Gorkhar* [*Equus onager*].
[4] This is the Surkhāb which rises in Sefīd-koh, and joins the Kābul river.
[5] [This must be the Persian gazelle (*Gazella subgutterosa*). Sterndale in his *Mammals of India*, pp. 466, states on the authority of Blanford that the name of this animal in the Tūrki of Yarkand and Kāshgar is *kik*, *sarkik*, or *jīrān.*]

deer is seldom to be met with so plump as near Ghazni. In the spring [a] there are many hunting grounds in Kābul. The great passage of the fowls and animals [b] is by the banks of the river Bārān, for that river is enclosed by mountains both on the east and west. Right opposite to this spot, that is, by the banks of the river Bārān, is the grand pass up Hindū-kūsh, and there is no pass but itself in this vicinity. On that account all the game ascend the mountain by this route. If there be wind, or if any clouds rest on the pass up Hindū-kūsh, the birds are unable to ascend it, and they all alight in the vale of Bārān, when multitudes of them are taken by the people of the neighbourhood. About the close of the winter, the banks of the river Bārān are frequented by multitudes of water-fowl, which are extremely fat. The cranes, the *karkareh* [1] (or *begla* heron), and the larger game afterwards arrive in innumerable flocks, and are seen in immense quantities. On the banks of the river Bārān, great numbers of cranes are caught in springes, which they make for that purpose, as well as the heron,[2] the *begla* heron, and the *khawāsil*.[3] This last-mentioned fowl is rare. The mode of taking these fowls is as follows : They spin a thin sliding springe, about an arrow's flight long, and to the one end of this cord fix a double-pointed arrow, while on the other end of it they fasten a cross handle of horn.[c] They then take a stick, of the thickness of the wrist, and a span in length, and commencing at the arrow, wind up the cord till it is all wound on, after which they make fast the horn handle, and pull out the stick of the thickness of the wrist, on which the cord had been wound; the cord remaining wound up

Modes of fowling.

[a] summer
[b] *Omit* and animals   [c] horn ring.

[1] [The Demoiselle Crane (*Anthropoides virgo*).]
[2] [This may be the Blue Heron (*Ardea cinerea*), which, according to Jerdon (*Birds of India*, vol. ii, p. 240), is found throughout Europe, Asia, and Africa.]
[3] [I think from the context that this must be a mistake for *Hawāsil*, or pelican, as *Khawāsil*, which means goldfinch, would be out of place here. There are two species of Pelican found in India, viz. the white (*Pelicanus onocrotalus*) and the grey (*P. Philipensis*).]

and hollow. Taking a firm hold of the horn handle, they throw the dart, having the cord attached to it, at any fowl that comes near. If it falls on the neck or wings of the bird it twists round it, and brings it down. All the people on the Bārān catch birds in this manner; but this mode of fowling is extremely difficult and unpleasant, as it must be practised on dark and rainy nights, for on such nights for fear of the ravenous animals and beasts of prey, they fly about constantly all night long, never resting till the morning; and at such times they fly low. In the dark nights they keep flying over the running water, as it appears bright and white, and it is at such times when, from fear, they fly up and down above the streams all night long, that the fowlers cast their cords. One night I threw the cord many times, but at last it severed and the bird escaped; next morning, however, they brought in both the bird and the severed cord twisted round it. In this manner the people of the Bārān catch great numbers of herons. The *kalk i tāj* [1] are of the heron's feathers. These plumes, or *kalk i tāj*, are one of the commodities carried into Irāk and Khorasān from Kābul. There is a body of slave fowlers,[2] whose trade and occupation is to act as fowlers; they may consist of about two hundred or three hundred houses. One of the family of Taimūr Beg first caused them to be brought from the neighbourhood of Multān. They have constructed tanks, and bending down the branches of trees,[a] have placed nets over the tanks; in this way they take every species of bird. These, however, are not the only persons who practise fowling, for all the inhabitants along the river Bārān are extremely skilful in throwing the cord, in laying nets, and in every other device for taking fowl; and they take birds of every description.

Slave fowlers.

Modes of fishing.

In the same season the migration of the fish takes place

[a] They excavate tanks and on their banks fix long branches of trees, in the middle of which they lay nets. [P. de C. explains that the word *milwah* used for 'long branches of trees' may mean a decoy bird.]

[1] Plumes [or aigrettes] worn on the cap, or turban, on great occasions.
[2] *Ghulāmān i sayyād* — slave, or royal fowlers.

in the river Bārān; they first of all take great quantities of them by the net, and by erecting gratings.[1] In the autumn season, when the plant named *kalān kāirūghi* (or wild-ass-tail) has come out, reached maturity, flowered and seeded, they take ten or twelve loads of it, and twenty or thirty loads of the plant named *gūk-shibāk*, and having brought them to the banks of the river, shred them down and throw them into the stream; the instant that the plants touch the water the fishes become intoxicated, and they begin to catch them. Farther down the river they construct gratings, in a convenient place, in the following manner: They take twigs of the *tāl*[2] tree, of the thickness of one's finger, and weave them into open gratings, lattice-wise; this lattice-work they place under a water-fall where there is a hollow, and lay heaps of stones all around it, so that the water rushes through the wicker-work with a loud noise, and runs off below, while the fish that come down the stream are borne along and retained by the wicker-work above; and thus the fishes that have been intoxicated, while they come in numbers floating down the current, are taken within these gratings. They catch great quantities of fish in this manner, in the rivers of Gulbehār, Purwān, and Istālīf.[3]

There is another singular way in which they catch fish in Lamghānāt during the winter. In places where the water falls from a height, they dig out hollow pits of about the size of a house, and laying them with stones in the form of the lower part of a cooking furnace, they heap on stones above the pits, leaving only one passage for the water to descend; and they pile the stones up in such a manner, that, except by this single passage, there is no other for any fish either to come or go. The water of the stream finds its way through these stones that have been heaped on, so that this contrivance answers the purpose of a fish pool. In winter, whenever fish are required, they

---

[1] The *chīch*, or gratings, are frames of open basket-work, which allow the water to pass, but retain the fish.
[2] [P. de C. has 'willow'. *Tāl* (= the Palmyra palm) seems unsuitable here.]
[3] These rivers all run into the Bārān.

open one of these pits, and take out forty or fifty fishes at a time. In some convenient place of the pit an opening is formed, and excepting at that outlet, all the sides of it are secured with rice straw, over which stones are piled up. At the opening they fasten a kind of wicker-work like a net, the two extremities of which are contracted and brought near each other. In the middle of this first wicker-net they fix another piece of wicker net-work, in such a way that the mouth of this last may correspond with that of the other, but its whole length be only about half of that of the one first mentioned. They make the mouth of this inner net-work very narrow. Whatever enters it must pass into the larger wicker-net, the lower part of which is so constructed that no fish can escape back. The lower part of the mouth of the inner wicker-net is so formed that, when fish have once entered the upper part, they must proceed one by one down to the lower part of its mouth. The sharpened sticks forming the lower part of the mouth are brought close together. Whatever passes this mouth comes into the larger wicker-net, the lower passage of which is strongly secured, so that the fish cannot escape; and should it turn and attempt to swim back, it cannot get up, in consequence of the sharpened prongs that form the lower mouth of the small inner wicker-net. Every time that they bring these nets, they fasten them in the water-course of the fish-pool, and then take off the covering of the fish-pool, leaving all its sides secured by the rice-straw. Whatever they can lay hold of in the hollow pit they seize, while every fish that attempts to escape by the only issue left necessarily comes into the wicker-net that has been mentioned, and is taken there. This mode of catching fish I never saw practised elsewhere.

Some days after the taking of Kābul, Mukīm requested permission to proceed to Kandahār; and, as had been settled by the capitulation, I dismissed him safe and sound, with all his baggage, effects, and followers, to join his father and elder brother. After his departure I partitioned out the country of Kābul among those Begs only who had lately taken service with me.[a] Ghazni and its dependencies

[a] among the Mirzas and Begs who had taken refuge with me.

I gave to Jehāngīr Mirza; the Tumān of Nangenhār, Mandrāwar, the Dareh-Nūr, the Dareh-Kuner, Nūrgil, and Cheghānserāi, I gave to Nāsir Mirza. Those Begs and young officers who had followed me in my expeditions and dangers, I rewarded; giving to one of them a village, to another an estate in land, but to none of them did I give the government of a district. Nor was this the sole occasion in which I acted in this manner; but uniformly, whenever the Most High God prospered my undertakings, I always regarded and provided for those Begs and soldiers who were strangers and guests, in the first place, and in a superior manner to the Bāburians,[1] and those who were of Andejān. In spite of this, it has been a great misfortune to me [a] that I have always been charged with favouring none but my own Bāburians and the Andejānians. There is a proverb,

(*Tūrki*)—What is it enemies will not say?
What is it dreams will not display?
(*Persian*)—The gates of a city you may shut;
You cannot shut the mouth of an enemy.

As many Īls and Ulūses had come to me from Hissār, Samarkand, and Kunduz, it appeared advisable, as Kābul was a confined country, and to be governed by the sword, not the pen, and incapable of supplying a contribution in money sufficient for all my people, that a levy of corn should be made and given to the wives, families, and followers of the Īls and Ulūses, to enable them to proceed with us in our wars and expeditions. It was therefore determined to raise thirty thousand loads of grain,[2] from Kābul, Ghazni, and their dependencies. As I was at that time very imperfectly acquainted with the revenues and resources of Kābul, the amount was excessive, and the country suffered extremely.

Levies a contribution on Kābul

[a] it is strange

[1] [i. e. Bābur's old adherents (P. de C.)]
[2] A *kharwār* [ass-load] is generally one hundred *man* of Tabrīz.—*Leyden.* Abul-Fazl says, that it is equal to 40 *kandahāri*, or 10 Hindustāni *mans*.—Vol. ii, p. 158. It is about 700 pounds avoirdupois.

It was at this time that I invented a kind of writing called the Bāburi hand.

Foray against the Masaūdi Hazāras.

I had imposed a large contribution of horses and sheep on the Sultan Masaūdi Hazāras, and sent collectors to receive it. In a few days I heard from them that the Hazāras[1] refused to pay, and were in a state of rebellion. Several times before, they had been guilty of depredations on the roads of Ghazni and Gerdēz.[2] On these accounts I took the field for the purpose of falling on them by surprise; and having advanced by way of Meidān, we cleared the pass of Nirkh[3] by night, and, by the time of morning prayers, fell upon the Hazāras in the territory of Chātū, and beat them to our heart's content. Returning thence by way of Sang-e-surākh, Jehāngīr Mirza took leave to go to Ghazni, while I returned to Kābul. When I reached Kābul, Yār Hussain, the son of Daryā Khan, came from Behreh[4] to offer me his services.

Bābur resolves on an irruption into Hindustān.

January 1505.

A few days afterwards, having mustered my army, and assembled the persons best acquainted with the situation of the country, I made particular inquiries regarding the state and condition of the different districts on every hand. Some advised that we should march against Dasht;[5] others preferred Bangash; while others proposed to advance against Hindustān. It was at last determined in council to make an irruption into Hindustān.

Reaches Adīnapūr.

In the month of Shābān, when the sun was in Aquarius, I set out from Kābul towards Hindustān; and proceeding by way of Badām-chashmeh and Jagdālīk,[6] in six marches reached Adīnapūr. I had never before seen the *garmsīl* (or countries of warm temperature), nor the country of

---

[1] It is not clear where the Sultan Masaūdi Hazāras lay; but it must have been west or south-west of Kābul, among the hills. [According to Raverty (*Notes*, p. 690), the country of the Sultan Mas'ūdi Hazāras is reached through the Sanglākh valley out of which the Kābul river issues.]

[2] Gerdēz lies upwards of 65 miles south-east from Kābul. [It is the chief village of Zurmat.]

[3] Nirkh lies west of Kābul. [The Nirkh Pass is now known as the *Kotal i takht*, or Pass of the Sepulchre. Raverty's *Notes*, p. 690.]

[4] Or Bhīreh, on the Behāt [or Jhelum].   [5] Dāmān.

[6] This is the straight road to Peshāwar and Attok from Kābul.

Hindustān. Immediately on reaching them,ᵃ I beheld a new world. The grass was different, the trees different, the wild animals of a different sort, the birds of a different plumage, the manners and customs of the Īls and Ulūses (the wandering tribes) of a different kind.[1] I was struck with astonishment, and indeed there was room for wonder.

Nāsir Mirza, who, a little before, had come to his government, now waited upon me at Adīnapūr. As the Aimāks of that neighbourhood, with their followers, had moved down with all their families into Lamghānāt, for the purpose of wintering there, I halted a day or two in that vicinity, till I was joined by them and the troops that were behind; and then taking them along with me, I went on to Kūsh-gumbez,[2] lower down than Jūi-Shāhi.[3] Nāsir Mirza having made ᵇ some provision for his dependants and followers from the country under his government, stayed behind by permission at Kūsh-gumbez, promising to follow in two or three days.

Marching from Kūsh-gumbez, when we halted at Garm-cheshmeh,[4] they brought me one Pekhi,[5] a head-man of the Gagiānis, who had been used to accompany the caravans. I carried on Pekhi along with me, in order to have the benefit of his information concerning the road and the country. In one or two marches I passed Kheiber, and

Passes Kheiber.

ᵃ Ningnahār,   ᵇ in order to make

---

[1] Mr. Forster, in travelling the same road, in an opposite direction, was sensible of a similar change. 'About three miles to the eastward of Gandamak, crossed a small fordable river, running to the southward. The air, hitherto hot, had assumed at this place a sudden coldness; not effected by any change of weather, but, agreeably to the observation of travellers, peculiar to the climate of this part of the country. The shortness of our stay would not permit an inquiry into the cause of this quick transition; nor could any of my associates, though used to the road, give a reasonable account of it.'—Forster's *Travels*, vol. ii, p. 68, second edition. The cause is no doubt to be found in the sudden rise of the ground, and the position of the neighbouring mountains.

[2] The Bird's Dome.
[3] The royal or chief stream.   [4] Hot-spring.
[5] Probably so called from the town of Muhammed Pekh afterwards mentioned.

encamped at Jām.¹ I had heard of the fame of Gurh-Katri,² which is one of the holy places of the Jogis of the Hindus, who come from great distances to cut off their hair and shave their beards at this Gurh-Katri. As soon as I reached Jām, I immediately rode out to visit Bekrām.³ I saw its stupendous tree, and surveyed the country. Our guide was Malik Bu-saīd Kamari. Although we asked particularly for Gurh-Katri, he did not show us where it was; but just as we had returned, and were close upon the camp, he said to Khwājeh Muhammed Amīn that Gurh-Katri was close upon Bekrām, but that he did not mention it, for fear of being obliged to go among its narrow caverns and dangerous recesses. The Khwājeh, exclaiming against him as a perfidious rogue, immediately repeated what he had said; but as the day was nearly spent, and the way long, I could not go back to visit it.

Marches against Kohat,

At this station I held a consultation about passing the river Sind, and which way I should direct my course. Bāki Cheghāniāni advised that, instead of crossing the Sind, we should proceed against a place called Kohat, which lay at the distance of two marches; that the inhabitants were very numerous and very wealthy; and he produced some Kābul men, who confirmed what he had stated. I had never even heard the name of the place; but as my principal man, and the one who possessed most influence and authority in the army, had urged our marching against Kohat, and had even called in evidence to fortify his opinion, I gave up my plan of crossing the river and invading Hindustān; and therefore, marching off from Jām, and crossing the Bārch,⁴ advanced up to Muhammed Pekh and Abāni, and encamped not far from them.

At this time the Gagiāni Afghans were in Peshāwar, and,

¹ Now Jāmrūd.

² Gurh-Katri is now the site of the Tehsīl head-quarters at Peshāwar.

³ [Bigrām is included in the present city of Peshāwar. In the *Ayīn i Akbarī* (p. 451) it is described as follows: 'Toman Bekram, commonly called Peishor, enjoys a delightful spring season. Here is a temple, called Gor Khatri, a place of religious resort, particularly for Jogis.']

⁴ The river of Peshāwar.

from dread of my army, they had all drawn off to the skirts of the mountains. At this encampment, Khosrou Gagiāni, one of the chief men of the Gagiānis, came and paid me his respects. I took him to accompany Pekhi, in order to have the benefit of their advice regarding the roads and the country.

Marching from this station about midnight, and passing Muhammed Pekh at sunrise, we fell upon and plundered Kohat[1] about luncheon-time,[2] and found a great many bullocks and buffaloes. We also made a great many Afghans prisoners; but the whole of these I sought out and released. In their houses immense quantities of grain were found. Our plundering parties pushed on as far as the river Sind, on the banks of which they stayed all night, and next day came and rejoined me. The army, however, found none of the riches which Bāki Cheghāniāni had led us to expect; and Bāki was greatly ashamed of his expedition.

and plunders it.

Having tarried two days and two nights in Kohat, and called in our plundering detachments, we held a council to consider whither we should now bend our course; and it was determined that we should ravage the lands of the Afghans in Bannu and Bangash, and then return back by way of Naghz[3] and Fermūl. Yār Hussain, the son of Daryā Khan, who had come and joined me in Kābul, and tendered his allegiance, requested that instructions might be issued to the Dilāzāks, the Yūsuf-zais, and Gagiānis,[4] to act under his orders, pledging himself that he would carry my power beyond the Sind. I granted him the authority which he required, and he took leave of me at Kohat.

Taking our departure from Kohat, we marched up[5] towards Bangash, by the route of Hangu. Between Kohat and

Marches by Bangash.

---

[1] The valley of Kohat lies south-east from Jām [Jamrūd]. It is about twelve miles in length.

[2] Eleven o'clock.

[3] [Naghz, or Naghr, is a town and district marked on Rennell's map as lying on the left bank of the Kurram river, Fermūl being opposite it on the right bank. It is situated between Bannu and Gardez about forty miles south-east of the latter.]

[4] [A full account of these Afghan clans and their countries will be found in Raverty's *Notes*.]

[5] The road from Kohat to Bangash is west by south.

Hangu there lies a valley, with a high mountain on each side, through which the road passes. When in the course of our march we had reached this glen, the Afghans of Kohat and that quarter having collected, occupied the hills that overhang the glen on both sides, raised the war-shout, and made a loud clamour. Malik Bu-saīd Kamari, who was well acquainted with the whole of Afghanistān, was our guide. He told us that, a little farther on, there was a small hill on the right of the road, and that, if the Afghans should pass from their mountain to that hill, which was detached, we might then surround them on all sides, and get hold of them. Almighty God accomplished our wishes. The Afghans having descended upon us, came and occupied that detached hill. I instantly dispatched a party of my men to take possession of the neck of ground between the mountain and the hill. I ordered the rest of the army to attack the hill on both sides, and, moving regularly forward, to punish them for their temerity. The moment my troops advanced upon them, the Afghans found that they could not stand their ground, and in an instant a hundred or a hundred and fifty of them were brought down; of these some were brought in alive, but only the heads of the greater part of them. The Afghans, when they are reduced to extremities in war, come into the presence of their enemy with grass between their teeth; being as much as to say 'I am your ox'. This custom[1] I first observed on the present occasion; for the Afghans, when they could not maintain the contest, approached us with grass in their teeth. Orders were given for beheading such of them as had been brought in alive, and a minaret[2] was erected of their heads at our next halting-place.

On the morrow I marched on and encamped at Hangu. The Afghans of that quarter had fortified a hill, or made it a *sanger*. I first heard the word *sanger*[3] on coming to

[1] It is as old as the time of the heroes of the *Shahnāmeh*, or at least of Firdausi.

[2] This barbarous custom has always prevailed among the Tartar conquerors of Asia.

[3] *Sanger* is now in constant use in Kābul and Persia for an entrenchment or field-work.

Kābul. They called a detached piece of a hill strongly fortified a *sanger*. The troops, immediately on coming up to the *sanger*, stormed and took it, and cut off a hundred or two hundred heads of the refractory Afghans, which they brought down along with them. Here also we erected a minaret of heads.

Marching from Hangu, the second stage brought us to a place called Til,[1] at the bottom of the upper Bangash. The soldiers set out to plunder the Afghans of the neighbourhood. Some of them, who had made an attack on a *sanger*, returned without success.[a]

Marching from thence, and proceeding in a direction in which there was no road, we halted one night, and on the day after reached a very precipitous declivity, where we were obliged to dismount, and descended by a long and steep defile, after which we encamped in Bannu.[2] The soldiers, as well as the camels and horses, suffered extremely in the steep descent and the narrow defile; and the greater part of the bullocks, which we had brought away as plunder in the course of this expedition, dropped down by the way. The common road was only a kos or two to our right; and the road by which we were conducted was not a horse-road. As the herds and shepherds sometimes drove their flocks of sheep and mares down this descent and by the defile, it was for that reason termed *Gosfend-liar*, or the Sheep-road, *liar* signifying a road in the Afghan language. Our chief guide was Malik Bu-saīd Kamari; and the soldiers in general attributed the taking of this left-hand road to some design in him.

Reaches Bannu.

Immediately on descending from the hills of Bangash and Naghz, Bannu appeared in sight. It has the appearance of a flat and level champaign. On the north are the hills[3]

[a] rather too lightly

[1] [Thal.]
[2] These last marches must have been southerly. [The Bannu here meant is not the modern town of that name, but 'the fertile plain south-west of the Salt Range, which is well watered by the Kurram river '.—Thornton's *Gazetteer of India*.]
[3] The Salt-range.

of Bangash and Naghz. The Bangash river [1] runs through the Bannu territory, and by means of it chiefly is the country cultivated. On the south are Choupāreh and the river Sind; on the east is Dīnkōt, and on the west is Dasht, which is also called Bāzār and Tāk.[2] Of the Afghan tribes, the Kerāni, the Kivi, the Sūr, the Isakhail, and Niāzai cultivate the ground in this country. On ascending into the Bannu territory, I received information that the tribes inhabiting the plain had erected a *sanger* in the hills to the north. I therefore dispatched against them a body of troops under Jehāngīr Mīrza. The *sanger* against which he went was that of the Kivi tribe. It was taken in an instant, a general massacre ensued, and a number of heads were cut off and brought back to the camp. A great quantity of cloth was taken on this occasion by the army. Of the heads a pile of skulls was formed in the Bannu country. After the taking of this *sanger*, one of the chiefs of the Kivis, named Shādi Khan, came to me with grass in his mouth, and made his submission. I spared and gave up to him all the prisoners who had been taken alive.

After the sack of Kohat, it had been resolved that, after plundering the Afghans about Bangash and Bannu, we should return back to Kābul by way of Naghz or Fermūl. After ravaging Bannu, however, persons perfectly acquainted with the whole routes represented to me that Dasht was near at hand; that the inhabitants were wealthy and the roads good; and it was finally determined that, instead of returning by Fermūl, we should plunder the Dasht, and return back by that road.[a][3]

[a] it was determined after making a raid on Dasht to return by Fermūl.

[1] The Kurram.

[2] All through his operations in Bannu, Bābur uses west for south, and the other points of the compass accordingly. Hence we have on the east Choupāreh and the Sind, on the north Dīnkōt, on the south Dasht or Dāmān. [Tāk, or Tank, is the head-quarters of a Tehsīl in the Derah Ismail Khân District, N.W.F.P. It is said to have long been the capital of Dāmān. Bāzār is described in Thornton's *Gazetteer* as a town in the District of Bannu on the right bank of the Kurram river, 60 miles north of Derah Ismail Khan town.]

[3] This road was more to the south, and more circuitous than the other.

On the morrow, we marched thence, and halted on the banks of the same river, at a village of the Isakhail.[1] The Isakhail having had notice of our approach, had betaken themselves to the Choupāreh mountains.[2] I next marched from the village of the Isakhail, and encamped on the skirts of the Choupāreh mountains, while the skirmishers, ascending the mountain, stormed a *sanger* of the Isakhail, and brought back sheep, cattle, and cloths, in great quantity. The same night, the Isakhail Afghans attempted a surprise; but as I had been particularly cautious, they did not succeed. The whole army had been drawn up in battle array, with right and left wing, centre and van, at their stations, armed and ready to maintain their posts; and there were foot-soldiers on the watch all round the camp, at the distance of rather more than a bowshot from the tents. In this manner the army passed the night. Every night I drew out the army in the same manner; and every night three or four of my most trusty chiefs [a] in turn went the rounds about the camp with torches. I myself also took one round. Such persons as had not repaired to their posts had their noses slit, and were led about the camp in that state. On the right wing was Jehāngīr Mirza, with Bāki Cheghāniāni, Shīrīm Taghāi, Syed Hussain Akber, and several other Begs; on the left wing were Mirza Khan, Abdal Razāk Mirza, Kāsim Beg, and some other Begs; in the centre there were none of the superior Begs, all of them were Begs of my own household; in the van were Syed Kāsim, the chamberlain, Baba Ughūl Allah-berdi, and several other Begs. The whole army was divided into six bodies, each of which, in its turn, was appointed to keep watch for one whole day and night.

Arrives in the Isakhail country.

Leaving the skirt of this mountain I marched towards the west,[3] and halted between Dasht and Bannu,[4] at a tank

Mode of finding water.

[a] the officers of my household

---

[1] The Isakhail are one of the principal tribes of Afghans. [The Niāzai are a section of the Isakheyls.]

[2] The Choupāreh mountains seem to be the ridge between Largi and the Sind.

[3] That is, as explained, the south.

[4] Bābur has now crossed the Kurram and Gambīla, and is advancing south to the Dasht or Dāmān. Between Dāmān and Bannu,

in which there was no water.ᵃ The soldiers here digging in the dry bed of a river, procured water for themselves, their flocks, mares, and cattle. By digging a gaz or a gaz and half into the dry channel, water was found; and it is not in this river alone that this occurs, but in all the beds of rivers in Hindustān, water is with certainty found by digging down a gaz or a gaz and a half. It is a wonderful provision of Providence, that though in Hindustān there is no permanently running water except in the large rivers, yet that water should be found so near the surface in all the dry channels of the rivulets.

Reaches the Dasht. Marching from this dry river in the morning, the light cavalry moving forward without anything to encumber them, about afternoon prayers reached the villages of Dasht.[1] The skirmishers immediately proceeded to ravage several of the villages, and brought off much spoil in raiment, flocks of sheep, and horses bred for sale. All this night, till morning, and all next day till night,ᵇ the beasts of burden, flocks of sheep, camels, and foot-soldiers of the army, which had been left behind on the road, continued to drop in. During the day that we remained here, the pillaging parties went out, and brought in numbers of sheep and oxen from the villages of Dasht. Having also fallen in with some Afghan merchants, they took a great quantity of white cloth, aromatic drugs, sugar, both candied and in powder, the stout species of horses called Tipchāk, and other horses which they had for sale. Mendi Moghul dismounted Khwājeh Khizer Lohāni,[2] who was one of the most noted and eminent of the Afghan merchants, cut off his head, and brought it to the camp. Shīrīm Taghāi had gone out in the rear of the pillagers. He met an Afghan on foot, who struck him a blow with his sword that cut off his fore-finger.

ᵃ in a waterless tableland.   ᵇ noon,

and also between Dāmān and Īsakhail, which Bābur considers as part of Bannu, there is a halt without water by whichever way you go.

[1] [The plain.]

[2] Lohāni is the general name for most of the tribes of Dāmān, the greatest merchants of Afghanistān.

On the next morning we marched forward, and halted at no great distance, among the villages of Dasht. Our next march was to the banks of the river Gumal. From Dasht there are two roads that lead to the west. One of them is the road of Sang-e-surākh, which reaches Fermūl by way of Būrek.[a] The other is along the banks of the Gumal which also conducts to Fermūl, but without passing Būrek. The road along the Gumal is generally preferred. During the few days that I had been in the Dasht, it had rained incessantly; and the Gumal had in consequence swelled so much, that it was with great difficulty that we found a ford by which we could pass. Persons who knew the road informed me that it would be necessary by the Gumal road to cross the river several times; which would be attended with extreme difficulty if the flooding should continue as high as it then was. Some hesitation still remained respecting the propriety of taking this route; nor were our opinions quite settled next morning when the drum beat for the march. It was my intention to have conversed over the matter as we mounted our horses,[b] and to have followed the route that should then appear best. It was the *Id e fitr*,[1] and I was engaged in performing the ceremonial ablutions required on account of that festival, while Jehāngīr Mirza and the Begs were conversing on the subject. Some of them suggested that the mountain on the west of the Dasht, which they call the Mehter Suleimāni mountain,[2] lies between Dasht and Dūki; that if we could turn the extremity[c] of the mountain we should come to a road that was level, although it might make a difference of a march or two. This plan meeting with their approbation, they directed the march of the army towards the edge of the mountain.[3] Before I had com-

Reaches the Gumal

March 7 1505.

[a] Barak.
[b] It was my intention when the drum had sounded the departure next morning to discuss the matter as we rode along,
[c] spur

---

[1] The *Id e fitr*, or *Greater Bairām*, is the feast on the conclusion of the fast of the Ramzān. It commences as soon as the new moon of Shawāl is seen.
[2] The mountain of the Prophet Solomon, called also the *Takht e Suleimān*, or Solomon's Throne.
[3] The army would seem to have marched by Pezū.

pleted my ablutions, the army was in full march for the skirts of the mountains, and many had even passed the river Gumal. As none of us had ever been this road, we were perfectly ignorant of its length or shortness. It had been adopted on mere idle surmise. The stated prayers of the *Id* were recited on the banks of the Gumal. In this year the *Nouroz*[1] fell remarkably near the *Id e fitr*, there being only a few days between them. On the subject of this approximation I composed the following *ghazel* :

They are blest who see the new moon and the face of their beloved at the same time :
But I, far from the countenance of my beloved and her eyebrow, experience only sorrow.

. . . . .

O Bābur, deem thou the face of thy love the best of new moons, and an interview the best of Ids !
For a better day than that thou canst not find, were there a hundred festivals of Nouroz, and a hundred Bairāms.

March southward. Leaving the banks of the Gumal, we directed our course towards the south, and marched along the skirts of the mountain. We had advanced a kos or two, when a body of death-devoted Afghans presented themselves on an eminence close upon the mountain. We instantly proceeded to charge them at full gallop; the greater part of them fled away; the rest foolishly attempted to make a stand on some small hills, which were on the skirts of the heights. One Afghan took his stand on a detached hillock, apparently because all its other sides[a] being steep and a direct precipice, he had no road by which to escape. Sultan Ali Chanāk rode up,[b] gained the summit, engaged and took him. This feat, which he performed in my presence, was the occasion of his future favour and advancement. In another declivity of the hill, Kūtluk Kadem engaged an Afghan in combat, and while they grappled, both of them fell tumbling from a height of ten or twelve gaz; at last, however, Kūtluk cut off his head, and brought it in. Kupek Beg grappled with another Afghan on a steep knoll, when both the combatants came rolling from

[a] further side　　　　　　　[b] *Add* all in mail,

[1] The *Nouroz* is the feast of the old Persian new-year.

the top midway down; but he also brought away the Afghan's head. A great many of these Afghans fell into my hands on this occasion, but I released them all.

After leaving Dasht, we marched for three stages in a southerly direction, keeping close to the skirts of the mountain of Mehter Suleimān; and at the close of the fourth halted at Bīlah,[1] a small district lying on the banks of the Sind, and which is dependent on Multān. The inhabitants in general took directly to their boats, and crossed the river; a few plunged into the water, and crossed it by swimming. Opposite to this village there was an island, on which we observed several natives who had not passed over to the mainland; many of our troops drove their horses, all armed as they were, into the river, and passed over. Several of them were carried down by the stream; of my followers one was Kūl Ahmed Arūk, another the chief of my tent-pitchers [2] and house servants[a]; of Jehāngīr Mirza's followers, one was Kaitmās Turkmān. In this island a considerable booty in clothes, furniture, and other property fell into the hands of our men. All the people of that neighbourhood passed the Sind in boats, and went to the other side. A party that had passed immediately opposite to the island, trusting to the breadth of the river, drew their swords, and began to flourish them in an insulting way. Among those who had passed over to the island, one was Kūl Bayezīd the cupbearer,[3] who alone, and on an unarmed horse, threw himself into the stream and pushed for them. The water on the other side of the island was twice as broad as on this side. After swimming his horse for the distance of a bowshot in the face of the enemy, who stood on the banks, it got footing and took ground, with the water reaching as high as the flap of the saddle. He stopped there as long as milk takes to boil; and having apparently made up his mind, seeing nobody following behind to support him, and having no hopes of receiving any assistance, he rushed with great speed on the enemy who occupied

Reaches the Sind.

[a] *Omit* and house servants

[1] Abul-Fazl says ' on the outside of Terbīlah '.
[2] *Mehter Farāsh.*   [3] *Bekāwel*—also a taster.

the bank: they discharged two or three arrows at him, but durst not stand their ground, and fled. Alone, on an unarmed horse,[1] devoid of all support, to swim across such a river as the Sind, to put the enemy to flight and occupy their ground, was a stout and manly feat. After the enemy had taken to flight, our troops passed over, and got a considerable booty in cloth, cattle, and other plunder. Although on several former occasions I had distinguished Kūl Bayezīd by marks of favour, in consequence of the services which he had done, and of the bravery which he had repeatedly displayed, and had promoted him from the office of cook to be one of my tasters, yet after this last courageous achievement, I was still more resolved to show him every possible mark of favour, and accordingly I did distinguish him in the most marked manner, as will be mentioned. In truth, he was worthy of every kind of attention and honour.

I made other two marches down the river Sind, keeping close to its banks. The soldiers had now completely knocked up their horses, from being perpetually on plundering parties, in the course of which too they had gained no booty worth the while. It consisted chiefly of bullocks; in the Dasht they had got some sheep, and in several places clothes, and such like articles. After leaving the Dasht, they got nothing but bullocks. In our marches along the Sind, however, these were found in such plenty, that the meanest retainer in the army often picked up three or four hundred bullocks and cows; but from their very numbers they were obliged to leave the greater part of them behind.[a]

Marches westward from the Sind.

For three marches I proceeded along the Sind, and separated from it right against the tomb of Pīr Kānū,[2] on reaching which we halted. As some of the soldiers had

[a] at least as many were left behind at each stage as were brought in.

[1] *Yedak* often signifies a led horse.
[2] [The tomb of Pīr Kānū is at Sakhi Sarwar near Derah Ghāzi Khan. The shrine of the saint is still a place of pilgrimage and held in deep veneration by both Hindus and Muhammedans. He was a Seyyid, named Ahmed Sultan Sakhi (Sarwar = spiritual guide), and was born about 1252 and died about A.D. 1291. Raverty's *Notes*, p. 12.]

wounded several of the attendants at the tomb, I ordered one of the culprits to be punished, and he was hewn to pieces as an example. This tomb is very highly respected in Hindustān. It lies on the skirts of a hill which is connected with the mountain of Mehter Suleimān.

Taking my departure from this tomb, I reached the top of a hill-pass,[1] where we halted. Marching from thence I gained Rūdi, a place dependent on the country of Dūki.[2] While moving from that station, Fāzil Gokultāsh, the Dārogha of Sīvi,[3] a servant of Shah Beg,[4] with twenty of his people, who had come to reconnoitre us, were seized and brought in; but as at that time we were not on bad terms, I dismissed them with their arms and horses.

Leaving this station, the second march brought us to Chotiāli, one of the villages of Dūki,[5] near which we encamped. Though the horses had undergone great fatigue in the continual plundering parties in which they had been engaged, both before reaching the Sind, and along its banks, yet they had plenty of corn, and abundance of grain cut in the ear, so that they did not flag. But when we left the banks of the Sind, and moved up by Pīr Kānū, there were no longer green cuttings, or at least in two or three marches a very inconsiderable quantity of young corn was occasionally met with. I could not even get corn for my own horse. In

Arrives at Chotiāli.

The pass of Pawat lies above Sakhi Sarwar.
[2] [Or rather, 'a stream belonging to the territory of Dūki (Leyden and P. de C.).]
[3] [Sībi is the head-quarters of a district of the same name in Belūchistan situated near the east bank of the Nari river, 88 miles SE. of Quetta in 29° 33′ N. and 67° 53′ E.]
[4] Shah Beg, Zūlnūn Beg's son, when expelled from Ghazni and Kābul, had occupied the country below Sīvistān. He finally conquered Sind.
[5] [Dūki (ceded to us in 1879) is west by north of Derah Ghazi Khan, lying between Thal and Loralai. Dūki is now a Tahsīl of the Loralai District, the head-quarters of which are situated near Dūki village, on an affluent of the Beji river. There are good pasture grounds in this tract, which is chiefly inhabited by Kākars, Khetrāns, and Mūsakheyls. In Bābur's time Dūki was probably the name of a tract which included a large portion of the present Loralai District. Chotiāli is due west of Derah Ghazi Khan, about midway between it and Thal. It now forms part of the Loralai District.]

the course of these marches, the horses of the army began to flag.[a] In the stage at which we halted after leaving Chotiāli, I was even forced to leave my pavilion-tent[1] behind for want of carriage. While there, such a rain fell during the night, that the water reached above the knee among the tents, and I was obliged to sit on carpets piled on each other; in which melancholy plight we were forced to wear away the night till morning appeared.

Conspiracy in Bābur's camp.

A march or two after, Jehāngīr Mirza came up to me, and whispered in my ear, 'I have a word to speak with you in private.' I retired with him, and he said to me, 'Bāki Cheghāniāni has been with me, and said, We intend to send the King, with seven, eight, or ten persons, over the Sind, and to raise you to the throne.' I asked, 'Who are his inferior associates in this plot?' He replied, 'Bāki Beg himself mentioned it to me just now, and I know not any one else.' I said, 'You must endeavour to learn who the other conspirators are, as it is probable that Syed Hussain Akber, Sultan Ali Chihreh, and other Begs and retainers of Khosrou Shah are concerned in the business.' In truth, Jehāngīr Mirza, on this occasion, conducted himself perfectly well, and in a brotherly manner; and his proceedings, on this emergency, were the exact counterpart of my own at Kahmerd, when this same worthless man,[2] by his machinations, attempted to stir up discord and hostility between us.

We marched from this station, and when I reached the next halting-place, I dispatched a body of soldiers, whose horses were still capable of service, under the command of Jehāngīr Mirza, to attack and plunder the Aughāns[3] in that vicinity. At this stage, the horses of the army began to be completely worn out, and every day[b] two hundred horses, or three hundred horses, were obliged to be left behind. Many brave partisans, and some of note, were

---

[a] As to corn there was absolutely none. So, after leaving these camps, the horses of the army began to flag.
[b] there came a day when

[1] *Khirgāh.*   [2] [i. e. Bāki Beg.]
[3] The Afghans are also called Aughāns, a different pronunciation of the same word.

reduced to march on foot. Shah Mahmūd Ughlākchi, who was one of the officers of my household, and a man of eminence, having lost all his horses, was forced to trudge it on foot. This continued to be the state of the horses of the army till we reached Ghazni.

Three marches afterwards, Jehāngīr Mirza, having plundered a party of Afghans, brought in a few sheep.

In one or two marches more, we reached Āb-istādeh,[1] when a wonderfully large sheet of water presented itself to our view. Nothing could be seen of the plains on the opposite side. The water seemed to join the sky; the hills and mountains on the farther side appeared inverted, like the hills and mountains on the farther side of the *mirāge*;[2] while the hills and mountains near at hand appeared suspended between earth and heaven.[a] In this spot are collected the waters arising from the inundations occasioned by the rains of spring, in the valley of Kattehwāz, the dale of Zurmet, the river of Ghazni, with the meadow of Karabāgh, and all the superfluous water of the spring season, that arises from the swelling of the rivers, and that remains after the purposes of irrigation are answered. When I came within one kos of Āb-istādeh, a singular phenomenon presented itself. From time to time, between this water and the heavens, something of a red appearance was seen, like the ruddy crepuscule, which again by and by vanished, and so continued shifting till we had come near it. When we came close up, we discovered that this appearance was occasioned by immense flocks of wild geese,[3] not of ten thousand or twenty thousand, but absolutely beyond computation, and innumerable;

He arrives at Āb-istādeh.

Its singular appearance.

[a] the mountains and hillocks in the distance seemed to hang suspended between heaven and earth like those in a mirage.

---

[1] The Standing-Water. This lake lies in north latitude 32° 35′, south-west from Ghazni.

[2] The *sarāb*, or mirage, is the appearance presented in desert countries, during the extreme heat of the sun, when a lake seems to be close at hand. The objects around are seen inverted in it as in a piece of water.

[3] *Baghlān-kāz.* The description would lead us to imagine it was a flock of flamingoes [*Phoenicopterus roseus*].

and in their flight, as they moved their wings, their red feathers sometimes appeared and sometimes were hid. But it was not wild geese alone; innumerable flocks of every species of bird settled on the banks of this water, and the eggs of countless multitudes of fowl were deposited on every corner of its banks. A few [a] Afghans who had come here, and were employed in gathering these eggs, on seeing us, fled, and threw themselves into the lake; but a party of my men pursued them for nearly a kos, and brought them back. As far as these went into the water, it was nearly of one uniform depth, reaching up to the horse's belly; indeed, the water, apparently in consequence of the levelness of the plain, did not seem to acquire any great depth. On reaching the banks of the river of the plain of Kattehwāz, which falls into Āb-istādeh, we halted. It is in general a dry river, not having any running water in it. I have passed its channel many times, but never found any water in it, except on this occasion, when, in consequence of the rains of spring, it was so flooded, that I could find no ford to pass; for though it is not very broad, yet it was extremely deep. All the horses and camels were crossed over by swimming. Many of the soldiers tied up their baggage in bundles, which they pulled over to the other side with cords. After passing this torrent, we proceeded by the way of Kuhneh-Nāni,[1] and, passing the water-mound [2] of Sardeh,[3] we reached Ghazni. Jehāngīr Mirza there entertained us, provided us with victuals, did the honours of the place for a day or two, and presented me with his *peshkesh*.[4]

Arrives at Ghazni.

This year the greater part of the streams and rivers came down in flood, so violently that we could get no passage over the river of Deh-Yākūb. I therefore made them carry a boat, which I caused to be constructed in

[a] Two

---

[1] Old Nāni. There are two Nānis; one the Old Nāni, to the north of the lake of Āb-istādeh, on a river that discharges itself into it. The other Nāni is a march south of Ghazni.
[2] [Dam.]
[3] Sardeh [Sar i deh] lies south-east of Ghazni.   [4] [Presents.]

a tank of water, and launch it in the river of Deh-Yākūb, opposite to Kamari,[1] and by means of this vessel all the army was passed over. In this way, after surmounting the hill pass of Sajāwend,[2] we proceeded directly forward, and passing the Kamari river in boats,[a] reached Kābul, in the month of Zilhijeh. *Reaches Kābul, May 1505.*

A few days before our arrival, Syed Yūsef Beg had been carried off by a colic, and departed to enjoy the mercy of God.

Nāsir Mirza, as was formerly mentioned, after providing his people with some necessaries from his government, had obtained leave to stay behind in Kūsh-gumbez, promising to follow me in two or three days. But we had no sooner separated, than, under pretence of quelling the refractory spirit of the men of Dareh-Nūr, though in reality the matter of complaint was very slight, he dispatched his whole army towards Dareh-Nūr. Fazli, who was the general of the army, did not keep up proper discipline, nor act with sufficient circumspection, considering the strength of the fort of Dareh-Nūr, that it was surrounded with rice-fields, and situated on the brow of a hill, as has been described. For in that mountainous tract, and in sight of the fortified hill, he divided his force and sent out a detachment to plunder. The men of Dareh-Nūr, immediately sallying forth, attacked the plunderers who were scattered for pillage, and routed them ; and no sooner were they discomfited, than the rest of the army, unable to maintain their ground, also took to flight. Many were slain, and many horses and arms taken. Such will always be the fate of an army that has a general like Fazli. Whether it was from this circumstance, or whether some disaffection influenced Nāsir Mirza, he did not follow me, but stayed behind. Another circumstance, which had some influence on his conduct, was that I had bestowed Alingār on Yūsef, and Alisheng on Bahlol, the two sons of Ayūb, than whom *Misconduct of Nāsir Mirza.*

---

[a] *Omit* passing the Kamari river in boats,

[1] Kamari and Deh-Yākūb are both in the district of Būtkhāk, south-east of Kābul.

[2] Sajāwend is in the district of Logar, south-east of Kābul.

more wicked, more seditious, more arrogant or haughty persons, were nowhere to be found. They also were to have made some levies from their governments, and to have come along with Nāsir Mirza to join me; but as Nāsir Mirza did not come, they also stayed behind, and were the favourite bottle companions and friends of Nāsir Mirza all that winter.

During the course of this winter he made one excursion against the Turkolāni Afghans, and ravaged their country. All the Aimāks, Īls, and Ulūses, from the upper country, who had descended into Nangenhār and Lamghānāt, he attacked and drove up, and then [a] encamped on the banks of the Bārān. While Nāsir Mirza was on that river, and in its neighbourhood, the tidings arrived of the defeat and slaughter of the Uzbeks, by the inhabitants of Badakhshān, and of the general rising of that country, which took place in the following manner.

Revolt of Badakhshān

Sheibāni Khan, having entrusted Kunduz to Kamber Bī, proceeded himself to Khwārizm. Kamber Bī, for the purpose of securing the submission of [b] the inhabitants of Badakhshān, had sent into that country Mahmūd, the son of Muhammed Makhdūmi; but Mubārek Shah, whose ancestors had been Begs of the Kings of Badakhshān, having rebelled, cut off the heads of Mahmūd, the son of Makhdūmi, and of several more of the Uzbeks, and seizing on the fort of Zafer,[1] formerly known by the name of Shāf-tiwār, fortified himself in it. He was the person who gave this fortress the name of Zafer. Besides this, Muhammed Korchi, who was one of the *Korchis*[2] of Khosrou Shah, and at this time had the command of Khamalangān,

[a] In the summer, dragging along with him the Aimāks and alien tribes, who had come down for the winter into the Lamghānāt, with their families and herds, he

[b] conciliating

---

[1] [Fort of Victory. This fort is on the Kokcha, a tributary of the Amu.]

[2] The office of *Korchi* seems to have corresponded to that of armour-bearer. In the Persian service, however, the term was applied to a body of cavalry, the most honourable as wel las ancient military force of the kingdom.

likewise rebelled; and having slain the *Sader* (or Justiciary) of Sheibāni Khan, with a number of Uzbeks in Rustāk, fortified himself in Khamalangān. An inhabitant of Rāgh,[1] too, whose forefathers had been nobles in the court of the kings of Badakhshān, at the same time rose in Rāgh. Jehāngīr Turkomān, who was one of the retainers of Wali, the brother of Khosrou Shah, and who, during the late confusions, had separated from his lord, having collected some fugitive soldiers, besides stragglers and Aimāks, drew off and revolted. Nāsir Mirza, on receiving this intelligence, inspired with the ambition of acquiring Badakhshān, at the instigation of certain senseless and short-sighted flatterers, passed over into that quarter by the route of Shibertū and Ābdareh, accompanied by some bodies of these Īls and Ulūses, who, on being expelled from the other side of the hills, had come hither and were moving about with their whole families and property.[a]

<small>Nāsir Mirza attempts to subdue it.</small>

Khosrou Shah, after flying from Ajer with Ahmed Kāsim, had proceeded with him to Khorasān; and having met with Badīa-ez-zemān Mirza and Zūlnūn Beg by the way, they all went together to Heri, and paid their court to Sultan Hussain Mirza. I alone was the cause that these men, who for a series of years had been at open enmity with the Mirza, and had subjected him to many insults, the old sores of which were still rankling in his heart, now all went in such a state of distress and humility, to present themselves before him. For had I not deprived Khosrou Shah of his army and retainers, and reduced him to his present helpless condition, and had not I taken Kābul from Mukīm, Zūlnūn's son, they never would have thought of going to wait upon the Mirza. Badīa-ez-zemān was only as dough in the hands of the other two, and never attempted to swerve from their advice. Sultan Hussain Mirza received them all in a gracious manner,

<small>Khosrou Shah resolves to return.</small>

---

[a] taking with him the families and herds of all those tribes who had emigrated here from their own country.

---

[1] [Rāgh is the name of a district of Badakhshān lying to the north-west of Rustāk on the left bank of the Panj river opposite Kilāb.]

without reminding them of their offences, and made them a variety of presents. After some time Khosrou Shah asked permission to return to his own country, alleging that, if he were allowed to go, he could now reduce the whole of it to subjection. As, however, he was without arms, and without any means of success for such an enterprise, objections were made to his return. On perceiving this, he only persevered with the greater importunity to be allowed to take his leave. As his importunities increased, Muhammed Berandūk retorted on him sharply: 'When you had thirty thousand men, and the whole country in your hands, what did you effect, that now you are so anxious to set out with five hundred men, and the country in the hands of the Uzbeks?' However judicious the remonstrances made to him were, as his destined end was drawing near, he refused to listen to them. The urgency of his representations increasing, he was at last permitted to take his departure; and, attended by three or four hundred men, he advanced directly to the confines of Dahāneh.

At this very juncture Nāsir Mirza had passed over to the same quarter. He had a conference with Nāsir Mirza in the territory of Dehāneh.[1] The chiefs of Badakhshān had invited Nāsir Mirza alone, and did not wish for Khosrou Shah's return; but all the efforts that Nāsir Mirza made to prevail on him to separate from him, and proceed to the hill-country, had no influence on Khosrou Shah, who saw the Mirza's motives. Khosrou Shah's plan was to employ Nāsir Mirza's name as a cover to his designs, and after acting in his name so as to get possession of these countries, to seize and put him to death.[a] As, however, they could not come to an understanding, each of them put his adherents in array in the territory of Ishkamish,[2] and having clothed them in armour, and drawn them out ready for action, they separated from each other, and Nāsir Mirza proceeded towards Badakhshān; while Khosrou Shah, having collected a naked and disorderly

Khosrou Shah advances to Kunduz,

[a] *Omit* to seize and put him to death.

[1] [i. e. near Dahāneh, a place which lies south from Balkh.]
[2] South-east from Kunduz.

rabble, to the amount of a thousand men, good and bad, went to lay siege to Kunduz, and took post at Khwājeh Chārtāk, one or two farsangs distant from that city.

After Muhammed Sheibāni Khan had taken Sultan Ahmed Tambol in Andejān, he had advanced against Hissār, upon which Khosrou Shah, without either battle or effort, had abandoned his territories and fled. Sheibāni Khan reached Hissār, in which was Shīrīm Chihreh with some brave soldiers, who, although deserted by their superiors, who had fled the country, would not surrender the fortress, but made every exertion for its defence. Sheibāni Khan left Hamzeh Sultan and Mahdi Sultan to conduct the blockade of Hissār, and himself proceeded against Kunduz; he conferred the government of Kunduz on his younger brother Mahmūd Sultan, and himself without delay marched for Khwārizm against Chīn Sūfi. He had not yet reached Samarkand, when his brother Mahmūd Sultan died in Kunduz, on which he gave the command in Kunduz to Kamber Bī of Merv. When Khosrou Shah arrived, Kamber Bī was in Kunduz; and instantly dispatched messengers to Hamzeh Sultan and the other Sultans who had been left behind, to call them in to his aid. Hamzeh Sultan having himself advanced as far as Serāi,[1] on the banks of the river Amu, sent on his army to Kunduz, under the command of his sons and Begs, who marched on to battle the instant they arrived. Khosrou Shah could not stand *is defeated* his ground, and his gross body was not sufficiently alert for flight; so that Hamzeh Sultan's men unhorsed him, and brought him in as a prisoner. They also slew Ahmed Kāsim, his sister's son, Shīrīm Chihreh, and a number of his best troops. They then carried Khosrou Shah to Kunduz, where they struck off his head, which they sent *and put to* to Sheibāni Khan at Khwārizm. Khosrou Shah had no *death.* sooner entered the Kunduz territory, than, as he had predicted, the conduct and demeanour of his old followers and retainers, who had taken service with me, was visibly changed. Numbers of them began to draw off, and marched

[1] Probably the Saliserāi so often mentioned in the history of Tamerlane. [Saliserāi is on a branch of the Amu south-east of Kabādiān.]

for Khwājeh Riwāj and the country in its vicinity. The greater part of my force at this time consisted of his old retainers. Several Moghuls of note went off, and the rest had begun to form combinations together; the moment the news of his death arrived, the spirit of discontent was quenched, as when water is thrown on fire.

EVENTS OF THE YEAR 911

Death of Bābur's mother.

In the month of Muharrem,[1] my mother, Kŭtluk Nigār Khanum, was seized with the pustulous eruption, termed *hasbeh*,[2] and blood was let without effect. A Khorasān physician, named Syed Tabīb, attended her; he gave her water-melons, according to the practice of Khorasān; but as her time was come, she expired, after six days' illness, on a Saturday, and was received into the mercy of God. Ulugh Beg Mirza had built a garden palace on the side of a hill, and called it Bāgh-e-Nourozi (the Garden of the New Year). Having got the permission of his heirs,[3] we conveyed her remains to this garden; and on Sunday I and Kāsim Gokultāsh committed them to the earth. During the period of mourning for my mother, the news of the death of the younger Khan, my uncle Alāchah Khan,[4] and of my grandmother Isān Doulet Begum, also arrived. The distribution of food on the fortieth day after the Khanum's decease was near at hand, when the mother of the Khans, Shah Begum, my maternal grandmother, Meher Nigār Khanum, the widow of Sultan Ahmed Mirza, with Muhammed Hussain Gurkān Dughlet, arrived from Khorasān. Our lamentation and mourning now broke out afresh. Our grief for the separations we had suffered was unbounded. After completing the period of mourning,[a] food and victuals were dressed and doled out to the poor

[a] mourning ceremonies,

[1] The Muhammedan year 911 began on June 4, 1505.
[2] [The word for measles is *haṣbah* (with a *ṣād*), but *hasbah* (with a *sīn*), which seems intended here, means slow fever.]
[3] It will be observed, from several instances in these Memoirs, that the Musulmans are most scrupulously cautious not to erect a burial-place in any ground gained by violence or wrong.
[4] [He had died a year before in 1504.]

and needy. Having directed readings of the Korān, and prayers to be offered up for the souls of the departed, and eased the sorrows of our hearts by these demonstrations of love, I returned to my political enterprises which had been interrupted,[a] and by the advice of Bāki Cheghāniāni, led my army against Kandahār. We had marched as far as the *auleng* (or meadow) of Kūsh-Nādir, where we had halted, when I was seized with a fever. It came most unseasonably. Whatever[b] efforts they made to keep me awake, my eyes constantly fell back into sleep. After four or five days, I got somewhat better.[c]

At this period there was such an earthquake that many ramparts of fortresses, the summits of some hills,[d] and many houses, both in the towns and villages, were violently shaken and levelled with the ground. Numbers of persons lost their lives by their houses and terraces falling on them. The whole houses of the village of Pamghān[1] fell down, and seventy or eighty respectable householders were buried under the ruins. Between Pamghān and Bektūt, a piece of ground, about a stone's throw in breadth, separated itself, and descended for the length of a bowshot; and springs burst out and formed a well in the place that it had occupied. From Isterghach to the plain,[e] being a distance of about six or seven farsangs, the whole space was so rent and fractured, that in some places the ground was elevated to the height of an elephant above its old level, and in other places as much depressed; and in many places it was so split that a person might have hid himself in the gaps. During the time of the earthquake,[2] a great cloud of dust rose from the tops of the mountains. Nūr-allah, the lutanist, happened to be playing

Great earthquake.

[a] *Omit this clause and translate,* I yielded to the insistence of Bāki Cheghāniāni and
[b] A curious effect of this malady was that whatever
[c] quite well.   [d] walls of gardens,   [e] Maidān (a place name),

[1] [Paghmān lies south-east of Kabul. The valleys of Paghmān and Bek-tūt, and the Ulang of Tīpah, are described in Raverty's *Notes,* p. 690.]
[2] [This was probably the earthquake felt at Agra on July 5, A.D. 1505. *E. B.,* p. 229.]

before me on the mandolin, and had also another instrument with him; he instantly caught up both the instruments in his hands, but had so little command of himself, that they knocked against each other. Jehāngīr Mirza was at Tībah, in the upper veranda of a palace built by Ulugh Beg Mirza. The moment the earth began to quake, he threw himself down, and escaped without injury. One of his domestics was in the same story, when the terrace [a] of this upper floor fell on him. God preserved him, and he did not sustain the slightest harm. Many rising-grounds [b] were levelled. That same day there were thirty-three shocks; and for the space of a month, the earth shook two or three times every day and night. The Begs and soldiers had orders to repair the rents and breaches in the walls and fortifications [c] of the fortress. By great diligence and exertions, in twenty days or a month, all the parts of the walls that had been damaged or thrown down were repaired and rebuilt.

Expedition against Kandahār.
My expedition against Kandahār had been delayed by my sickness and the earthquake; but as soon as I had regained my health, and restored the defences of the fortress, I immediately resumed my former plan. When we halted below Shnīz,[1] we had not yet finally decided between marching against Kandahār, and sending out detachments to scour the hills and plains. I called Jehāngīr Mirza and the Begs to a council of war; when Jehāngīr Mirza and Bāki Cheghāniāni warmly supporting the proposition for proceeding against Kalāt, it was settled that we should move and attack it. On reaching Tāzi, I gained information that Sher Ali Chihreh and Kūchek Bāki Diwāneh, with some others, had formed the plan of deserting. I instantly had them seized; and as Sher Alī Chihreh had been notoriously guilty of various seditious and mutinous practices, both while in my service, and when in the service

[a] roof   [b] The majority of the houses in Tīpah
[c] towers and battlements

[1] Shnīz is north of Shashgou, to the west of the road between that and Lora. [The Shnīz valley lies to the east of the Lohgar valley, and is inhabited by Karlarni Wardags (Afghans). Raverty gives a full description of it in his *Notes*, pp. 693 et seq. Tāzi is on the east bank of the Tarnak.]

of others, and in various countries, he was delivered over
to the executioner. Having deprived the others of their
arms and horses, I let them go.

When we reached Kalāt,¹ without having arrayed ourselves in armour, or erected any engines for an attack, we instantly made an assault. The conflict was severe. Kūchek Beg, the elder brother of Khwājeh Kalān, was a most courageous and gallant man, and had many a time wielded his sword with great effect in my presence, as has already been mentioned in these Memoirs. He had clambered up a tower on the south-west of Kalāt, and had nearly gained the top, when he was wounded in the eye with a spear; and he died of this wound two or three days after Kalāt was taken. Kūchek Bāki Diwāneh, who had been seized while attempting to desert with Sher Ali, here atoned for that act of treachery, being killed with a stone under the rampart, while attempting to enter. Two or three other persons of note were killed. The fight continued in this way till about the time of afternoon prayers; when, just as the assailants, who had fought bravely, and exerted all their vigour, were almost exhausted, the garrison demanded quarter, and surrendered. Zūlnūn Arghūn had bestowed Kalāt on Mukīm, and two of Mukīm's partisans, Farrukh Arghūn and Kara Bilūt, held it at this time on his part. They came out with their bows,ᵃ quivers, and scimitars hanging round their necks, and I forgave them. It was not my wish to treat this family harshly; for had anything severe been practised among us at a time when such an enemy as the Uzbeks was close at hand, what would not have been said, both far and near, by those who either saw or heard of it? As this enterprise had been undertaken at the instance of Jehāngīr Mirza and Bāki Beg, I gave up Kalāt to the charge of the Mirza, but he would not accept of it; neither would Bāki Beg undertake to keep it, though he could offer no satisfactory excuse for declining; so that all our exertions and our

Kalāt taken by storm.

ᵃ *Omit* bows

¹ Kalāt, east of Kandahār, in the vale of Tarnak, and now called Kalāt-e-Ghilji.

success in the assault and taking of the place, were completely thrown away.

Bābur returns to Kābul.

Proceeding southward from Kalāt, we plundered the Afghans of Sawa-Sang, Alatāgh,[1] and that neighbourhood, and then returned to Kābul. The night that I arrived in Kābul, I proceeded to the fortress, leaving my tents and horses at the Chārbāgh. That same night a Khirilchi thief came and stole from the Chārbāgh a bay horse of mine, caparisoned as it was, and one of my own sabres.[a]

Bāki Cheghāniāni discontented.

From the time that Bāki Cheghāniāni had joined me on the banks of the Amu, no person about me had been in higher estimation or authority than himself. Whatever was done or said, was said or done by his ascendancy; although I had never experienced from him that duty which was to have been expected, or that propriety of conduct which is indispensably necessary. Indeed, on the contrary, he had done many unjustifiable acts, and shown me many marks of disrespect. He was mean, sordid, malicious, narrow-minded, envious, and cross-tempered. He carried his meanness to such a length, that when he broke up from Termez, and came and joined me with his family and property, though his own flock of sheep amounted to thirty or forty thousand, and though every march numbers of them passed before our face, while my servants and retainers were tortured with hunger, he did not give us a single sheep; at last, when we reached Kahmerd,[2] he then gave them fifty sheep! Although he had himself acknowledged me as his King, he used to have the nagarets beaten before his tent. He liked nobody, and could see no one prosper. The revenue of Kābul arises from a *tamgha*[3] (or stamp-tax). This *tamgha* I bestowed on him; and made him at the same time Dārogha of Kābul and Penjhīr; gave him the property-tax levied

---

[a] daggers.

[1] Ala-tāgh lies south-east of Kalāt. Sawa-Sang may be Torkani (black stone).
[2] [Kamard is north of Bāmiān.]
[3] All animals, goods, clothes, &c., brought into the country are stamped or marked, and a tax collected.

from the Hazāras,[a] and conferred on him the office of Captain of my Guards,[b] with absolute power in my household. Though distinguished by such marks of favour, he was never either thankful or contented; but, on the contrary, cherished the most wicked and dangerous projects of treason, as has been mentioned. I never, however, upbraided him with them, nor mentioned them to him. He constantly affected great chariness, and asked leave to go away. I gave in to his dissimulation, and in a tone of apology, refused him the permission he solicited.

Every day or two he returned again, and used again to begin asking his discharge. His dissimulation, and eternal requests for liberty to depart, at length exceeded all bounds; so that, wearied to death with his conduct and teasing,[c] I lost patience, and gave him his discharge. Disappointed and alarmed at this, he was now in the utmost perplexity;[d] but to no purpose. He sent to remind me that I had made an agreement with him, that I would not call him to account till he had been guilty of nine offences towards me. I sent him by Mulla Bāba a list of eleven grievances, the justice of which he was forced to acknowledge one after another. He submitted, and having obtained leave, proceeded towards Hindustān with his family and effects. A few of his own retainers accompanied him as far as Kheiber, and then returned back. Having joined the caravan of Bāki Gagiāni, he passed by Nilāb. At this time Yār Hussain Deryā Khan was in Kacheh-Kot. This man had converted into a *sanad* the *firmān* which he had received from me on leaving Kohat; and having enlisted[e] in his service a number of followers, who were partly Afghans of the tribes of Dilazāk and Yusefzai, and partly men of the Jāt[1] and Gujer tribes, his sole occupation now was ravaging the

Has leave to retire.

[a] the Kedı Hazāras and the Kushluk,
[b] Grand Chamberlain,   [c] character,
[d] he repented and tried hard to get out of it;
[e] On the strength of the order he had got from me in Kohat he enrolled

---

[1] The Jāts compose the greater part of the agricultural population over the west of India, down to the mouth of the Indus.

country, and robbing on the highways. Having got notice of Bāki's approach, he occupied the road, and took prisoner Bāki himself, and every person that was along with him. He put Bāki to death, and took his lady. Though I gave Bāki his discharge, and did him no harm, yet he was caught in his own evil, and taken in his own toils.

His death.

> Do thou resign to Fate him who injures thee;
> For Fate is a servant that will not leave thee unavenged.

Bābur attacks the Turkomān Hazāras.

This winter we remained encamped in the Chārbāgh, during one or two of the first falls of snow.[a] Down to the time of my arrival in Kābul, the Turkomān Hazāras had been guilty of numerous insults and depredations; I therefore determined to make an excursion against them, and having gone into the city, and taken up my residence in the palace of Ulugh Beg Mirza, called Bostān-serāi, I set out from thence in the month of Shābān,[1] with the intention of making a foray on the Turkomān Hazāras. A detachment was pushed on, which made a sudden attack on a small party of Hazāras at Jangelik, in the mouth of the valley of Khesh,[b] and dispersed them. A few Hazāras had lain in ambush in a cave near the valley of Khesh. Sheikh Dervīsh Gokultāsh had been in many an action along with me, held the office of *Korbegi*,[2] and was distinguished for the strength with which he drew the bow, as well as the sureness of his aim. He had gone up close to the mouth of this den, without suspecting anything, when a Hazāra from within shot him with an arrow under the nipple, and he died the same day. The great body of the Turkomān Hazāras had erected their winter habitations in the valley of Khesh; we now pushed forward to fall upon them.

The valley of Khesh is a particular kind of glen. For about half a kos from its mouth there is a strait, which makes it necessary for the road to pass along the face of the hill. Below this road is a precipice of fifty or sixty gaz

[a] until snow had fallen once or twice.
[b] Khush.

[1] Shābān commenced on December 28, 1505.
[2] [Keeper of the Arsenal.]

perpendicular descent. Higher up than this road runs a pathway, by which one horseman only can pass at a time. Having passed this strait, we proceeded forward the same day till between noonday and afternoon prayers, when, not having come upon the enemy, we halted. A fat *shuterlūk* [1] belonging to the Hazāras was found, brought in, and killed. We ate part of its flesh roasted, part of it sun-dried.[a] I never ate such fine-flavoured camel's flesh ; many could not distinguish it from mutton.

Marching thence next morning, we began to approach the place where the Hazāras had taken up their winter quarters. It was about the end of the first watch,[2] when a man came from the advance with information, that, in a narrow defile, the Hazāras had fortified and strengthened a ford with branches of trees, and had stopped the advance of our troops who were now engaged with them. On hearing this, we instantly quickened our pace, and when we had advanced a little way, reached the place where the Hazāras had made their stand, and were in hot action. That winter the snow lay very deep, which rendered it dangerous to leave the common road. The banks of the stream, about the ford, were all covered with ice ; and it was impossible to pass the river at any place off the road, on account of the ice and snow. The Hazāras had cut down a number of branches of trees, with which they had fortified [b] the opposite landing-place. They ranged themselves both on horseback and foot, as well in the channel as along the banks of the river, and maintained the fight by discharges of arrows. Muhammed Ali Mubashar Beg, one of the new Amirs, whom I had distinguished by particular marks of favour, and who was a very brave and able man, and a deserving young officer, had neglected to put on his coat of mail ; as he advanced rather near to the place where the road was blocked up by the branches, he was struck by an arrow in the kidneys, and expired on the spot. We had come up

[a] the rest was boiled in vessels.
[b] which they had piled up in masses at

[1] The *shuterlūk* is a species of camel which has very little hair and is used for carrying burdens.
[2] [About 9 a.m.]

hurriedly, and many of us had not taken time to put on our armour. One or two arrows passed whizzing by, and missed us. Ahmed Yūsef Beg, in evident alarm, said every time, 'You should not have come here unarmed—you must go back. I have observed two or three arrows graze close by your head.'—I replied, 'Be you bold : as good arrows have many a time passed my head.' At this very moment, on our right, Kāsim Beg, with his band, discovered a place where the stream could be crossed, and having gained a footing on the opposite side, no sooner pushed on his horse to the charge, than the Hazāras, unable to keep their ground, took to flight. The party that had got in among them, followed them in close pursuit, dismounting and cutting numbers of them down. In reward for his bravery on this occasion, I bestowed Bangash on Kāsim Beg as a provision. Khātim Korbegi also signalized himself on this expedition, on which account I gave him the office of *Korbegi*, which had been held by Sheikh Derwīsh Gokultāsh. To Kupūk Kuli Baba, for his good conduct, I gave Muhammed Ali Mubashar Beg's office. Sultan Kuli Chanāk went in pursuit of them, but it was impossible to leave the road on account of the quantity and depth of the snow. I myself accompanied the pursuers ; we fell in with the sheep and herds of horses of the Hazāras, near their winter habitations. I collected, for my own share, to the number of four or five hundred sheep, and twenty or twenty-five horses. Sultan Kuli, and two or three other persons [a] who were at hand, were joint sharers. I myself went twice on a plundering party. This was one of the times. The other was also

[A.D. 1506–1507.] against these very Turkomān Hazāras, when, on my return from Khorasān, I led a foray against them, and brought off numbers of their horses and sheep. The wives and little children of the Hazāras escaped on foot to the snow-covered hillocks, and there remained. We were rather remiss in following them. The day, too, was far spent ; we therefore went and halted at the huts of the Hazāras.

This winter the snow lay very deep. At this place, off the road, it reached up to the horses' cruppers ; the picket [1]

[a] personal attendants

Chaghdāwel.

appointed for the night-watch round the camp were obliged to remain on horseback till daybreak, in consequence of the depth of the snow.

Next morning we began to move back, and passed the night in the winter huts of the Hazāras, within the valley of Khesh. Marching thence we halted at Jangelik. Yārek Taghāi and some others having lagged a little behind, I directed them to proceed and take the Hazāras who had shot Sheikh Dervīsh. These wretches, infatuated by the blood on their heads,[a] still remained in the cave. Our people, on coming up, filled the cave with smoke, took seventy or eighty Hazāras, and passed the greater number under the edge of the sword.

On finishing this inroad against the Hazāras, we moved down the river Bārān, into the vicinity of Ai-tughdi, for the purpose of collecting the revenue of Nijrau. While I remained at Ai-tughdi, Jehāngīr Mirza waited upon me from Ghazni.

Goes to Ai-tughdi

At this time, on the 13th of Ramzan, I was attacked with so severe a lumbago, that for forty days I was unable to move, and was obliged to be turned from one side to the other by my people. Among the glens of the valley of Nijrau, that of Bachghān is the chief, and is the principal district in the valley. The headman, Hussain Ghaibi Agha, and his younger brother, were noted for [b] their rebellious and contumacious spirit. I dispatched a division against him, under the command of Jehāngīr Mirza, whom I made Kāsim Beg accompany. The detachment went, attacked, and took by storm, a rough stone fort, or *sanger*, which had been thrown up, and inflicted on part of them the punishment they deserved. In consequence of the pain I suffered from my lumbago, they made a sort of litter, in which I was conveyed from the banks of the Bārān to the city, where I was lodged in the Bostān-serāi, and spent there some part of that winter. My first complaint was not removed, when I was seized with boils on my right cheek, which I got lanced. I also used laxatives for this disorder.

His illness, Feb. 7, 1506

[a] whose blood had curdled through fear,
[b] Among the valleys of Nijrau, the Glen of Bajgān, and particularly its headman, Hosain Ghaibi Agha, were noted for

Defection of Jehāngīr Mirza.

On getting better I moved into the Chārbāgh. Jehāngīr Mirza came thither to pay his respects to me. Yūsef and Bahlol, the sons of Ayūb, from the time they had joined the Mirza, had been instigating him to seditious and treasonable practices. I did not on this occasion find Jehāngīr Mirza what he had formerly been. In the course of a few days he set out from his quarters, put on his mail, and went off hastily for Ghazni. Having taken Kila Bāki,^a and killed several of the men in it, he completely plundered the place. He then pushed on, accompanied by all his retainers of every description, and directed his route through the midst of the Hazāras towards Bāmiān.[1] Almighty God knows that neither from me, nor any person dependent on me, did he receive any provocation by word or deed to occasion such violent measures. I afterwards learned that he assigned the following cause for his flight. At the time when Jehāngīr Mirza came from Ghazni, and Kāsim Beg and the rest of the Begs went out to meet him, the Mirza had thrown off a falcon at a *budīneh*, or quail. When the falcon had overtaken it, and was in the act of seizing it in his pounces, the quail dashed itself on the ground. There was a cry, 'Has he taken it or not?' Kāsim Beg observed, 'When he has reduced his enemy to such a plight, he will not let him off. No doubt, he will take him.' This expression struck him, was misinterpreted, and was subsequently one of the causes of the Mirza's elopement. They also noted and treasured up one or two expressions still more idle and unmeaning than even this. In a word, having acted at Ghazni in the manner that has been mentioned, they passed through the midst of the Hazāras, and repaired to the Aimāks.[2] At that time the Aimāks had left Nāsir Mirza, but were in a state of hostilities with the Uzbeks, and lived in Yāi, Asterāb, and the summer habitations in that quarter.

Causes of it.

At this very juncture Sultan Hussain Mirza having come

^a Nāni,

---

[1] Bāmiān, or Būt-Bāmiān, lies north-west from Ghazni, among the hills.

[2] The Aimāks inhabit the hill-country west of the Hazāras, towards Herāt. This, however, appears to have been only one wandering tribe of them.

to a determined resolution to check the progress of Muhammed Sheibāni Khan, summoned all his sons to attend him. He also sent Syed Afzal, the son of Syed Sultan Ali Khāb-bīn (the dreamer), to summon me. It appeared to me expedient to march towards Khorasān on many accounts. One of these was, that when a mighty prince like Sultan Hussain Mirza, who filled the throne of Taimūr Beg, had collected his sons and Amirs from every quarter, with the intention of attacking so formidable an enemy as Sheibāni Khān, if others went on their feet, it became me to accompany them were it on my head; if others went against him with sticks, it was my business to go were it only with stones. Another consideration was, that Jehāngīr Mirza having shown his hostility, it became necessary either to remove his animosity, or to repel his aggressions.

SultanHussain Mirza resolves to oppose Sheibāni Khan. Summons Bābur.

This year Sheibāni Khan besieged Hussain Sūfi[1] in Khwārizm, which he took after a siege of ten months. In the course of this siege a number of desperate actions were fought, and the men of Khwārizm displayed many deeds of consummate bravery, and distinguished themselves by their gallant exertions; they discharged their arrows with so much force that often they pierced through both shield and mail, and frequently right through the double cuirass. For ten months was the siege protracted; when, there being no hope of succour from any quarter, some mean and dastardly wretches among the inhabitants,[a] having lost heart, entered into an understanding with the Uzbeks, and introduced them into the fortress. Hussain Sūfi, on hearing the alarm, repaired to the spot, charged those who had scaled the walls, and while in the act of driving them out, was struck with an arrow, and died.[b] This put an end to the contest, and the place was taken. The blessing of God rest on Hussain Sūfi, who never hesitated for a moment, in the midst of danger and distress, gallantly to expose his life at the call of duty.

Sheibān takes Khwārizm

[a] soldiers,
[b] was killed by an arrow discharged by his page from behind.

[1] [Chīn Sūfi in the *T. R.* Khwārizim at this time belonged to Hosain Mirza Baikara, King of Khorasān. *E. B.*, p. 237.]

Sheibāni Khan having committed Khwārizm to the care of Kūchek Bī,[1] himself repaired to Samarkand.

Death of Sultan Hussain Mirza.

In the latter part of this year, in the month of Zilhijeh,[2] Sultan Hussain Mirza, when he had collected an army for the purpose of acting against Sheibāni Khan, and had advanced as far as Baba Ilāhi, was called to the mercy of God.

His birth and extraction. 1438.

He was born in the year 842 at Heri, in the time of Shahrokh Mirza. Sultan Hussain was the son of Mansūr, the son of Baikara, the son of Omer-Sheikh, the son of Amīr Taimūr. Mansūr Mirza and Baikara Mirza never mounted the throne. His mother was Firōzeh Begum, a granddaughter of Taimūr Beg. Sultan Hussain Mirza was also the grandson of Mirānshah.[3] He was of exalted birth, and of royal race by both parents. There were born of that marriage, two brothers and two sisters of the full blood, Baikara Mirza, Sultan Hussain Mirza, Aka Begum, and another sister, whom Ahmed Khan married. Baikara Mirza, though elder than Sultan Hussain Mirza, served under him, but did not attend in the Diwān.[a] Except when in the Diwān, they were accustomed to sit on the same cushion. The younger brother bestowed on him the government of Balkh, which he held many years. He had three sons, Sultan Muhammed Mirza, Sultan Weis Mirza, and Sultan Iskander Mirza. Aka Begum was the Mirza's elder sister; she married Sultan Ahmed Mirza, the grandson of Mirānshah. She had one son named Kūchek Mirza, who at first entered into the service of his maternal uncle; but afterwards, renouncing the military life, devoted himself to letters. He is said to have become very learned, and had a genius for poetry. The following is one of his *rubāis* (quatrains):

(*Persian*)—For a while I plumed myself on my virtuous life;
I vaunted myself on my adherence to the rules of piety:
When Love came, what became of Virtue and Devotion?
Thanks be to God that I have proved myself.

[a] did not occupy the place of honour in the Divān.

---

[1] It will be remarked, that several of Sheibāni's officers are called Bī, as Kamber Bī, Kūchek Bī, &c. This title of Bī is still given among the Uzbeks to the heads of families or clans.

[2] The 1st of Zilhijeh corresponds to April 25, 1506.

[3] [The eldest son of Amir Taimūr (A.D. 1367–1408).]

There is a coincidence between these lines and a quatrain of the Mulla (Jāmi's). Latterly [a] he went on the pilgrimage of Mekka. Badkeh Begum was the Mirza's younger [1] sister. She was given in marriage to Ahmed Khan, the Khan of Hāji-tarkhān.[b][2] She had two sons by him, who came to Heri, and were long in the Mirza's service.

He had straight narrow eyes, his body was robust and firm;[3] *His figure* from the waist downwards he was of a slenderer make. Although he was advanced in years and had a white beard, he dressed in gay-coloured red and green woollen [c] clothes. He usually wore a cap of black lamb's skin, or a *kilpāk*.[4] Now and then, on festival days, he put on a small turban tied in three folds, broad and showy,[d] and having placed a plume nodding over it, went in this style to prayers.

On first mounting the throne, he took it into his head that *His manners and character* he would cause the names of the twelve Imāms [5] to be recited in the *khutbeh*. Many used their endeavours to prevent him.[e] Finally, however, he directed and arranged everything according to the orthodox Sunni faith. From a disorder in his joints, he was unable to perform [6] his prayers, nor could he observe the stated fasts. He was a lively, pleasant man. His temper was rather hasty, and his language took after his temper. In many instances he displayed a profound reverence for the faith ; [f] on one occasion, one of his sons having slain a man, he delivered him up to the avengers of blood to be carried before the judgement-seat of the Kazi. For about six or seven years

[a] Towards the end of his life
[b] *Add* during the period of his troubles.
[c] silken   [d] very loose and carelessly tied,
[e] Ali Sher Beg and others prevented him.   [f] religious law ;

[1] [P. de C. has 'elder'.]
[2] Hāji-tarkhān was the old name of Astrakhān.
[3] Literally, he was lion-bodied.
[4] The *kilpāk* is the Turkomān cap.
[5] This was a proof that he was then a Shīa. The *khutbeh* is the prayer for the prince.
[6] The word *perform* may be excused in speaking of Musulman prayers, as a great part of them consists in ceremonial bendings and prostrations. Hence the disease in his joints made it difficult for Sultan Hussain Mirza to observe the injunctions of the law

after he first ascended the throne, he was very guarded in abstaining from such things as were forbidden by the law; afterwards he became addicted to drinking wine. During nearly forty years that he was King of Khorasān, not a day passed in which he did not drink after midday prayers; but he never drank wine in the morning. His sons, the whole of the soldiery, and the townspeople, followed his example in this respect, and seemed to vie with each other in debauchery and lasciviousness. He was a brave and valiant man. He often engaged sword in hand in fight, nay, frequently distinguished his prowess hand to hand several times in the course of the same fight. No person of the race of Taimūr Beg ever equalled Sultan Hussain Mirza in the use of the scimitar. He had a turn for poetry, and composed a *diwān*. He wrote in Tūrki. His poetical name was Hussaini. Many of his verses are far from being bad, but the whole of the Mirza's *diwān* is in the same measure. Although a prince of dignity, both as to years and extent of territory, he was as fond as a child of keeping butting rams, and of amusing himself with flying pigeons and cock-fighting.

His wars and battles. One of his exploits was on the banks of the river of Kurkān,[1] when he plunged into the stream, passed it, and completely routed a party of Uzbeks. Another was, when Sultan Abūsaīd Mirza nominated Muhammed Ali Bakhshi to the command of three thousand horse, with instructions to proceed without halt, and attack him by surprise. Sultan Hussain Mirza advanced to meet them with only sixty men, fell upon them straightway, and fairly discomfited them.[2] This was a gallant and most distinguished achievement of Sultan Hussain Mirza. On another occasion he had a battle with Sultan Mahmūd Mirza at Asterābād, and defeated him.[3] He had also another fight at Asterābād, when he beat Hussain Turkomān Saadlīmek.[4] Another of

---

[1] Kurkān, or Gurgān, lies on the south-east of the Caspian.

[2] [The battle of Tarshīz (A. D. 1463), *Tazkiratu-sh-shu'arā* of Daulat Shah (Browne's Edition (London, 1901), p. 527).]

[3] [The battle of Jauzi Wali, near Asterābād (A. D. 1460), Daulat Shah, p. 523.]

[4] [P. de C. has S'ad, son of Hosain, the Turkomān.]

his battles was after mounting the throne, when he engaged and routed Yādgār Muhammed Mirza in Khabārān.[1] Another of his exploits was when, passing the bridge of the Murghāb,[2] he proceeded by forced marches, and surprised and took prisoner Yādgār Muhammed Mirza, who was lying in a state of intoxication in the Bāgh-Zāghān (or Raven Garden),[3] after a debauch, and by this success gained the undisturbed possession of Khorasān.[4] Another of them was at Chekmān,[5] in the vicinity of Andekhūd and Shaberghān,[6] where he encountered and defeated Sultan Mahmūd Mirza. Another of them was, when Ababeker Mirza came from Irāk, accompanied by the Turkomāns of the Black-sheep, defeated Ulugh Beg Mirza in Takāneh and Khimār, and took Kābul, which he abandoned in consequence of the confusions in Irāk, passed by way of Kheıber, traversed the territory of Khushāb and Multān, and entered Sīvī, from whence he proceeded and occupied Karmān ; but being unable to retain it, he again entered the country of Khorasān, when Sultan Hussain Mirza came upon him by surprise, and took him prisoner.[7] On another occasion, at the bridge of Chirāgh, he defeated Badīa-ez-zemān Mirza, one of his own sons.[a][8] At another time he raised an army, with which he besieged Kunduz, but was forced to abandon the siege ; on another occasion he besieged Hissār, but not succeeding, he

[a] *Add* On another occasion he defeated at Halwa-Chashmeh two other sons of his, Abul Muhsin Mirza and Kūpak Mirza. [A.D. 1498.]

---

[1] [The battle of Janārān (A. D. 1469), *Daulat Shah*, p. 531. This, according to P. de C., was a town and district between Sarakhs and Abiward, the birthplace of the poet Anvari.]

[2] Pul-e-murghāb—perhaps the name of a village.

[3] [This was a celebrated garden outside the north-west angle of the walls of Herat. It is said to have been founded by Shah Rukh and his wife Gauhar-shād Agha in the first half of the fifteenth century. *T.R*, p. 83.]

[4] [This incident occurred in A. D. 1470. *Daulat Shah*, p. 531.]

[5] [The battle of Chikmān Serai was fought in A. D. 1471. *Daulat Shah*, p. 532.]

[6] About sixty miles west from Balkh.

[7] [Abā Bakr was defeated on the banks of the river Jurjān, near Asterābād, taken prisoner, and executed in A. D. 1480.]

[8] [This was probably the battle that resulted in Badi'uzzemān's expulsion from Balkh in A. H. 902 (A. D. 1497). *E.B.*, p. 199.]

raised the siege.¹ Another of his enterprises was when he marched against Zūlnūn Beg's country; the Dārogha of Bast surrendered the place,² but he could effect nothing further, and was obliged even to abandon Bast and retreat.³ Sultan Hussain Mirza, though a great and warlike prince, accomplished nothing worthy of his dignity in these two or three enterprises, and returned baffled. At another time, he engaged and defeated in the Auleng-Nīshīn his son Badīa-ez-zemān Mirza, who had advanced, accompanied by Shah Shujā Beg, the son of Zūlnūn Beg.⁴ On this occasion a singular coincidence occurred. Sultan Hussain Mirza, having divided his army, had sent the main body towards Asterābād. On the very day of the battle, the army that had been dispatched against Asterābād returned and joined him : and the very same day, Sultan Masaūd Mirza, from whom Hissār had been wrested by Baiesanghar Mirza, made his appearance from another quarter, and also joined Sultan Hussain Mirza.ᵃ

His dominions.

His kingdom was that of Khorasān, which on the east has Balkh, on the west Bistām ⁵ and Damghān, on the north Khwārizm, and on the south Kandahār and Sīstān. After the fine city of Heri fell into his hands, his whole time was devoted, night and day, to revelry and enjoyment; and there was not one of his servants or dependants, who, in like manner, did not give himself up to pleasure and riot. The cares of ambition and the necessary toils of military disci-

---

ᵃ *Add* Haidar Mirza, who had gone to meet Badiuzzamān Mirza at Sabzewār (chief town of the district of Baihak), was the third to arrive at the strange rendezvous.

¹ [This event occurred in A. D. 1496. *E.B.*, p. 197.]
² Bast is situated on the left bank of the Helmand, below its junction with the Argendāb. This expedition of Sultan Husain Mirza was against Zamīn-dāwer, which is higher up on the opposite bank of the Helmand.
³ [In A. D. 1497. *E.B.*, p. 270.]
⁴ [This defeat was inflicted on Badi'uzzamān Mirza in A. D. 1497. Aulang Nīshīn (Meadow of Nīshīn) lies near Herat.—*E.B.*, p. 270.]
⁵ [Bistām (the modern Bostān) and Dameghān are places in Khorasān. The former (36° 30′ N., 55° 2′ E.) is south-east of Asterābād, and the latter (36° 12′ N., 54° 38′ E.) lies on the edge of the great Salt Desert due south of Chārdeh.]

pline were consequently neglected. Hence, down to the time of his death, his dominions and servants went on diminishing, without getting any corresponding increase.

He had fourteen sons and eleven daughters who lived. The eldest of his sons was Badīa-ez-zemān Mirza, whose mother was the daughter of Sanjer Mirza of Merv.

Another was Shah Gharīb Mirza. Although his form was not prepossessing,[a] he had a fine genius; and though his constitution was feeble, he had a powerful style. He assumed the poetical name of Gharbi, and composed a *diwān*. He wrote verses both in Persian and Tūrki. The following is his:

I had a passing glance of a fairy face, and became inflamed to madness with her love;
What is her name, where her abode, I know not.

Sultan Hussain Mirza gave Shah Gharīb the government of Heri for some time. He departed in his father's lifetime, leaving no son nor daughter.

Another was Muzaffer Hussain Mirza, who was the favourite son of Sultan Hussain Mirza, although there was nothing in his manners or conduct to justify such marked favour. In consequence of the decided partiality which he showed to this son, several of the others were induced to revolt. Khadījeh Begum, who had been a concubine of Sultan Abūsaīd Mirza's, was the mother of the two last-mentioned Mirzas. She had likewise a daughter by the Mirza, named Ak Begum.[1]

Another of his sons was Abul Hassan Mirza. Another was Kīpek Mirza,[2] as he was generally called, but his name was Muhammed Muhsin Mirza. The mother of these two was Latīfeh Sultan Aghācheh.

Another was Abu Tarāb Mirza, who in early life was highly extolled for his rapid acquirements. When his father's illness increased and became extreme, having heard something to alarm him, he went to Irāk, accompanied by his younger brother, Muhammed Hussain Mirza. He there

[a] *Add* and he was deformed,

[1] The Fair Princess.—*Leyden.*
[2] Kīpek Mirza, from being round-shouldered.—*Leyden.*

renounced the profession of arms, and betook himself to that of a dervīsh. I never heard of him afterwards. He had one son, Sohrāb Mirza, who was in my service when [A.D. 1511.] I defeated Hamzeh Sultan, Mahdi Sultan, and the other Sultans, and took Hissār. This young man was blind of one eye. He was singularly ill-favoured, and his manners corresponded with his looks. Having been guilty of something extremely reprehensible, he found it impossible to remain in my employment, and repaired to Asterābād, where Najem Sāni inflicted on him condign punishment for his misdeeds.

Muhammed Hussain Mirza.

Another son was Muhammed Hussain Mirza. He and Shah Ismāel [1] were once imprisoned in the same place in Irāk, at which time he became one of Shah Ismāel's disciples, and from that period was a rank heretic.[2] Although his father, his elder brother, and his younger brothers were all orthodox Sunnis, he continued a blind and confirmed *rāfizi* (heretic) till his death in Asterābād. His character stood high as a brave and courageous warrior; but I never heard any of his exploits that deserve to be recorded. He had a genius for poetry; the following is his:

(*Persian*)—In the pursuit of what game dost thou range thus dust-defiled ?
From the ardours of whose warm heart art thou thus bathed in perspiration ?

Ferīdūn Hussain Mirza.

Another was Ferīdūn Hussain Mirza. He was a powerful archer, and an excellent marksman. They say that his *gūrdehieh* (or double-stringed [3] bow) required forty *mans* [4] weight to make the ears meet.[5] He was himself a man of bravery, but not fortunate in battle. He was beaten wherever he engaged. At Rabāt-e-dodez, Ferīdūn Hussain Mirza, and his younger brother Ibn Hussain Mirza, engaged

---

[1] Shah Ismāil was the founder of the Safevi dynasty in Persia. He was a rigid Shīa, and a man of great learning and piety.
[2] That is, he became a Shīa.
[3] [*Gūrdehieh*, according to P. de C., means 'round'.]
[4] If the Tabrīz *man*, this would be about 290 pounds. [P. de C. reads *batmans* for *mans*. A *batman* = 82 English pounds. 'Batman est pondus LV libr. sive LXXXII libr. Angl.' See De Laet, *De imperio Magni Moghalis*, &c. Elzevir 1631, 2nd issue, p. 136.]
[5] [To draw or bend.]

Taimūr Sultan and Ubeid Sultan, and were defeated. On that occasion, Ferīdūn Hussain Mirza distinguished himself by his strenuous exertions. At Damghān, Ferīdūn Hussain Mirza and Muhammed Zemān Mirza [1] fell into the hands of Sheibāni Khan. He killed neither of them, but set them at liberty. Afterwards, when Shah Muhammed Diwāneh fortified Kalāt [2] for a siege, he repaired thither; and when the Uzbeks took Kalāt, was made prisoner, and put to death. These three last-mentioned princes were all by Mingeli-bī Aghācheh, an Uzbek concubine of the Mirza's.

Another was Haider, whose mother was Payandeh Sultan Begum, the daughter of Sultan Abūsaīd Mirza. In his father's lifetime he for some time enjoyed the government of Meshhad and Balkh. At the siege of Hissār, Sultan Hussain Mirza betrothed this son to the daughter of Sultan Mahmūd Mirza by Khanzādeh Begum, concluded a peace, and raised the siege of Hissār. By her he had one daughter, called Shād Begum, who lived to grow up. She latterly came to Kābul, and was given to Ādil Sultan. Haider Mirza also departed this life before his father.

Haider Mirza.

Another was Muhammed Maasūm Mirza, to whom Kandahār was given by his father, Sultan Hussain Mirza. On that occasion a daughter of Ulugh Beg Mirza was betrothed to this son. After she was brought to Heri he made a grand festival, and erected a magnificent pavilion [3] for the occasion. Though he bestowed Kandahār on this prince, yet everything that was done, be it black or be it white, was done by Shah Beg Arghūn; [4] the Mirza had neither power nor influence in the matter; for which reason he would not continue at Kandahār, but returned to Khorasān, where he died in his father's lifetime.

Muhammed Maasūm Mirza.

Another was Farrukh Hussain Mirza, who did not reach any great age, and did not survive his younger brother Ibrahīm Hussain Mirza.

Farrukh Hussain Mirza.

Another was Ibrahīm Hussain Mirza, whose talents were

Ibrahīm Hussain Mirza.

---

[1] A son of Badia-ez-zemān Mirza.
[2] This is the Kalāt [ı Nādırı] in Khorasān, famous as the birthplace of Nādir Shah.   [3] *Chār-tāk.*
[4] [Son of Zunnūn, who was Governor of Kandahār, and for whom he was acting as Deputy.]

thought respectable. He was eternally drinking the wine of Heri to excess, and died of hard drinking in his father's lifetime.

Ibn Hussain Mirza, and Muhammed Kāsim Mirza.

Another was Ibn Hussain Mirza, who, with Muhammed Kāsim Mirzá, will be mentioned in the sequel. The mother of these five Mirzas was Pāpa Aghācheh, who was a concubine.

Sultānim Begum.

His eldest daughter was Sultānim Begum, who had no brother or sister of the full blood. Her mother, Jūli Begum, was the daughter of one of the Begs of the Azāks. Sultānim Begum was very eloquent and ingenious,[a] but her remarks in conversation were frequently rude and ill-timed.[b] Her elder brother[1] gave her in marriage to Sultan Weis Mirza, the son of Miāngi Baikara Mirza, by whom she had one son and one daughter. This daughter was given to Īsān Kuli Sultan, the younger brother of Dilbars [c] Sultan, one of the Shābān Sultans. Sultan Muhammed Mirza, on whom I have conferred the government of Kanauj,[2] is the son of this marriage. Sultānim Begum set out along with her grandson for Hindustān, but expired at Nilāb on the journey. Her attendants returned back with her remains, while her grandson continued his route and joined me.

Ak Begum.

Again, by Payandeh Sultan Begum, Sultan Hussain Mirza had four daughters. The eldest of them was Ak Begum, who was married to Muhammed Kāsim Arlat, the grandson of Begah Begum, Bābur Mirza's[3] younger sister. By him she had one daughter named Karagūz Begum (the black-eyed princess), who was married to Nāsir Mirza.

Kīchek Begum.

The second of the daughters was Kīchek Begum. Sultan Masaūd Mirza was extremely attached to her, but whatever efforts he made, Payandeh Sultan Begum, having an aversion

---

[a] She spoke with much elegance and remarkable facility,
[b] *Omit this clause.* [c] Ilburs

---

[1] [or, perhaps, 'the middle son'.]
[2] [In 1527. Kanauj is a town in the U.P., situated on the right bank of the Kāli nadi near its confluence with the Ganges.]
[3] Probably Bābur Mirza, the grandson of Shahrokh Mirza, who was for several years King of Khorasān, and whose transactions in Khorasān, Persia, and Māweralnaher, make a great figure in the history of the times. This able prince died in 1457.

to him, would not consent to the match. She was afterwards married to Mulla Khwājeh, who was of the family of Syed Āta. The third sister, Begah Begum, and the fourth, Agha Begum, were given to Bābur Mirza,[1] and Sultan Murād Mirza, the sons of his younger sister Rabīah Sultan Begum.

Begah Begum, and Agha Begum.

By Mangeli-bī Aghācheh he had two daughters; the elder was given to Syed Abdallah Mirza, who was descended of the Syeds of Andekhūd, and the grandson, by a daughter, of Baikara Mirza. She had one son named Syed Barkeh. When I took Samarkand, he came and entered my service. He afterwards went to Urganj,[2] and aspired to the sovereignty. The Kizelbashes[3] slew him in Asterābād. The name of the other daughter was Fātimeh Sultan. She was married to Yādgār Muhammed Mirza, who was of the line of Taimūr Beg.

Fātimeh Sultan.

By Pāpa Aghācheh he had three daughters. The eldest was Sultan Nizhād Begum. Sultan Hussain Mirza gave her in marriage to Sikander Mirza, the younger son of his elder brother. The second daughter was Begum Sultan, who was bestowed on Sultan Masaūd Mirza, after the loss of his eyesight. By him she had one son and one daughter. The daughter was taken charge of, and brought up by Apāk Begum, one of Sultan Hussain Mirza's ladies. She came to Kābul from Heri, and Apāk married her to Syed Mirza.[a] After the Uzbeks had put to death Masaūd Sultan, Begum Sultan set out with her son, for Mekka. I have received information that she and her son are now in Mekka. The third daughter was married to one of the Syeds of Andekhūd, well known under the name of Syed Mirza.

Sultan Nizhād Begum.

Begum Sultan.

He had one other daughter, called Aisha Sultan, by a concubine. Her mother was Zobeideh Aghācheh, the granddaughter of Hussain Sheikh Taimūr, of the race of the

Aisha Sultan

[a] where she was married to Seyyid Mirza Apāk.

---

[1] This is evidently a different Bābur Mirza from the one last mentioned.

[2] In Khwārizm.

[3] The Kizelbashes, or red bonnets, are the Persians, so called from a red cap worn by their soldiers.

Shābān Sultans.[a] This daughter was given in marriage to Kāsim Sultan. By him she had one son, Kāsim Hussain, who came to Hindustān, entered into my service, and was in the holy war against Rāna Sanka. I gave him the government of Budāūn.[1] After Kāsim Sultan, she married Burān Sultan, one of his relations, by whom she had another son named Abdallah Sultan, who is at present in my service, and although young, acquits himself very respectably.

His wives and concubines.
Begah Sultan Begum.

The first wife whom he married was Begah Sultan Begum, the daughter of Sanjer Mirza of Merv. By her he had Badīa-ez-zemān Mirza. She was extremely cross-tempered, and fretted Sultan Hussain Mirza beyond endurance, till the Mirza, driven to extremities by her insufferable humour, divorced her. What could he do? The Mirza was in the right;

(*Persian*)—A bad wife in a good man's house,
Even in this world, makes a hell on earth.[2]

May the Almighty remove such a visitation from every good Moslem; and God grant that such a thing as an ill-tempered, cross-grained wife, be not left in the world!

Jūli Begum.

Another of his wives was Jūli Begum, the daughter of one of the chiefs of the Azāks, by whom he had Sultānim Begum.

Shaher-bānu Begum.

Another was Shaher-bānu Begum, the daughter of Sultan Abūsaīd Mirza, whom he married after he ascended the throne. At the battle of Chikmān, when all the Mirza's ladies descended from their litters and mounted on horseback, this princess, relying on her younger brother,[3] did not leave her litter nor take to horse. This was reported to the Mirza, who thereupon divorced her, and married her youngest sister, Payandeh Sultan Begum. After the Uzbeks took Khorasān, Payandeh Sultan Begum went to Irāk, where she died in distress.

Payandeh Sultan Begum.

[a] *This clause is put after the next sentence, viz.* Kāsim Sultan of the race of Shābān Sultans.

[1] [In 1527 Budāūn lies above Kanauj in Rohilkand, U.P.]
[2] From the *Gulistān* of Sadi [chap. ii, story 31.]
[3] The battle of Chikmān was fought between Sultan Hussain Mirza and Sultan Mahmūd Mirza, who was the son of Sultan Abūsaīd Mirza, and the brother of Shaher-bānu Begum.

Another was Khadījeh Begum, who had been a concubine of Sultan Abūsaīd Mirza, and borne him one daughter, who was named Ak Begum (or the Fair Lady). After the defeat of Sultan Abūsaīd Mirza in Irāk, this lady came to Heri, where Sultan Hussain Mirza took her, and being passionately fond of her, raised her from the rank of concubine to that of Begum. She finally managed him entirely according to her will and pleasure. It was by her intrigues that Muhammed Mūmin Mirza [1] was put to death. She was the chief cause of the rebellions of Sultan Hussain Mirza's sons. She regarded herself as a personage of profound sense, but was in truth a foolish, talkative woman. She was, besides, heretical in her religious opinions. She had two sons, Shah Gharīb Mirza and Muzaffer Hussain Mirza.

<small>Khadījeh Begum.</small>

Another of his wives was Apāk Begum, by whom he had neither son nor daughter. Pāpa Aghācheh, who was so much attached to her,[a] was her foster sister; having no children herself, she brought up the sons of Pāpa Aghācheh as her own. She attended the Mirza with very tender care during his illnesses; indeed, no lady of his family equalled her in dutiful attentions. The year that I came to Hindustān [2] she arrived from Heri. I showed her all the respect and kindness in my power. While I was besieging Chanderi,[3] I learned that, at Kābul, she had departed to the mercy of God.

<small>Apāk Begum.</small>

Of Sultan Hussain Mirza's concubines, one was Latīf Sultan,[b] by whom he had Abul Hassan Mirza, and Kīpek Mirza.

<small>His concubines. Latīf Sultan.</small>

Another of them was Mangeli-bī Aghācheh, who was an Uzbek, and one of Shaher-bānu Begum's people. She was the mother of Abu Tarāb Mirza, of Muhammed Hussain Mirza, and of Ferīdūn Mirza. She had also two daughters.

<small>Mangeli-bī Aghācheh.</small>

Another of them was Pāpa Aghācheh, the foster-sister of Apāk Begum. The Mirza having seen and liked her, took

<small>Pāpa Aghācheh.</small>

---

[a] to whom he (i. e. the Mirza) was so much attached,
[b] *Add* Agācha, belonging to the Chār-shambah,

---

[1] This young prince was the son of Badīa-ez-zemān Mirza, the eldest son of Sultan Hussain Mirza.
[2] [In 1526.]
[3] [In 1528.]

her; and she was the mother of five sons and four daughters, as has been mentioned.[1]

Begi Sultan Aghācheh. Another was Begi Sultan Aghācheh, by whom he had neither son nor daughter.

He had many other concubines and women [a]: those whom I have mentioned were the most eminent of his wives and concubines. There was no prince of his time who could be compared to Sultan Hussain Mirza in power, nor any city of Islām like Heri; yet it is remarkable, that of his fourteen sons,[2] only three were legitimate. The consequences of vice and debauchery manifested their baleful influence on himself, his sons, his tribes, and hordes (Īls and Ulūses). It was one of the judgements which they drew down, that of so large a family, in seven or eight years, not a trace or vestige remained, except only Muhammed Zemān Mirza.[3]

His Amirs. Muhammed Berendūk Birlās. With regard to his Amirs, one of them was Muhammed Berendūk Birlās, who was descended of Jākū Birlās; his genealogy runs thus: Muhammed Berendūk,[4] the son of Jehān-shah, the son of Jākū Birlās. He was first a Beg in the service of Bābur Mirza, and was afterwards in high favour with Sultan Abūsaīd Mirza,[5] who gave Kābul to him and Jehāngīr Birlās, and appointed him governor to his son Ulugh Beg Mirza.[6] After the death of Sultan Abūsaīd Mirza, Ulugh Beg Mirza formed designs to rid himself of the two Birlās; but they, having discovered his plans, placed him under custody, moved away with their Īls and Ulūses, and marched for Kunduz. On reaching the top of Hindū-kūsh, they sent back the Mirza in the handsomest manner to Kābul; while they themselves proceeded on to Khorasān to Sultan Hussain Mirza, who gave them the most favourable

---

[a] *Add* of inferior rank:

[1] [Only three are previously mentioned.]

[2] Badīa-ez-zemān Mirza, Shah Gharīb Mirza, and Muzaffer Hussain Mirza.

[3] This prince was in Bābur's service in India.

[4] In the margin of the Tuzuk is the following note: Muhammed Ferīdūn bin Muhammed Kuli Khan bin Mirza Ali bin Berendūk Birlās.—*Leyden*. [P. de C. adds after Berendūk in the text 'Son of 'Ali, son of Berendūk'.]

[5] The grandfather of Bābur. [This prince died in 1469.]

[6] Afterwards King of Kābul.

reception. Muhammed Berendūk Beg was a very prudent and wise man, and incomparably the first in distinction at the court of Heri.[a] He was extremely fond of his hawks, insomuch, that if he at any time learned that one of his hawks was dead or lost, he used to take the name of one of his sons, and say, 'Had such a son died, or such an one broken his neck, I would have thought nothing of it in comparison with the death or loss of such a hawk.'

Another of his Amirs was Muzaffer Birlās, who attended him in all his wars. I know not in what manner he contrived to ingratiate himself so much with the Mirza, but that prince loaded him with favours. Such was the Mirza's familiarity with him, that in his first campaigns they entered into an agreement, that whatsoever country should be conquered, four parts should belong to the Mirza and two to him. A strange agreement! How could it possibly answer for a monarch to adopt a servant as the partner of his sovereignty? Such an agreement could never have answered even with his own brother or son. How could it succeed with one of his Amirs or Captains? After he had mounted the throne he became ashamed of this compact, but to no purpose. This wrong-headed man, singularly distinguished as he had been by the Mirza's favour, only presumed the more on it, and behaved factiously. The Mirza, not being able to retain him within the limits of his duty, is said finally to have poisoned him. The omniscient God knows with truth what befell him.

Muzaffer Birlās.

Another of them was Ali Sher Beg Nawāi, who was not so much his Amīr as his friend. In their youth they had been schoolfellows, and were extremely intimate. I know not for what offence he was driven from Heri by Sultan Abūsaīd Mirza; but he went to Samarkand, where he remained for several years, and was protected and patronized by Ahmed Hāji Beg. Ali Sher Beg was celebrated for the elegance of his manners; and this elegance and polish were ascribed to the conscious pride of high fortune: but this was not the case; they were natural to him, and he had precisely the same refined manner when he was in Samarkand. Indeed, Ali Sher Beg was an incomparable person. From

Ali Sher Nawāi.

[a] *Omit this clause.*

the time that poetry was first written in the Tūrki language, no man has written so much and so well. He composed six *masnevis* in verse, five in imitation of the *Khamsah*[1] (of Nizāmi), and one in imitation of the *Mantik-ut-teir*[2] (the Speech of the Birds). This last he called *Lissān-ut-teir* (the Tongue of the Birds). He also composed four *diwāns* of *ghazels* (or odes), entitled, The Singularities of Infancy, The Wonders of Youth, The Marvels of Manhood, and The Benefits of Age.[a][3] He likewise composed several other works, which are of a lower class and inferior in merit to these. Of that number is an imitation of the Epistles of Moulāna Abdal Rahmān Jāmi, which he partly wrote and partly collected. The object of it is to enable every person to find in it a letter suited to any business on which he may desire to write.[b] He also wrote the *Mizān-al-auzān* (the Measure of Measures) on Prosody, in which he is very incorrect; for, in describing the measures of twenty-four *rubāis* (quatrains), he has erred in the measures of four; he has also made some mistakes regarding other poetical measures, as will be evident to any one who has attended to the structure of Persian verse. He besides completed a *diwān*[4] in Persian, and in his Persian compositions he assumed the poetical name of Fāni.[5] Some of his Persian verses are not

[a] *Add* He also composed some very good quatrains.

[b] Among these is a collection of letters which he wrote in imitation of the Epistles of Maulāna 'Abdur-rahmān Jāmi and in which he collected all the letters he had written to different people on all possible topics.

---

[1] [The *Khamsah* (Quintet), or five poems of Nizāmī Ganjavī, are: The Treasury of Secrets (Makhzan ul asrār); The Romance of Khusru and Shīrīn; The Romance of Leilah and Majnūn; The Romance of Alexander the Great (Sikander-nāmah); and The Seven Effigies (Haft paikar). Nizāmī, who was one of the most celebrated poets of Persia, died in A. D. 1202–3.]

[2] The *Mantik-ut-teir* was written by the celebrated Sheikh Ferīd-ed-dīn Attār [A.D. 1119–1230], better known in Europe as the author of a *Pand-nāmeh*.

[3] [*Gharā'ib us sighar, Nawādir ush shahāb, Badā'i ul wasat*, and *Fawā'id ul kibr*.]

[4] The Persian *diwān* is a series of poems, in which each letter of the alphabet in its turn furnishes the rhyme.

[5] Every Persian poet has a *takhallus*, or poetical name, which he introduces into the last couplet of each ode.

bad, but the greater part of them are heavy [a] and poor. He has also left excellent pieces of music; they are excellent both as to the airs themselves and as to the preludes. There is not upon record in history any man who was a greater patron and protector of men of ingenuity and talent than Ali Sher Beg. Ustād [1] Kuli Muhammed, the celebrated Sheikhi,[2] and Hussain Ūdī,[3] who were so distinguished for their skill in instrumental music, attained their high eminence and celebrity by the instructions and encouragement of Ali Sher Beg. Ustād Behzād and Shah Muzaffer owed the extent of their reputation and fame in painting to his exertions and patronage; and so many were the excellent works which owed their origin to him, that few persons ever effected anything like it. He had no son, nor daughter, nor wife, nor family: he passed through the world single and unencumbered. At first he was keeper of the signet; in the middle part of his life he was invested with the dignity of Beg, and held the government of Asterābād for some time. He afterwards renounced the profession of arms, and would accept of nothing from the Mirza; on the contrary, he annually presented him with a large sum of money as an offering. When Sultan Hussain Mirza returned from the Asterābād campaign, the Beg came out of the city to meet him; between the moment of the Mirza's saluting him and his rising, he was affected with a sudden stroke, which prevented his getting up, and he was obliged to be carried off. The physicians were unable to render him any assistance,[b] and next morning he departed to the mercy of God.[4] One of his own couplets was highly applicable to his situation:

(*Tūrki*)—I perish of a mortal disease, though I know not what it is;
In this disease, what remedy can physicians administer?[c]

Another of Sultan Hussain's Begs was Wali Beg, who was of the race of Hāji Seifed-dīn Beg. He was one of the

Wali Beg.

[a] weak   [b] could not diagnose the disease,
[c] *Add* Ahmed, the son of Tawakkul Birlās, who for a time held the government of Kandahār, was another.

---

[1] [The Master.]   [2] [P. de C. adds 'the fluté-player'.]
[3] [i. e. 'Ūdī the lute-player.]
[4] ['Alisher was born in 1440 and died in 1500.]

Mirza's principal Begs, but did not long survive that Prince's accession to the throne.[a]

Sheikh Hassan Taimūr. Another of them was Sheikh Hassan Taimūr, who had been in high favour with Bābur Mirza, by whom he was elevated to the rank of Beg.

Nuyān Beg. Another of them was Nuyān Beg. His father was of the Syeds of Termez, and his mother was of the same extraction.[b] Sultan Abūsaīd Mirza patronized him greatly, and he was the Beg who stood highest in the confidence of Ahmed Mirza.[1] When he went to Sultan Hussain Mirza, he was received by him with marked favour and promoted. He was a profligate, jolly, drinking, debauched libertine. Hassan Yākūb, from having been in his father's service, was frequently called Hassan Nuyān.

Jehāngīr Birlās. Another was Jehāngīr Birlās, who was for some time joint governor of Kābul with Muhammed Berendūk. He afterwards went to the court of Sultan Hussain Mirza, and was graciously received. His manners and deportment were remarkable for elegance and politeness.[c] He was of a gay lively temper, and a great favourite of Badīa-ez-zemān Mirza. He never forgot that Prince's attachment to him, and always spoke of him in terms of praise.

Mirza Ahmed Ali Fārsi. Another was Mirza Ahmed Ali Fārsi.[d]

Abdal Khālik Beg. Another was Abdal Khālik Beg, whose grandfather, Firoz-Shāh Beg, having received high marks of favour from Shahrokh Mirza, this nobleman was from him called Abdal Khālik Firoz-Shāhi. He held the government of Khwārizm for some time.

Ibrahīm Duldāi. Another of them was Ibrahīm Duldāi, who was profoundly skilled in the revenue accounts, and in the course of public business. He was a second Muhammed Berendūk.

[a] *Add* He was a good Moslem, being regular in his devotions, and a simple and loyal man.

[b] on his mother's side he was related to Sultan Abu Sa'īd Mirza and Sultan Husain Mirza.

[c] *Add* As he was skilled in hunting and hawking, Sultan Husain Mirza generally referred to him in all matters relative to these sports.

[d] *Add* Though he composed no verse, his sound judgement enabled him to appreciate good poetry. Owing to his taste he was a remarkable man, in fact one in a thousand.

[1] One of Sultan Abūsaīd's sons, and king of Samarkand.

Another was Zūlnūn Arghūn, a brave man. He distinguished himself above all the other young warriors, in the presence of Sultan Abūsaīd Mirza, by his use of the scimitar, and afterwards, on every occasion on which he went into action, he acquitted himself with distinction. His courage is unimpeached, but certainly he was rather deficient in understanding. He left the service of our Mirzas, and took himself to Sultan Hussain Mirza, who conferred on him the government of Ghūr and the Nukderi country. With only seventy or eighty followers, he performed several very gallant exploits in that quarter. With but a handful of men he bravely vanquished and reduced large and numerous bodies of Hazāras and Nukderis; and these tribes were never so effectually settled and kept in order by any other person. Some time afterwards he also got the Zamīn-dāwer.[1] His son Shah Shujā Arghūn, though a boy, accompanied his father in his expeditions, and sword in hand displayed great valour. Sultan Hussain Mirza, to gratify the father's feelings, gave Kandahār to be held by the father and son in common. Afterwards, however, this father and son stirred up dissension between their sovereign and his son, and were the cause of dangerous rebellions. In the same year in which I took Khosrou Shah, and separated him from his adherents and retainers, I likewise took Kābul from Mukīm,[2] the youngest son of Zūlnūn Arghūn; in consequence of which, Zūlnūn and Khosrou Shah, being both reduced to great difficulties, repaired to Sultan Hussain Mirza's court. After the demise of Sultan Hussain Mirza, Zūlnūn rose to very high rank, and the countries on the Dāmenkoh (skirts of the mountains) of Heri, such as Ubeh and Chakhcherān,[3] were given to him. He was Badīa-ez-zemān's prime adviser, as Muhammed Berendūk Birlās was Muzaffer Mirza's.[a] Though a man of courage, he was ignorant, and somewhat

Zūlnūn Arghūn.

[a] *Add* when these two Mirzas exercised sovereign power jointly (in Herat).

---

[1] The country of Zamīn-dāwer lies west of Kandahār, on the right bank of the Helmand, reaching from Sirbesha, under the Hazāra hills, to the Helmand. [2] [In 1504.]

[3] Ubeh lies about one degree east of Herāt; Chakhcherān lies four degrees east by south among the Hazāra hills.

crazed. Had it not been for this craziness and ignorance, he never would have made himself the dupe of such gross flattery, and exposed himself to scorn in consequence. The story is this: When he was prime minister, and in the chief confidence at Heri, several Sheikhs and Mullas came and told him that they had had an intercourse with the spheres, and that the title of Hizaber-ullah (the Lion of God) had been conferred on him; that he was predestined to defeat the Uzbeks, and make them all prisoners. He, implicitly believing all this flattery, tied a kerchief round his neck, and returned thanks to God. When Sheibāni Khan fell upon the Mirzas in the territory of Badghīs, prevented their junction and discomfited them, Zūlnūn was in Kara Rabāt with a hundred or a hundred and fifty men, and relying on this prediction, boldly kept his ground, and made head against Sheibāni Khan. No sooner had Sheibāni's numerous troops come up, than this small body was surrounded and taken on the spot. Zūlnūn was made prisoner and put to death. He was a pious and orthodox believer, never neglected saying the appointed prayers, and frequently repeated the supererogatory ones. He was madly fond of chess; if a person played at it with one hand, he played at it with his two hands.[1] He played without art, just as his fancy suggested. He was the slave of avarice and meanness.

Derwīsh Ali Beg. Another of the nobles was Derwīsh Ali Beg, who was the younger brother of the full blood of Ali Sher Beg, and for some time held the government of Balkh, which he managed creditably. He was, however, a muddle-brained, wrong-headed, dull man. Sultan Hussain Mirza, when he first advanced against Kunduz and Hissār, was baffled through his stupidity, and forced to retreat; on which account he was dismissed from his government of Balkh. In the year **1510.** 916, when I went to Kunduz, he joined me. He was a buffoon, and a silly fellow, as unfit for the exercise of dignified authority, as incapable of the virtues of social life. The favour which he experienced was entirely on account of his brother Ali Sher Beg.

Moghul Beg. Another of them was Moghul Beg, who for some time

---

[1] This is an idiom expressive of his great keenness.

possessed the government of Heri, and afterwards got that of Asterābād. From Asterābād he fled to Irāk to Yākūb Beg. He was of a low turn, and eternally gambling with dice.

Another was Syed Bader, who was a man of great strength,[a] and of very sweet manners. He was highly skilled in the elegant arts, and danced singularly well, exhibiting dances of the most uncommon sort, of which he was generally himself the inventor.[b] He was always in the Mirza's immediate service, was his boon companion, and his comrade in his drinking-bouts.[c] *Syed Bader.*

Another was Sultan Juneid Birlās, who latterly went into the service of Sultan Ahmed Mirza. This is the Sultan Juneid Birlās whose father is at present associated with him in the government of Jaunpūr. *Sultan Juneid Birlās.*

Another was Sheikh Abūsaīd Khan Dar-mian (in the midst). I do not know whether it was from having brought the Mirza a horse *in the middle* of a fight, or from warding off the blow of an enemy by interposing *between* him and the Mirza, that he gained this appellation. *Sheikh Abūsaīd Khan.*

Another was Behbūd Beg, who at first served in the band of young soldiers.[d] As he did good service in the Mirza's expeditions, in reward of it, his name was inscribed on the *tamgha* and *sikka*.[1] *Behbūd Beg.*

[a] *Add* of very graceful carriage,
[b] one graceful dance he used to execute of which probably he was the inventor.
[c] *Add* Another was Islīm Birlās, a simple straightforward man, who was well versed in the art of hawking, and an expert in many feats of skill. He used to draw a bow of the power of thirty to forty *batmans* with such vigour that his arrow would pierce the board that served as a target. He would enter the shooting ground at one end at a gallop, turn round, let the bow fall (on the ground), replace it in his hand, draw it, and hit the target. Again, he would fasten a ring to a string a cubit or a cubit and a half long, and tie the other end to a piece of stick (a post), and give it (the string) a rotary motion; then, seizing his opportunity, he would let fly his arrow, and shoot it through the ring (as it revolved). In this manner he used to perform a lot of tricks with remarkable skill. He never left the Mirza's service, and accompanied him in all his parties of pleasure
[d] the corps of pages.

[1] That is, on the royal seal or stamp, and on the coin. This seems a singular compliment to a subject not of the highest rank. [The legend *bihbūd* (it was good) on Hosain's coins (of which several

Sheikhim Beg.

Another was Sheikhim Beg. As he bore the poetical name of Suheili, he was generally called Sheikhim Suheili.[1] He composed a sort of verse, in which both the words and sense are terrific, and corresponding with each other. The following is one of his couplets:

During my sorrows of the night, the whirlpool of my sighs bears the firmament from its place;
The dragons of the inundation of my tears bear down the four quarters of the habitable world.

It is well known that, on one occasion, having repeated these verses to Moulāna Abdal Rahmān Jāmi, the Mulla said, 'Are you repeating poetry, or terrifying folks?' He composed a *diwān*, and was likewise the author of various *masnevis*.

Muhammed Wali Beg

Another was Muhammed Wali Beg, the son of the Wali Beg who has been mentioned. He latterly became a great Beg in the Mirza's court; but notwithstanding his high rank, he never abated of his service, but day and night was constantly at court; insomuch that he even paid his allowances to his retainers, and made his distributions of food, at the palace. One who pays such assiduous court is sure to meet with corresponding favour. It is a heavy calamity nowadays, when one who gets the name of Mīr invites and calls in to him five or six scabbed, blind fellows, to create trouble and confusion in the palace.[a] But where is the other kind of service to be found? The present practice of the Begs only serves to evince their want of liberality. The food and distributions of victuals made by Muhammed Wali Beg, on the contrary, were always respectable. He kept his servants in a good style, and in handsome attire. He bestowed much with his own hand on the poor, and on mendicants. He was, however, a foul-mouthed, bad-tongued man. When I took Samarkand in

A.D. 1511. the year 917, Muhammed Wali Beg, and Derwīsh Ali

[a] It is a pity that nowadays a man that calls himself a Beg, and has a following of only five or six scabbed and blind fellows, cannot be made to attend court without an effort.

were in my collection) was simply a currency mark, and its application to Behbūd, the Beg, must have been an afterthought.]

[1] His name was Mīr Ahmed Suheili. The *Anwār i suheili* is dedicated to him.

Kitābdār (the librarian), were with me. At that time he had been struck with a palsy, and had no remains of anything agreeable either in his language or manners. He did not seem equal to the favours that had been shown him; and probably the assiduity of his service had assisted in elevating him to his high rank.

Another of Sultan Hussain Mirza's nobles was Bāba Ali, the Ishek-Agha (or Master of Ceremonies). He was at first in the service of Ali Sher Beg, but afterwards, on account of his bravery, he was taken into the Mirza's service, and appointed Ishek-Agha. He attained the rank of Beg. Yunis Ali, who is now a Beg with me, and in my intimate confidence, and hereafter will be mentioned, is a son of his. Bāba Ali.

Another was Badereddīn, who first served with Mīrek Abdalrahīm, the Sadder (or Justiciary) of Sultan Abūsaīd Mirza. He was a very alert and nimble man; it is said that he could leap over seven horses at once. He and Bāba Ali were intimate friends. Badereddīn.

Another was Hassan Ali Jalāir. His proper name was Hussain Ali Jalāir; but he was generally called Hassan Ali. His father, Ali Jalāir, was in the service of Bābur Mirza, by whom he was raised to the rank of Beg. Afterwards when Yādgār Muhammed Mirza took Heri, there was no man in higher estimation in his service than Ali Jalāir. Hassan Ali Jalāir was grand Falconer[1] to Sultan Hussain Mirza. He was a poet, and assumed the poetical name of Tufeili. He wrote many beautiful *kasīdehs*, and was the most eminent of his age in that species of composition. When I took Samarkand, in the year 917, he joined me, and was in my service five or six years. He addressed to me some very fine *kasīdehs*; he was an extravagant, shameless man, and kept catamites; he was everlastingly playing at draughts, or at dice. Hassan Ali Jalāir.

A. D. 1511.

Another was Khwājeh Abdallah Marwarīd, who was at first Sadder[2]; but afterwards entered the service, and becoming a retainer and courtier, was raised to the dignity Khwājeh Abdallah Marwarīd.

---

[1] *Kūsh-begi.*
[2] The Sadder, or Chief Justice, is properly an ecclesiastical law appointment. This nobleman laid aside his legal character, and entered into the military and political department

of Beg. He was a man full of accomplishments; and no person could match him in playing on the *kānūn* (or dulcimer). The mode of shaking on this instrument is his invention. He excelled in writing the various hands, and in particular wrote the *taalīk* character in a very beautiful and superior manner. He was well versed in the epistolary style of composition.[1] He was a very pleasant companion, and was also a poet. He assumed the poetical name of Bayāni, but his poetry fell far below his other merits, though he was an excellent critic in poetry. He was profligate and debauched. From excess of sensual indulgence, he was attacked with boils all over his body, and lost the use of his hands and feet. After enduring various and exquisite pain and torture for several years, he was finally carried off by this disease.

Muhammed Syed Urūs.

Another was Muhammed Syed Urūs. His father was Urūs Arghūn, who, when Sultan Abūsaīd Mirza seized the throne, was a Beg of the first rank, and his prime adviser. At that time many brave young men signalized their courage. One of the most eminent of them was this Muhammed Syed Urūs. His bow was strong, and his arrow long, and its range was far, and its aim sure. He for some time held the government of Andekhūd.

Mīr Ali.

Mīr Ali, the Mīr Akhūr (or Master of the Horse), was another. This was the man who sent a person to Sultan Hussain Mirza, and brought him to fall upon Yādgār Muhammed Mirza, when off his guard, and defenceless.

Syed Hussain Ughlākchi.
[A.D. 1511.]

Another was Syed Hussain Ughlākchi, the son of Syed Ughlākchi, and elder [a] brother of Syed Yūsef Beg. He had a son named Mirza Farrukh, a man of great acquirements and talents, who joined me when I took Samarkand in 917. He was a poet, and though he wrote little, he wrote that little well. He was well acquainted with the use of the astrolabe, and the science of astronomy. He was also an agreeable friend and companion. He was rather addicted

[a] younger

---

[1] The Persian style of letter-writing is very artificial. Great care must be taken to address each man according to his proper rank or situation. The style, too, differs very much from that of common conversation. Hence it is regarded as a particular art.

to wine, and was riotous in his cups. He fell in the battle of Ghajdewān.¹

Another was Tengri Berdi, of the Samānchi tribe. He was an honest, brave man, and an accomplished swordsman. By a well-conducted surprise, he seized and carried off, from the gates of Balkh, Nazar Bahāder Khosrou Shah's head-man, as has been mentioned.[a]

Tengri Berdi.

There were, besides, several Turkomān Begs, who had come and joined the Mirza, and had been well received by him. Of the first comers, one was Alı Khan Baiendūr. Ased Beg, and Tahemtan Beg, who were brothers, were also of the number. It was the daughter of this Tahemtan Beg whom Badīa-ez-zemān Mirza married, and had by her Muhammed Zemān Mirza. Another was Ibrahīm Chaghatāi; another Amir Omer-Beg, who was afterwards in Badīa-ezzemān's service. He was a brave, plain, honest man. A son of his, named Abul Fateh, came to me from Irāk, and is still with me; he is a lazy, inactive, good-for-nothing fellow. Such a father to have such a son!

Sultan Hussain Mirza's other Begs

Of the later comers, who joined him after Shah Ismāel had conquered Irāk and Azarbāijān, one was Abdal Bāki Mirza. He was of the race of Taimūr Beg, by the Mirānshāhi branch. From the very first, though of such illustrious extraction, when he came into those countries, he laid aside[b] all pretensions to sovereignty, and entered into the service of the kings of the country, by whom he was treated with great favour. The paternal uncle of this Abdal Bāki Mirza, named Taimūr Osmān, was a nobleman of high estimation and consequence with Yākūb Beg. On one occasion, having marched with a large army, it was supposed that he had moved to invade Khorasān. Immediately on Abdal Bāki Mirza's arrival at court, he met with a gracious reception from Sultan Hussain Mirza, who made him his

---

[a] I have already related with what spirit he vanquished Nazi Bahādur, the chief of Khusru Shah's officers, at the gates of Balkh.
[b] The princes of this family, when they came into those countries, laid aside

---

¹ This was the great battle fought in November 1512, in which Bābur and his Persian auxiliaries were defeated and driven out of Bokhāra.

son-in-law by giving him in marriage Sultānim Begum, who was the mother of Muhammed Sultan Mirza.

Another of the later comers was Murād Beg Bayandūr.

The Sadder Mīr Sar barahneh. As for the heads of the Sadder,[1] one was Mīr Sar barahneh (the bare-headed Mīr). He was from a village in Andejān. He affected to be a Syed. He was of an amiable disposition, an agreeable companion, and elegant in his conversation. Among the men of letters and poets of Khorasān, his judgement and opinion were reckoned of the greatest weight and a law. He wasted his life in an attempt to rival the story of Amir Hamzeh,[2] and in composing a far-fetched, long-winded, improbable tale, an employment altogether absurd, and quite unworthy of his genius.[a]

Kamāled-dīn Hussain Gāzergāhi. Another of them was Kamāled-dīn Hussain Gāzergāhi, who, though not a Sūfi, affected Sūfi principles. Many who affected these Sūfi principles gathered about Sher Ali Beg, pretended to raptures and ecstasies, and studied the doctrines of the sect. Of all these this man had made the greatest progress in these mystical fancies,[b] which probably was the reason of the distinctions that he had received, as he showed no ability in anything else. He composed one work, the *Majālis-ul-ushāk* (the Assembly of Lovers), which he ascribes to Sultan Hussain Mirza. It is very dull, full of fiction, and of tasteless fiction, and contains passages so profane, that they subjected him to the imputation of infidelity. He has, for example, represented some of the prophets, and many saints, as engaged in amours, and has provided each of them with a lover and a friend. It was certainly a strangely absurd thing, after, in the preface, ascribing the work to Sultan Hussain Mirza as its author, in the body of the work to introduce odes and pieces of poetry

[a] opposed to nature and good sense.
[b] He was superior by birth to most of these mystics.

---

[1] The *Sadder*, or chief court of justice in Persia, is superseded at the present day by that of the Sheikh-ul-islām. The various offices in Persia are extremely fluctuating, both as to their names and duties, which makes it difficult to assign their exact meaning and extent at different periods.

[2] The story of Amir Hamzeh is a wild story in the Persian language, and filled with tales that shock all probability.

known to be written by Kamāled-dīn Hussain, by saying that 'they are by the writer of this work'. It was in consequence of the flattery of this same Kamāled-dīn Hussain that Zūlnūn Arghūn got the name of Hizaber-ullah (the Lion of God).

Of the Wazīrs of Sultan Hussain Mirza, one was Majd-ed-dīn Muhammed, the son of Khwājeh Pir Ahmed Khawāfi, who was the chief counsellor in the Diwān [1] of Shahrokh Mirza. Before his time, Sultan Hussain Mirza's Diwān was conducted without regularity or method, and the greatest disorder and waste prevailed. The subjects suffered from exactions, and the soldiers were not satisfied. At the time when Majd-ed-dīn Muhammed held the office of Parwānchi [2] (or issuer of the royal firmāns), he went by the name of Mīrek; the Mirza happened on one occasion to want a little money, and sent for the officers of the Diwān, who told him that there was none, and that none could be got. Majd-ed-dīn, who was present, smiled; the Mirza asked him the reason, and retired with him; when Majd-ed-dīn told him his whole mind, and added, ' If your majesty will make an agreement with me, by consenting to give me full power, and not to deviate from my plans, I will undertake, in a very short time, to make the subjects comfortable, the army satisfied, and the treasury full.' The Mirza entered into the agreement with great willingness, placed the whole revenues of Khorasān entirely under his management, and gave him the unlimited direction of everything. Majd-ed-dīn, on his part, spared no pains nor labour, exerted his utmost ability, and in a short time made both the peasantry and soldiery contented and happy, while he, at the same time, replenished the treasury, and rendered the country flourishing and populous. He, however, conducted himself with envious hostility towards [a] Ali Sher Beg, and the Amirs who were in his interest, as well as towards all men who were in office; on which account all of them were ill disposed

Wazirs. Majd-ed-dīn Muhammed.

[a] He nevertheless continued on bad terms with

[1] The Wazīr was a sort of minister of finance. The Diwān was the office of revenue receipts and issues.
[2] [A secretary for writing out royal orders (Steingass).]

towards him, and their endeavours to ruin him finally effected his overthrow, and got him dismissed, when Nizām-ul-mulk was made Diwān in his place. In a short time, Nizām-ul-mulk was in his turn seized and put to death, when Khwājeh Afzal was brought from Irāk and appointed Diwān. At the time when I came to Kābul, Khwājeh Afzal had been made a Beg, and held the seal of the Diwān.

Khwājeh Atā.

Another was Khwājeh Atā,[1] who although he was not, like those who have been mentioned, of the first rank nor Diwān, yet, in the whole extent of the Khorasān dominions, nothing was done without his advice. He was a man of piety, strictly observant of the accustomed prayers, and devoted to religious exercises. He was, besides, diligent in business. Such were the principal advisers and ministers of Sultan Hussain Mirza.

Theologians and Metaphysicians.

The age of Sultan Hussain Mirza was certainly a wonderful age, and Khorasān, particularly the city of Heri, abounded with eminent men of unrivalled acquirements, each of whom made it his aim and ambition to carry to the highest perfection the art to which he devoted himself. Among these was the Moulāna Abdal Rahmān Jāmi,[2] to whom there was no person of that period who could be compared, whether in respect to profane or sacred science. His poems are well known. The merits of the Mulla are of too exalted a nature to admit of being described by me; but I have been anxious to bring the mention of his name, and an allusion to his excellencies, into these humble pages, for a good omen and a blessing.

Jāmi.

Seif-ed-dīn Ahmed.

Another was the Sheikh-ul-Islām, Seif-ed-dīn Ahmed,

[1] [This was Atā ullah bin Muhammed al Husaini Naishapūri, author of a history of Muhammed, named *Rauzat ul ahbāb*, which was dedicated to 'Ali Sher in 1494. He also wrote the *Kitāb i takmīl us san'at*, on the art of writing poetry. He was a Wazīr of Sultan Husein Mirza, and died in 1511.—Beale's *Biog. Dict.*]

[2] No moral poet ever had a higher reputation than Jāmi. His poems are written with great beauty of language and versification, in a captivating strain of religious and philosophic mysticism. He is not merely admired for his sublimity as a poet, but venerated as a saint. [Jāmi (A. D. 1414-92) composed the *Haft Aurang*, *Sikander-nāmah*, *Bahāristān*, *Nafahāt ul uns*, and many other poetical works.]

who was descended of the stock of Mulla Saad-ed-dīn Taftazāni,[1] which for several generations had occupied the situation of Sheikh-ul-Islām in the kingdom of Khorasān. He was eminent for his knowledge, and particularly versed in the sciences of the Arabs,[2] and the sciences dependent on theology. He was a man of great piety, and devoted to religion. Though of the sect of Shāfi,[3] he cherished persons of every persuasion. It is said, that for nearly seventy years he had never omitted the appointed prayers in the public worship. Shah Ismāel, when he took Heri,[4] put him to death, and he was the last of his family.

Another was Moulāna Sheikh Hussain. Although he was in his greatest eminence and celebrity in the time of Sultan Abūsaīd Mirza, yet, as he continued to flourish in the reign of Sultan Hussain Mirza, he is mentioned here. He was profoundly skilled in philosophy, logic, rhetoric, and metaphysics. He had the faculty of extracting a great deal of meaning from a very few words, and of commenting with great subtlety on them. In the time of Sultan Abūsaīd Mirza, he enjoyed a high degree of influence and intimacy with that prince, and was consulted on all affairs of national importance. Nobody performed the office of *Muhtesib*[5] with more ability. In consequence of the great favour in which he had been with Sultan Abūsaīd Mirza, this incomparable person was but harshly treated in the time of Sultan Hussain Mirza.

Moulāna Sheikh Hussain.

Another was the Mulla-zādeh Mulla Osmān, who was from the village of Chirkh, which lies in the Tumān of Lohūger,[6] one of the Tumāns of Kābul. As, in the time of Ulugh Beg Mirza, when only fourteen years of age, he had commenced giving instructions as a teacher, he was denominated the

Mulla Osmān.

---

[1] [A. D. 1322-90.]
[2] The sciences of the Arabs are those connected with grammar and rhetoric.
[3] The Shāfi is one of the four orthodox sects.
[4] [In 1510. *E.B.*, p. 305.]
[5] The *Muhtesib* takes cognizance of all offences against good morals, such as drinking, gambling, intriguing; whence he is often alluded to with terror by the jovial poets of Persia. He had also the superintendence of the markets.
[6] Or Logar.

Mother-born Mulla. When he was on his journey from Samarkand to Mekka, as he was passing through Heri, Sultan Hussain Mirza stopped him by the way, and detained him at his court. He was a man of most extensive knowledge. There was not in that age any one who equalled him in the extent of his acquirements. Many affirmed that he had attained the degree of *ijtihād*,[1] but he never pretended to it. It was he who said, ' When a man has heard anything, how can he forget it ? ' He had a most retentive memory.

Jamāleddīn Muhaddis. Another was Mīr Jamāleddīn *Muhaddis* (or the traditionalist), who, in the science of tradition, was unequalled in all the country of Khorasān. He is of a very advanced age, and is still alive at the present date.

Mīr Murtāz. Another was Mīr Murtāz, who was well versed in the sciences of practical philosophy and of metaphysics. He received the name of *Murtāz* (the Ascetic) from the frequency of his fasting. He was madly fond of the game of chess; to such a degree, indeed, that when he met with two persons who understood the game, while he played with one of them, he used to lay hold of the skirts of the other's clothes to prevent his going away.

Mulla Masaūd. Another of them was Mulla Masaūd, who was of Sherwān.

Abdal Ghafūr Another was Abdal Ghafūr of Lār, who was both the scholar and disciple of Moulāna Abdal Rahmān Jāmi. He had read many of the Mulla's works, under his immediate guidance,[2] and wrote a sort of exposition or commentary on the *Nafahāt*[3] (or Breeze of Affection) of that author. He was extremely versed in the profane sciences, besides

[1] The rank of *Mujtahid*, which is not bestowed by any individual or class of men, but which is the result of slow and imperceptible opinion, finally prevailing and universally acknowledged, is one of the greatest peculiarities of the religion of Persia. The *Mujtahid* is supposed to be elevated above human fears and human enjoyments, and to have a certain degree of infallibility and inspiration. He is consulted with reverence and awe. There is not always a *Mujtahid* necessarily existing.—See Kaempfer, *Amoenitates Exoticae*.

[2] The works of the Mulla Jāmi were extremely refined and mystical. To have the advantage of reading them over in the author's presence, to receive the benefit of his explanatory comments and remarks, was therefore of the first importance.

[3] The *Nafahāt ul uns* is a poem of Jāmi's, written on the principles of the Sūfis, or Mystic Latitudinarians.

having made great proficiency in mystical knowledge. He was a remarkably unassuming and unceremonious man. If any person had but the name of a Mulla, he was never ashamed to take out a section of any work, and enter into discussion with him;[a] and if any derwīsh was mentioned to him as being in a particular place, he was never satisfied till he had sought him out and seen him. When I visited [A.D. 1506] Khorasān, Mulla Abdal Ghafūr was sick; and when I went and circumambulated the Mulla's shrine (Jāmi's), I at the same time went and inquired after the health of Mulla Abdal Ghafūr. He was at that time in the Mulla's[1] college. A few days afterwards he died of the disease of which he was then ill.

Another of them was Mīr Atā-ullah of Meshhad, who was well versed in Arabic literature. He wrote a treatise in Persian, on the *kāfiah* (rhyme or versification), which is extremely well composed; but has this fault, that all his examples are taken from his own verses, and he introduces each example by saying, 'as is to be observed in this couplet of mine.'[b] He wrote another very excellent work on the kinds and measures of verse, which he called *Badāī-us sanāi* (the wonders of art). He was not quite orthodox in his religious opinions.

Mīr Atā-ullah.

Another was Kazi Ikhtiyār, who executed the duties of Kazi with great propriety. He wrote a treatise, in Persian, on Jurisprudence.[2] It is an excellent treatise. He formed a collection of passages, for the purpose of elucidating and explaining the texts of the Koran.[3] When I met the Mirzas at Murghāb, Kazi Ikhtiyār and Muhammed Mīr Yūsef accompanied them, and they were introduced to me. The conversation turned on the Bāburi character. I sent for the letters, and wrote them,[c] and at that same meeting he

Kazi Ikhtiyār.

[a] He never failed to explain some point of doctrine to any one who was called a Mulla;

[b] *Add* Certain of his opponents have made some well-founded criticisms on this treatise.

[c] The Kazi asked me to write out the letters for him, one by one, which I did.

---

[1] I have now by me a small Persian manuscript, containing anecdotes of Jāmi, by his friend Moulāna Abdal Ghafūr Lāri.

[2] *Fikh*.   [3] *Bahr i mazmūn*.

read the characters, comprehended the rules of writing, and wrote a little.

Muhammed Mīr Yūsef.

Another was Muhammed Mīr Yūsef, the scholar of the Sheikh-ul-Islām, and afterwards his successor. In many parties, Kazi Ikhtiyār had the upper place; and in others, Muhammed Mīr Yūsef. He finally was so much carried away and infatuated by his fondness for soldiership and generalship, that, except where these two matters were concerned, one could discover neither learning in his conversation, nor sense in his communications. Although he had neither good fortune nor talents in either of these pursuits, he, in the end, on their account, gave to the wind his wealth, his life, his family, and his reputation.[a][1]

The Poets.

Of the poets of Sultan Hussain Mirza's court, the most distinguished and the most eminent by far was Moulāna Abdal Rahmān Jāmi. Sheikhim Suheili, and Hassan Ali Tufeili Jalāir, whose names and characters have been mentioned in the short account which has been given of Sultan Hussain Mirza's principal Begs and courtiers, were also distinguished as poets.

Jāmi.
Suheili.
Tufeili.

Āsafi.

Another of the poets was Āsafi,[2] who was the son of a Wazīr, whence he obtained the poetical name of Āsafi.[3] His poems want neither colouring of style nor sentiment, although not possessed of passion or enthusiasm. He had

[a] *Omit* and his reputation *and add* He was a Shi'a.

[1] It is singular that Bābur, in this minute mention of the men who adorned the court of Sultan Hussain Mirza, makes no mention of Mīr-Khāwend Shah, or Mirkhond, the celebrated historian, and, if we perhaps except Jāmi, the most eminent man of his time. After a youth of pleasure, he was induced by his friend and patron, Ali Sher, to devote himself to history; and while he lived in the Khānekeh Khulāsia, in habits of constant intercourse with that distinguished encourager of letters, composed the eight volumes of the *Rauzet-es-safā*, or Pleasure-Garden. He died A. D. 1498, eight years before Bābur visited Herāt. His son Khāwend, or Khwānd-amīr, or Khond-amīn, also an excellent historian, the author [of the *Khulāsat-ul akhbār*, &c., visited Bābur at Agra in 1528.

[2] [Son of Ni'amat ullah, Wazīr of Sultan Abū Sa'īd Mirza, was a contemporary and friend of the poet Jāmi, who instructed him in the art of poetry. He was the author of the *Divān Asafi*, and a *Masnevi*. He died in 1514.—Beale's *Biog. Dict.*]

[3] Asaf being Solomon's famous vizir.—*Leyden.*

a pride in saying, 'I have never composed any of my odes with the intention of collecting them.' This was probably mere affectation. His odes were collected by his friends, and those about him.[a] He wrote few poems except odes. When I went to Khorasān, he waited on me.

Another of them was Banāi[1] of Heri, whose father's name was Ustād Muhammed Sabz Banā, whence he himself derived his poetical name. His odes possess both colouring of style and enthusiasm, and he composed a *diwān*. He also wrote *masnevis*, among which there is one on the qualities of fruits, in the *mutakārib* measure. It is a sorry composition, of no value. Another of them was a short *masnevi* in the *khafīf* measure; and another of greater extent, also in the *khafīf* measure; this last he completed in his latter days. At first he was unacquainted with the science of music, and Ali Sher Beg had taunted him with his ignorance; but, one year, the Mirza having spent a winter at Merv, whither he was accompanied by Ali Sher Beg, Banāi remained behind at Heri, applied himself to the study of music, and made such rapid progress, that, before the summer, he was even able to compose some pieces. In the summer when the Mirza returned to Heri, he sang in his presence, and that to music of his own composition, to the great astonishment of Ali Sher Beg, who complimented him on the occasion. He composed several pieces of music, one of which is denominated the *Nuh-rang* (or nine measure). The parts of this *Nuh-rang*, and of the *Yaldai Naksh* (or Midwinter-Night's Air), have their modulations in tenor.[b] He was a decided rival and opponent of Ali Sher Beg, whence he suffered much trouble and molestation; and finally, being unable to maintain his ground, went to Irāk and Azarbaijān to Yākūb Beg,

<small>Banāi.</small>

---

[a] His Odes were collected by his younger brother or one of his relations.

[b] The theme of this air and its variations are on the measure styled *rāst*.

---

[1] [Banāi was the son of an architect of Herāt, and hence his pen-name (Banā = a builder). He was killed in Shah Ismaïl's massacre in 1512. He wrote the *Bahrām o Bahroz*, besides other poems.—Beale's *Biog. Dictionary*.]

by whom he was well received, and became his companion in all his parties. After the death of Yākūb Beg,[1] he was obliged to leave those countries, and returned to Heri. He still retained his humour and his spirit of opposition, of which the following, among other instances, is related. One day at a chess-party, Ali Sher Beg happening to stretch out his foot, it touched the hinder parts [2] of Banāi; on which Ali Sher Beg said, in a joking way, 'It is a sad nuisance in Heri, that you cannot stretch out your foot without coming in contact with the backside of a poet.' 'Nor draw it in again,' said Banāi, 'without coming in contact with a poet's backside.' At last his sarcasms drove Banāi from Heri, and he went to Samarkand.[3] As Ali Sher Beg was the author and patron of many and useful inventions, every man who made any discovery or invention in his art or profession, in order to give it credit or currency, called it *the Ali Sheri*. Some carried their imitation of him to such an excess, that Ali Sher Beg having tied a handkerchief round his head, on account of an earache, that style of tying a handkerchief came to prevail,[a] under the name of the *Ali Sheri fashion*. When Banāi left Heri for Samarkand, as he was setting out, he ordered rather an uncommon sort of pad for his ass, and called it *the Ali Sheri*. The *Ali Sheri pad* became common, and is now well known.

Seifi Bokhāri.

Another was Seifi Bokhāri, who was a tolerable Mulla. He used to point to the numerous volumes he had read, as a proof of his undoubted claim to the title. He composed a *diwān*. There is another *diwān* of his which he composed for the use of tradespeople. He wrote many fables, but left no *masnevi*, as may be gathered from the following verses:

[a] women took to tying a blue kerchief round their heads,

---

[1] [Ya'qūb Beg succeeded his father, Ūzūn Hassan, in 1477, as chief of the White Sheep Turkmans. He died in 1491.—Beale's *Biog. Dict.*]

[2] It is to be recollected that the Asiatics sit on the ground, on a carpet, with their feet drawn up under them.

[3] Here Dr. Leyden's translation ends. One other fragment which he translated will be found under the year 925.

(*Persian*)—Although the *masnevi* be deemed the test of a poet's orthodoxy,
I take the *ghazel* as my creed;
Five couplets that afford delight,
I hold better than many [a] *khamsehs*.

He left a Persian Prosody,[1] which is very brief in one respect, and prolix in another. It is brief as it has omitted to treat of several useful and difficult subjects; and prolix inasmuch as such subjects as are plain and clear are treated of in their minutest particulars, down to their points and discriminating marks. He was addicted to wine, and troublesome in his cups. He was remarkable for the force with which he could inflict a blow with his fist.

Another was Abdallah Masnevigoi (the *masnevi* writer), who was of Jām. He was the nephew of the Mulla by his sister. He took the poetical name of Hātifi.[2] He wrote some *masnevis* in emulation of the *khamsehs*. He also composed the *Taimūr-nāmeh* in rivalry to the *Haft-paiker* (or seven statues [b]). Of his *masnevis*, the best-known is the *Leili-Mejnūn*, though its excellence does not equal its reputation.

Abdallah Masnevigoi.

Another was Mīr Hussain Maamāi (the Enigmatist). None perhaps ever equalled him in his conundrums and riddles. His whole time was spent in devising enigmas. He was a humble, unpretending, and, in his way, incomparable [c] man.

Mīr Hussain Maamāi.

Another was Mulla Muhammed Badakhshi, who was from Ishkamish. Ishkamish is not in Badakhshān,[3] which makes it odd that he should have taken the poetical name of Badakhshi. His poems are not equal to those of the

Mulla Muhammed Badakhshi.

[a] two
[b] The *masnavi* which he composed in imitation of the *Haft paikar* (seven effigies) was called by him *Haft manzar* (seven faces). His *Timūr-nāmah* corresponds to the *Sikander-nāmah*.
[c] inoffensive

---

[1] [This work, entitled '*Urūzi Saifi*, was written in 1491, and was translated into English by Blochmann in 1872.—Beale's *Biog. Dict.*]
[2] [Abdullah Hātifi, the poet Jāmi's nephew, was born at Jām in Khorasān, and died there in 1521. Towards the close of his life he enjoyed the patronage of Shah Ismaīl Safavī. He wrote, in imitation of Nizāmī's Quintet, *Lailī wa Majnūn*, *Khusrū wa Shīrīn*, *Haft manzar*, *Timūr nāmeh*, and *Futūhāt i shāhī*, which he did not live to complete.—Beale's *Biog. Dict.*]
[3] It lies south of Kunduz.

poets whose names I have mentioned.¹ Though he has written a treatise on enigmas, his enigmas are not particularly good; but he was a pleasant companionable man. He waited on me when I was at Samarkand.

Yūsef Badīaī. Another was Yūsef Badīaī, who was from the country of Ferghāna, and composed very respectable *kaṣīdehs*.²

Āhī. Another was Āhī,³ who wrote pretty good *ghazels*.⁴ He latterly went and lived with Ibn Hussain Mirza. He composed a *diwān*.

Muhammed Sālih. Another was Muhammed Sālih.⁵ He wrote sweet *ghazels*, but their correctness is not equal to their sweetness. He also composed verses in the Tūrki tongue, and good ones. He finally went to the Khan's court, and was received with every kind of favour. He wrote a Tūrki *masnevi*, which he addressed to Sheibāni Khan, in the measure of *ramal musaddas makhbūn*,⁶ which is that of the *Sabhat*⁷ (of Jāmi). It is very dull and flat. One soon gets tired of reading Muhammed Sālih's poems.ᵃ One good couplet of his is the following:

> Tambal (lubber) has gained the land of Ferghāna;
> He converts Ferghāna into a Tambal-Khāneh (lubberland).

The country of Ferghāna is also called Tambal-Khāneh. I am not quite certain, however, that this couplet is to be found in his *masnevi*. He was wicked, tyrannical, and unfeeling.

Shah Hussain Kāmi. Another was Shah Hussain Kāmi. His poems are very fair. He composed *ghazels*, and also wrote a *diwān*.

ᵃ When you have read his poems you cease to believe in the author's talents.

---

¹ One of his couplets on the succession of good and bad fortune is striking: 'The fortune of men is like a sand-glass; one hour up, the next down.'—See D'Herbelot on the poet.

² [Professor E. G. Browne defines a *qasīdeh* as a 'purpose poem', generally a panegyric, elegy, or satire.]

³ [Āhī, who was the author of a *divān*, which he dedicated to Gharīb Mirza, son of Sultan Hosain Baiqara, died in 1520.—Beale's *Biog. Dict.*]   ⁴ Odes.

⁵ [This was Muhammed Sāleh, the author of the *Shaibāni-nāmeh*, an historical poem in Turki (ed. Vambery, 1885). He died in 1534 at Bukhara (Rieu's *Catalogue of Turkish MSS.*, p. 274). Very little is known of his poetry, but Persian verses of his are quoted in the *Ātashkadah*, and the *Majma'ul fusuha* of Rizā Qulī Khān.]

⁶ This is a particular measure of Persian verse.

⁷ The Sabhat-ul-abrār, or Rosary of the Virtuous, is a mystic poem of Jāmi's.

Another was Hilāli,[1] who is still alive. His *ghazels* are Hilāli. correct and elegant, but leave little impression behind. He also wrote a *diwān*, and a *masnevi* entitled *Shah-va-derwīsh* (the king and the derwīsh), in the *khāfīf* measure: although many verses in it are excellent, yet the general plan of this poem and its structure are exceptionable and vicious. Former poets who have treated of love stories have made a man the lover and a woman the mistress. Hilāli has made the derwīsh the lover, and the king the object of his passion. The upshot of the verses in which he describes the words and actions of the king is, that he makes the king a catamite and an abandoned creature. So that the moral example afforded by this *masnevi* of his is that of a young man, a king, acting the part of a prostitute and catamite, which surely is no commendable or decent thing. He had a most retentive memory, and remembered thirty or forty thousand couplets. It is said that his recollection of most of the verses of the different[a] *khamsehs* was of great service to him, in regard to prosody and rhyming.

Another was Āhili,[2] who could neither write nor read.[b] Āhili. His poems are excellent. He also composed a *diwān*.

Although there were many beautiful penmen,[3] yet the Penmen. person who excelled all others in the Nastālīk character was Sultan Ali Meshadi.[4] He copied many books for the Mirza and Ali Sher Beg. He every day copied thirty couplets for the Mirza, and twenty for Ali Sher Beg.

Of the painters or limners, the most eminent was Behzād. Painters. He was a very elegant painter, but did not draw young Behzād.

[a] two   [b] who was a man of low origin.

---

[1] [Badr ud dīn Hilālī was the author of a *diwān* and also of the following works: *Shāh wa darwish, Lailī wa Majnūn*, and *Sifāt ul 'āshiqīn*. He was executed as a Shiah in 1533 by the orders of the Uzbeg chief, 'Ābid Khan.—Beale's *Biog. Dict.*]

[2] [This may have been Ahlī Shīrāzī (died in 1535), an elegant poet in the service of Shah Ismāīl, and the author of *Sihr i hilāl, Shama' wa parwānah*, and other poems. But there was another minor poet with the same pen-name, though not so distinguished, namely, Āhlī Khorāsānī, who died in 1527.—Beale's *Biog. Dict.*]

[3] In the eastern countries in which no printing is used, the art of penmanship is a source of much higher distinction than in Europe at the present day.

[4] [Sultan 'Alī Meshadī was more distinguished as a calligrapher than as a poet. He was born about 1487.---Beale's *Biog. Dict.*]

beardless faces well. He made the neck¹ too large. Bearded faces he painted extremely well.

Shah Muzaffer.

Another was Shah Muzaffer. He took likenesses very beautifully,[a] but he did not live long, and died when he was rising to eminence.

Musicians. Kūl Muhammed.

Of the musicians, there was none performed on the *kānūn*² in a style to be compared with Khwājeh Abdallah Marwārīd, as has been observed. Another was Kūl Muhammed Ūdī (the lutanist). He also performed well on the guitar. He added three strings to it. No vocal or instrumental performer ever composed so many and such excellent overtures.³

Sheikhi Nāyi.

Another was Sheikhi Nāyi (the flute-player). He also played well on the lute and guitar.⁴ From the age of twelve or thirteen, he played well on the flute.⁵ On one occasion he played an air beautifully before Badia-ez-zemān Mirza on the flute. Kūl Muhammed attempted, but was unable to play it on the guitar. He said, ' The guitar is an imperfect instrument.' Sheikhi immediately took the guitar out of Kūl Muhammed's hand, and played the same air completely and delightfully upon it. They tell of Sheikhi, that he was so accomplished in music, that on hearing any air whatever, he said, ' Such a tune of such a person resembles this.'[b] He did not compose much. They preserve two or three of his airs.⁶

Shah Kuli Ghicheki.

Another was Shah Kuli Ghicheki (the performer on the *ghichek* or guitar). He was a native of Irāk, who came into Khorasān, and rose to fame by his excellence as a composer.⁷ He composed many tunes, preludes, and airs.⁸

Hussain Ūdī.

Another was Hussain Ūdī (the lutanist), who played with great taste on the lute, and composed elegantly. He could play, using only one string of his lute at a time. He had the fault of giving himself many airs when desired to play. On one occasion Sheibāni Khan desired him to

---

[a] *Add* and painted the hair with a most artistic touch,
[b] This is such and such a tune, and by so and so.

---

¹ *Ghabghab* signifies the double-chin. [According to P. de C. the sentence runs : ' he exaggerated the lines of the chin '.]
² *Kānūn* [or dulcimer] is their largest stringed instrument.
³ *Pishrau.*   ⁴ *Ūd* and *Ghichek.*   ⁵ *Nai.*   ⁶ *Naksh.*
⁷ *Mashk-sāz.*   ⁸ *Naksh va pishrū va kārhā* [pieces].

play. After giving much trouble he played very ill, and besides, did not bring his own instrument, but one that was good for nothing. Sheibāni Khan, on learning how matters stood, directed that, at that very party, he should receive a certain number of blows on the neck. This was one good deed that Sheibāni Khan did in his day; and indeed the affectation of such people deserves even more severe animadversion.

Ghulām Shādi was also a musical composer. He was the son of Shādi the singer. Though a performer, yet he did not play so as to deserve to be ranked with the performers who have been mentioned. He composed sweet airs, and some finished pieces;[a] there were few compositions of that day that could be compared to his. At last Sheibāni Khan sent him to Muhammed Amīn Khan Kara Khāni,[1] since which I have not heard of him.

Ghulām Shādi

Another was Mīr Azū. He was not a performer, but composed. Though his productions are few, yet they are exquisite of their kind.

Mīr Azū.

Banāi was likewise a composer. He left many excellent *nakshes* and *sūts*.[2]

Banāi.

Another peerless man was Pahlewān[3] Muhammed Busaīd. He was unequalled as a wrestler. He was a poet too, and likewise composed various musical *sūts* and *nakshes*. He composed one beautiful (air or) *naksh* in the *chārgāh* key.[4] He was an agreeable man in society. The degree of excellence which he reached in athletic exercises was quite wonderful.

Pahlewān Muhammed Busaīd, the wrestler

[a] excellent themes and delightful airs;

---

[1] [Or rather, according to P. de C., Muhammed Amīn, Khan of Kāzān.]
[2] [P. de C. translates these terms by 'themes and airs'.]
[3] [Wrestler.]
[4] I have not been able to translate, with any degree of certainty, the musical terms used in the preceding pages. *Pardeh*, I understand to be a mode,—*pīshrau*, a prelude,—*naksh*, *kār*, and *sūt* are tunes of various kinds. The same uncertainty prevails as to the musical instruments: *Ūd* is applied to any stringed instrument. The *kānūn* is an instrument with many strings, and is generally placed on the ground when it is played on. The *ghichek* resembles our guitar, but has a large round bulb *Nāi* is a pipe or flute.—See Kœmpfer's *Amœnitates Exoticæ*, p. 740. [*Chārgāh* four time.]

Badīa-ez-zemān and Muzaffer Hussain made joint kings.

When Sultan Hussain Mirza expired, Badīa-ez-zemān Mirza and Muzaffer Hussain Mirza were the only Mirzas at hand. As Muzaffer Hussain Mirza was his favourite son, and as Muhammed Berendūk Birlās, the Amir and minister in chief credit, was that prince's *atkeh* (or tutor), and as, besides, his mother Khadījeh Begum had the most influence of all the Mirza's wives, the greater part of the people who were about the Mirza gathered round Muzaffer Hussain Mirza, and looked up to him as his father's successor. Badīa-ez-zemān Mirza being alarmed at this, intended not to go to head-quarters. Muzaffer Mirza and Muhammed Beg, however, having mounted and gone to wait upon him, removed all uneasiness from his mind, and prevailed upon the Mirza to accompany them thither. Sultan Hussain Mirza was conveyed in a royal style, and with all due pomp, to Heri, where they interred him in his own college. At this time Zūlnūn Beg was likewise on the spot. Muhammed Berendūk Beg, Zūlnūn Beg, and other Amirs, who had been with Sultan Hussain Mirza, and had accompanied the Mirzas, having now met and consulted together, finally resolved to place Badīa-ez-zemān Mirza, with Muzaffer Hussain Mirza, on the throne of Heri, as joint kings. At the court of Badīa-ez-zemān Mirza, Zūlnūn Beg was prime minister, and Muhammed Berendūk Beg held the same office in the court of Muzaffer Hussain Mirza. On the part of Badīa-ez-zemān Mirza, Sheikh Ali Taghāi was Dārogha of the city; as Yūsef Ali Gokultāsh was on the part of Muzaffer Mirza. This was a strange arrangement. A joint kingship was never before heard of. The well-known words of Sheikh Sādi in the *Gulistān* are very applicable to it: 'Ten Derwishes can sleep on one rug; but the same climate of the earth cannot contain two kings.'[1]

[1] [Chap. i, story 3 of the *Gulistān*.]

CPSIA information can be obtained
at www.ICGtesting.com
Printed in the USA
LVHW081234160822
726060LV00004B/55